1 JANUARY

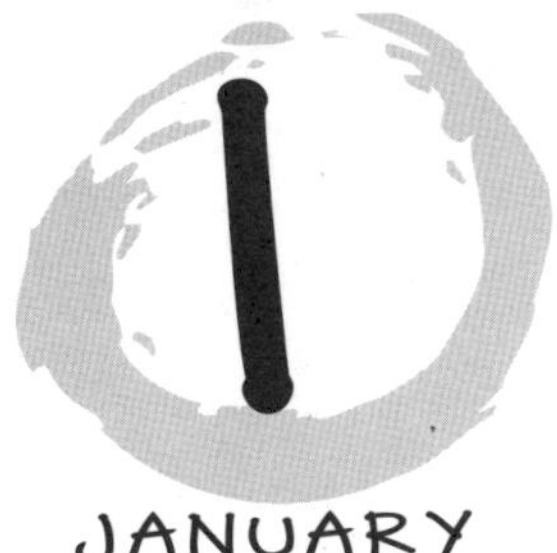

Adam was the first man.
He named every creature.

Can you find 15 white flowers in the picture?
You can find the story of Adam and Eve in Genesis 2:8–25.

AF207515

Color me!

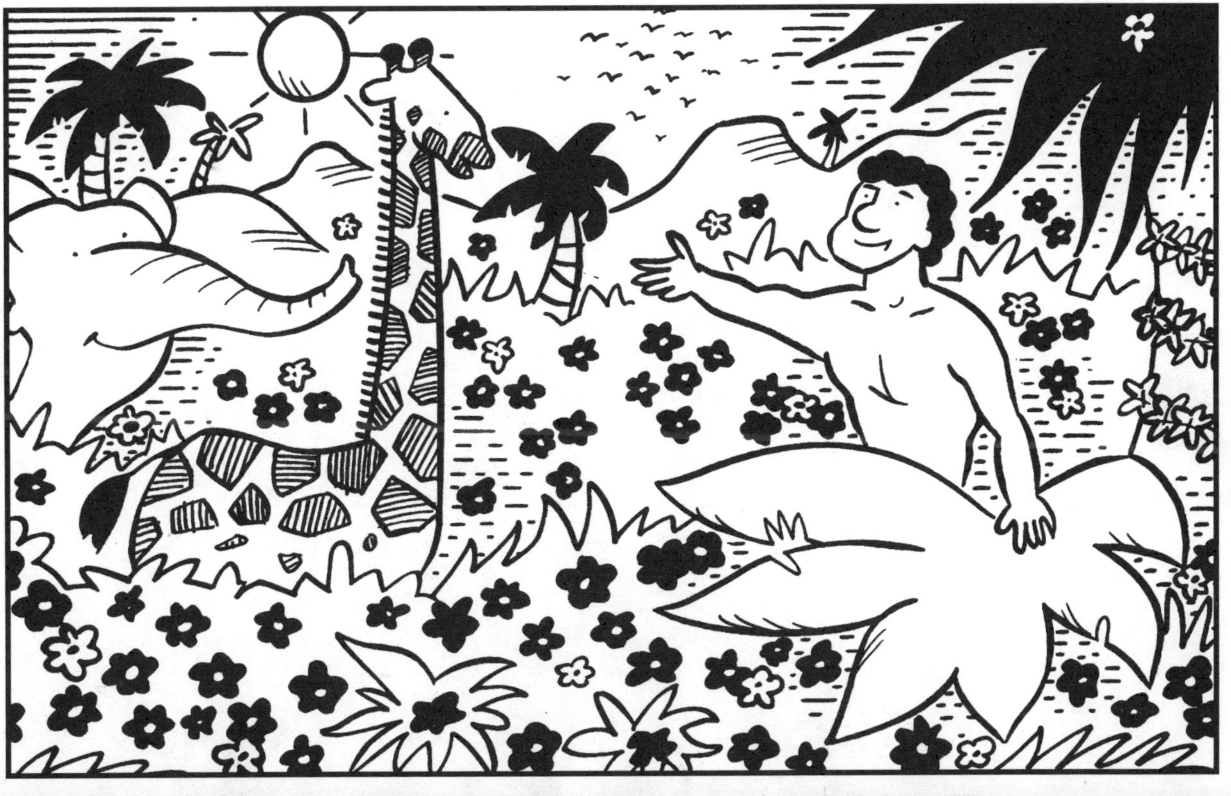

2

JANUARY

Here is another picture of Adam naming all the animals and birds. How many deliberate mistakes can you find?

You can read this story in Genesis 2:19–20.

Color me!

31

DECEMBER

An angel told Joseph that Herod wanted to kill baby Jesus. So Mary and Joseph took the baby away to safety in Egypt.

You can read this story in Matthew 2:13.

Color me!

3

JANUARY

Here are some of the animals named
by Adam. What are they?

**Complete the drawings and
then color the whole picture.
See Genesis 2:19–20.**

Color me!

Finally, the wise men found Jesus.
They gave the baby king gifts.
Find out what the gifts were in your Bible.

Read Matthew 2:11.

Color me!

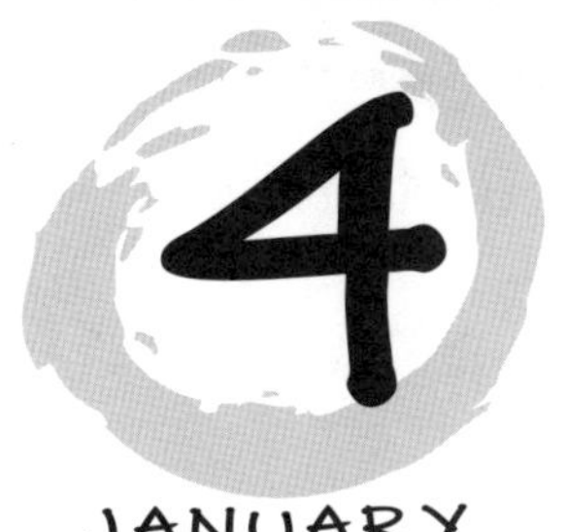

4
JANUARY

Join up the dots. What creature is going to trick Eve into doing wrong?

You can find the story of Adam and Eve in the Garden of Eden in Genesis 3:1–7.

DOT-TO-DOT

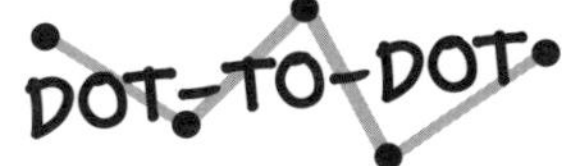

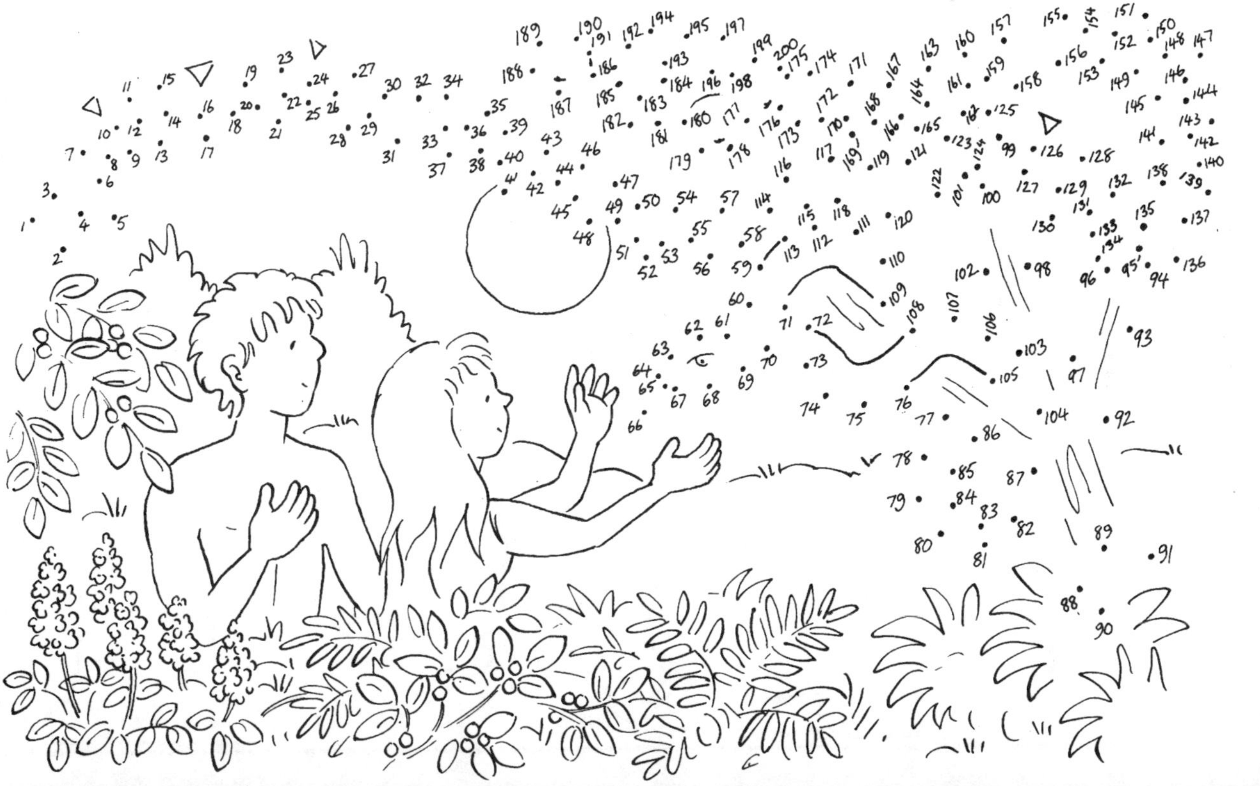

29

DECEMBER

When the wise men arrived in Jerusalem, they asked King Herod where they might find the newborn king, announced by the star.

You can read this story in Matthew 2:7.

Color me!

5

JANUARY

Put a circle around all the differences in the second picture of Eve being tempted.

Can you find at least 10?
See Genesis 3:4–5

28 DECEMBER

maze

One of the wise men has lost his camel. Help him find his camel through the sand dune maze.

You can read about the wise men in Matthew 2:1–2.

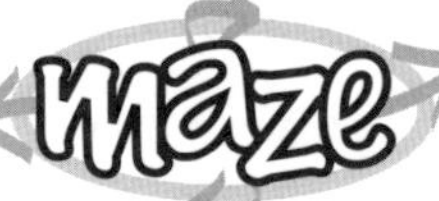

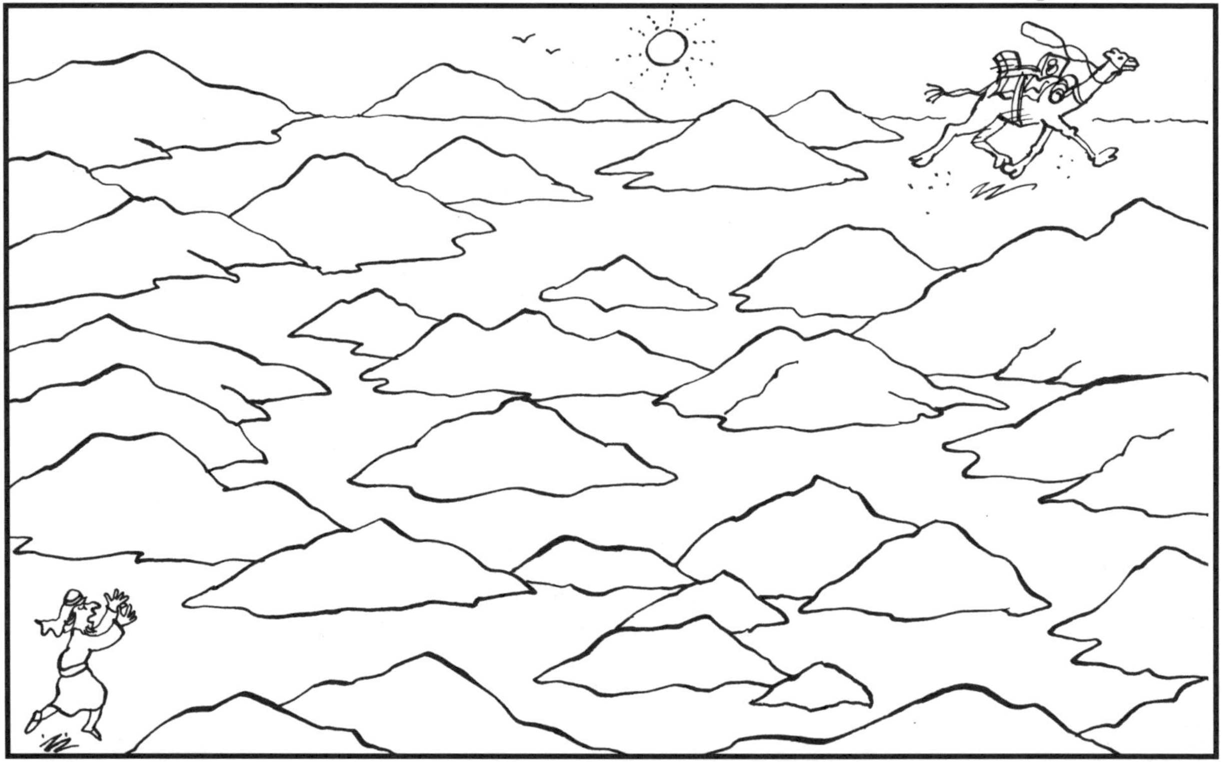

6

JANUARY

Here is another picture of Eve eating the fruit.

Can you find at least 9 hidden apples?
What is coiled around the tree?
See Genesis 3:1–6

Color me!

27

DECEMBER

The wise men set off on a long journey, following the star they had first seen in the east.

You can read this story in Matthew 2:9–10.

Color me!

Adam's son Cain attacked his brother Abel. Find 10 differences between these two pictures.

You can read what happened to the two brothers in Genesis 4:1–16.

26

DECEMBER

In the East, wise men were watching the skies. They saw a new star in the sky. 'We must follow this star,' they said.

You can read this story in Matthew 2:2.

Color me!

8 JANUARY

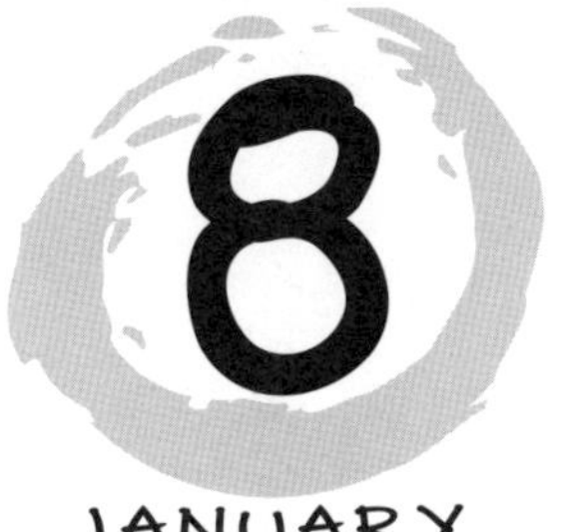

You can see Noah and two of his sons. What are they building? Join up the dots to find out.

You can find the story of Noah and his great task in Genesis 6:9—7:23.

DOT-TO-DOT

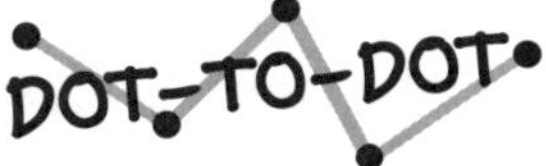

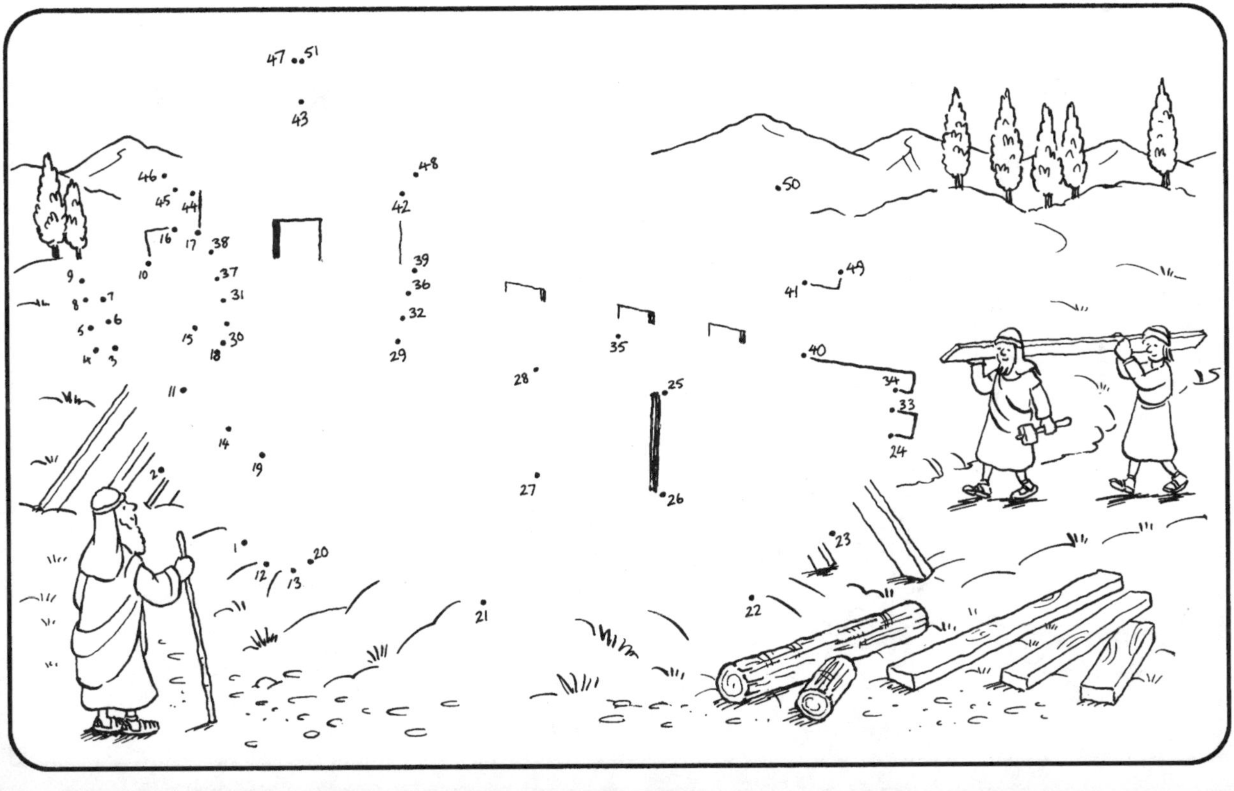

Christmas Day

25

DECEMBER

The shepherds went to the stable in Bethlehem to see the baby Jesus. They told Mary what the angels had said.

You can read this story in Luke 2:16–17.

Color me!

9

JANUARY

Noah and his three sons are building the ark. Find ten differences between the two pictures.

You can read this story in your Bible in Genesis 6:9–22.

24

DECEMBER

An angel of the Lord appeared to the shepherds, and the glory of God shone over them. What did the shepherds do after this?

Find out by reading Luke 2:15.

Color me!

10

JANUARY

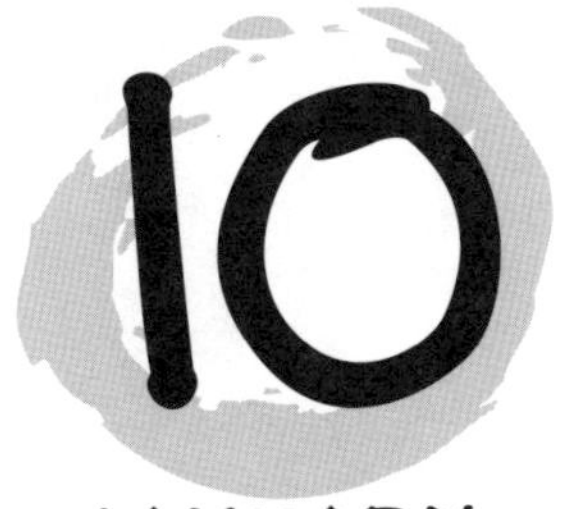

God told Noah to collect two of each kind of bird and animal.

Follow the lines to match up the pairs of creatures.
See Genesis 6:19–21

Puzzle

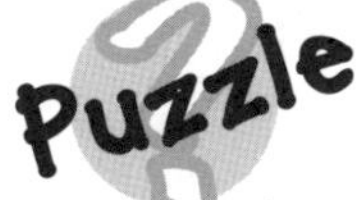

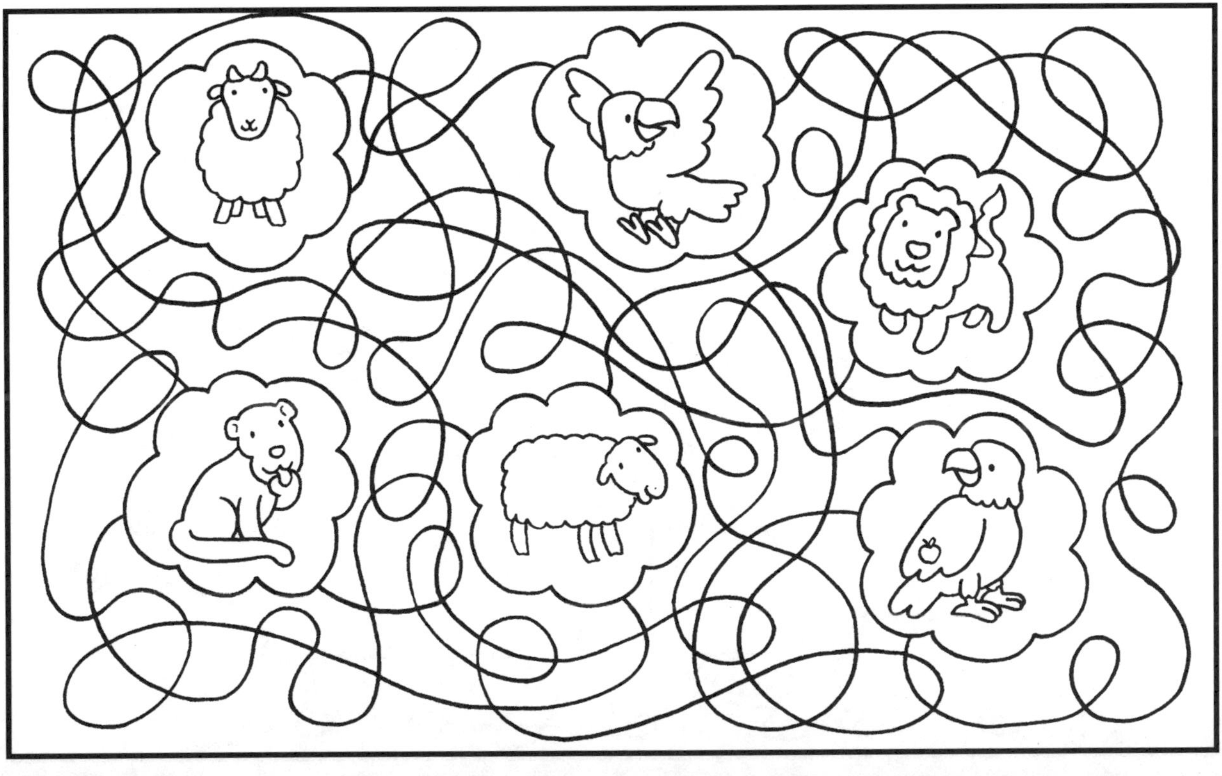

23

DECEMBER

In fields near Bethlehem, shepherds were looking after their sheep. What happened next?

Find out in Luke 2:8–9.

Color me!

11 JANUARY

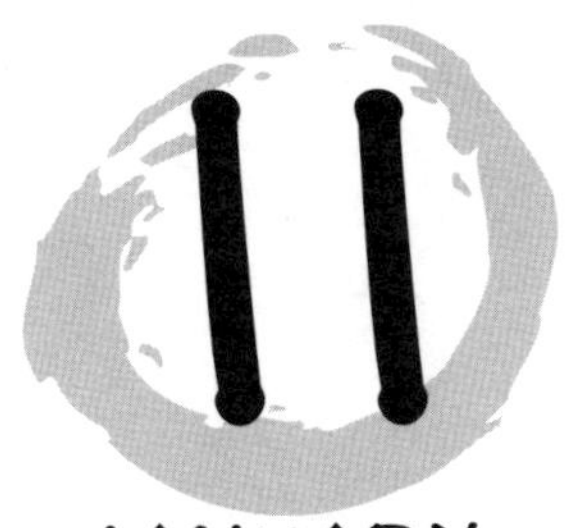

Noah puts the animals into the ark he has just built. How many of each kind of creature went into the ark?

You can read this story in Genesis 6:9–22.

DOT-TO-DOT

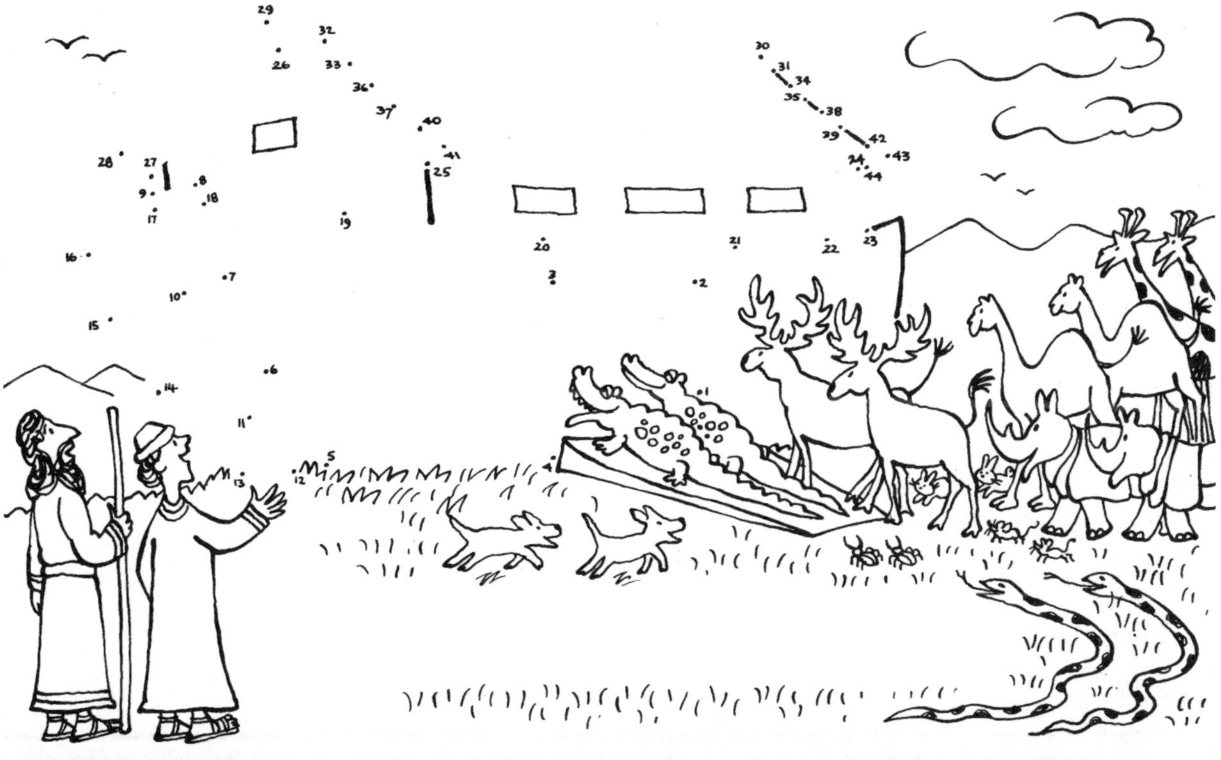

22 DECEMBER

The animals in the stable watched as visitors came to see baby Jesus. Which picture has all the pieces needed to make the cow?

You can read about this in Luke 2:7–8.

Puzzle

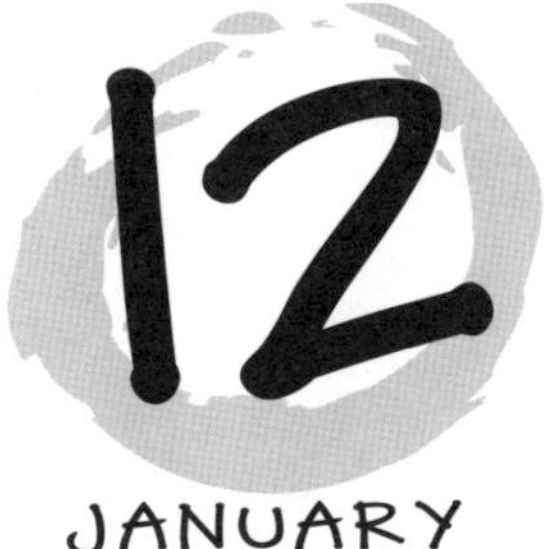

12 JANUARY

Noah and his wife are loading their luggage and the animals into the ark.

Can you find 12 luggage labels hidden in the picture?
Read Genesis 7:6–10

Puzzle

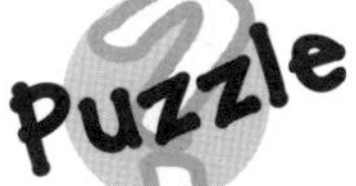

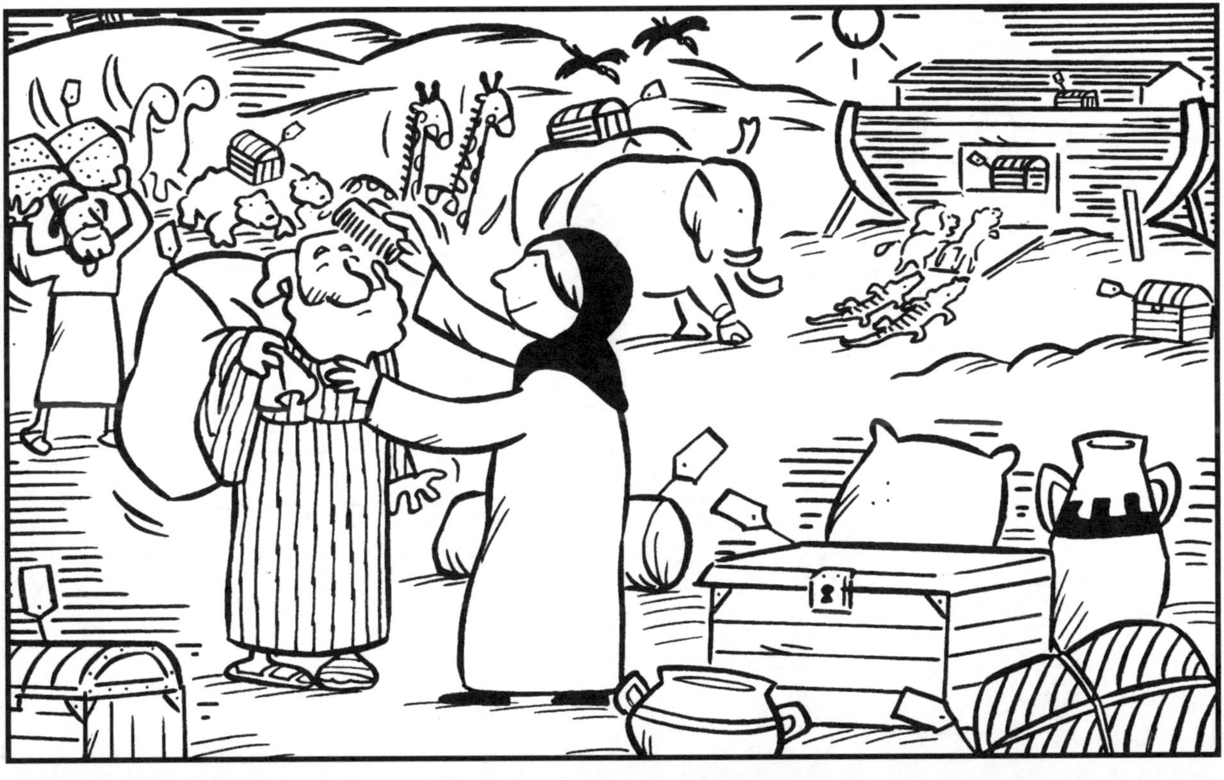

21

DECEMBER

So Jesus was born in a stable.
Mary wrapped him in strips of cloth
and laid him in a manger.

You can read about this in Luke 2:7.

Color me!

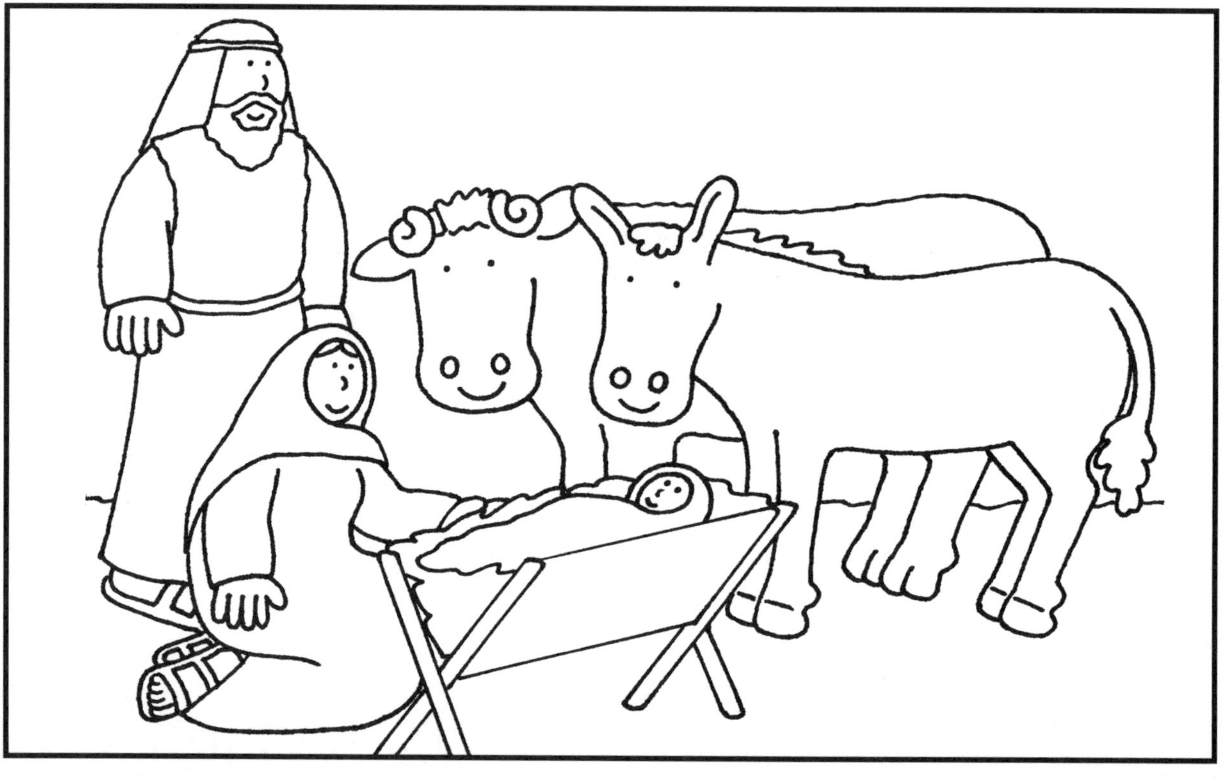

13

JANUARY

The artist hasn't finished this picture of the animals waiting to enter the ark.

Complete the picture—then color it in.
Read Genesis 7:6–10.

Color me!

When they arrived in Bethlehem, they found that there was no room for them at the inn.

Where did they stay instead?
You can read about this in Luke 2:7.

Color me!

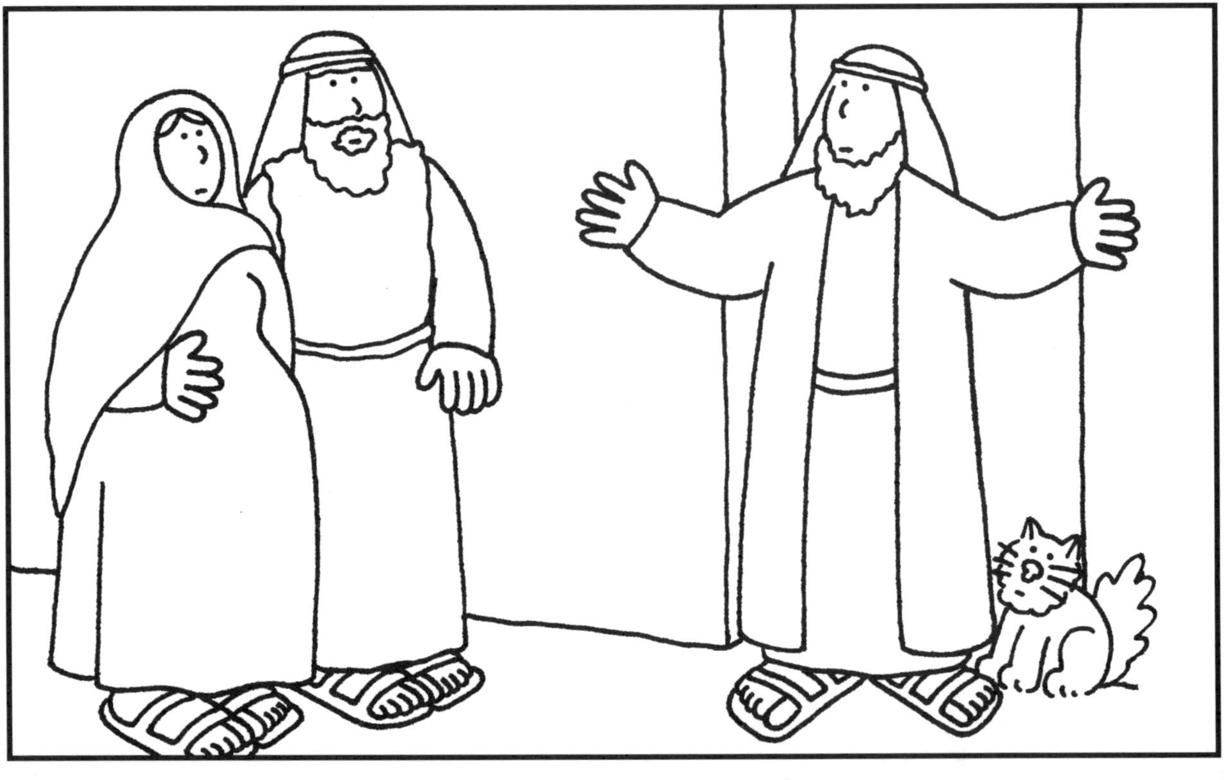

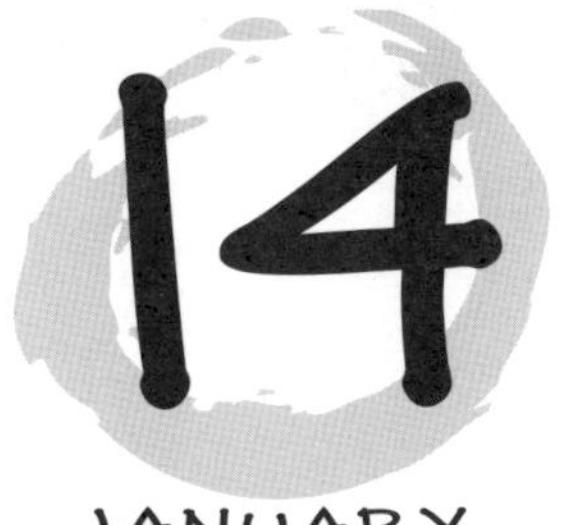

14 JANUARY

Noah is making sure the animals all enter the ark safely.

How many deliberate mistakes can you find?
Read Genesis 6:9–22.

Color me!

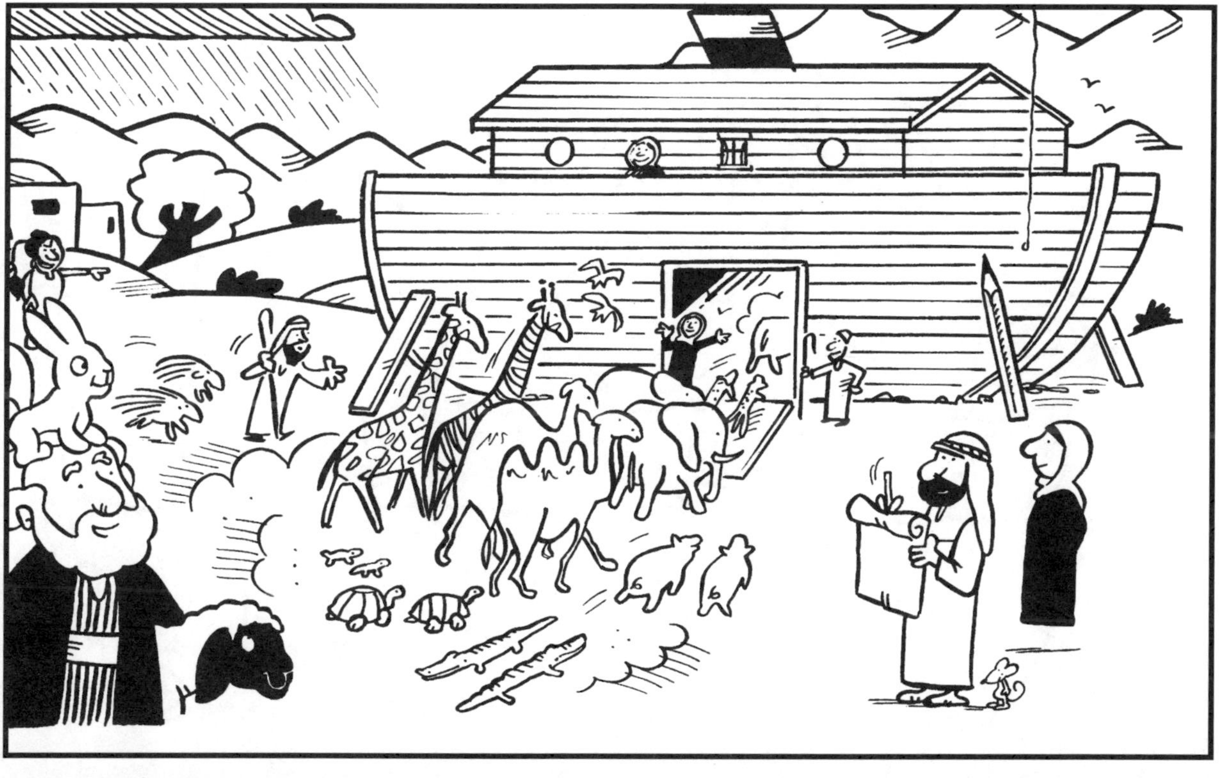

19
DECEMBER

Mary was expecting a baby soon. Joseph and Mary had to travel to Bethlehem to register their names.

You can read about this in Luke 2:4.

Color me!

The animals are now nearly all in the ark.

Put a circle around at least 10 differences between the two pictures.
Read Genesis 7:13–16.

DECEMBER

Mary's husband, Joseph, was a carpenter in the little village of Nazareth. What sort of things do you think he made?

You can read about him in Luke 1:27.

Color me!

16

Everyone is now safely aboard
the ark and the great flood has begun.

Can you find 10 upside-down raindrops in this picture?
Read Genesis 7:13–16.

Color me!

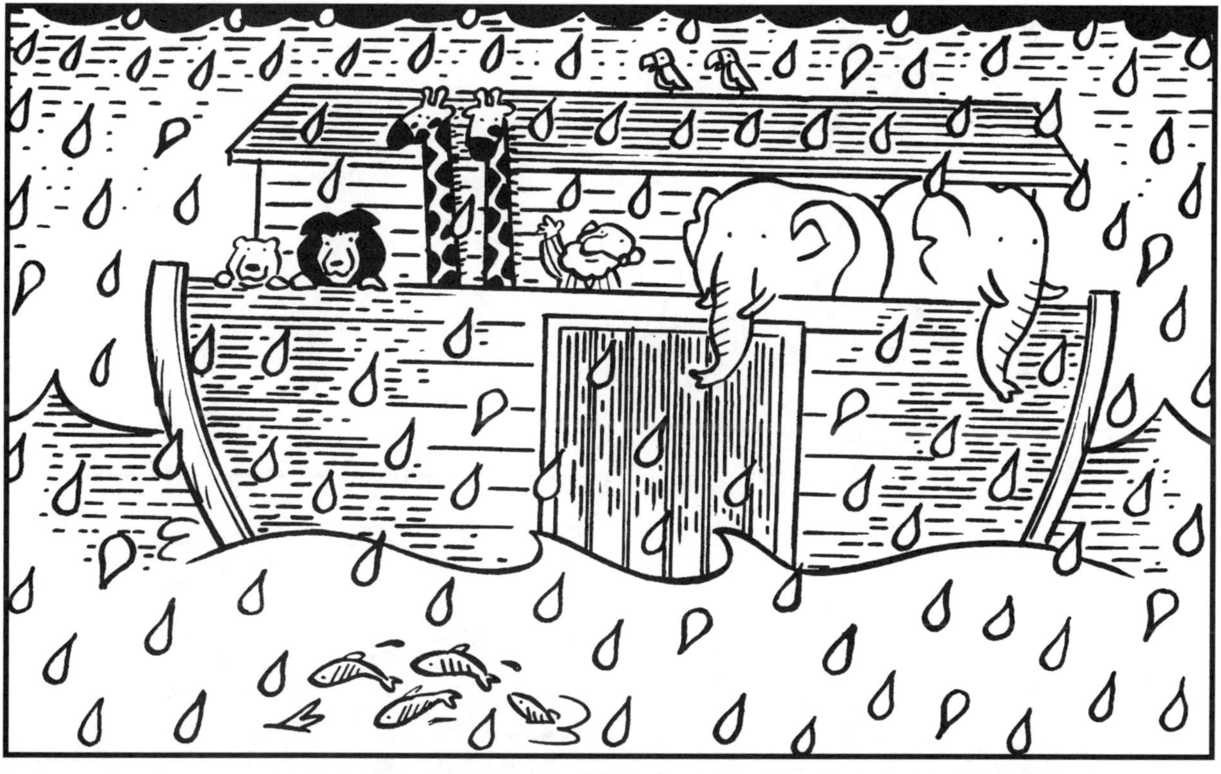

17

DECEMBER

We are getting very near Christmas. For the last days of December, we will re-look at the story of Christmas.

You may like to use these pictures to color and stick on card to make your own Christmas cards.

Here is a prophet foretelling the coming of Jesus.

Color me!

17

JANUARY

At last, after 40 days, the rain stopped. Join up the dots to discover which creature Noah sent out of the ark.

What did it carry back in its beak?
See Genesis 8:6–12.

DOT-TO-DOT

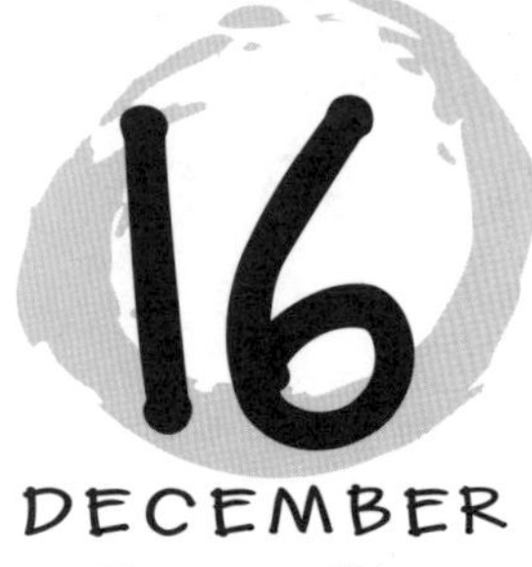

16 DECEMBER

Paul visited many countries to tell people about Jesus. He was shipwrecked more than once.

Can you help Paul to reach land without crossing any lines?
Read this story in Acts 27:39–44.

maze

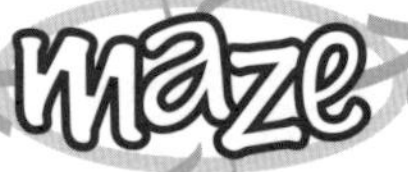

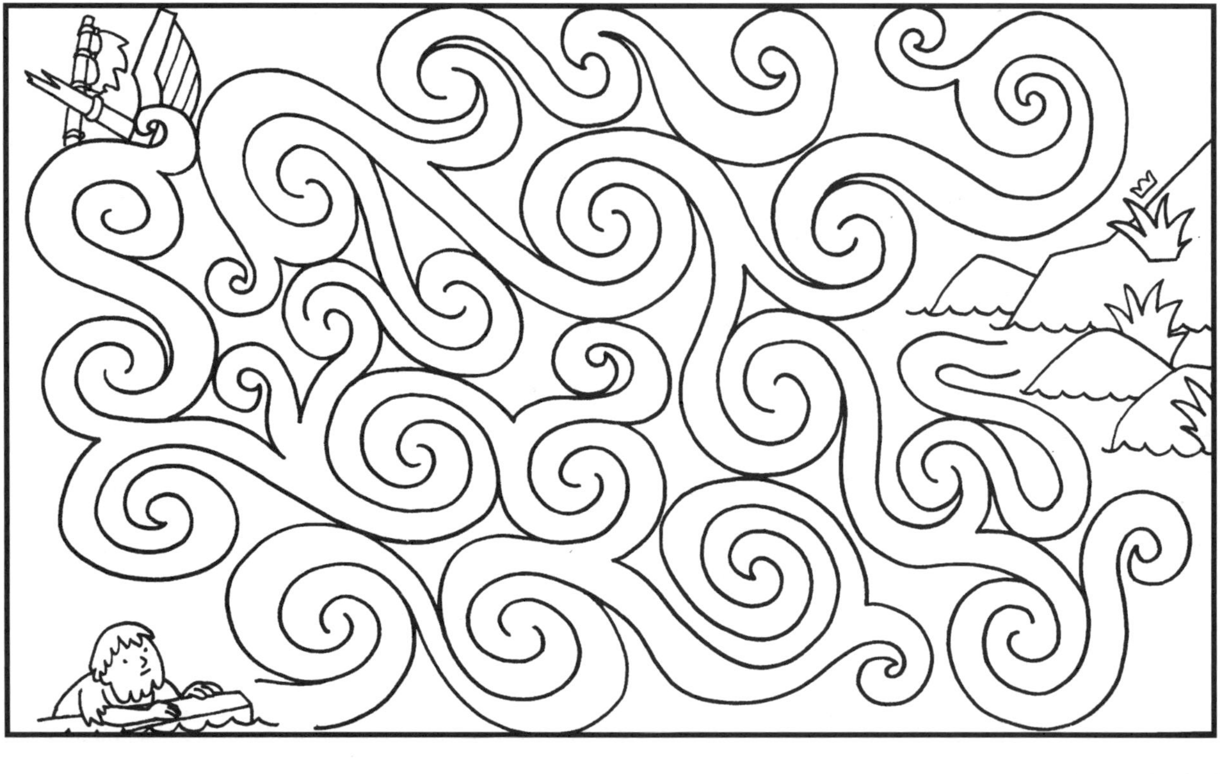

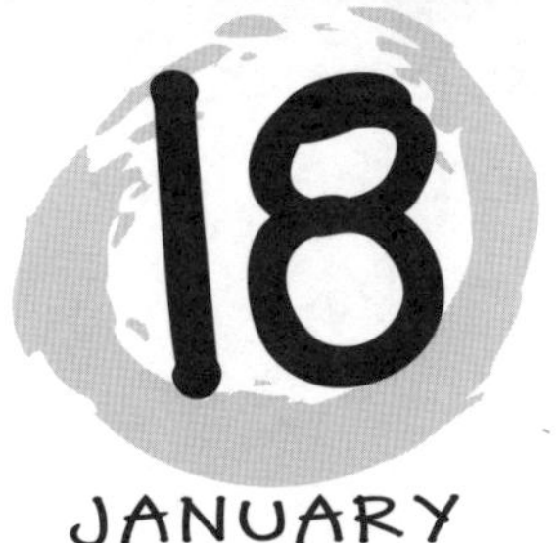

18

JANUARY

Help the dove find its way to the tree without crossing any waves in the water.

You can read this story in Genesis 8:6–12.

maze

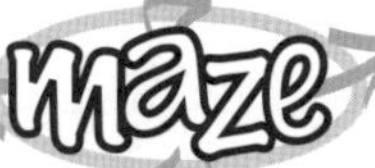

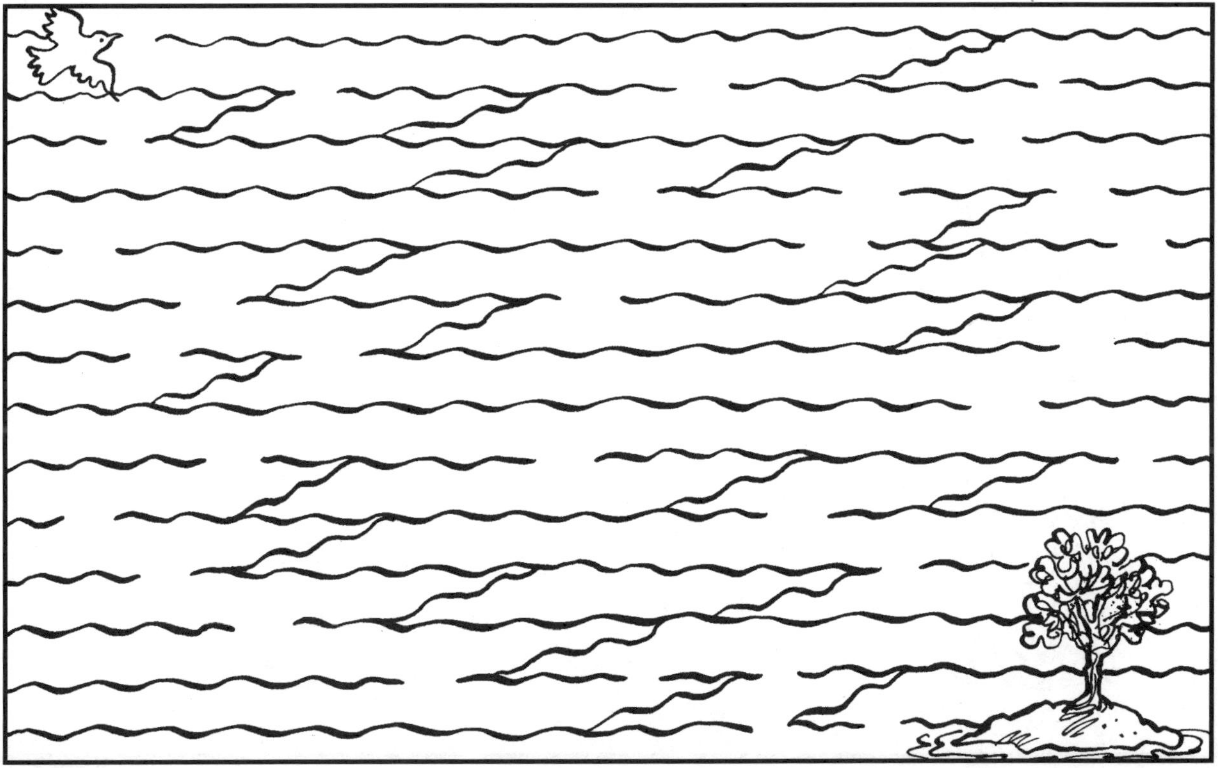

15
DECEMBER

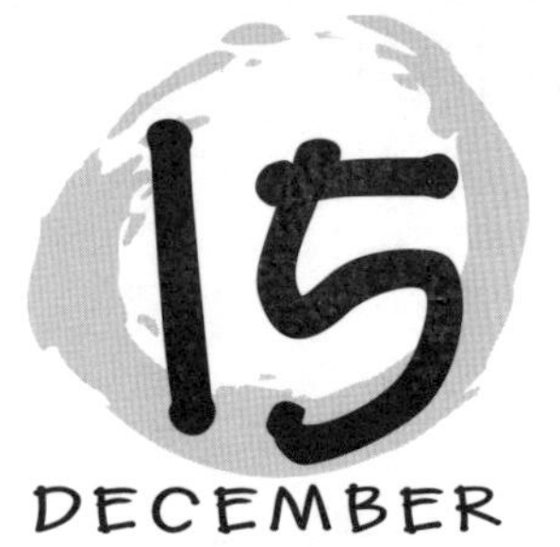

The artist has only finished one picture of a Roman soldier. Try to complete the other two pictures, then color them with felt-tips.

Find the name of a Roman soldier in Acts 10.

Color me!

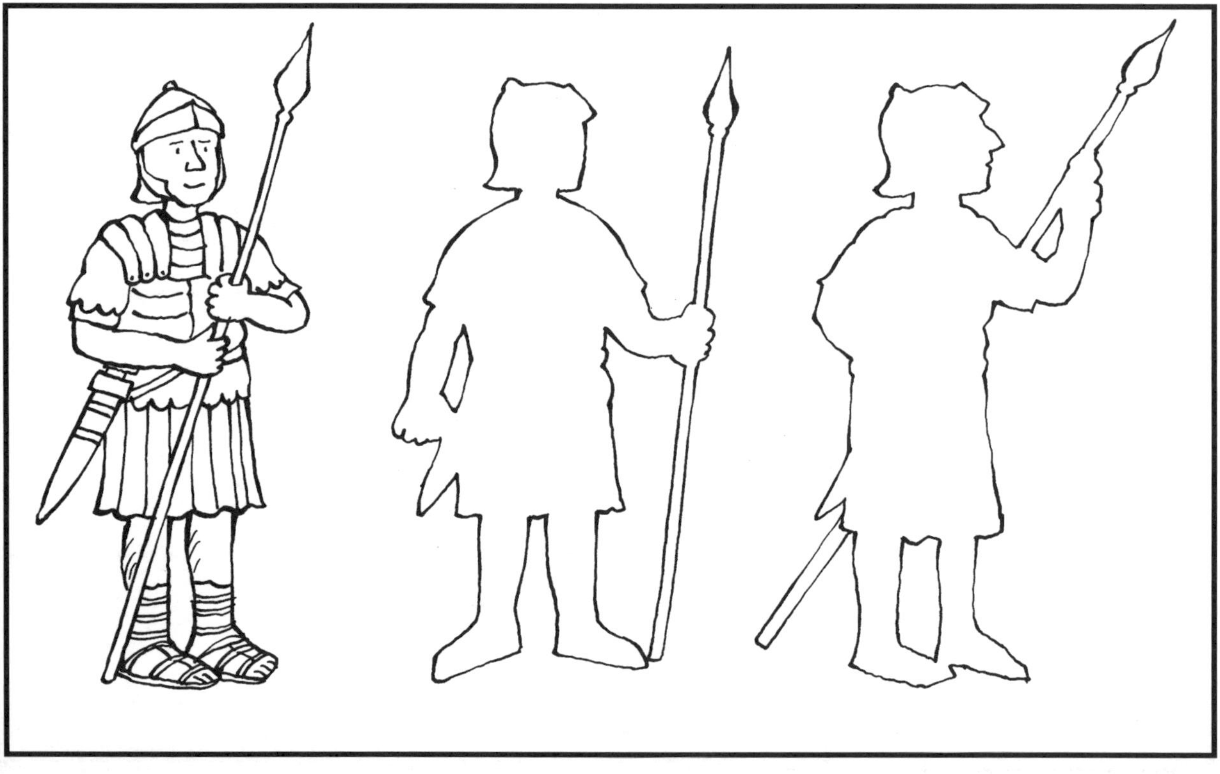

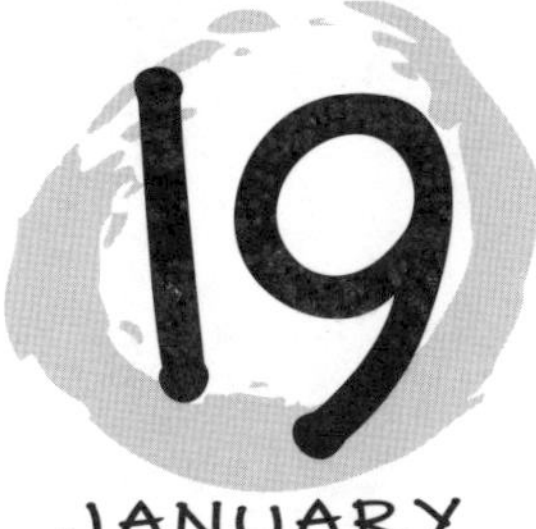

19

JANUARY

Now work out a clear path for the dove carrying the olive leaf to fly back to Noah's ark.

You can read what happened when the rain stopped in Genesis 8.

maze

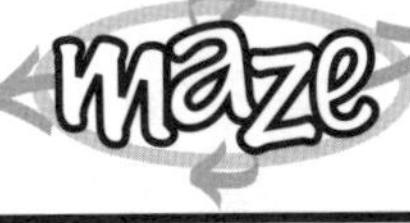

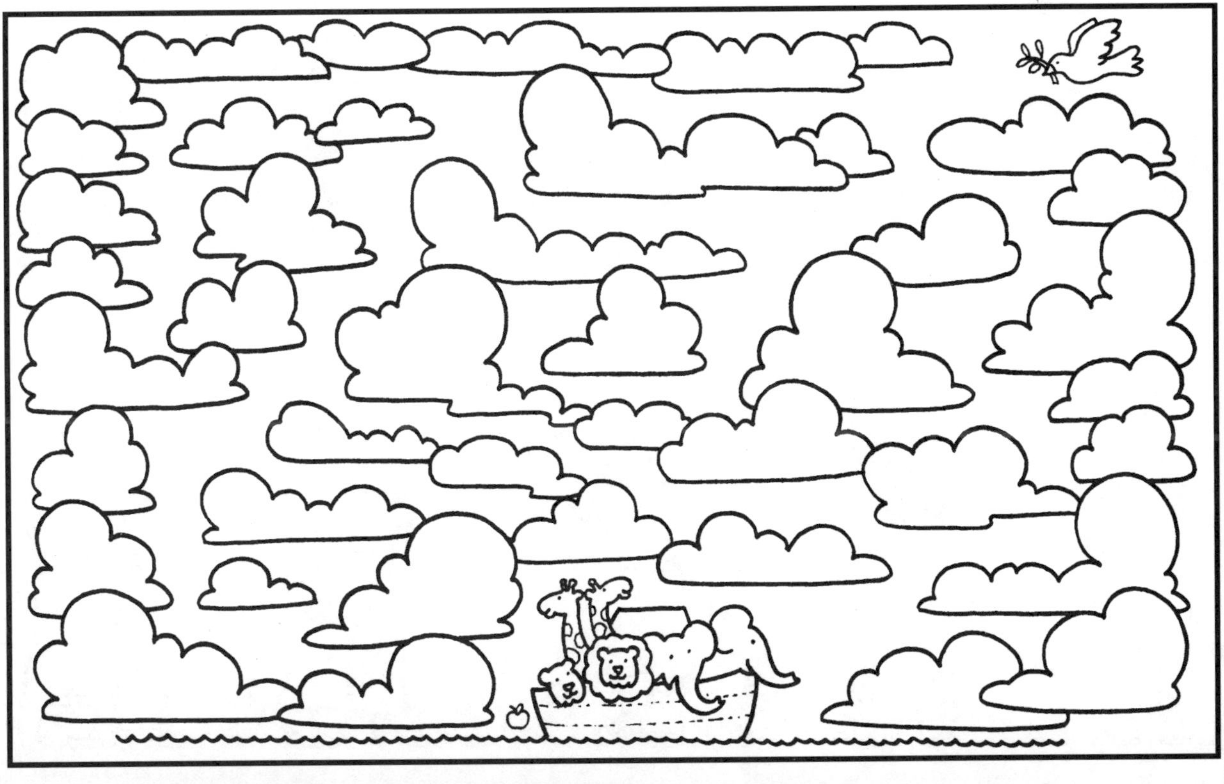

Match up these people with the objects from their work.
Draw a line to link them together.

Read about the Good Shepherd in John chapter 10.

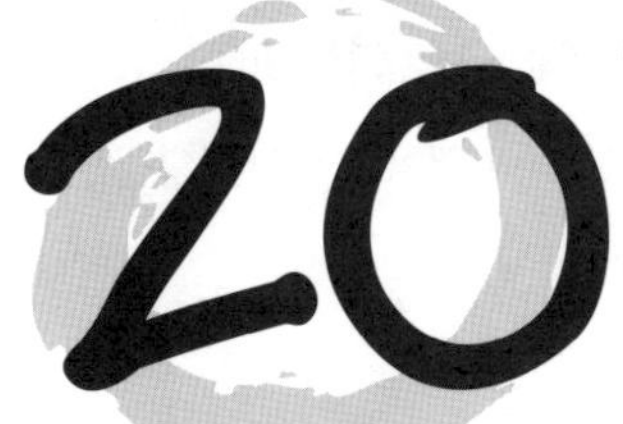

20

JANUARY

Here is another maze. Find the best route for the ark to reach dry land without crossing any lines.

You can read this story in Genesis 8:13–14.

maze

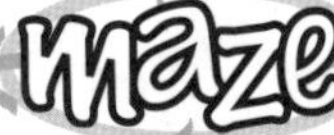

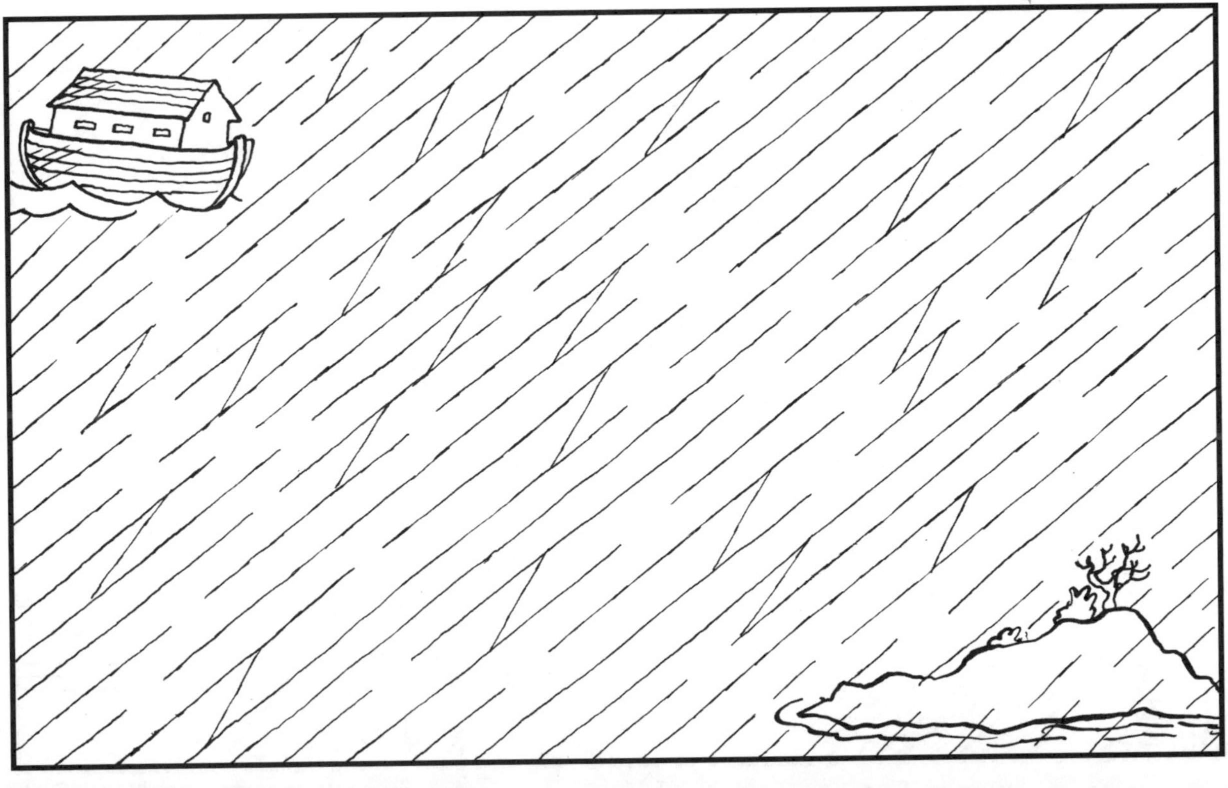

13 DECEMBER

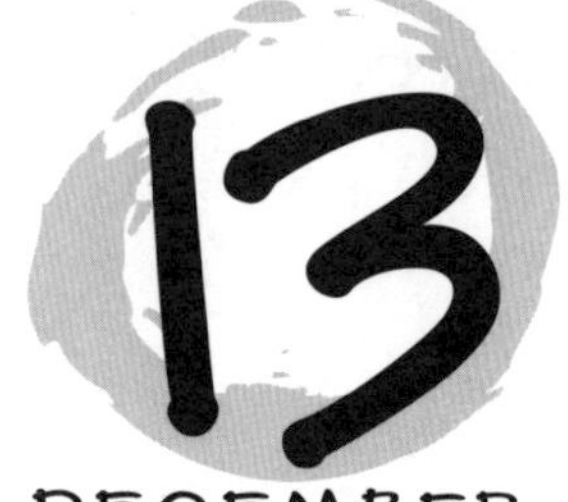

Priscilla made tents with her husband, Aquila. They were good friends of the missionary Paul. Can you find 15 needles hidden here?

Read about Aquila and Priscilla in Acts 18:1–4, 18–26.

Puzzle

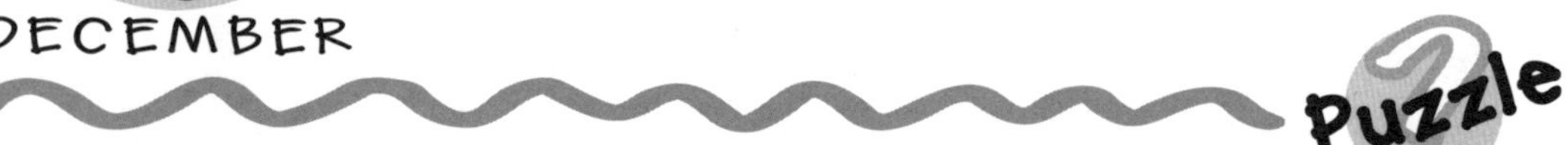

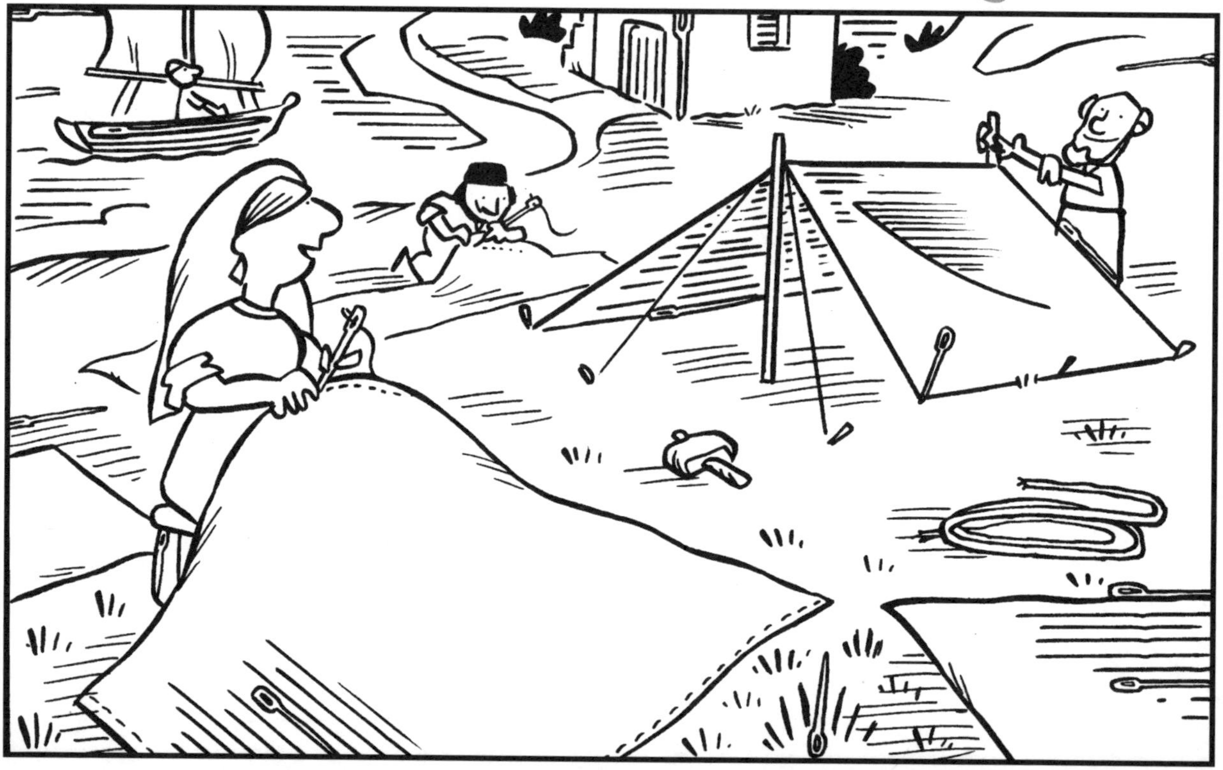

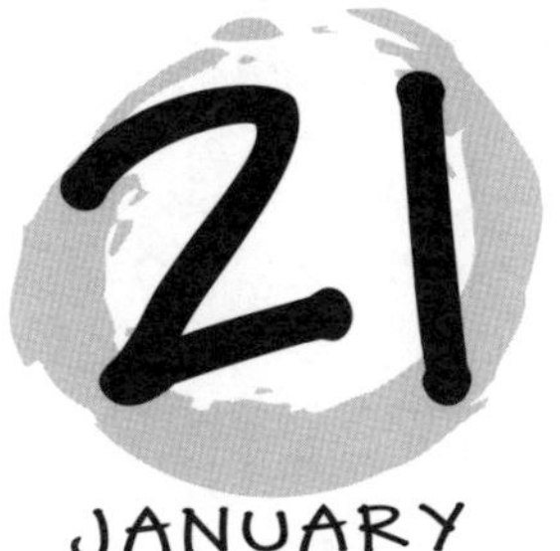

21 JANUARY

When Noah, his family and all the animals finally left the ark, God sent a sign promising never to flood the world again.

Join up the dots to discover what God's sign was.
See Genesis 9:12–17.

DOT-TO-DOT

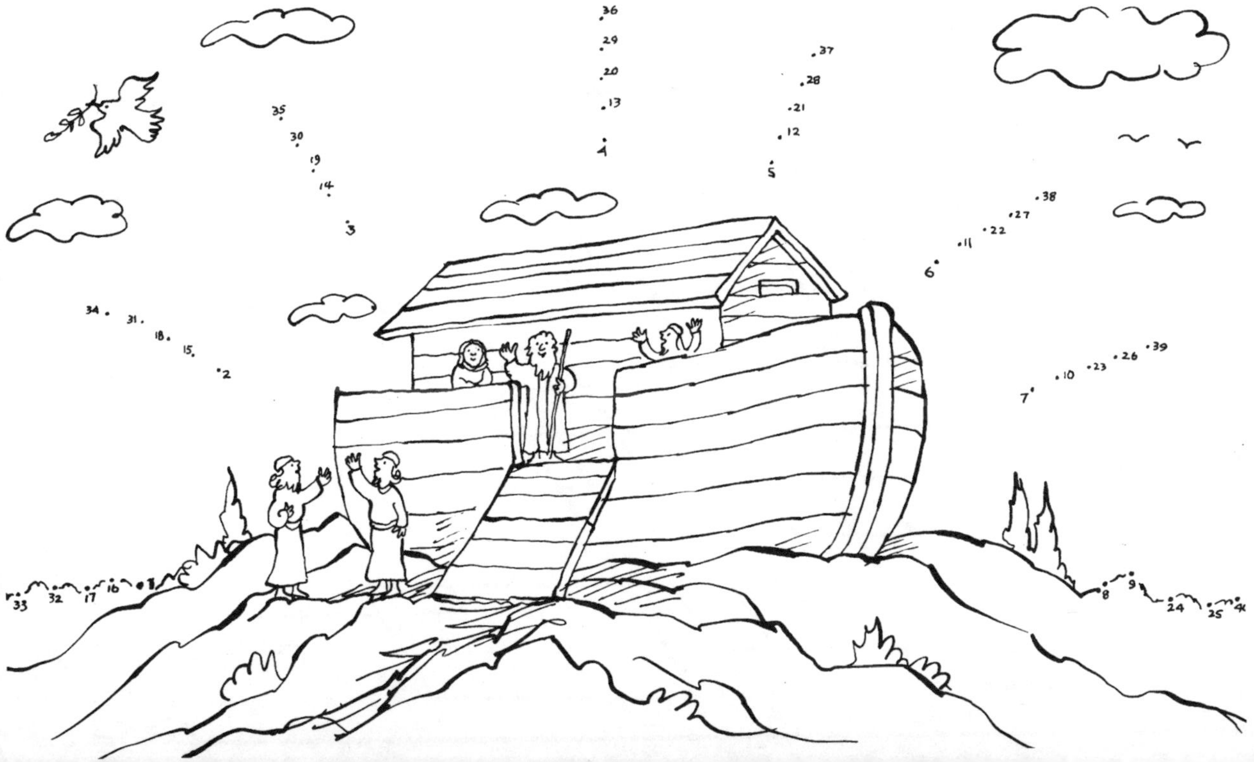

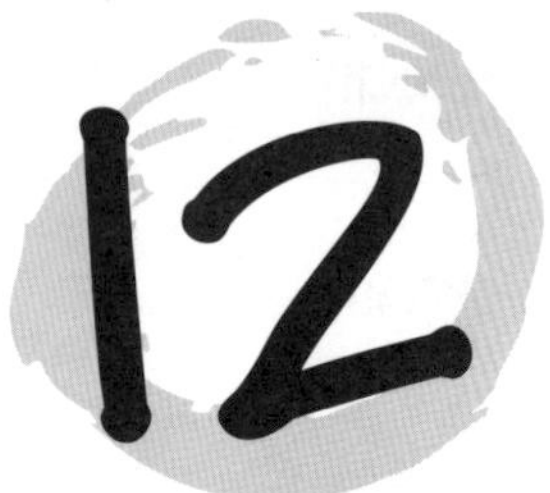

12 DECEMBER

Paul and Barnabas traveled together, telling people the good news about Jesus. Can you match up 2 pairs of brothers and 2 friends?

Read Acts 13:42–52.

Puzzle

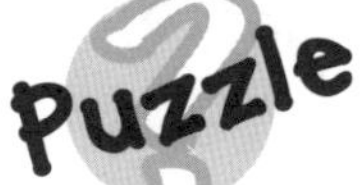

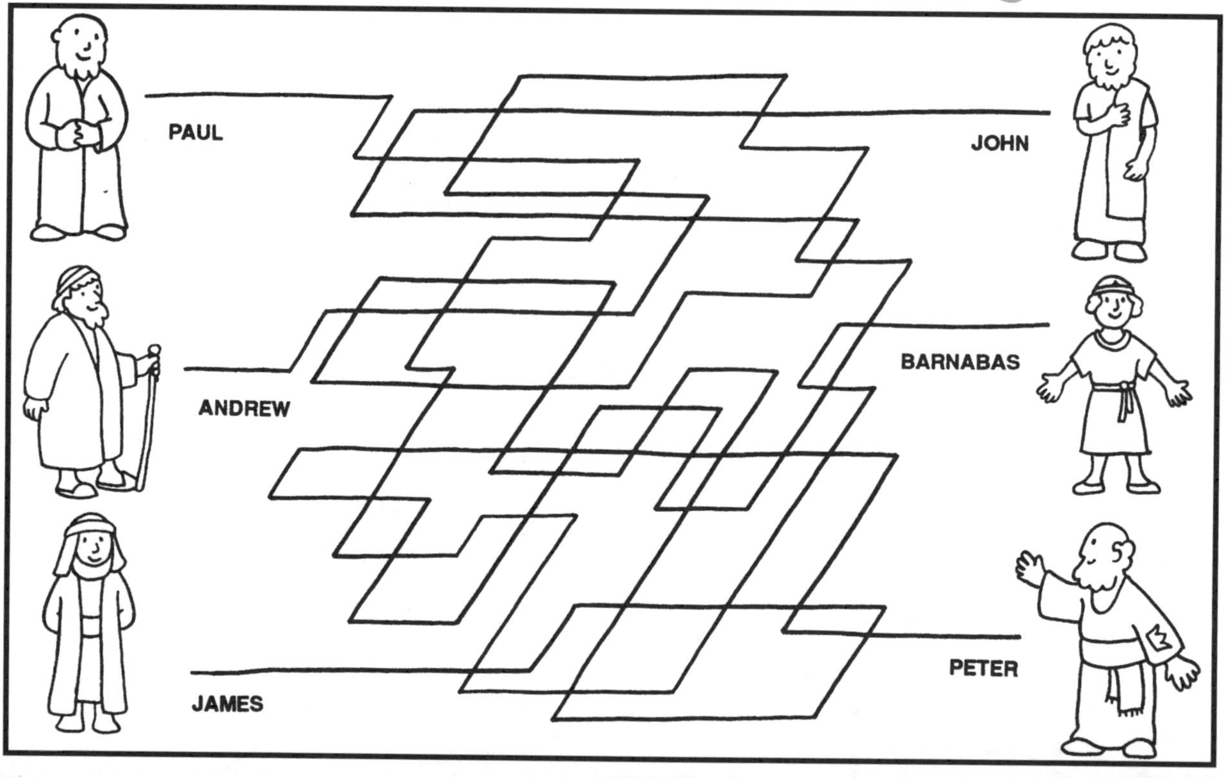

22

Here are six pictures telling the story of Noah. Number them in the right order.

You can read this story in Genesis chapters 6—9.

Puzzle

11

DECEMBER

Can you help Paul escape from Damascus by finding the way through the wall maze to reach the ground, without crossing any lines?

Read the whole story in Acts 9:19b–30.

maze

23

JANUARY

After Noah's time, some people started building a great tower that would reach the sky.

Help the builder find a way to his ladder without climbing over anything. See Genesis 11:1–4.

maze

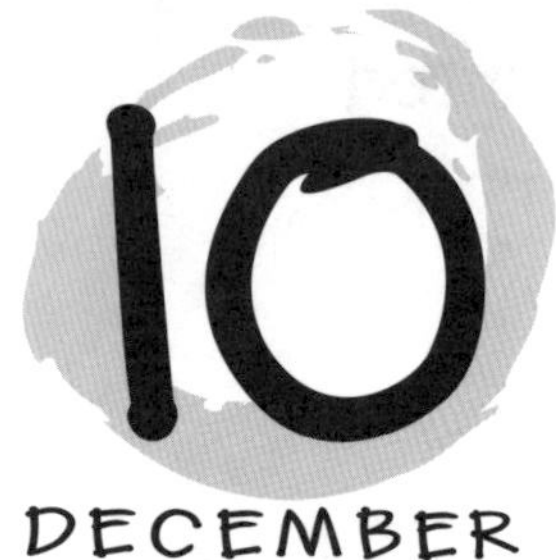

10 DECEMBER

Paul became a Christian himself, after meeting Jesus on the road to Damascus. He had to escape in a basket.

Find 10 differences between these two pictures.
See Acts 9:19b–30.

SPOT THE DIFFERENCE

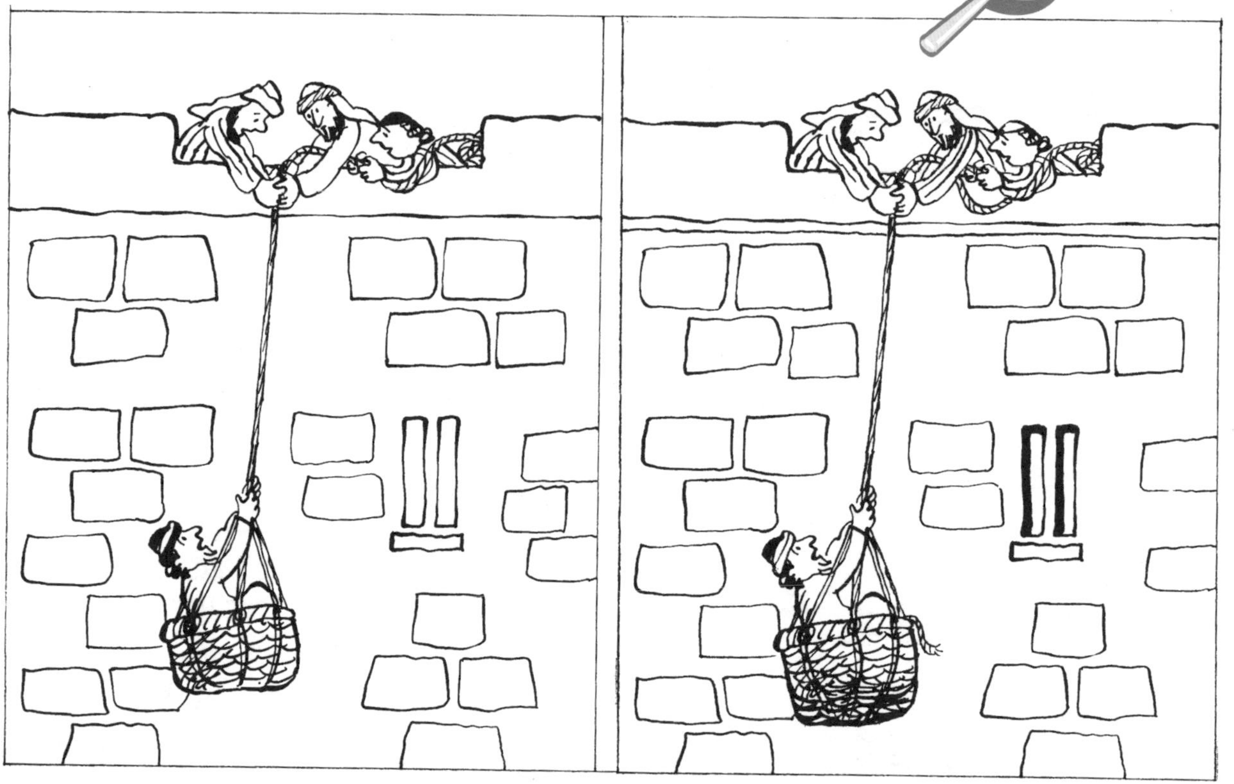

24
JANUARY

Circle every deliberate mistake you can find in this picture of the Tower of Babel.

You can find the story of the building of the great tower in Genesis 11:1–9.

Color me!

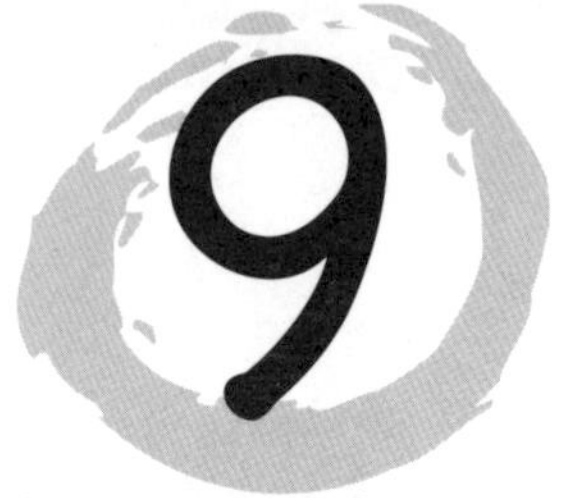

9 DECEMBER

On his way to Damascus, Paul was struck blind as Jesus spoke to him. Can you find 8 plants hidden in this picture?

Read the story in Acts 9:1–19.

Puzzle

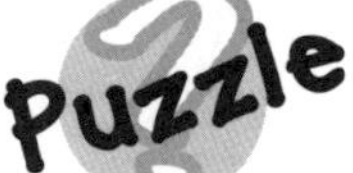

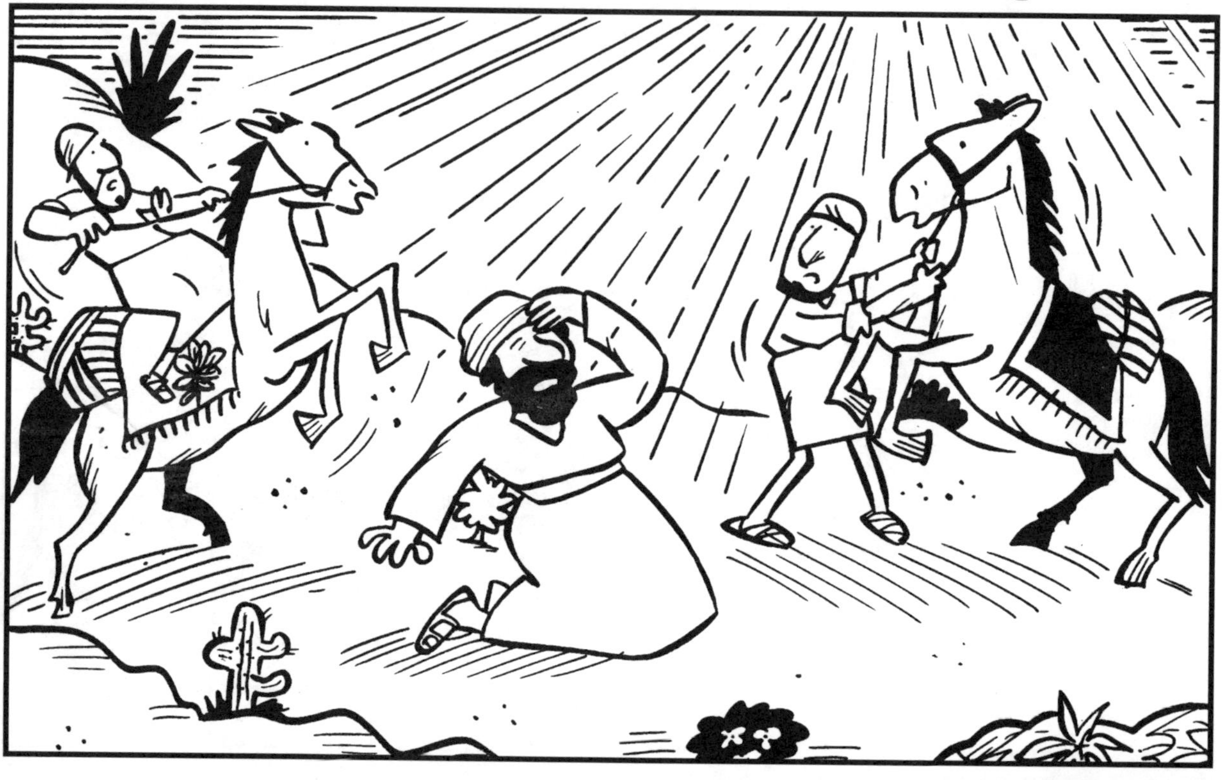

25

JANUARY

Can you find at least 10 differences between these two pictures of the building of the Tower of Babel?

Is the tower finished?
See Genesis 11:8–9.

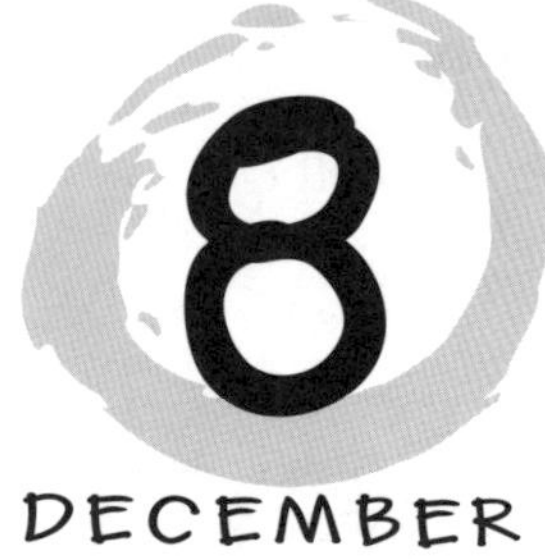

8

DECEMBER

Paul traveled to Damascus to harm the Christians living there. On the way, Jesus spoke to him.

Can you help Paul find his way to Damascus?
Read the whole story in Acts 9:1–19.

maze

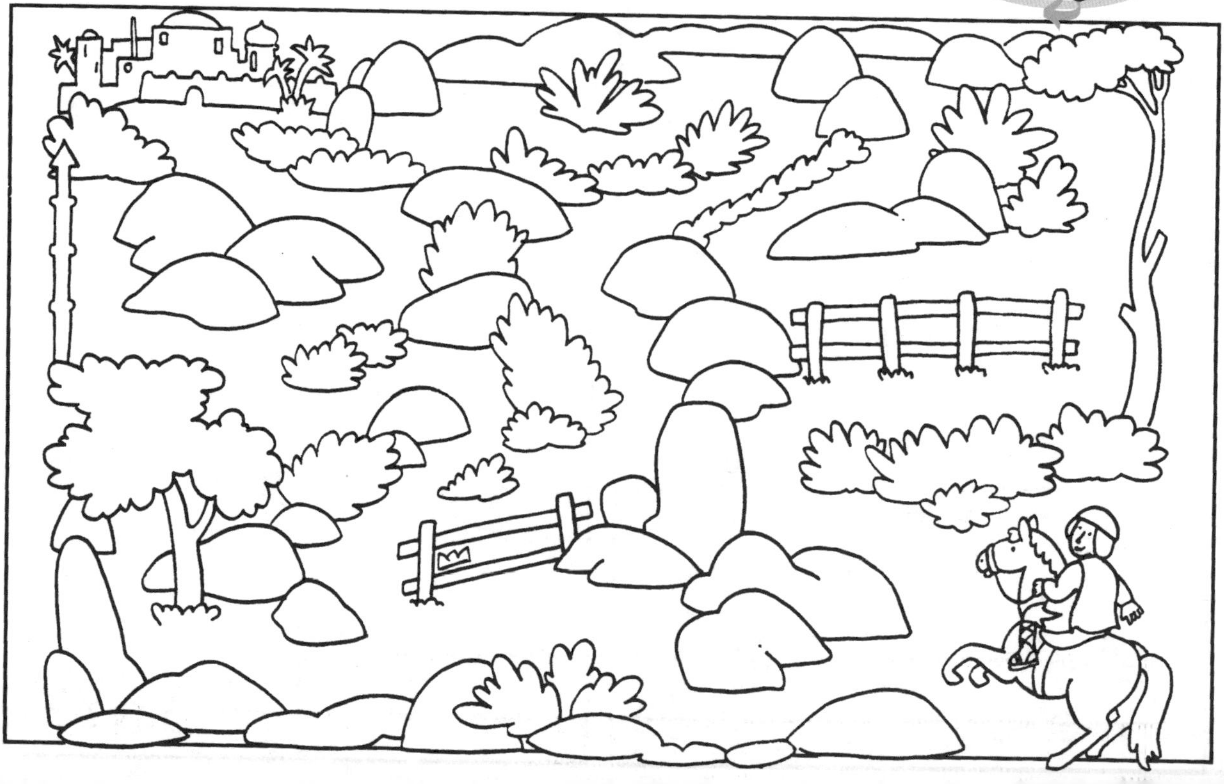

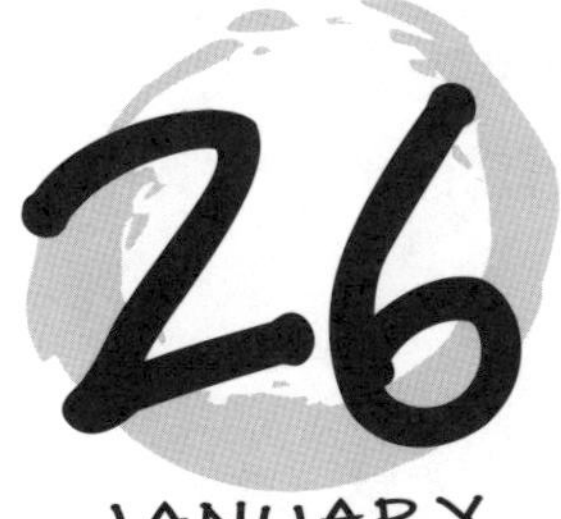

26

JANUARY

God called Abram to travel from his home in Ur to the Promised Land.

Find a clear path for Abram and his family to get from Ur to the Promised Land.
Read Genesis 12:1–8.

maze

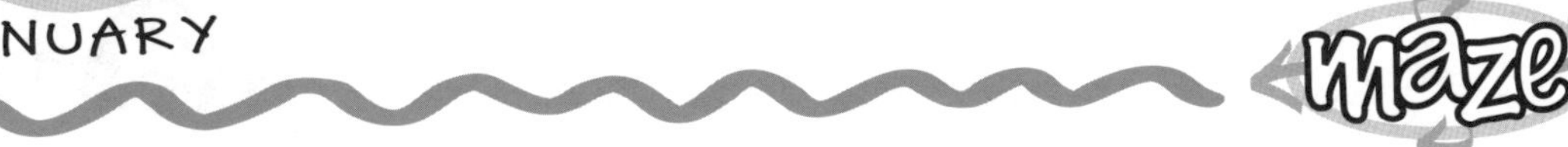

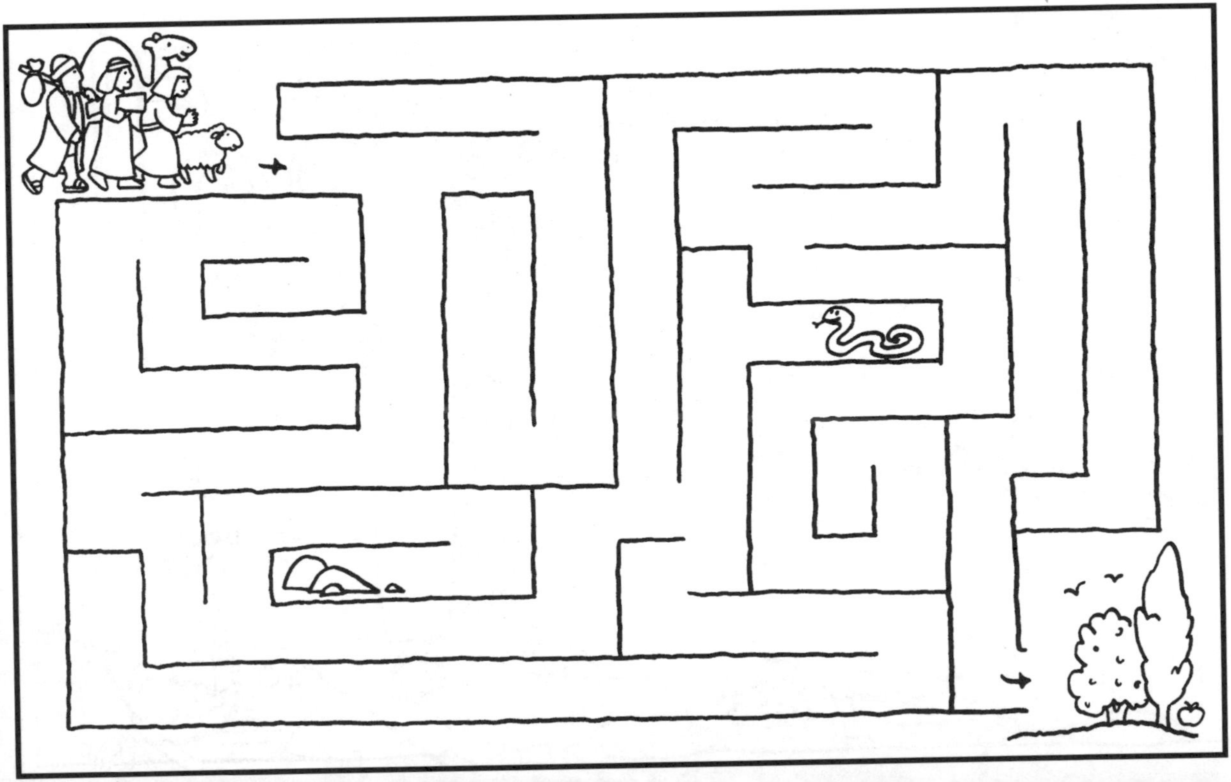

7 DECEMBER

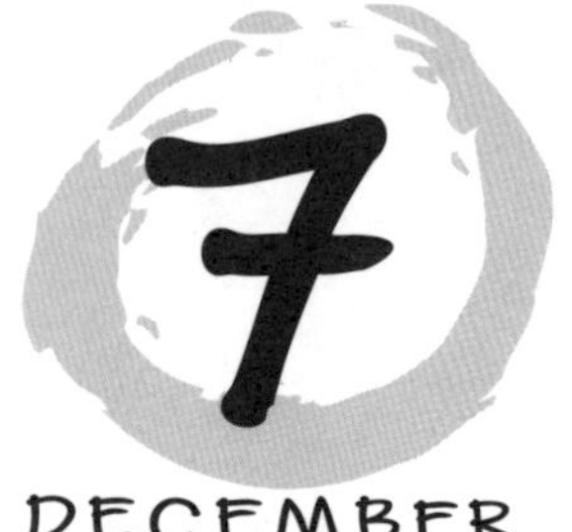

Dorcas was a good woman who helped the poor. When she died, Peter brought her back to life again.

Can you find 10 lamps hidden in this picture?
Read the story of Dorcas in Acts 9:36–42.

Puzzle

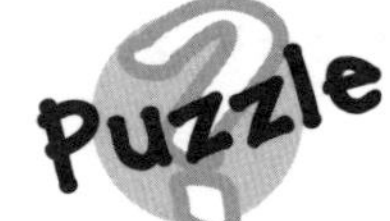

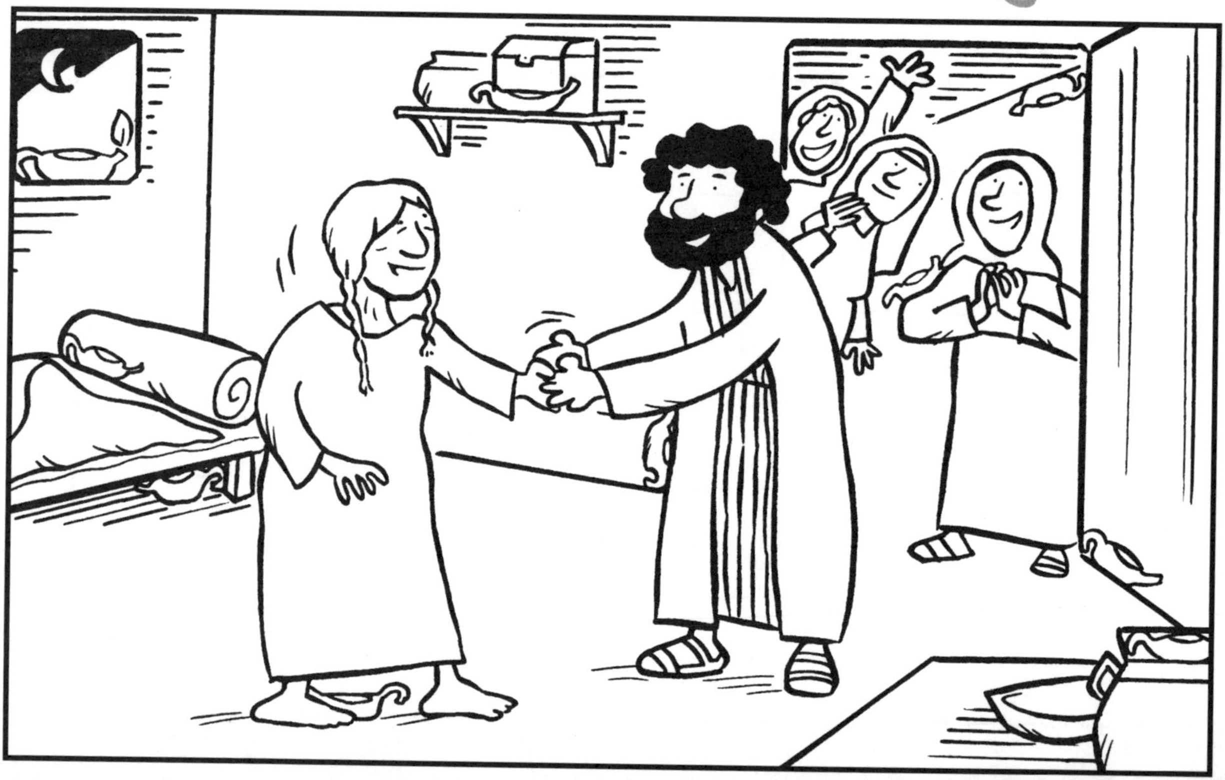

27
JANUARY

How many deliberate mistakes has the artist made in this picture of Abram leaving home? List them all.

You can find this story in Genesis 12:1–9.

Color me!

6

DECEMBER

There are two pairs of identical Roman soldier's helmets here.
Can you find them?

Read about Peter and a Roman centurion in Acts 10:1–48.

Puzzle

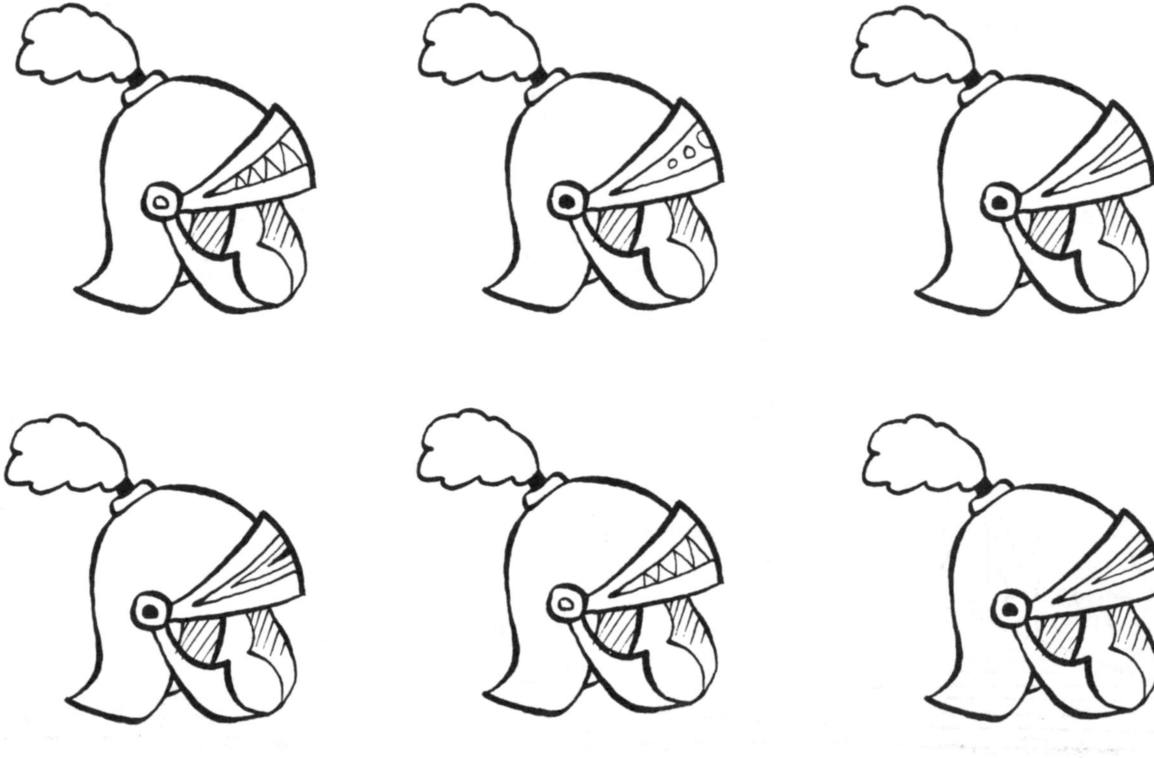

28

Can you find 6 hidden palm trees in this picture of Abram and his family traveling through the desert to the Promised Land?

You can find this story in Genesis 12:1–9.

Color me!

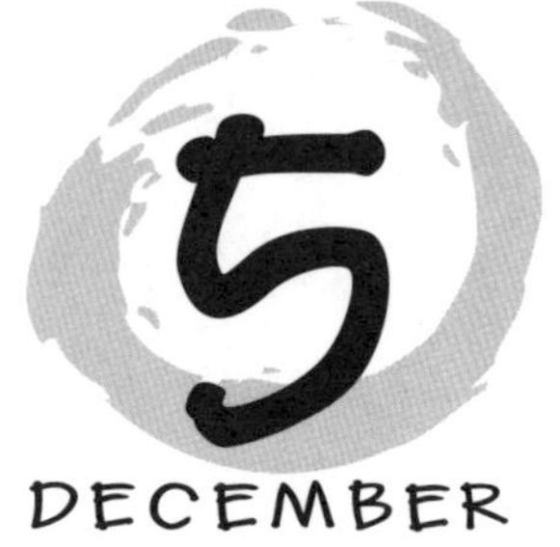

5

DECEMBER

Rhoda the servant girl answered the door to Peter when he escaped from prison. She was so happy that she forgot to open it!

Can you find 11 dogs hiding in this picture?
Read the whole story in Acts 12:1–18.

Puzzle

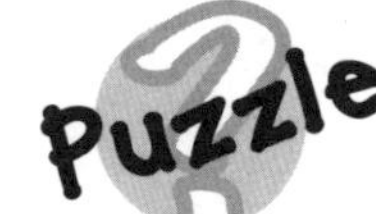

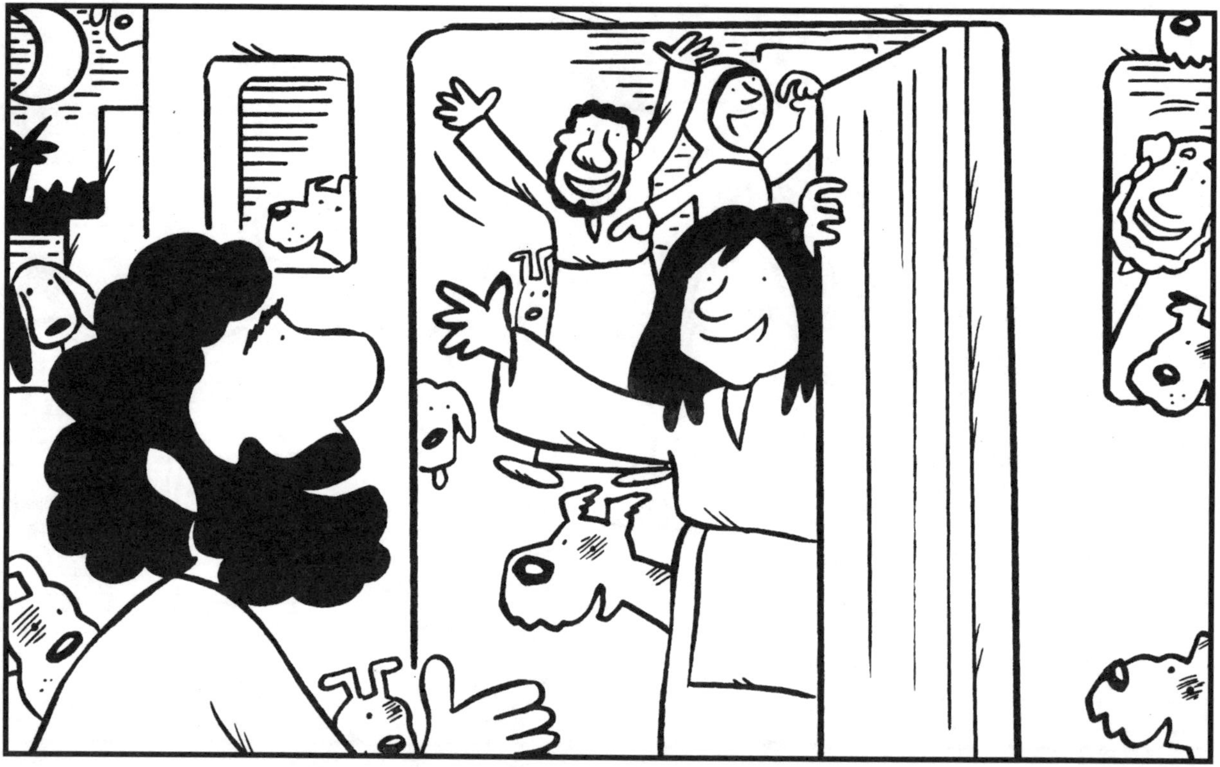

29
JANUARY

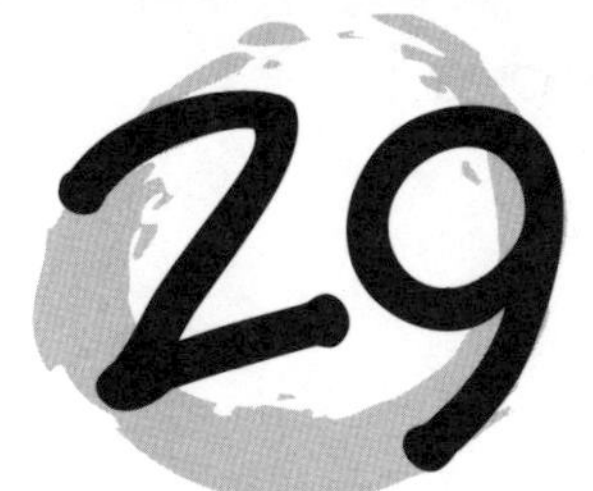

Join up the dots to find out where Abraham and Sarah lived.

You can find out in Genesis 18:1.

DOT-TO-DOT

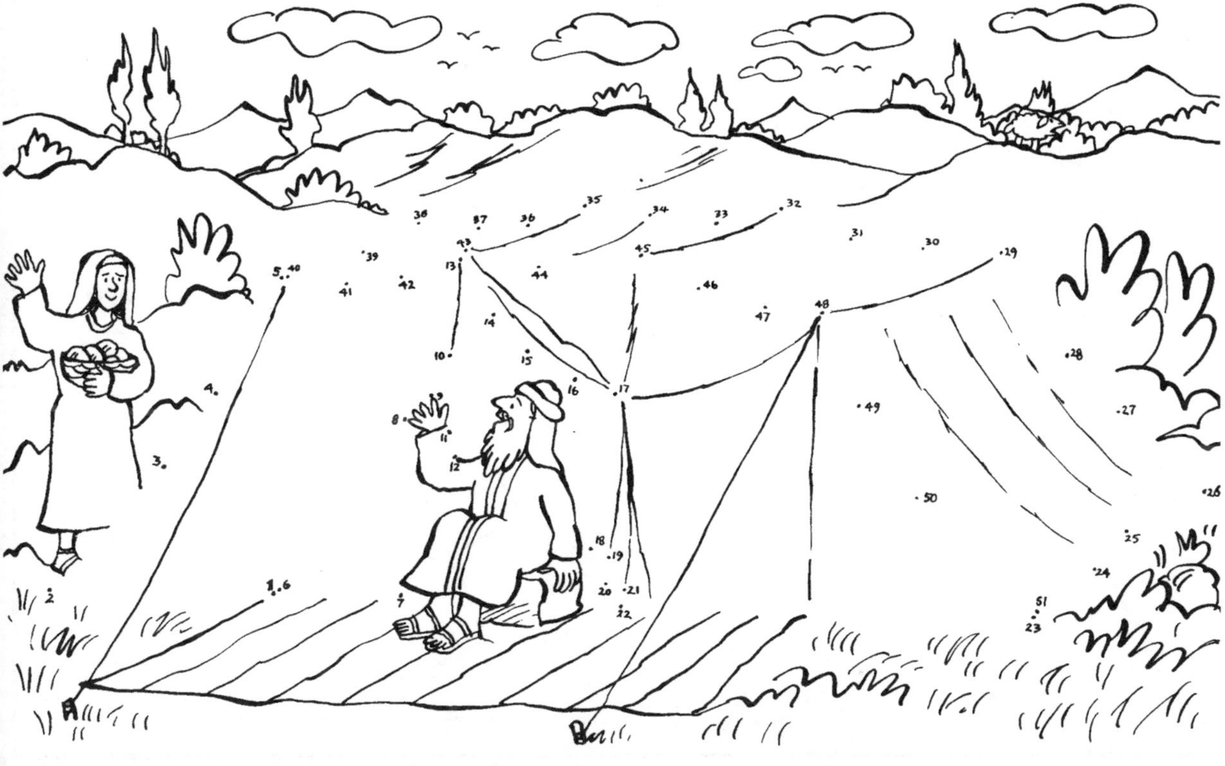

4 DECEMBER

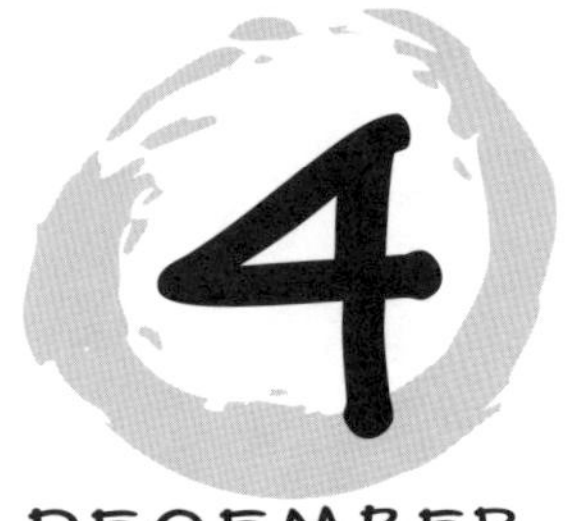

Matthew was a tax-collector before he followed Jesus;
Luke was a doctor.

Follow the lines to find which object belongs to which follower of Jesus.

maze

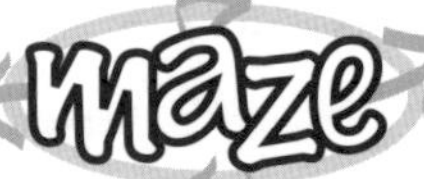

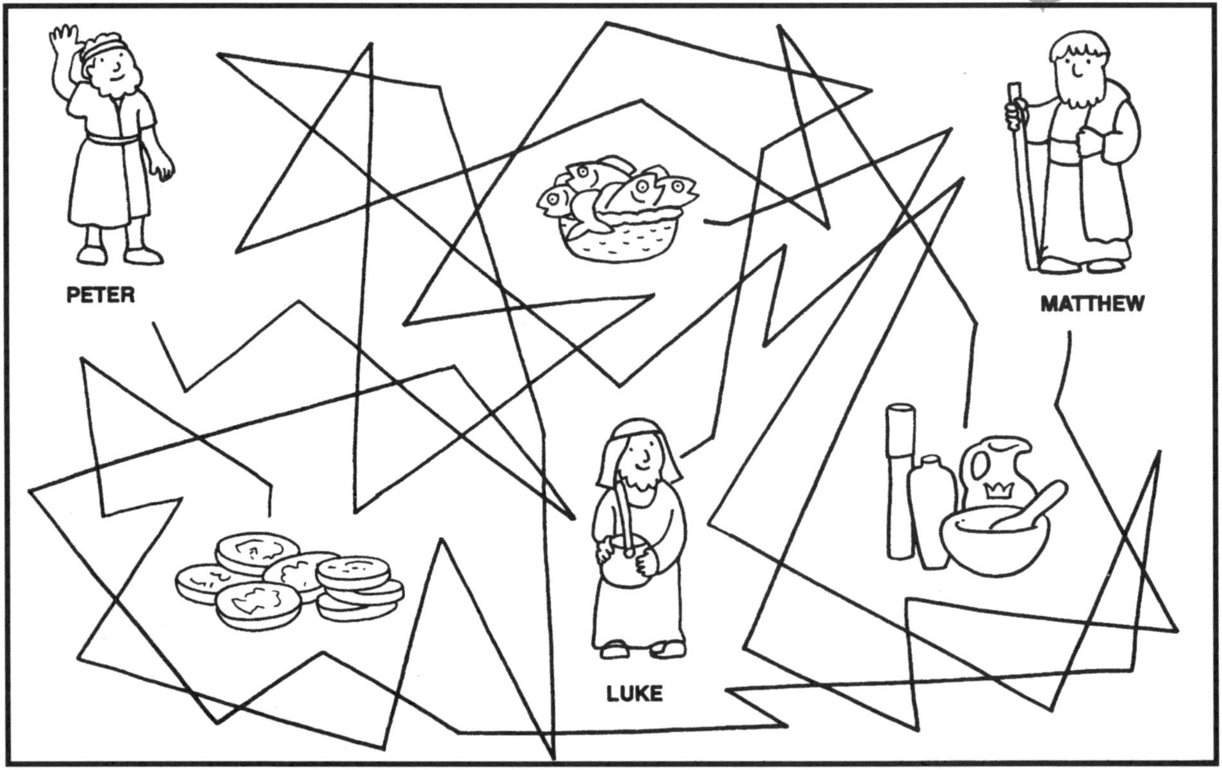

Abraham and his family lived in tents.

These tents all look the same—
but only two are exactly the same. Which two?

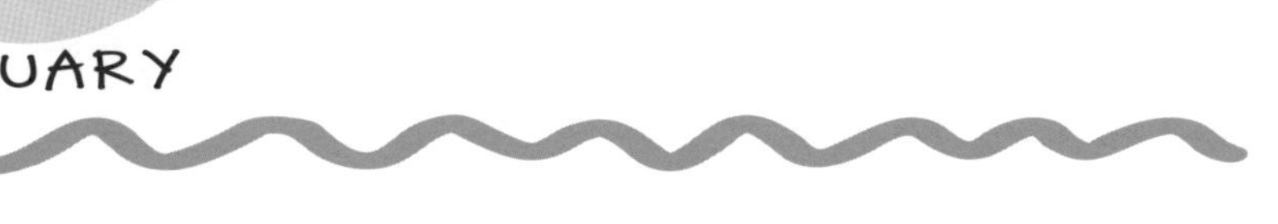

3

DECEMBER

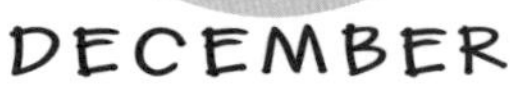

One of these drawings of a Roman chariot is a bit different from the other three.

Which is different from the other three?
What is the difference?

31

God told Abraham to count the stars.
Find out why in Genesis 15:5.

Find 10 differences between these two pictures.

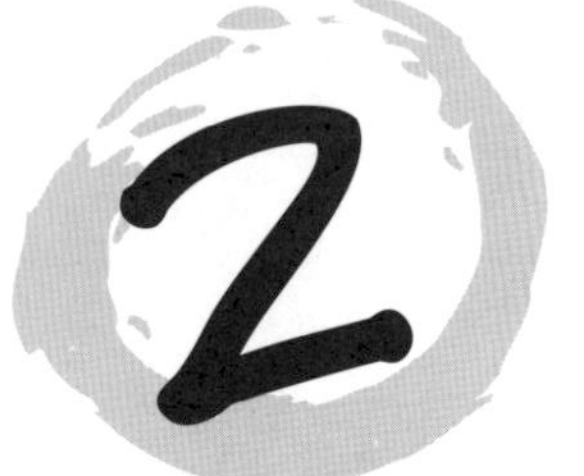

2

DECEMBER

Dr. Luke wrote the story of Jesus in the Gospel of Luke. Can you find all 11 pens hidden in this picture of him writing his Gospel?

Read the first words of his Gospel in Luke 1:1–4.

Puzzle

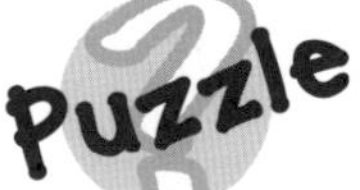

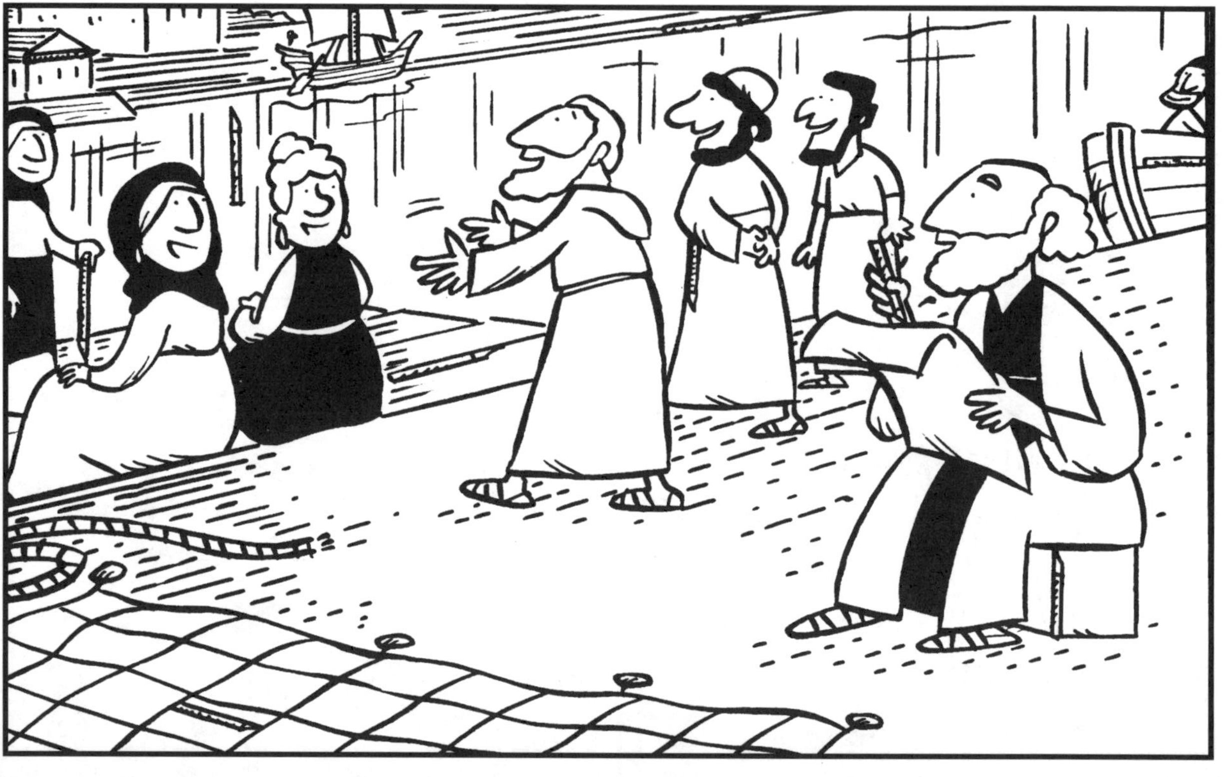

1 FEBRUARY

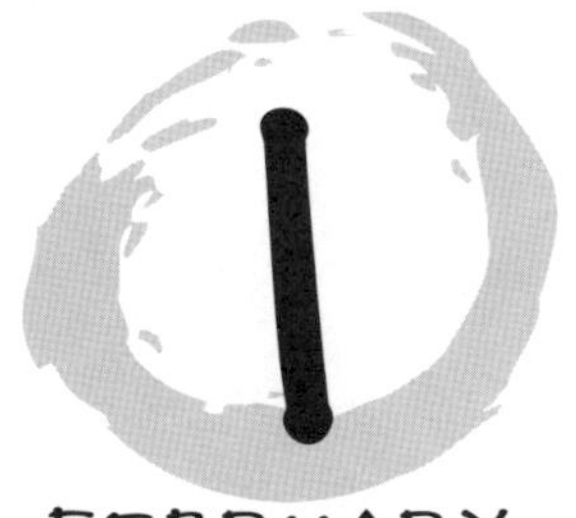

Three special messengers visited Abraham and Sarah. Join up the dots to find out where he was sitting.

You can read the story of Abraham's visitors and their message in Genesis 18:1–15. Who were the messengers?

DOT-TO-DOT

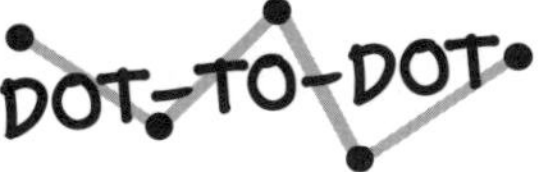

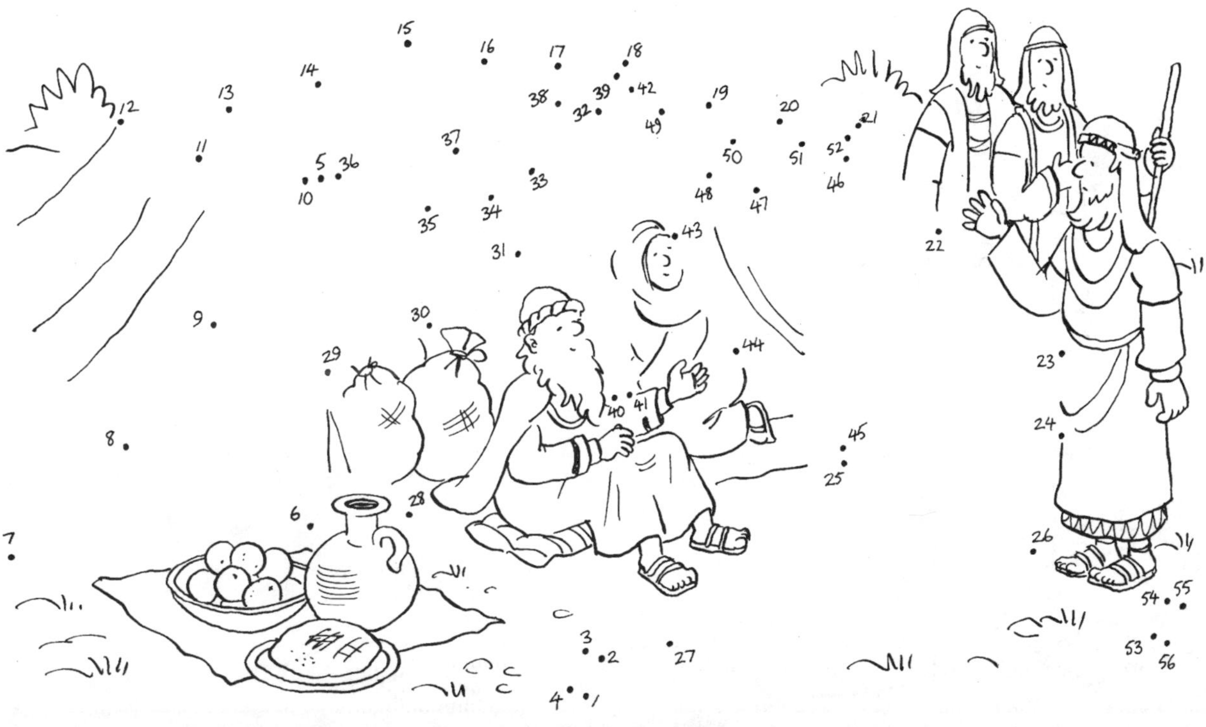

1

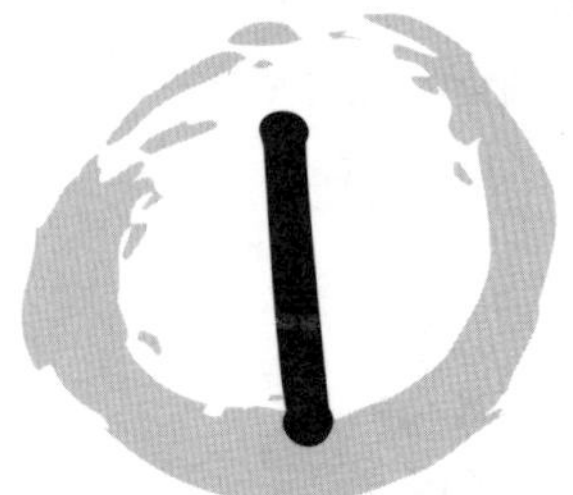

DECEMBER

Join up the dots to find out what the risen Lord Jesus is doing here. Who is he waving to?

Read John 21:1–14 to find out.

DOT-TO-DOT

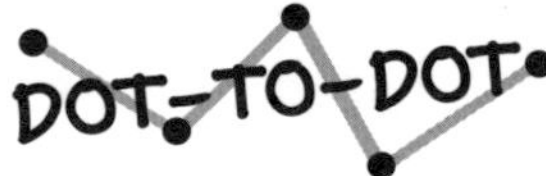

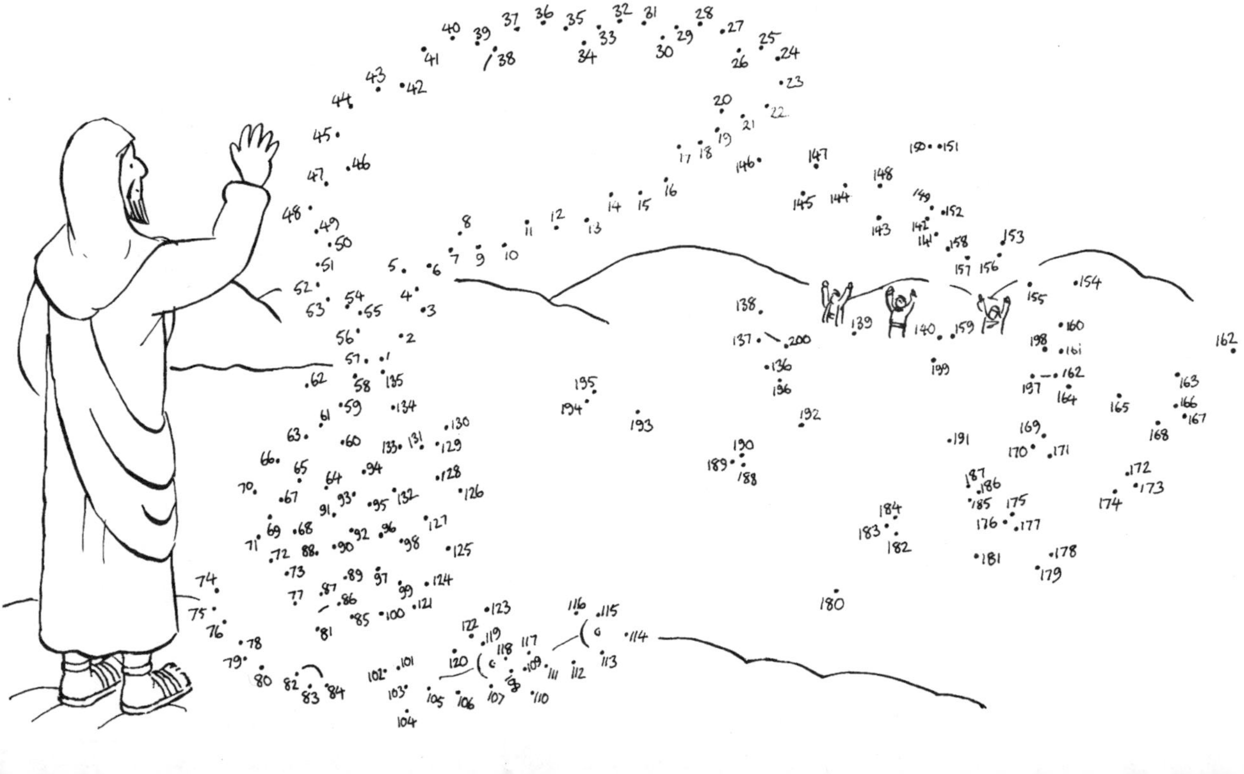

2
FEBRUARY

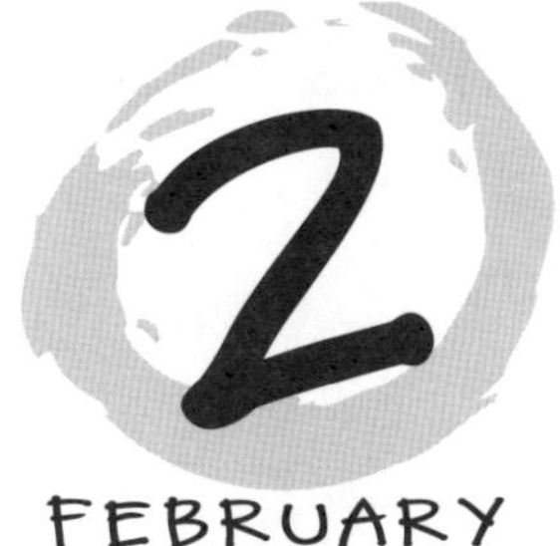

Abraham's wife Sarah was very old. She laughed when she heard the visitor say she would have a baby son.

Can you find 15 dishes hidden in this picture?
Read this story in Genesis 18:1–15

Color me!

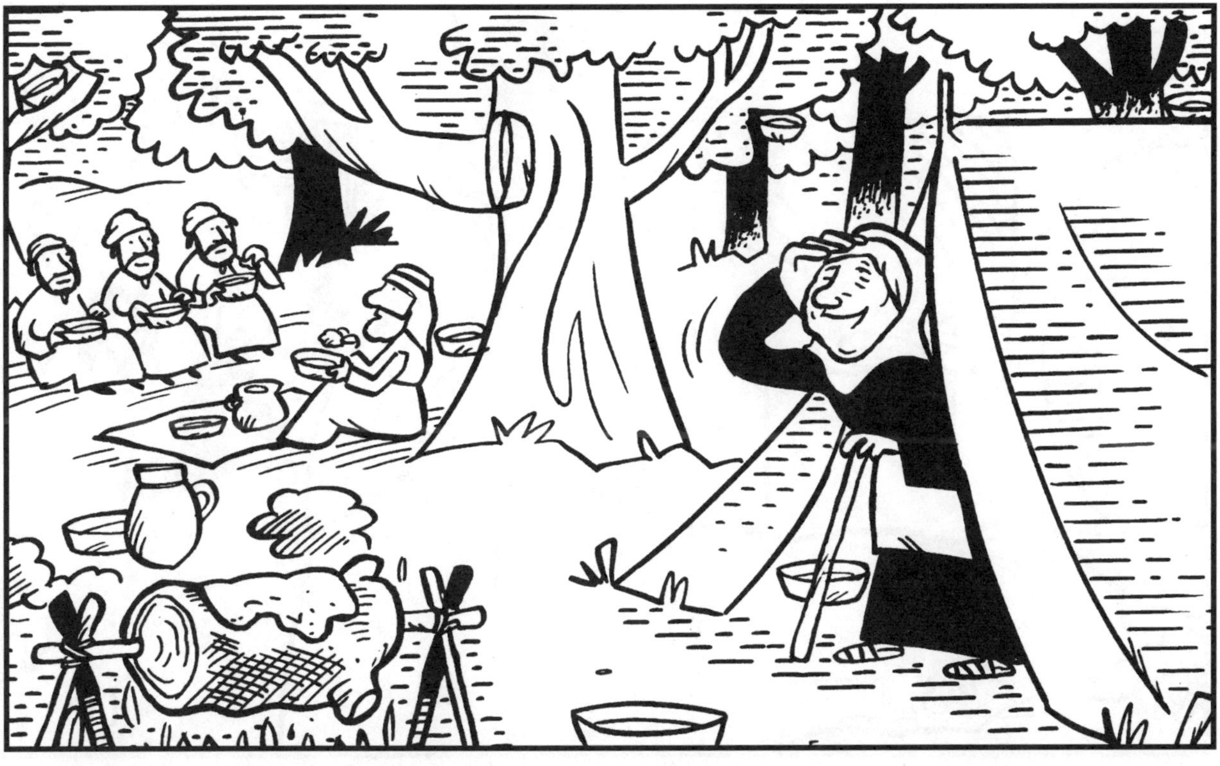

30

NOVEMBER

Mary Magdalene was very sad when she saw that Jesus' tomb was empty. She thought someone had stolen his body.

Can you find 13 butterflies hidden in this picture?
Read the whole story in John 20:10–18.

Puzzle

3 FEBRUARY

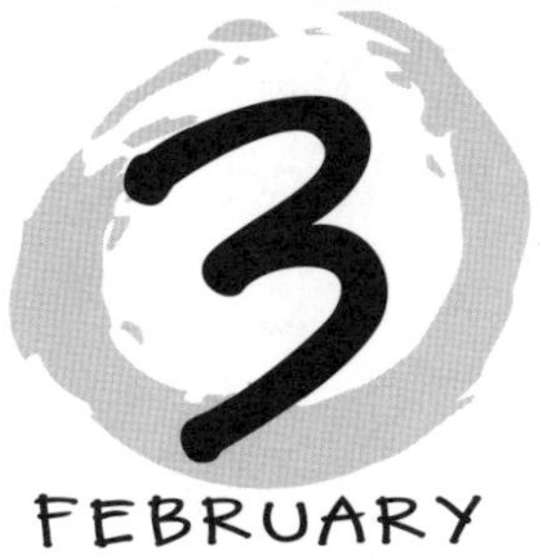

God told Abraham's nephew Lot to leave the wicked city of Sodom. Help him find the way.

You can read the story of Lot, and what happened to Lot's wife, in Genesis 19:1–29.

maze

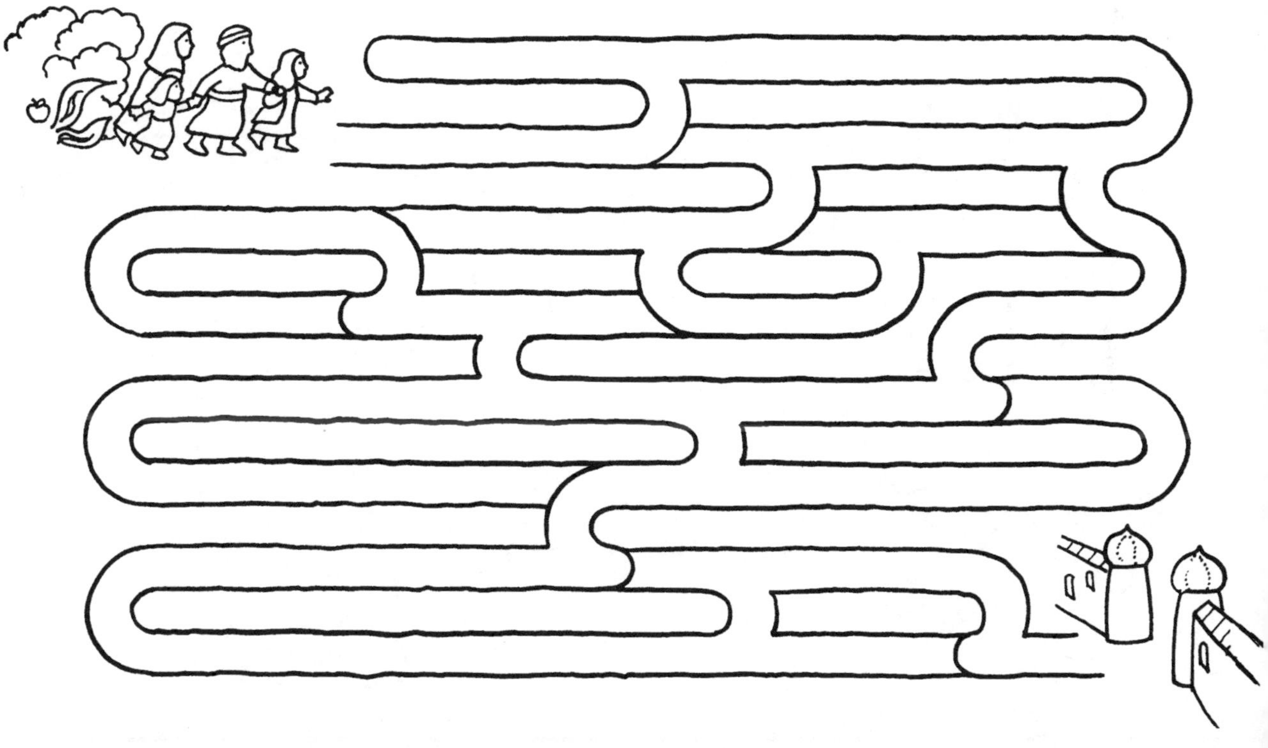

29

NOVEMBER

Jesus' friends Peter and John ran to the tomb. They found it was empty. Jesus had risen from the dead!

You can read about this in Luke 24:12.

Color me!

4

FEBRUARY

DOT-TO-DOT

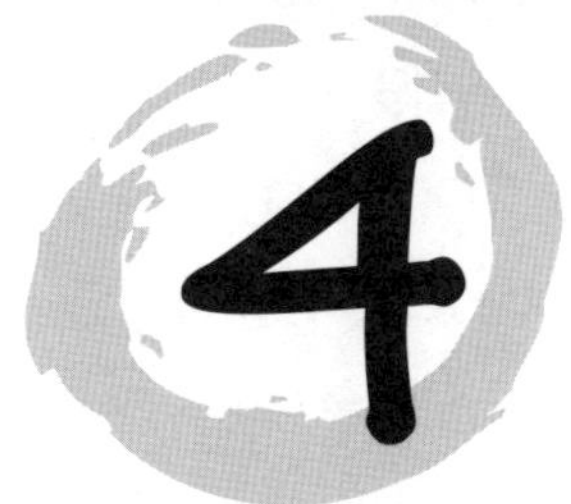

Join up the dots to find out what Abraham's sons, Isaac and Ishmael, are playing with.

You can find the story of Abraham's two sons in Genesis 21:1–20. Who were their mothers?

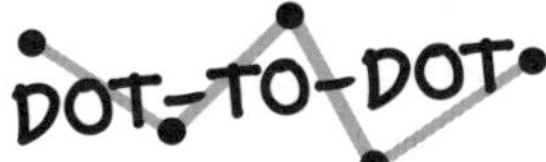

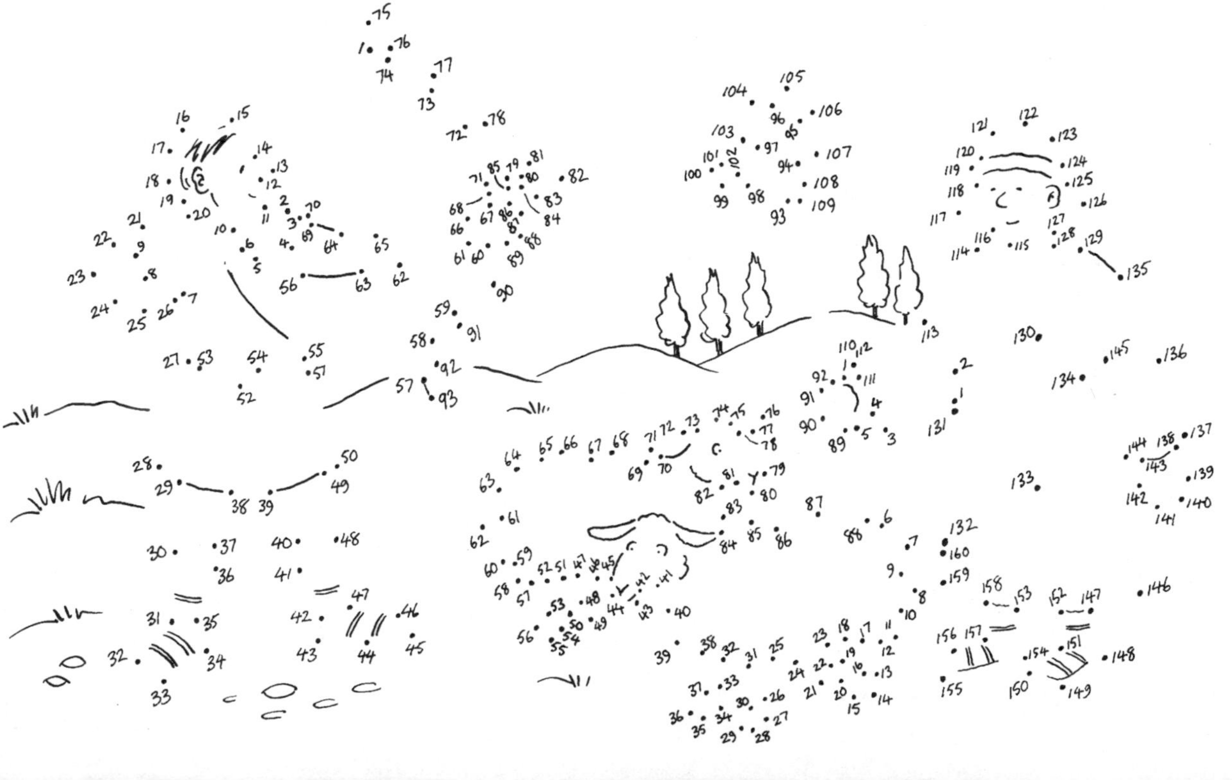

28

NOVEMBER

After Jesus died on the cross, he was buried in a cave. Join up the dots to find what the three women discovered when they visited his tomb.

Read this story in Luke 24:1–12.

DOT-TO-DOT

5

FEBRUARY

Hagar's son Ishmael grew jealous of his little brother, Isaac, Sarah's son.

Can you circle at least 10 differences between these two pictures of Abraham's family?
See Genesis 21:8–20

27

NOVEMBER

A Roman guard stood at the door of the tomb where Jesus was buried. They wanted no visitors!

You can read about this in Matthew 27:65.

Color me!

God tested Abraham, telling him to sacrifice Isaac. Find 10 differences between the pictures.

You can find this story in Genesis 22:1–19. Was Isaac safe?

26 NOVEMBER

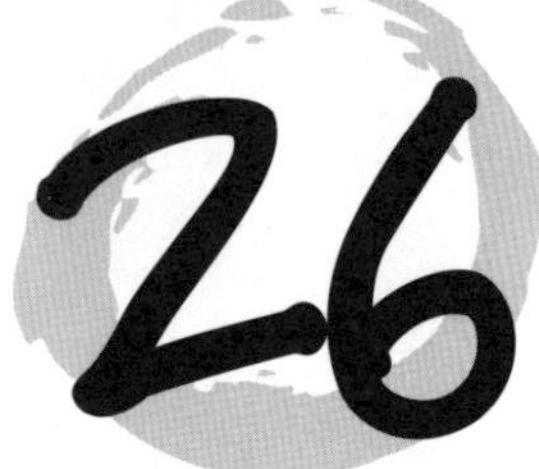

Judas was paid 30 pieces of silver to betray Jesus. Can you match the 3 pairs of Roman coins?

Read the story in Matthew 27:1–10.

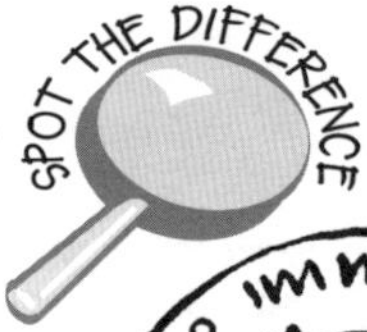

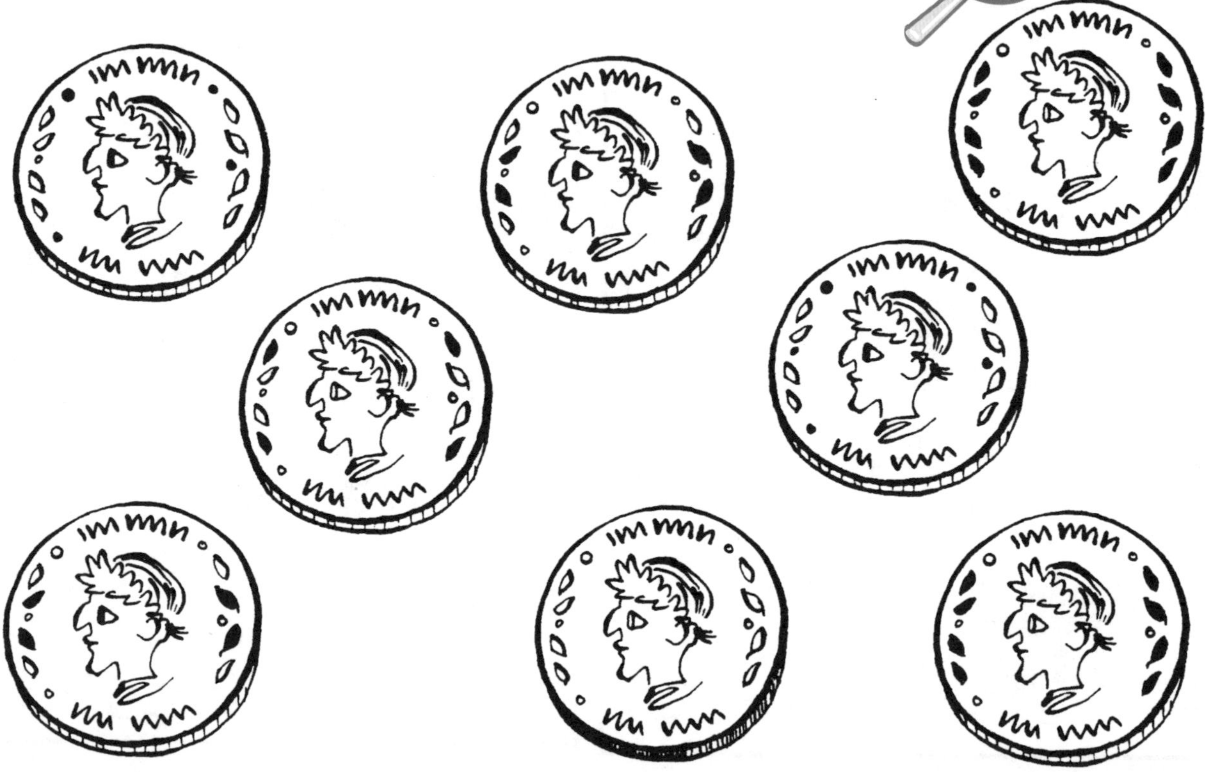

Even when he was an old man, Abraham moved his flocks and herds from place to place.

Find at least 10 differences between the two pictures that the artist has drawn. See Genesis 20:1–2; 22:19.

25 NOVEMBER

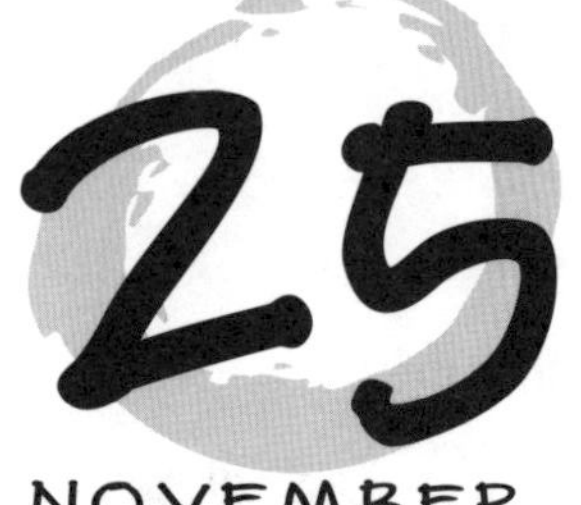

Judas Iscariot gave back the 30 pieces of silver that he had been paid to take the soldiers to arrest Jesus in the garden.

Can you find 10 silver coins hidden here?
Read the story in Matthew 27:1–10.

Puzzle

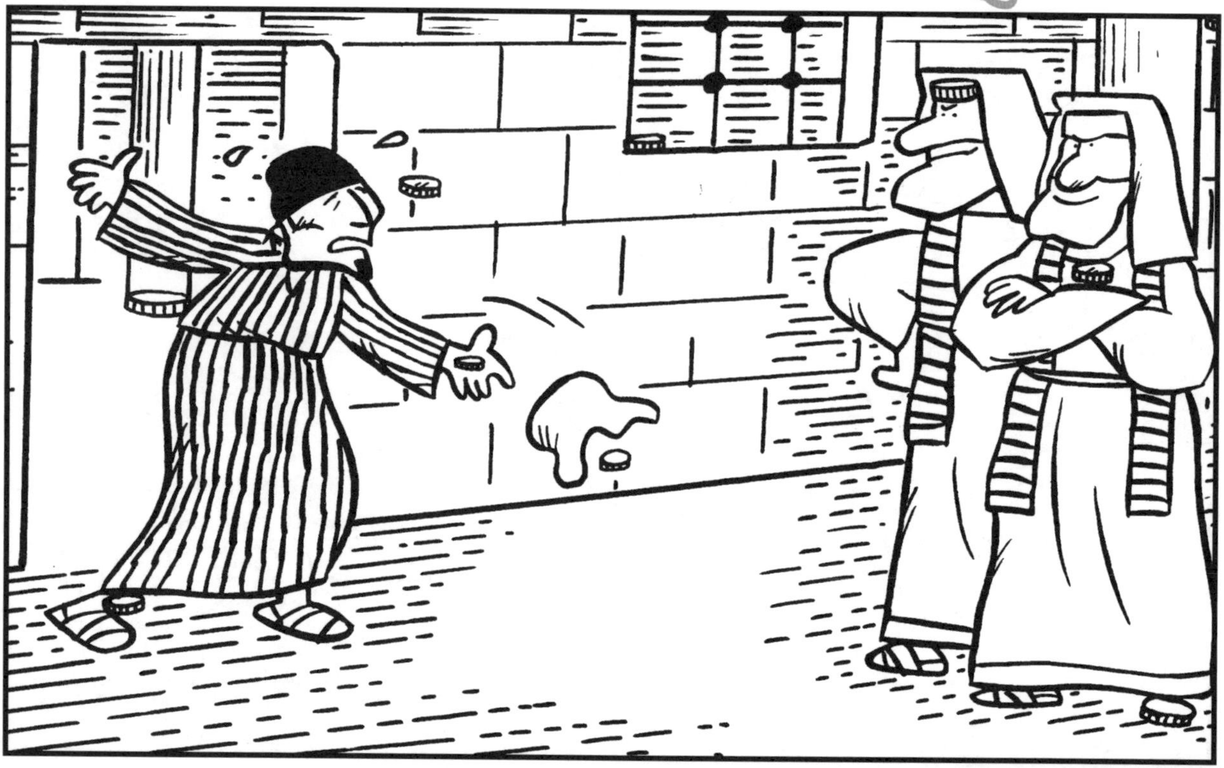

8
FEBRUARY

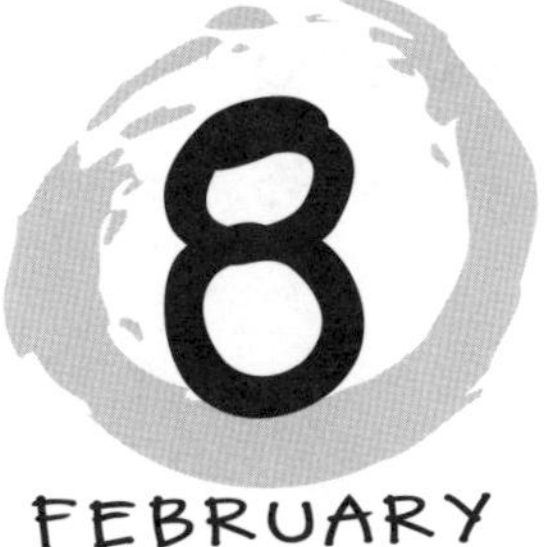

Abraham sent his servant to find a wife for Isaac. The servant found Rebekah filling pots with water for thirsty camels.

Can you find 9 water pots in the picture?
Read this story in Genesis 24:1–25.

Color me!

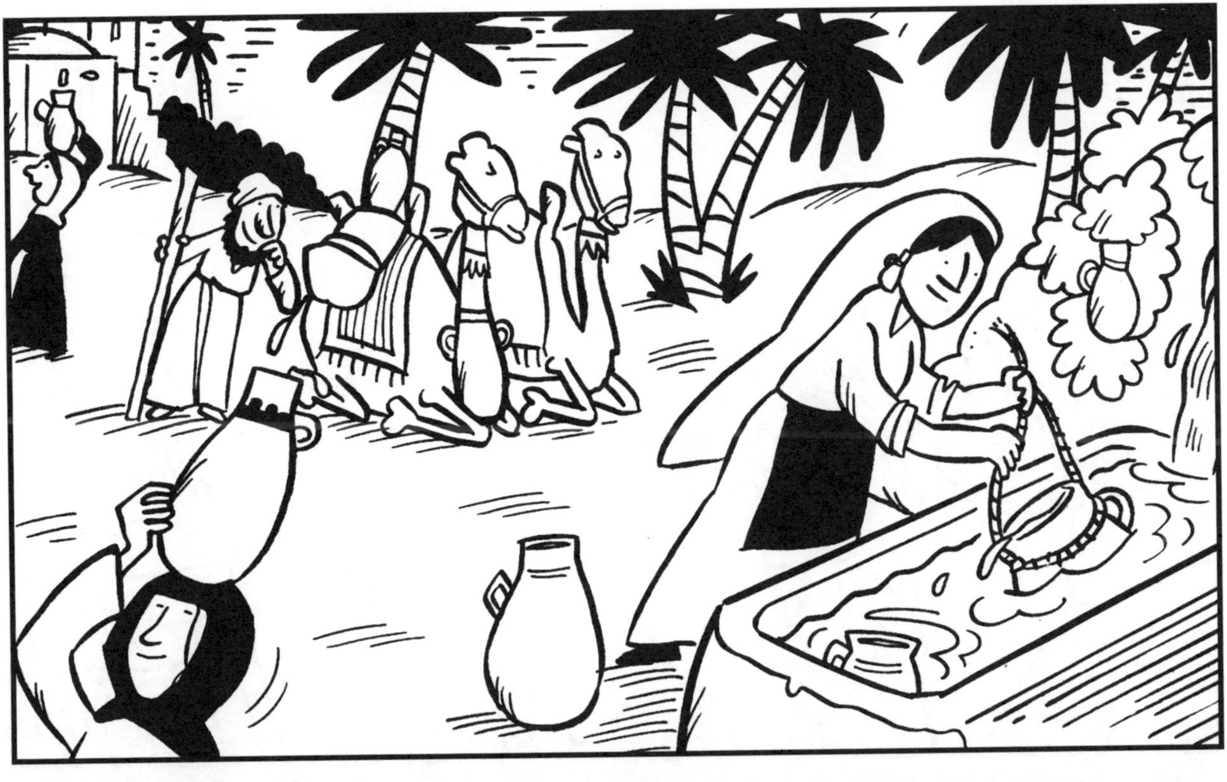

24

NOVEMBER

The soldiers took Jesus to a place called Skull Hill and killed him on a cross. He was between two thieves.

You can read about this in Luke 23:33.

Color me!

9

FEBRUARY

Here is a picture of Rebekah with a jar on her head. Which silhouette matches the complete drawing?

Complete the other silhouettes and color them.
Read Genesis 24:15.

Puzzle

23 NOVEMBER

Pontius Pilate washed his hands to show he didn't want to take the blame for having Jesus put to death on the cross.

Can you find 6 bowls hidden in the picture?
Read this story in Matthew 27:11–26.

Puzzle

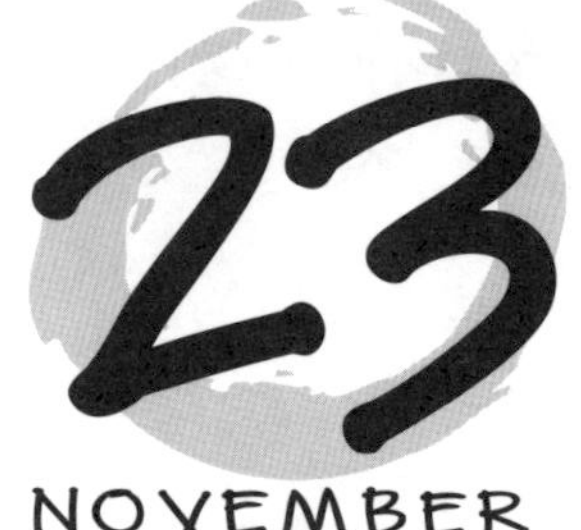

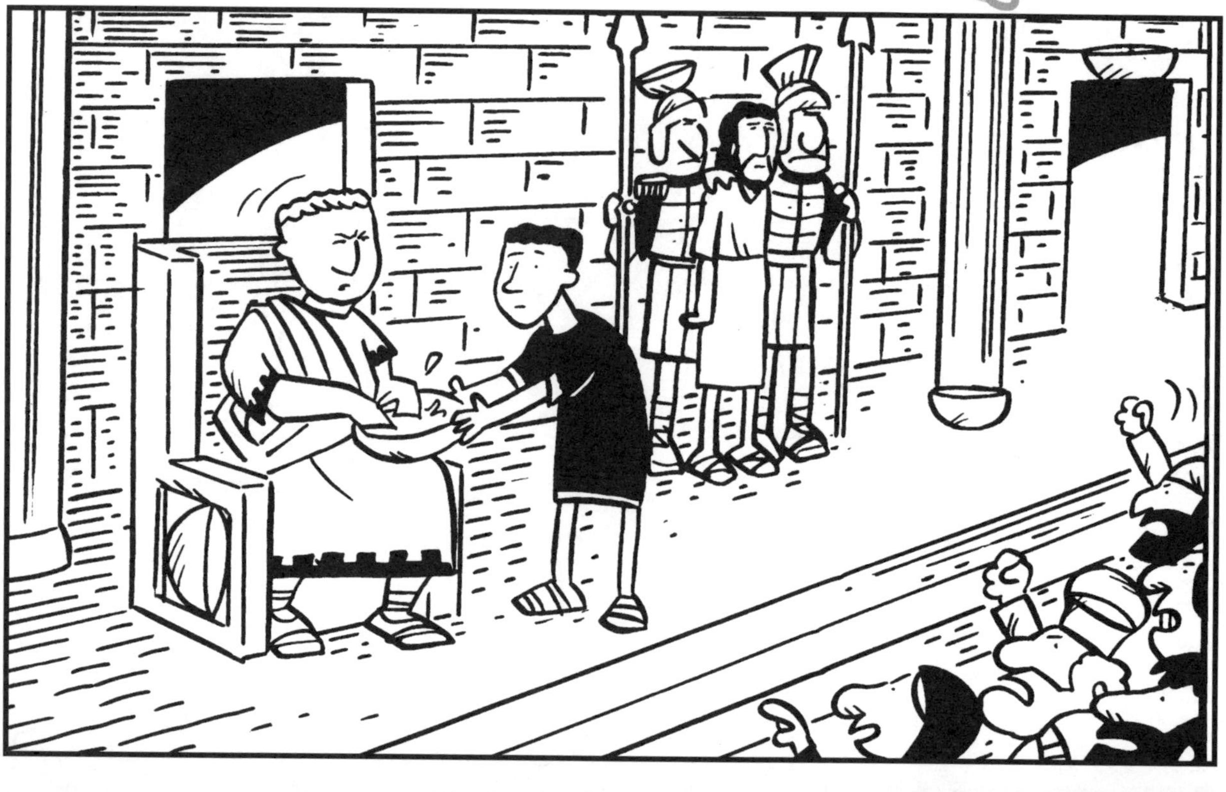

Rebekah went back with the servant to marry Isaac. Find 10 differences between the pictures.

You can find this story in Genesis 24.

22

NOVEMBER

The Roman leader said that Jesus had done nothing wrong, but the people shouted, 'Crucify him! Crucify him!'

You can read this in Luke 23:20.

Color me!

11

FEBRUARY

Many years later, Isaac and Rebekah had twin sons, named Jacob and Esau. Jacob had to run away, and slept in the open one night

Join up the dots to find out what he dreamed about.
Read Genesis 28:10–17.

DOT-TO-DOT

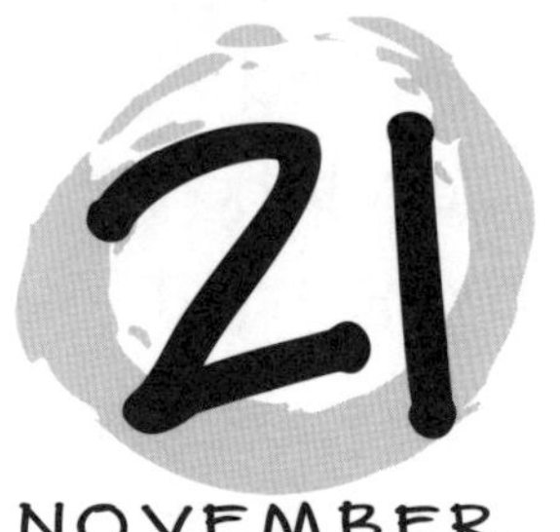

21

NOVEMBER

The artist has only finished one picture of a Roman soldier. One of the outlines will fit over the finished picture. Which one?

Finish the other pictures and color them all in.
Soldiers made fun of Jesus (Mark 15:16–20).

Puzzle

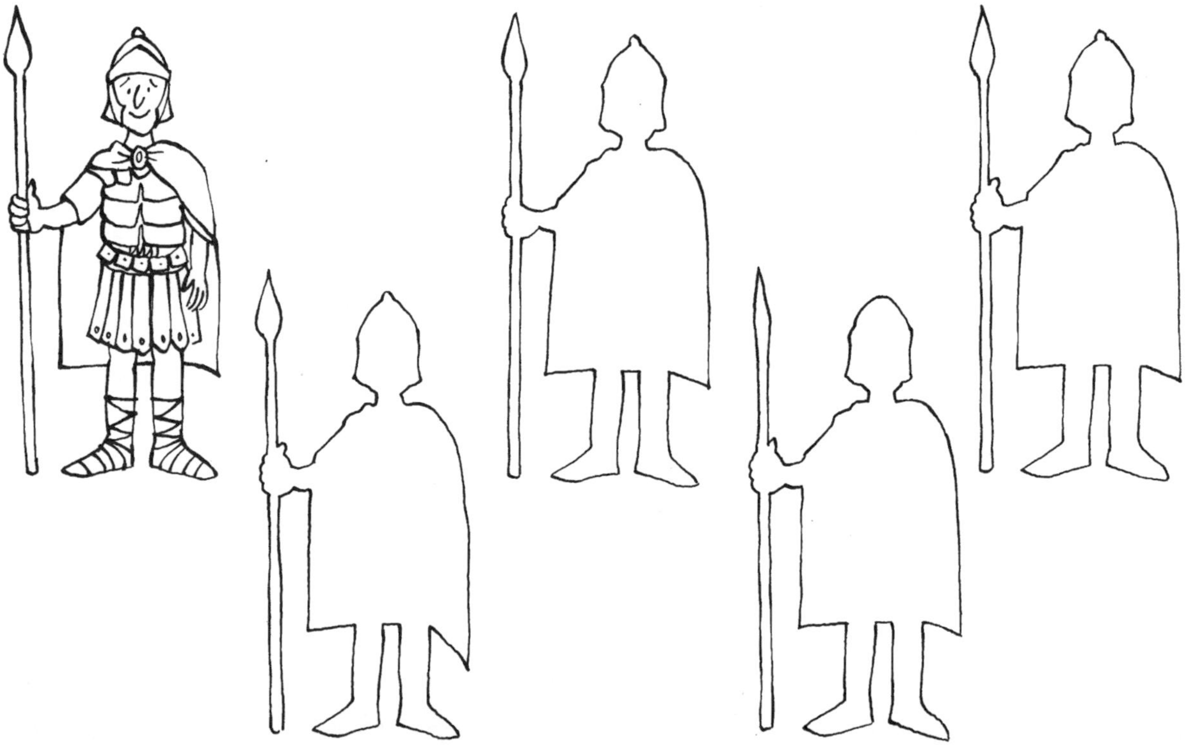

FEBRUARY

Here is Jacob dreaming about a stairway to heaven. Can you find 13 triangles?

You can read the story of Jacob and his dream in Genesis 28:10–22.

Color me!

20

NOVEMBER

Join up the dots to find out what is happening to Jesus here. Find out the name of another man in the picture.

Read this story in John 18:28–38.

DOT-TO-DOT

13

FEBRUARY

Jacob saw angels going up and down the stairway to heaven.

Circle at least 10 differences between these two pictures.
What did Jacob call the place?
See Genesis 28:19.

19

NOVEMBER

After Jesus was arrested, Peter heard a rooster crow. Which picture has all the pieces to make the rooster?

You can read this story in Mark 14:66–72.

Color me!

14
FEBRUARY

In this picture of Jacob dreaming, the artist has made lots of deliberate mistakes. Put a circle around each mistake.

How many have you found? Which is the silliest?
Read Genesis 28:10–22

Color me!

18

NOVEMBER

After Jesus was arrested, he was taken before the Jewish High Priest, who was called Caiaphas.

You can read about this in Matthew 26:57.

Color me!

15 FEBRUARY

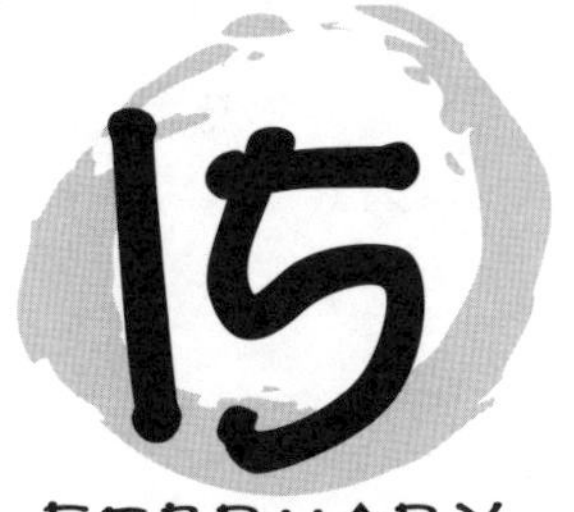

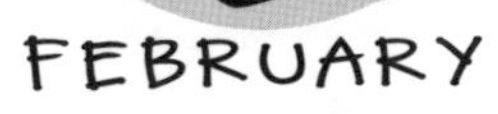

Here are Abraham, his son Isaac, and his grandson Jacob.

Can you connect them all up to their wives? Then color in all the family neatly.

Puzzle

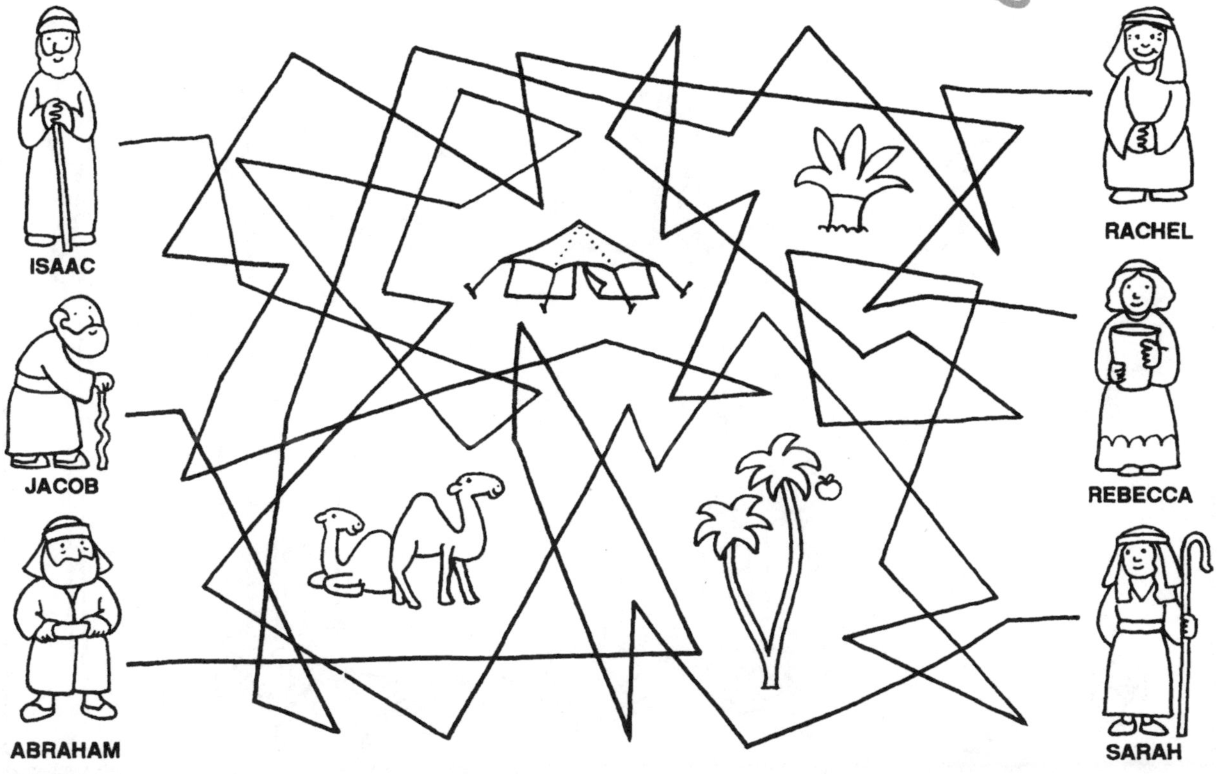

17

NOVEMBER

The soldiers arrested Jesus in the Garden of Gethsemane. What is Jesus' friend doing?

You can read this story in Matthew 26:47–54.

Color me!

16 FEBRUARY

Jacob had many sons—but Joseph was his favorite. Join up the dots to find out what Jacob is giving his favorite son.

Read Genesis 37:3–4.

DOT-TO-DOT

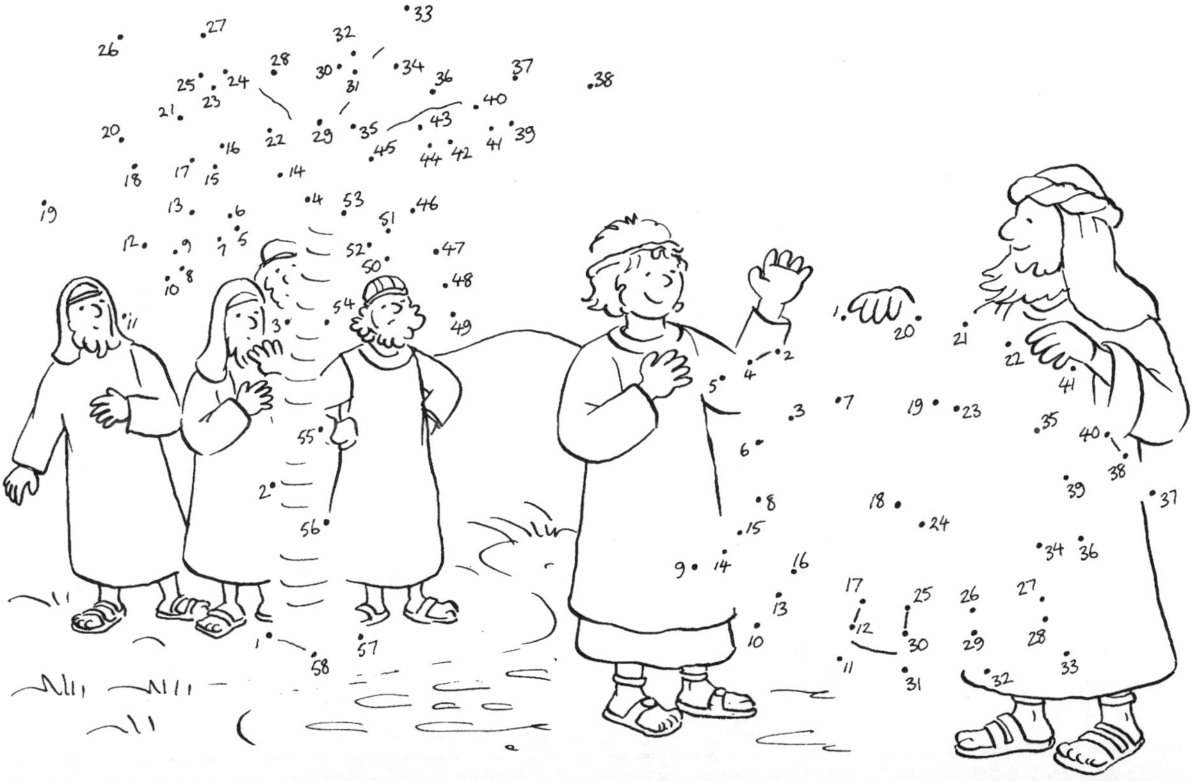

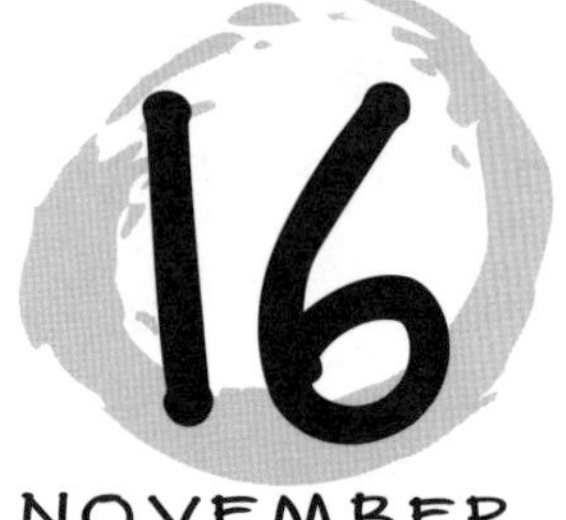

16
NOVEMBER

Jesus went to pray at night in the Garden of Gethsemane. The soldiers are coming to arrest Jesus. Which path will they take?

Read this story in Matthew 26:36–56.

maze

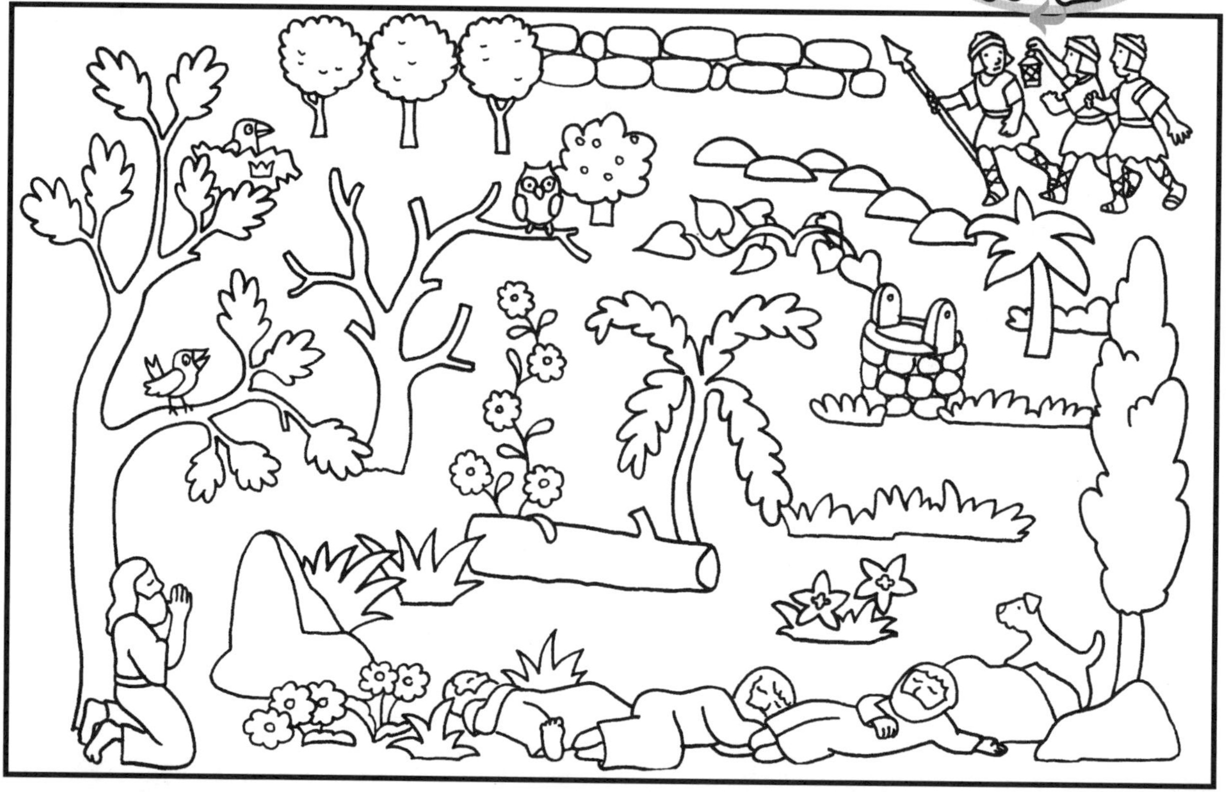

17

FEBRUARY

Here is a picture of Jacob's 12 sons. One appears twice. Which one?

For fun, give them all names
— see Genesis 35:23–26.

Puzzle

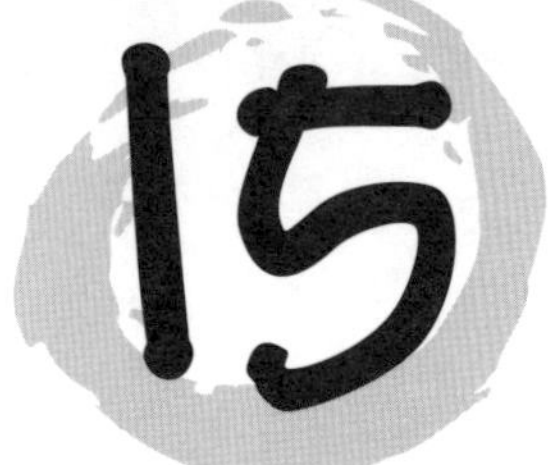

15
NOVEMBER

Here is a picture of some of Jesus' friends eating and drinking. How many hidden drinking cups can you find?

Read about the Last Supper in Matthew 26:17–30.

Puzzle

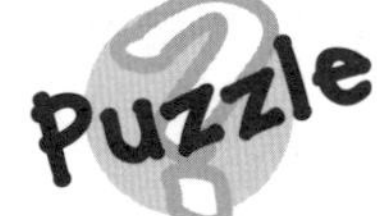

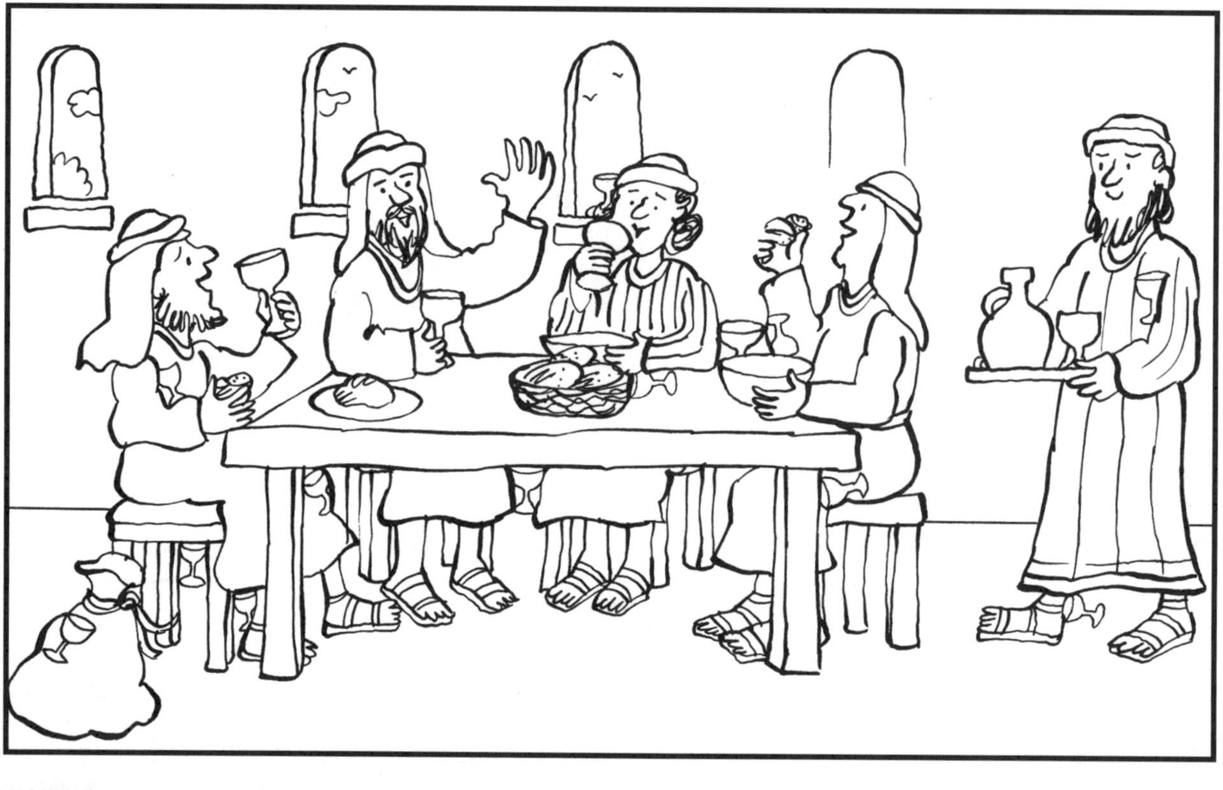

FEBRUARY 18

Here is Joseph in his special coat. Can you find 12 black-headed sheep in this picture?

You can find the story of Joseph and his coat in Genesis 37:1–4.

Color me!

14

NOVEMBER

Jesus had a special supper with his twelve disciples in an Upper Room in Jerusalem. Jesus broke the bread for them.

Read about this in Matthew 26:26.

Color me!

19

FEBRUARY

Here is Joseph showing off his special coat. Can you discover 10 differences between the two pictures?

Were Joseph's brothers happy for him?
See Genesis 37:1–4.

SPOT THE DIFFERENCE

13

NOVEMBER

Join up the dots to find out what Jesus is doing in the market at the Jerusalem Temple. Are the people pleased?

You can read the whole story in John 2:13–22.

DOT-TO-DOT

20

FEBRUARY

In this picture of Joseph and his coat, the artist has made lots of deliberate mistakes.

Find at least 10.
Read Genesis 37:1–4.

Color me!

This shepherd has separated his sheep from the goats. Find 10 differences between the two pictures.

You can read what Jesus said about sheep and goats in Matthew 25:31–43.

21 FEBRUARY

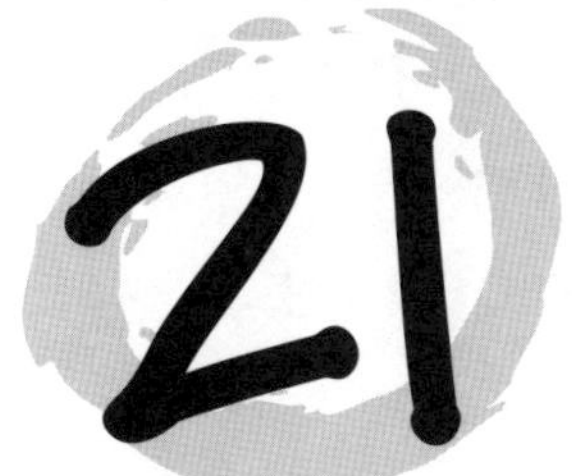

Joseph's brothers got so jealous of him, that they sold him. Join up the dots to find where they kept him until they sold him.

See Genesis 37:12–28.

DOT-TO-DOT

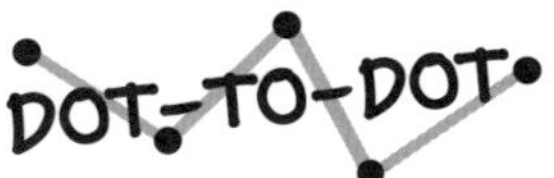

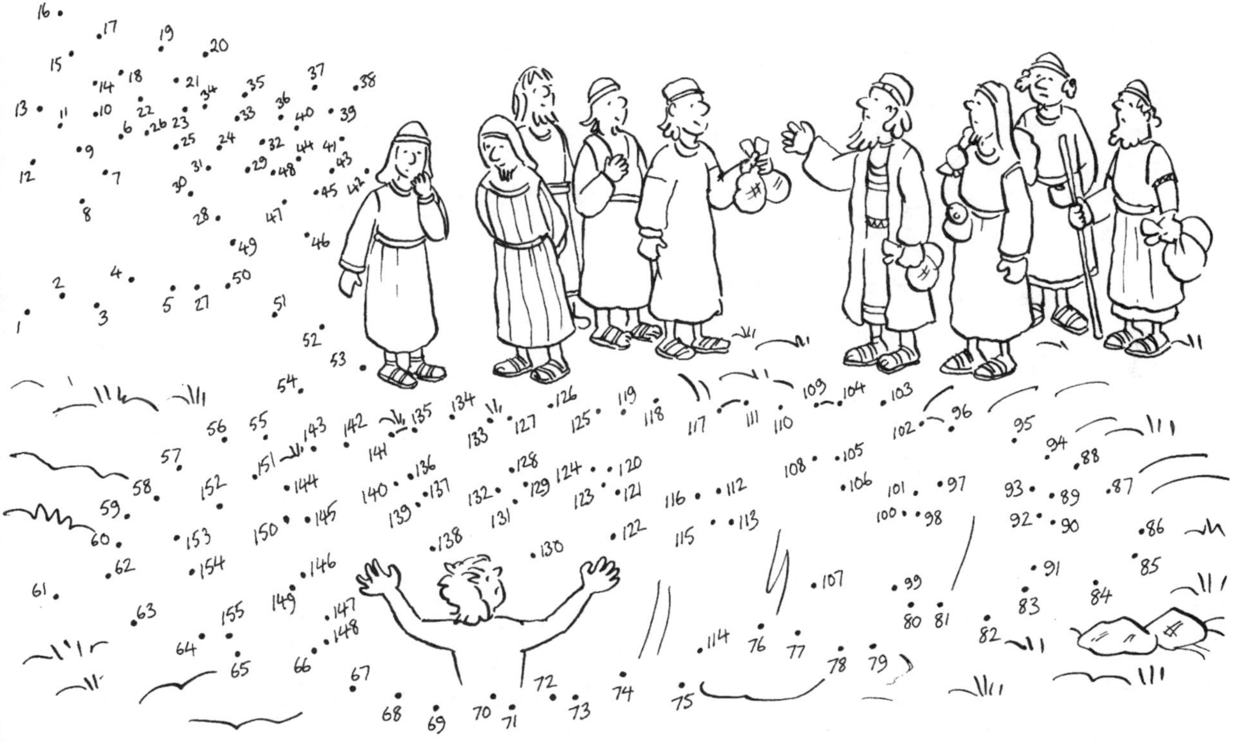

11
NOVEMBER

These bridesmaids are all waiting for the bridegroom to celebrate the wedding.
Find 10 differences between the pictures.

Read Jesus' story about the bridesmaids in Matthew 25:1–13.

22 FEBRUARY

Find at least 10 deliberate mistakes in this picture of Joseph being sold to the Midianites.

You can read this story in Genesis 37:12–36.

Color me!

10

NOVEMBER

Jesus said that, when he comes again,
two women might be milling grain together
with a hand mill.

**Read Matthew 24:41 to find out
what will happen to them.**

Color me!

23 FEBRUARY

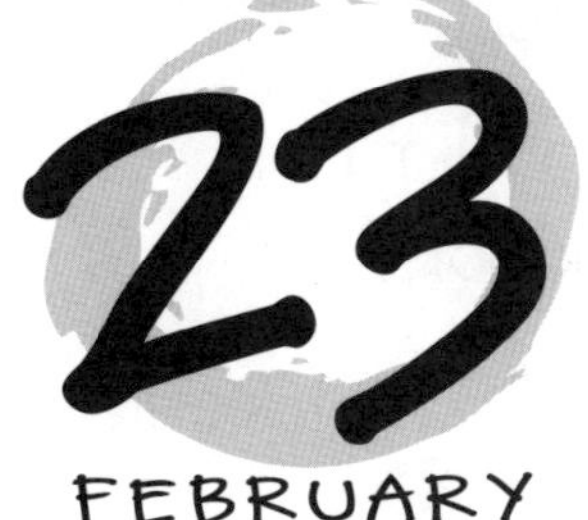

The traders took Joseph across the desert to Egypt. Find the path that takes them to the pyramids of Egypt without climbing over any trees.

You can read this story in Genesis 37:25–36.

maze

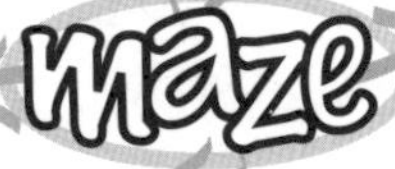

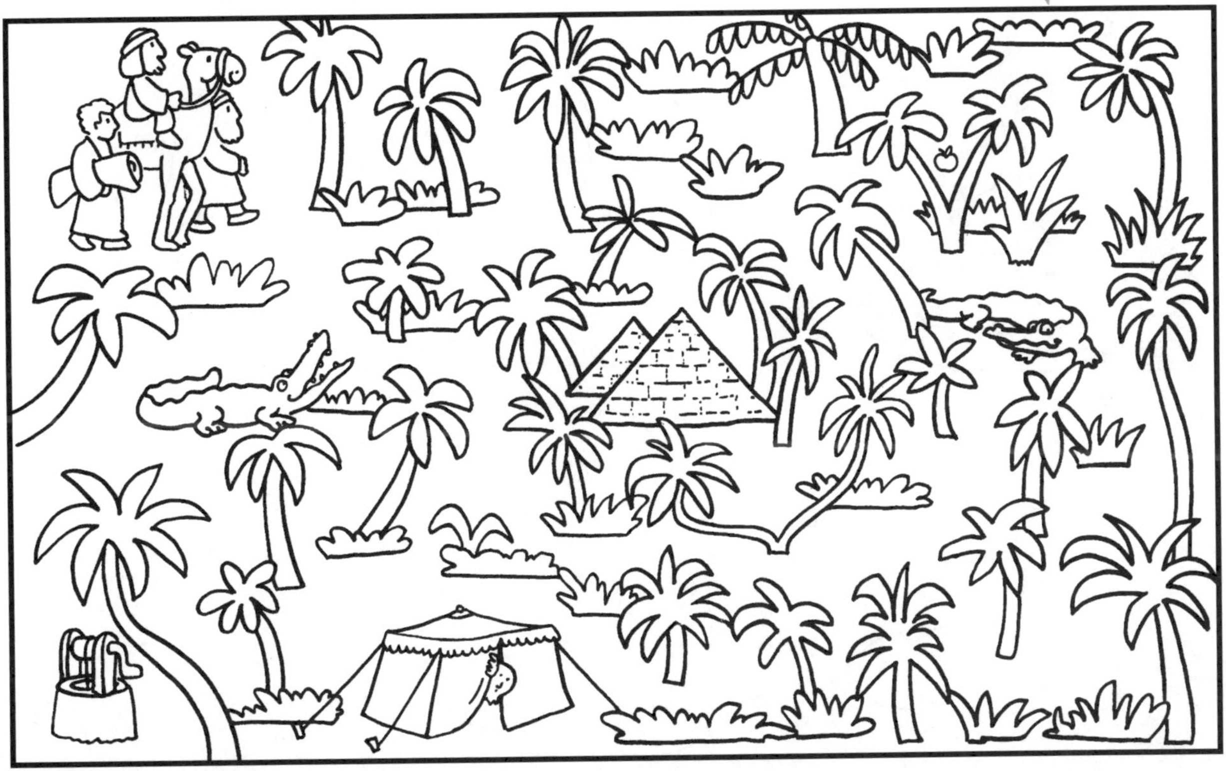

9

NOVEMBER

Here is a picture of a woman grinding grain to make flour. Which outline will fit exactly over the picture of the woman?

Finish the outline drawings and color them in.
See Matthew 24:41.

Puzzle

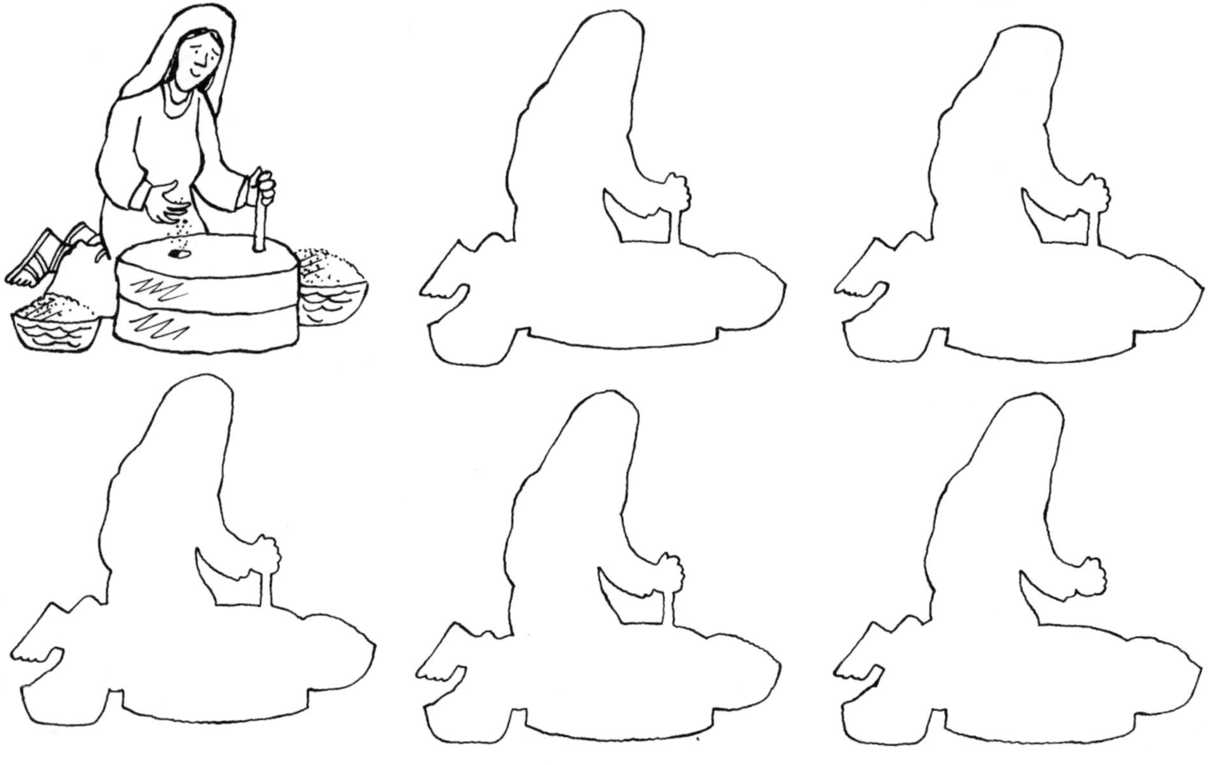

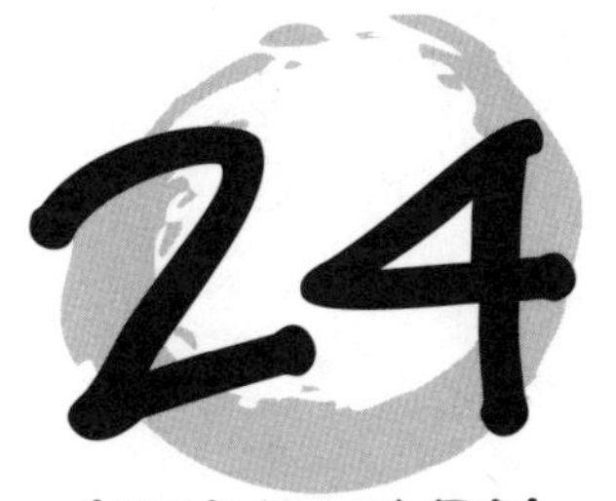

24
FEBRUARY

In Egypt, Joseph was thrown into prison.
A baker and butler had special dreams.

Follow the lines to find out by their dreams which is the butler and which is the baker.
Read Genesis 40:1–23.

DOT-TO-DOT

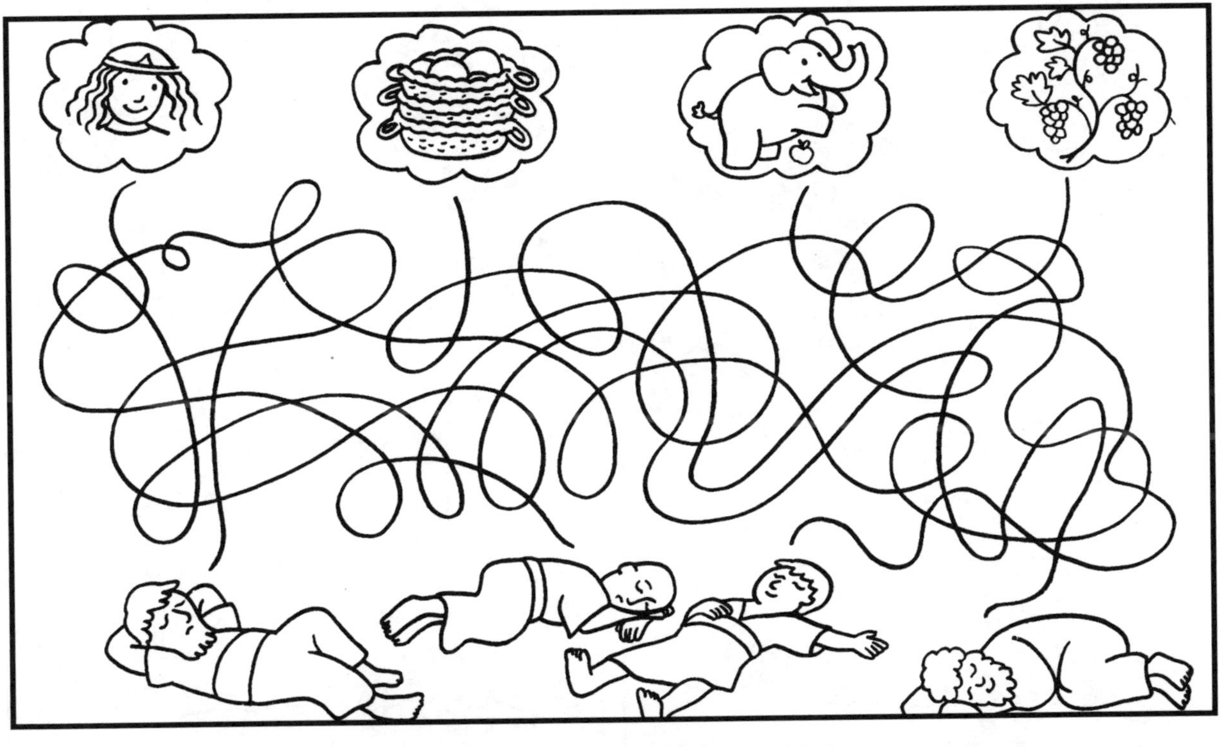

The farmer wants every branch of his vine to grow lots of big bunches of grapes. Find 10 differences between the two pictures.

You can read about the farmer's vine in John 15:1–7.

25

FEBRUARY

Here is Joseph in prison in Egypt. Which picture is the odd one out?

Read how Joseph came to be in prison in Genesis 39:1–23.

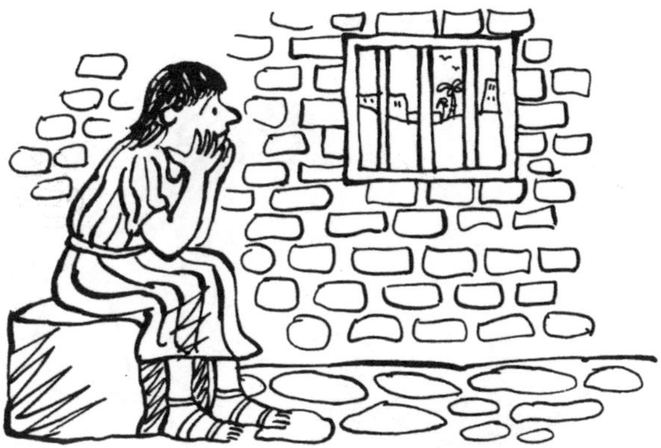

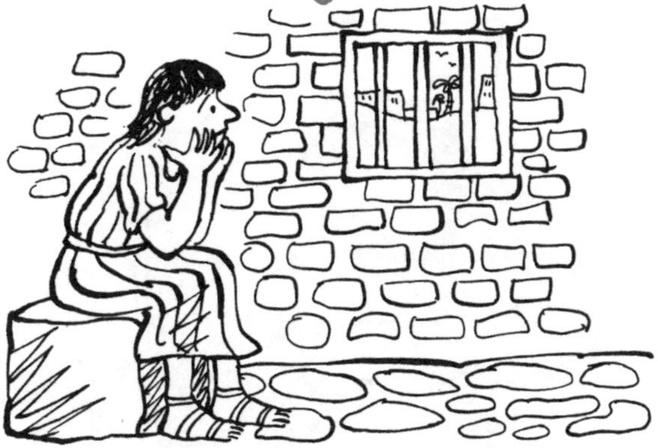

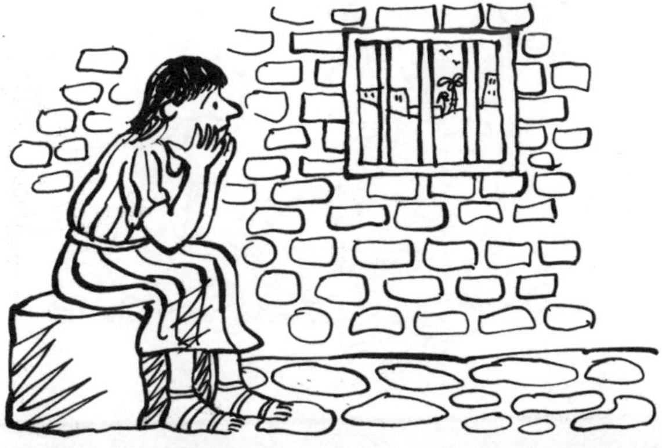

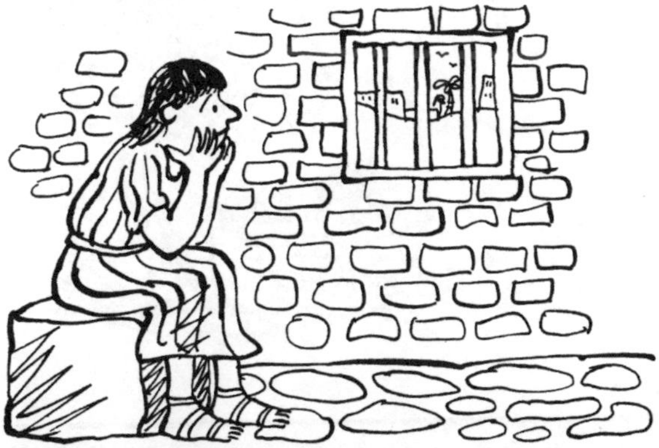

This man is picking grapes from the vine. Find 10 differences between the reflected pictures.

You can read the story of the workers in the vineyard in Matthew 20:1–16.

Joseph was taken out of prison to explain the dreams of Pharaoh. Find at least 10 differences between these two pictures.

Then draw one of Pharaoh's dreams in the bubble.
Read Genesis 41 to help you.

The grapes that were picked were used to make wine. How many drinking cups can you find here? Have you found more than 15?

You can read the story of the workers in the vineyard in Matthew 20:1–16.

puzzle

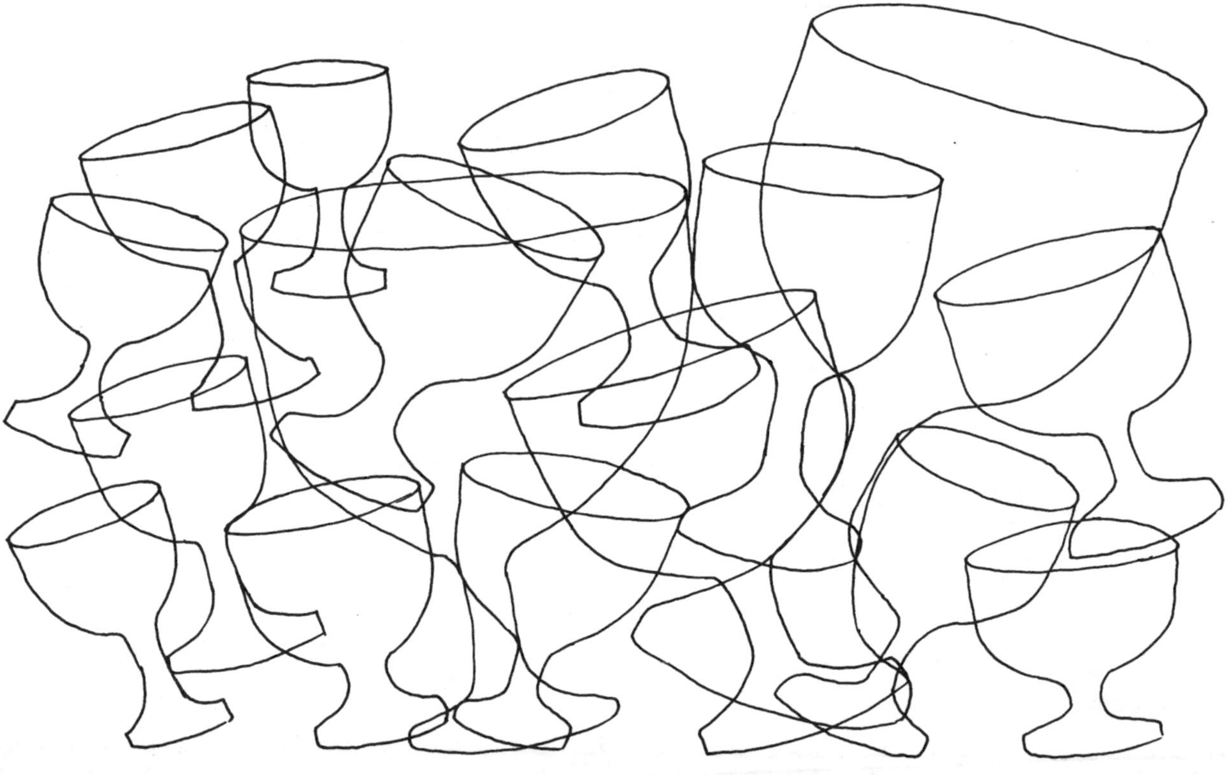

27
FEBRUARY

In this picture of Joseph explaining Pharaoh's dreams, the artist has made lots of deliberate mistakes. Circle them all.

How many have you discovered? There are at least 10 mistakes. Read Genesis chapter 41.

Puzzle

5

NOVEMBER

Follow the three paths through the vineyard to discover which servant picked the most grapes for his master.

How many bunches has he picked? You can read the story of the vineyard workers in Matthew 20:1–16.

Puzzle

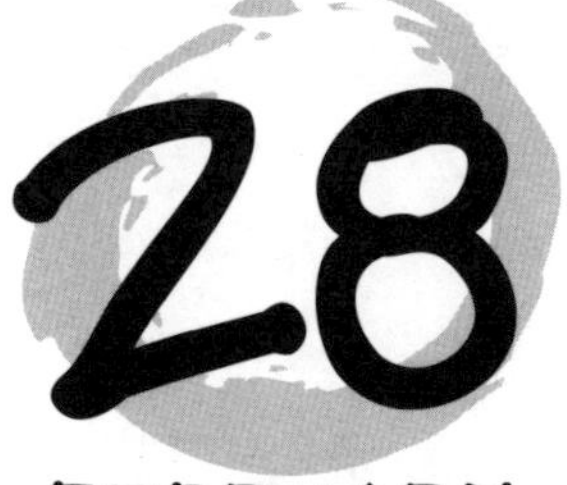

28

FEBRUARY

When he was a baby, Moses' mother put him in a basket in the River Nile.

Which path does the princess of Egypt have to take to reach baby Moses, without crossing any lines? See Exodus 2:1–7.

maze

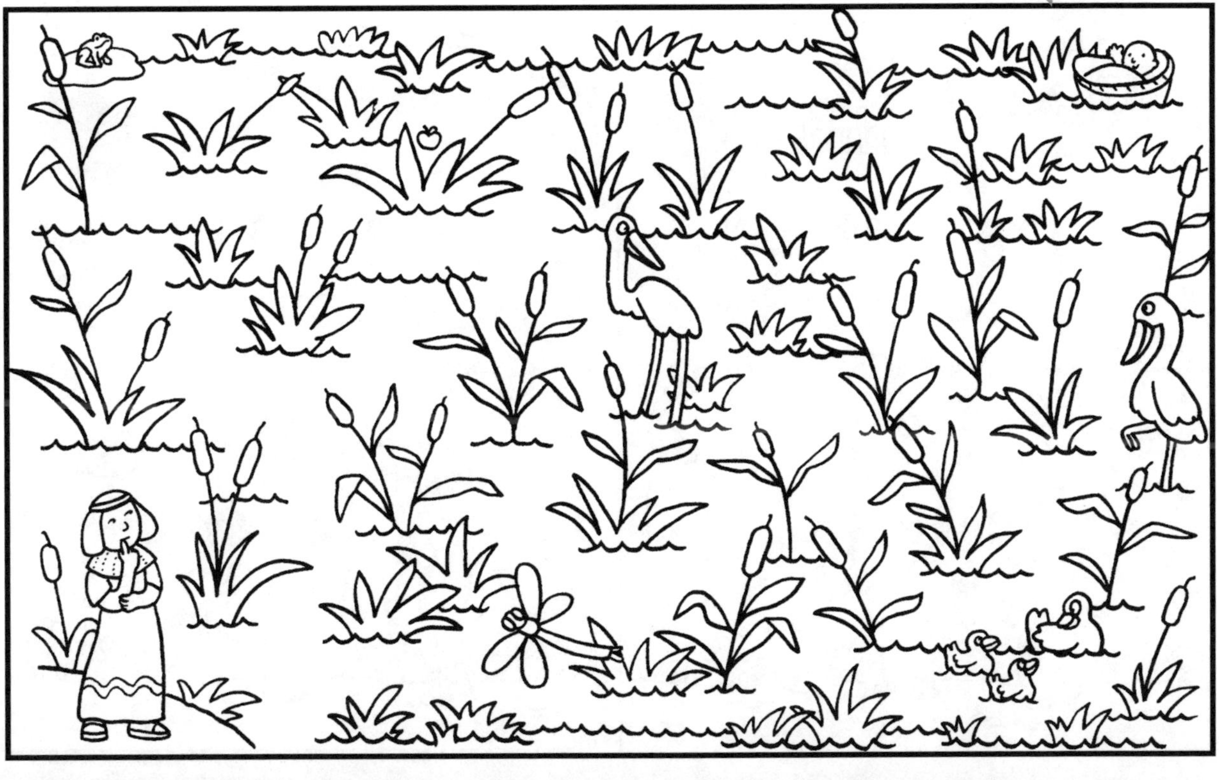

4

NOVEMBER

Jesus told a story about men who came to work in a vineyard.
Some started early, some later.

You can read this story in Matthew 20:1–16.
Find 10 differences between these two pictures.

1 MARCH

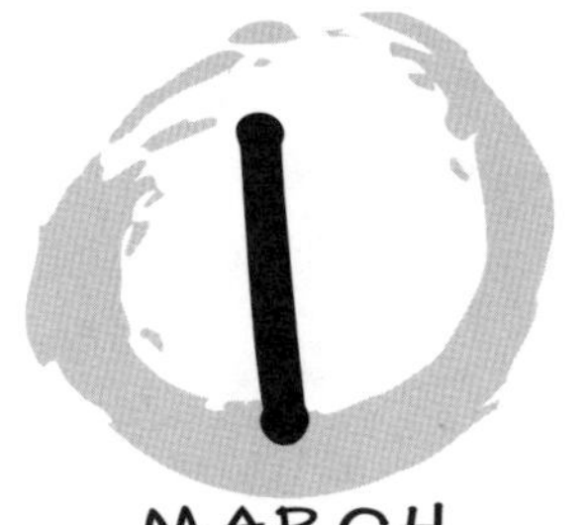

Join up the dots to find what Moses' sister Miriam is doing here.

You can read the story of baby Moses and his sister Miriam in Exodus 2:1–10.

DOT-TO-DOT

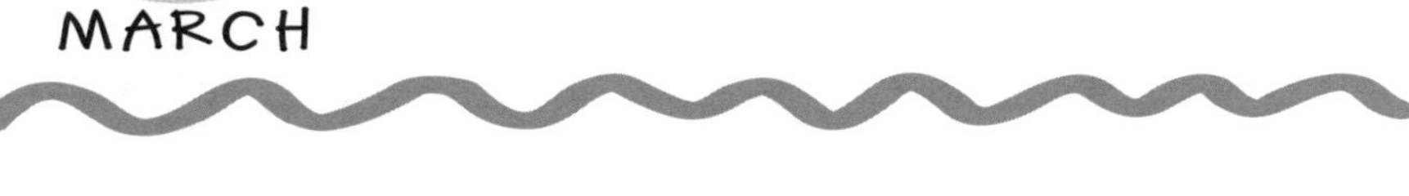

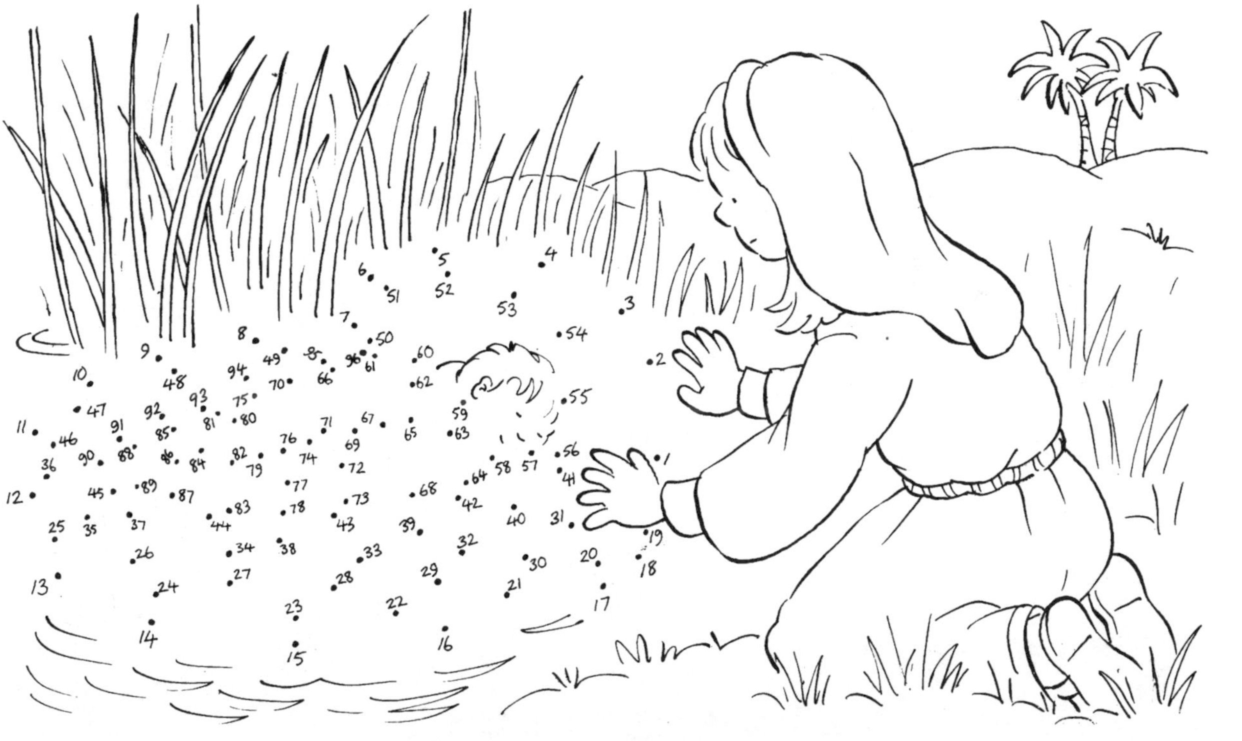

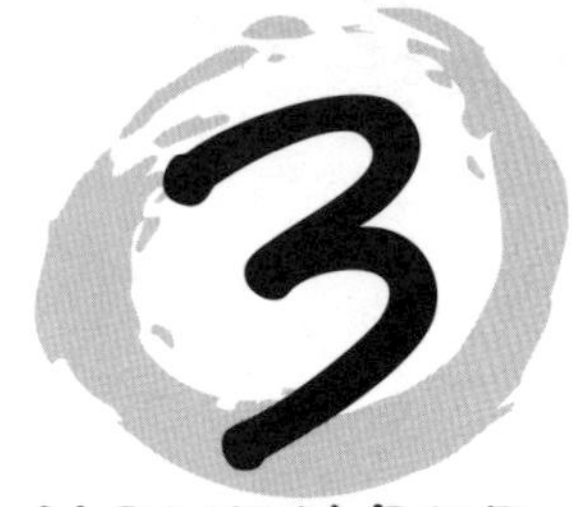

3 NOVEMBER

Are these people holding anything in their hands? Join up the dots to find out.

You can read this whole story in John 12:12–19.
What did the people shout?

DOT-TO-DOT

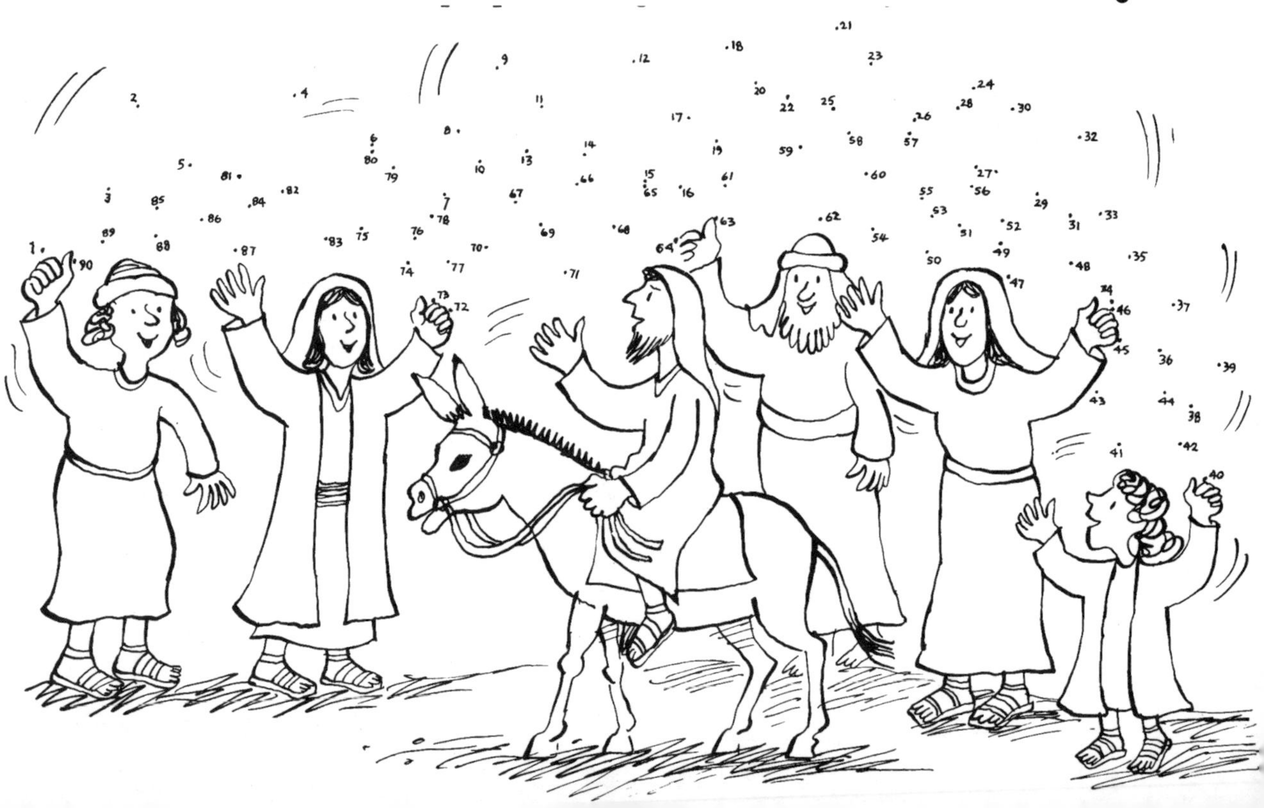

2 MARCH

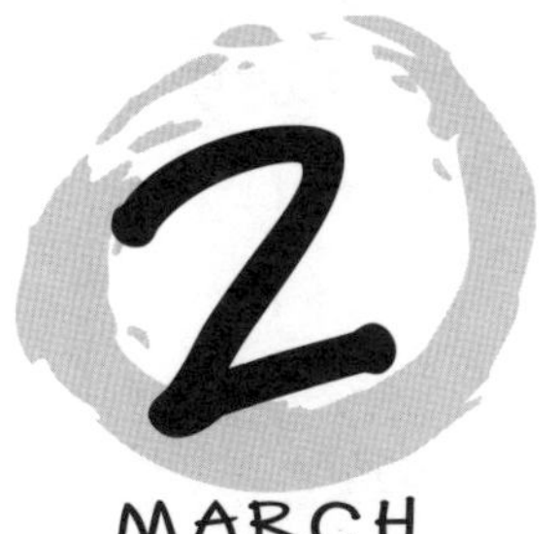

Join up the dots to discover where Pharaoh's daughter found baby Moses. What was she doing by the river?

You can read this story in Exodus 2:5–6.

DOT-TO-DOT

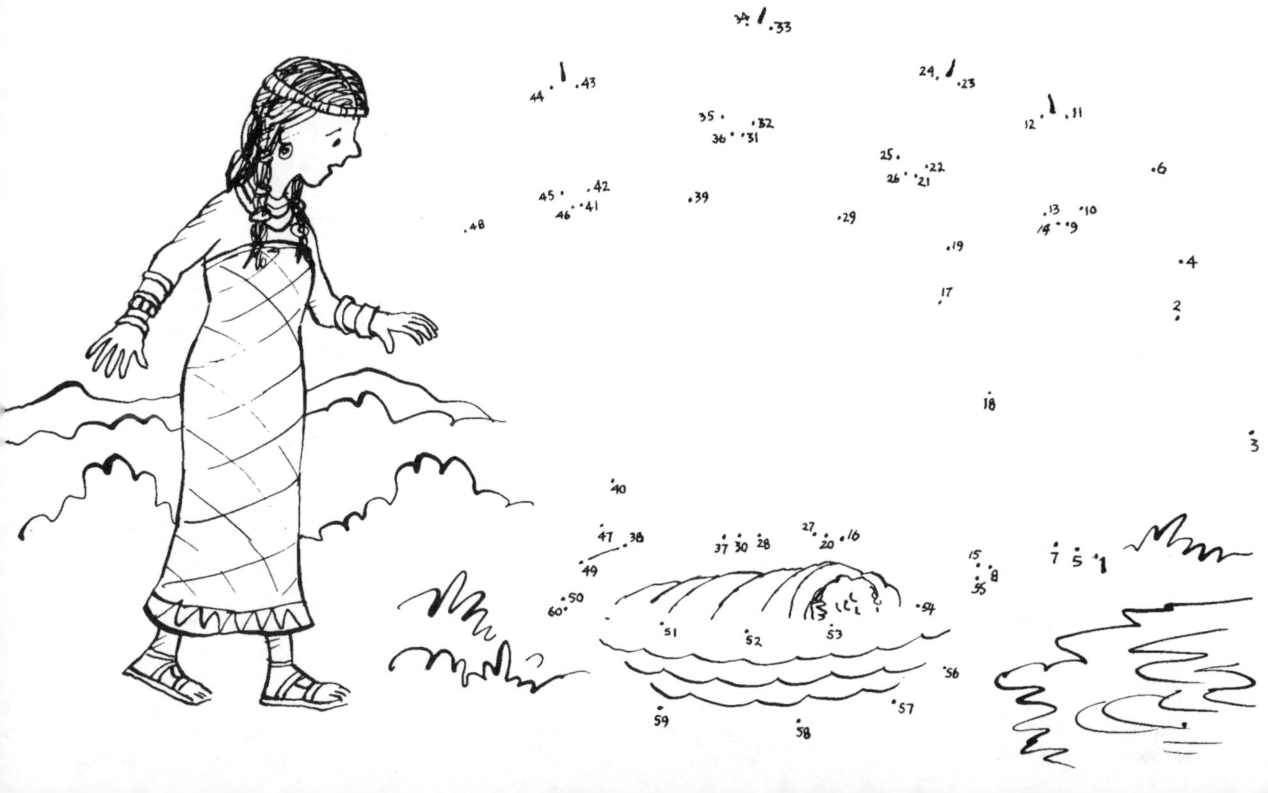

2 NOVEMBER

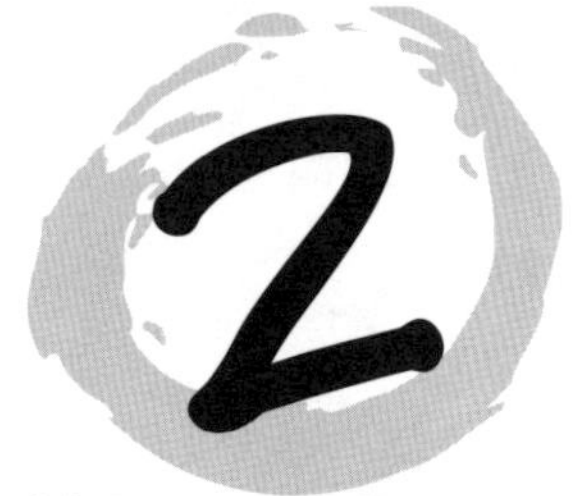

Here are 6 drawings of people waving palms. How many exactly matching pairs can you find?

You can read this story in John 12:12–19.

SPOT THE DIFFERENCE

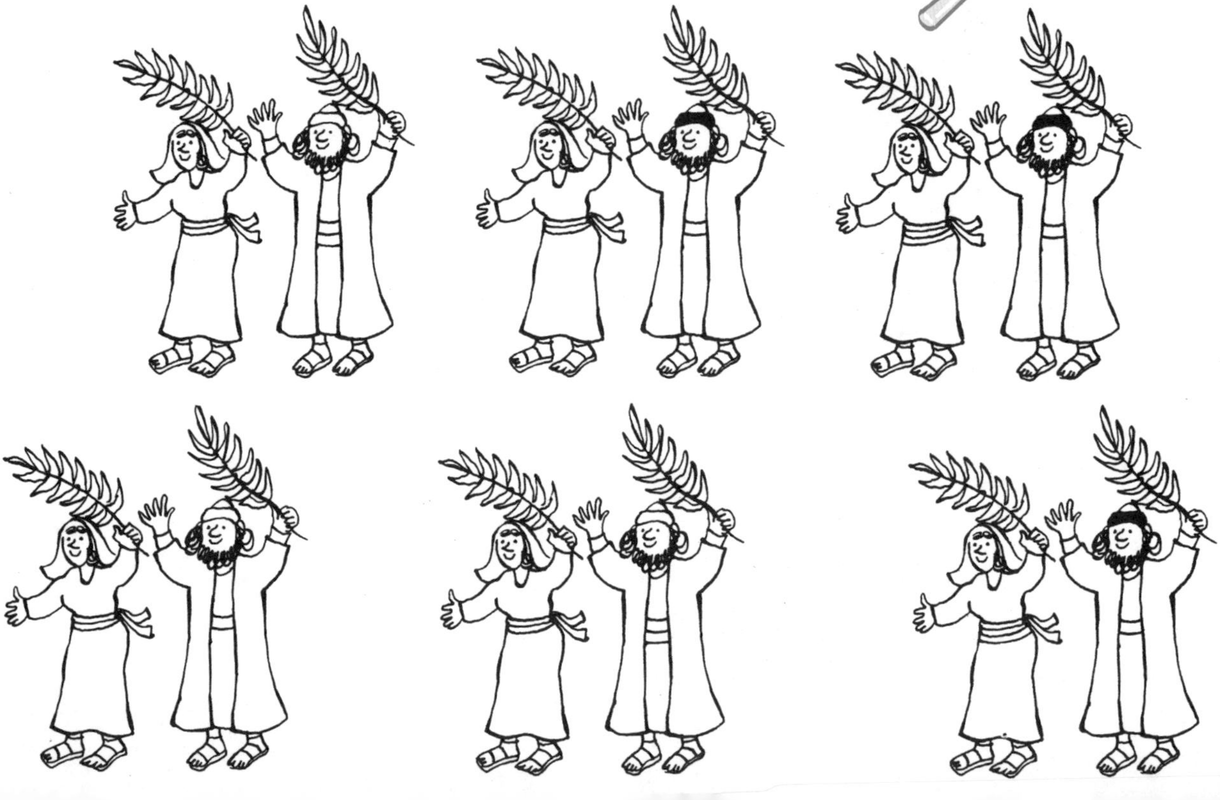

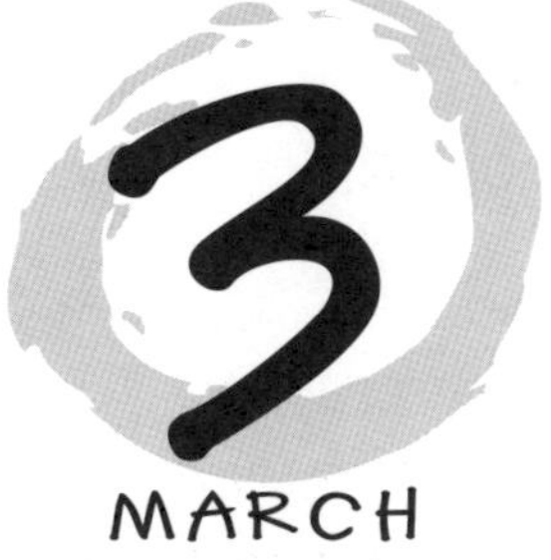

3
MARCH

The artist has hidden 10 frogs in this picture of Moses in the basket in the Nile. Can you find them all?

Now color the picture in with felt-tips or colored pencils.
You can read this story in Exodus 2:5–6.

Color me!

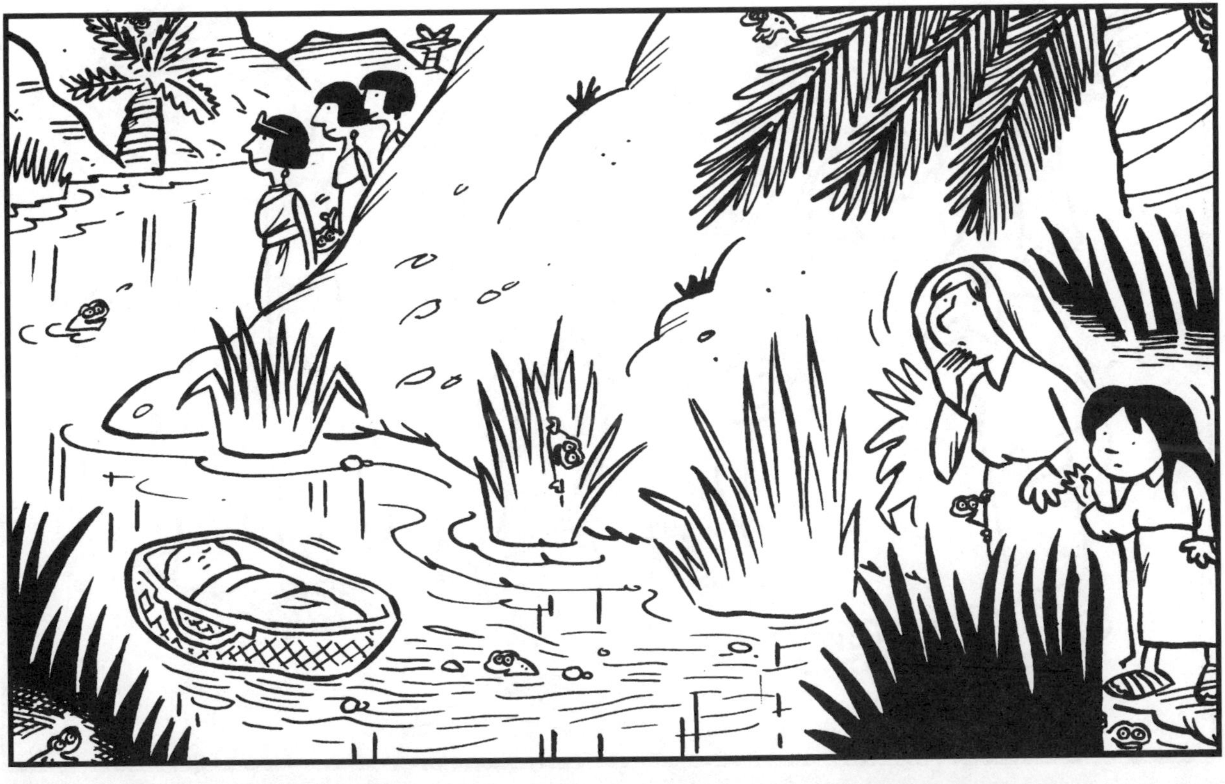

1

NOVEMBER

When Jesus rode on a donkey into Jerusalem, people waved palm branches.

Find out what they threw on the ground by reading this story in Luke 19:28–35.

Color me!

4

MARCH

The artist has missed out Moses and the basket in this picture. Draw them in and then color the whole picture.

You can read this story in Exodus 2:1–7.

Color me!

31

OCTOBER

Join up the dots to discover what the people are waving at Jesus as he rides into Jerusalem on a borrowed donkey.

You can read this story in John 12:12–19.

DOT-TO-DOT

5 MARCH

Circle all the deliberate mistakes the artist has made in this picture of Moses in the basket.

Do you think the princess would have worn a swim suit? You can read this story in Exodus 2:1–6.

Color me!

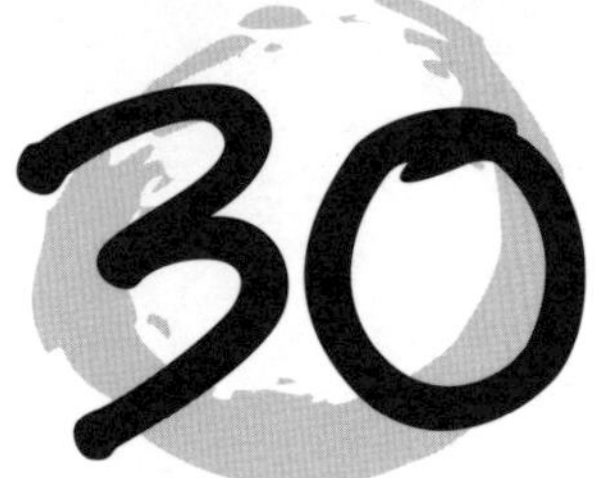

30 OCTOBER

Jesus asked his friends to borrow a donkey for him. Which picture has all the pieces to make up the donkey?

You can read this story in Luke 19:28–35.

Puzzle

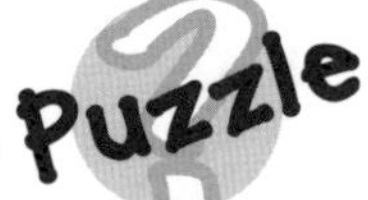

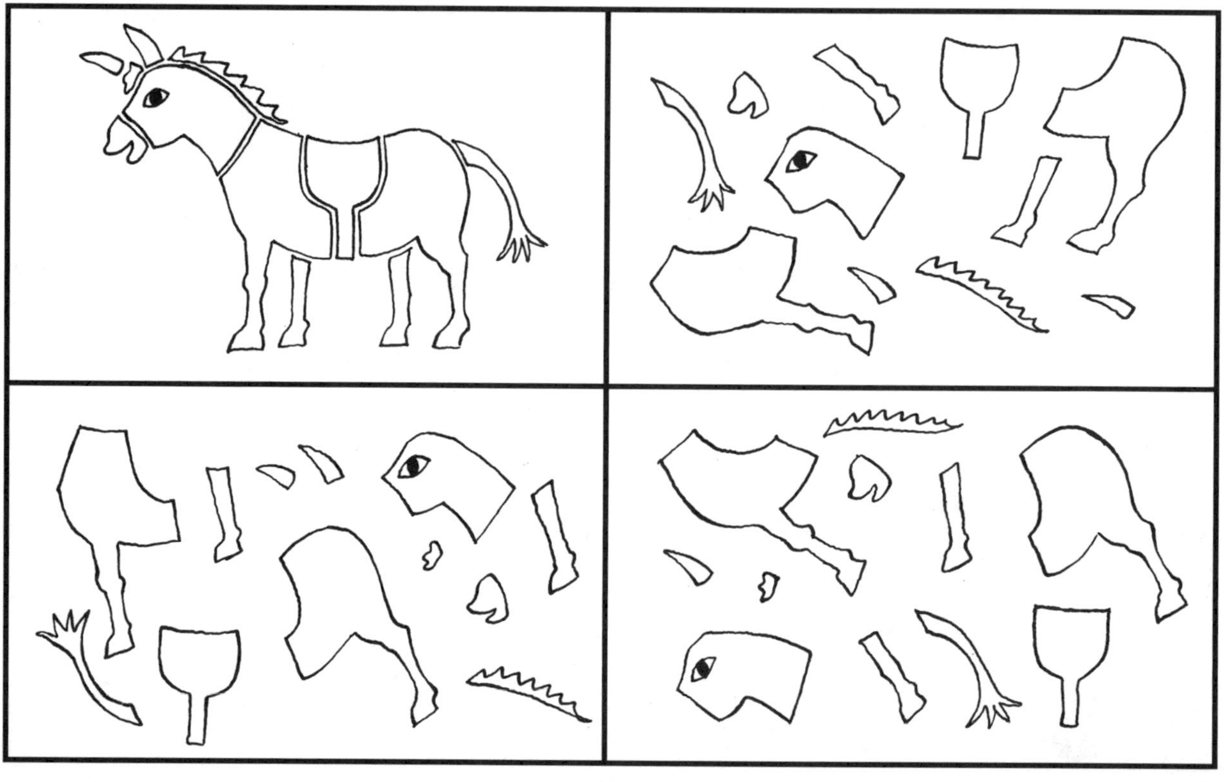

6
MARCH

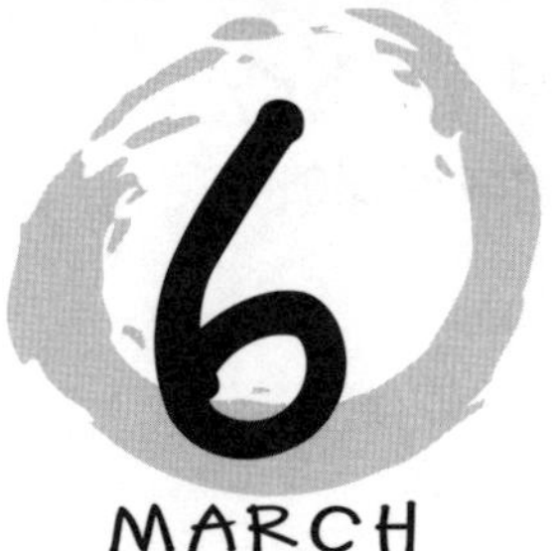

Later Moses went to work as a shepherd in the desert. Where are the sheep?

Draw in some sheep and color the picture.
You can read this story in Exodus 2:15–25.

Color me!

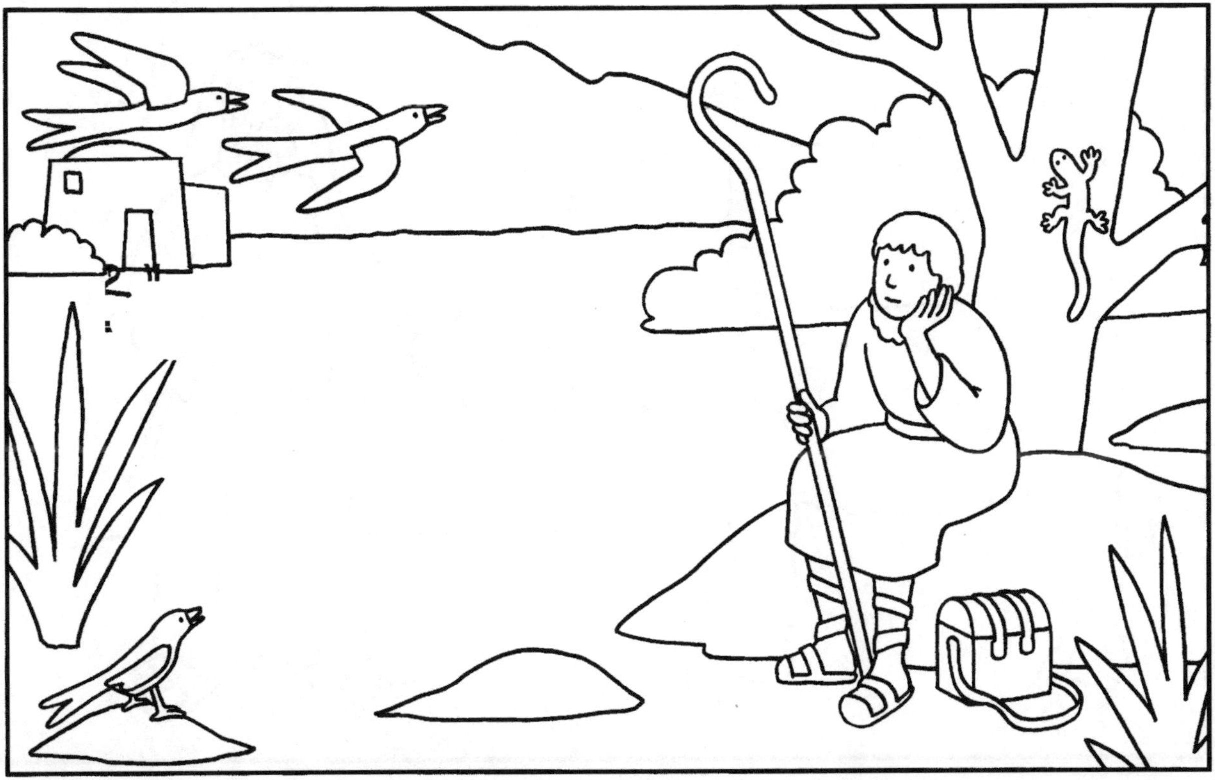

29

OCTOBER

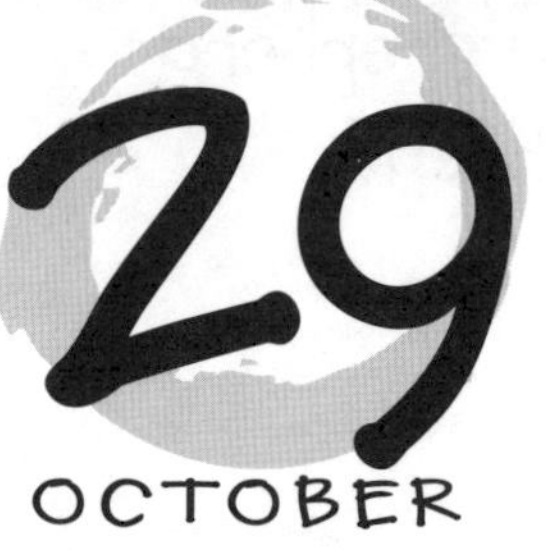

Jesus told his friends to borrow a donkey for him to ride into the city of Jerusalem.

You can read this story in Matthew 21:7.

Color me!

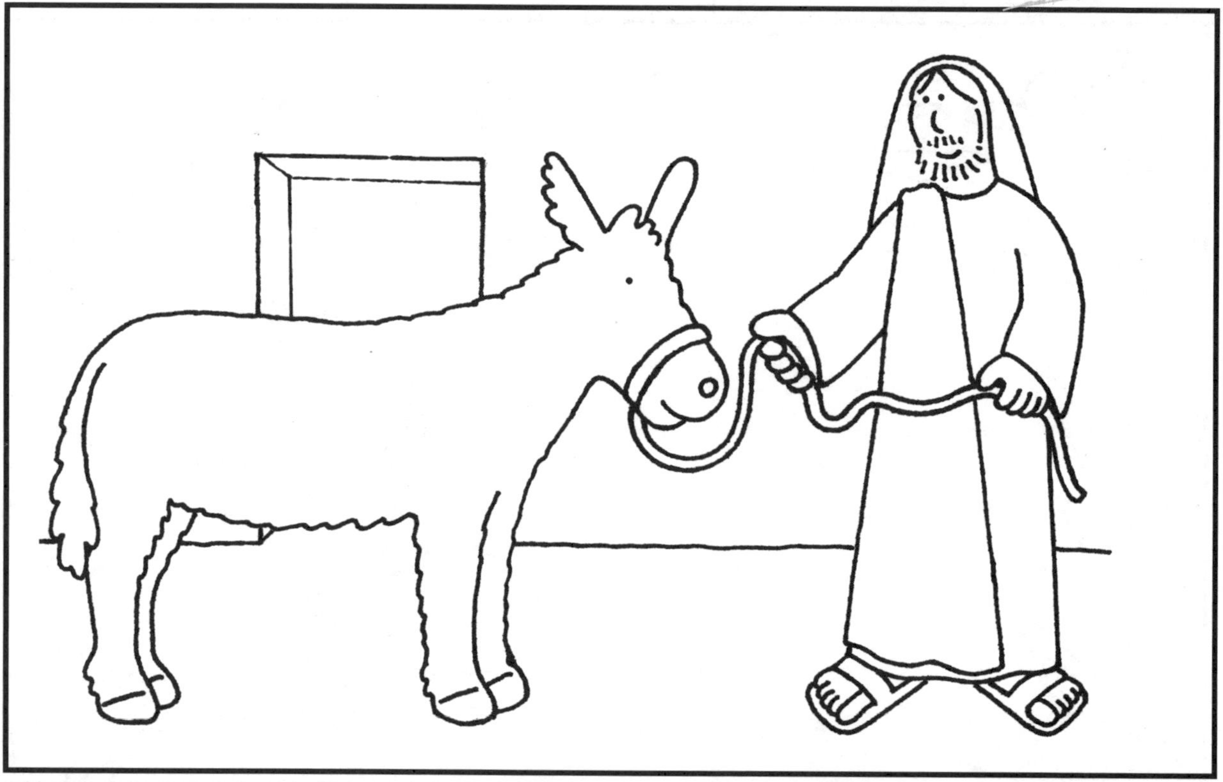

One day, Moses saw a bush burning in the desert. Find 10 differences between the two pictures.

You can read what happened when Moses saw the bush in Exodus 3:1–14.

28
OCTOBER

Martha got very cross with her sister Mary when she talked to Jesus instead of helping her get dinner ready for him.

Find 11 things to eat in this picture.
Read this story in Luke 10:38–42.

Puzzle

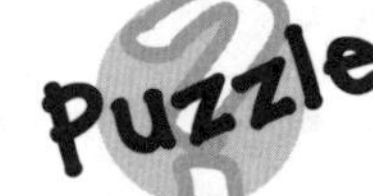

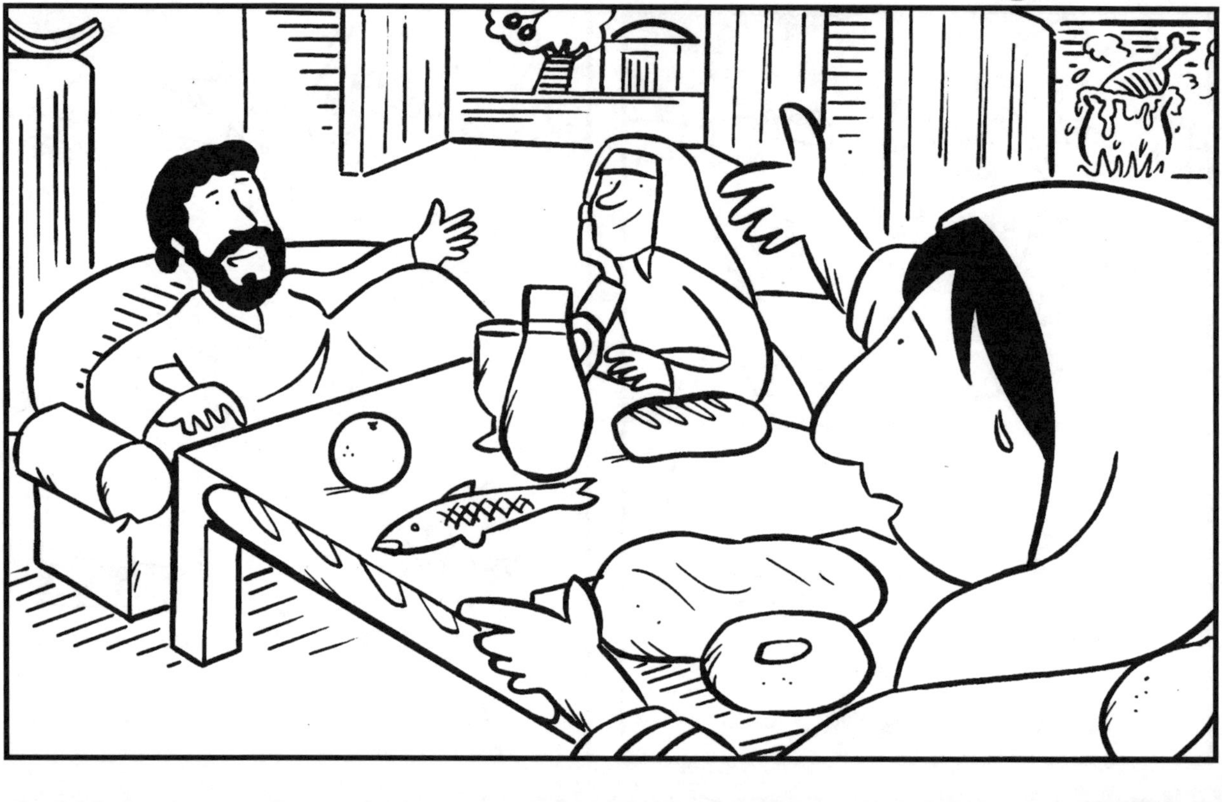

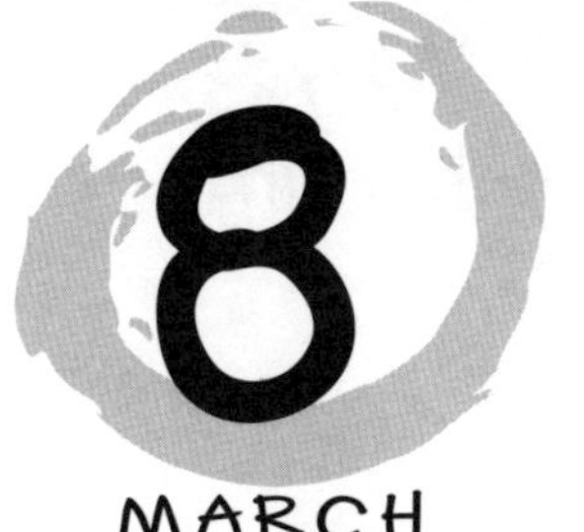

8
MARCH

Here is another picture of Moses listening to an angel of God in the desert.
Draw in the burning bush.

You can read this story in Exodus 3:1–21.

Draw me!

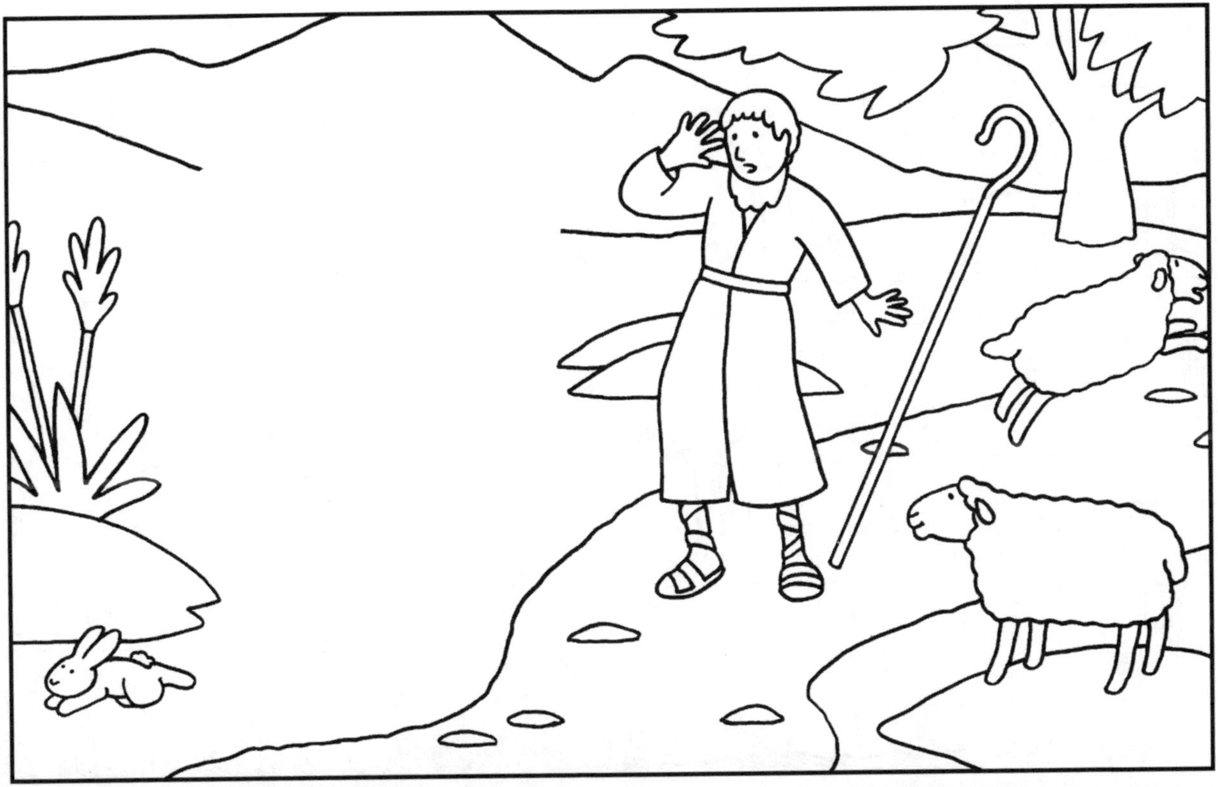

27

OCTOBER

Here is Jesus visiting the house of Mary, Martha and Lazarus. Can you help him find the way without crossing any lines?

See Luke 10:38–42.

maze

There are 10 differences between these two reflected pictures of Moses and the burning bush. Can you find them all?

You can read this story in Exodus 3:1–14.

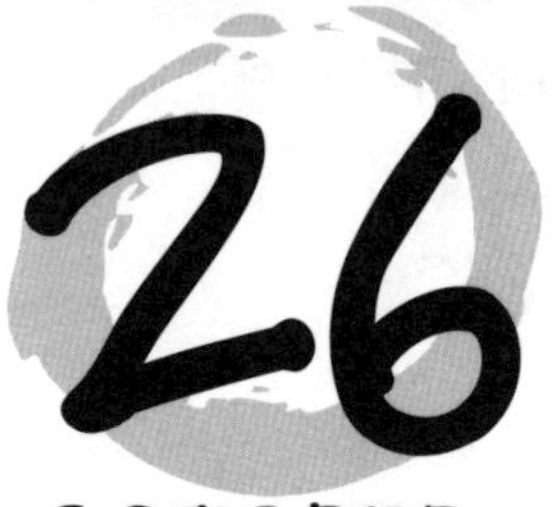

26 OCTOBER

Mary, Martha and Lazarus sometimes looked after Jesus in their house in Bethany. Can you help Martha reach the flowers?

Read this story in Luke 10:38–42.

maze

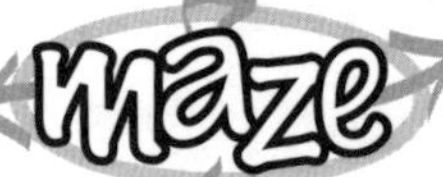

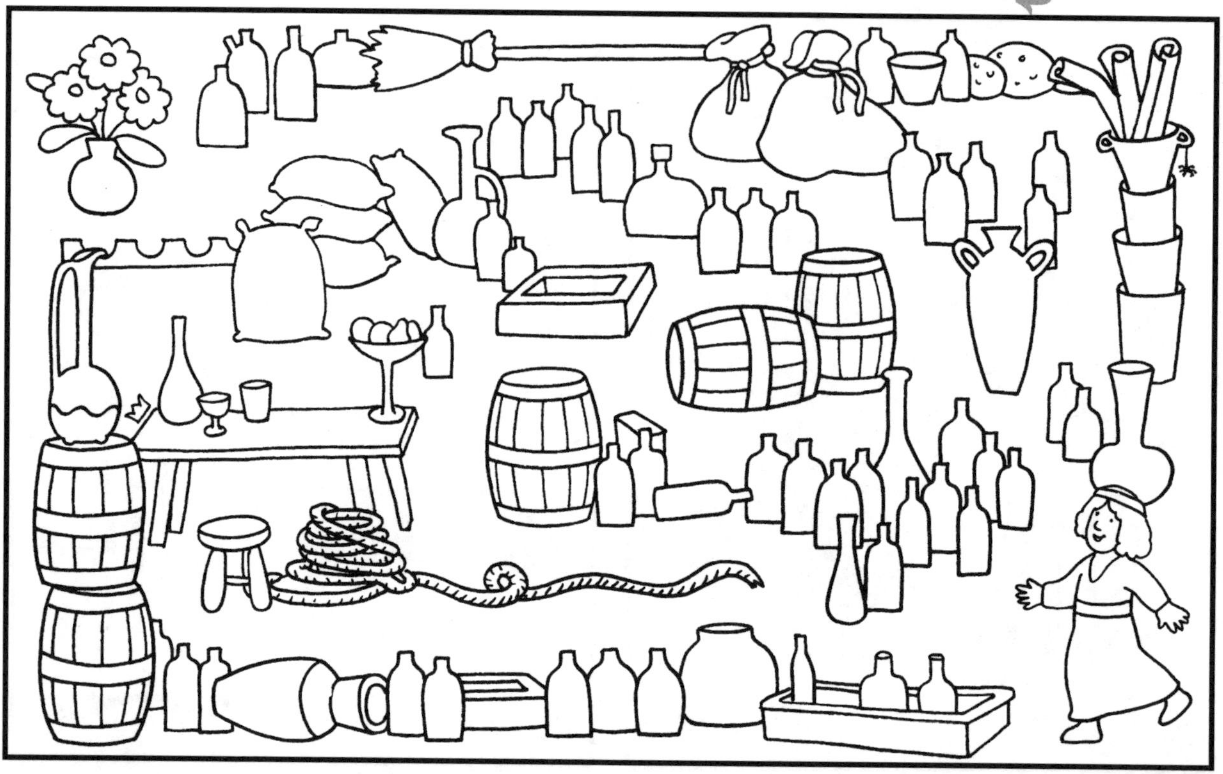

10

MARCH

In Moses' time, God made dreadful things happen in Egypt. Once, thousands of frogs swarmed all over the land.

Circle 10 differences between these two pictures.
Read about this plague in Exodus 8:1–15.

25
OCTOBER

In this picture of Zacchaeus in the sycamore tree, the artist has made lots of deliberate mistakes. List all those you can see.

Ask your friends if they can find any more.
Now read Luke 19:1–10.

Puzzle

Can you find 10 differences between these two drawings of the Egyptian Pharaoh?

Read what happened when Moses met Pharaoh in Exodus 7:8–13.

24

OCTOBER

Can you find 10 differences between these two pictures of Jesus talking to Zacchaeus in the sycamore tree?

Read Luke 19:1–10 for the whole story.

12

MARCH

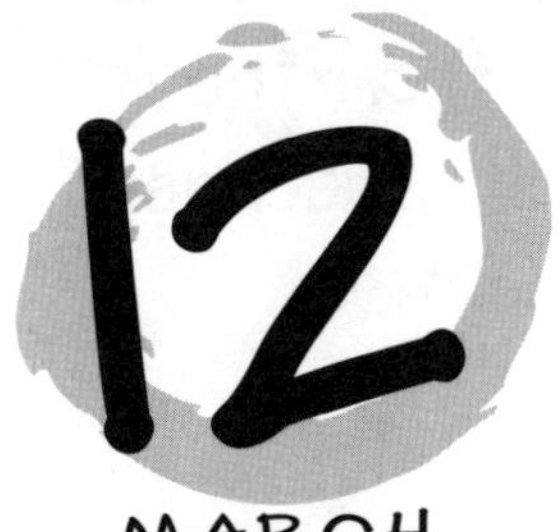

God sent a terrific hailstorm on Egypt.
Add great hailstones to this picture.

You can read this story in Exodus 9:13–35.

Draw me!

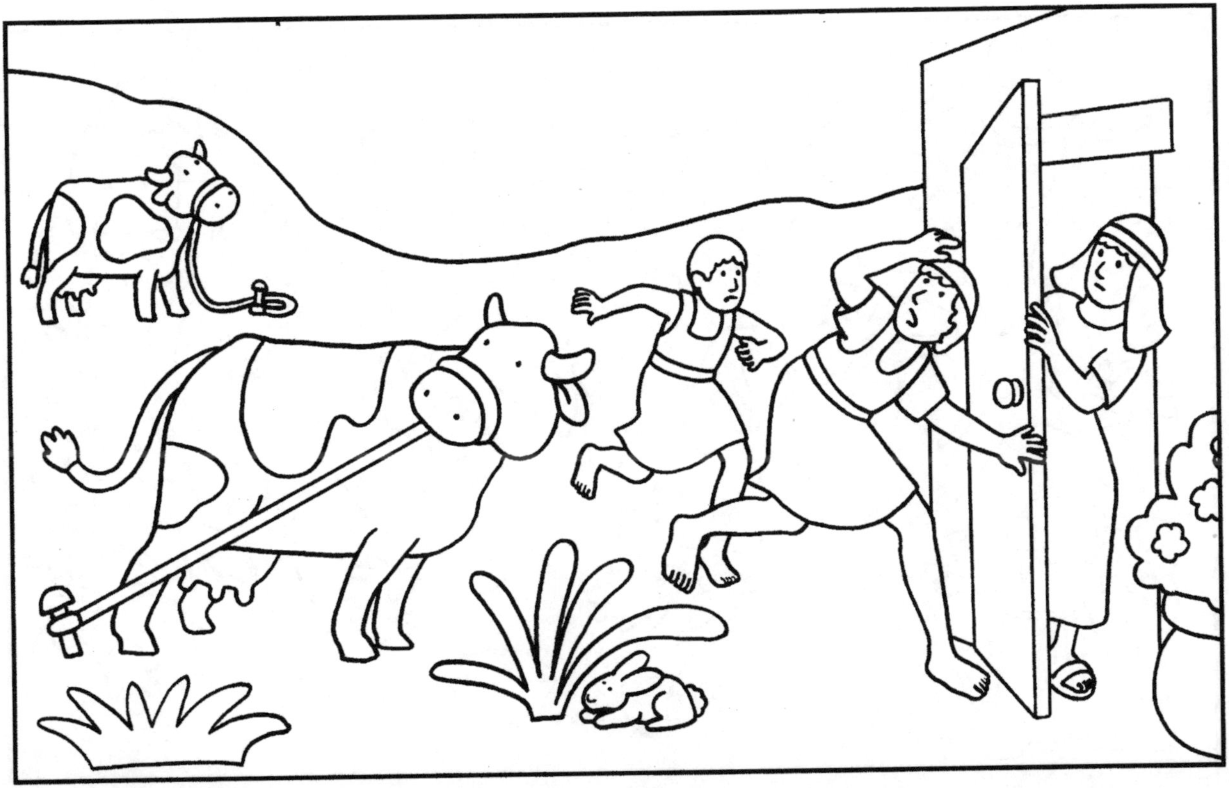

23
OCTOBER

Jesus told Zacchaeus, 'Come down from the tree; I'm coming to your house.' Help Zacchaeus find the right way down the tree without crossing leaves or branches.

Read this story in Luke 19:1–10.

maze

MARCH

There are lots of mistakes in this picture of the frogs invading Egypt.
Try to find all of them.

You can read this story in Exodus 8:1–15.

Color me!

22

OCTOBER

Zacchaeus was so small that unless he climbed a tree he knew he wouldn't be able to see Jesus.

Can you find 10 animals in this picture of Zacchaeus?
Read this story in Luke 19:1–10.

Puzzle

14

MARCH

At last Pharaoh told Moses he could lead his people out of Egypt. Draw Pharaoh sitting on his great throne.

You can read this story in Exodus 12:31–36.

Draw me!

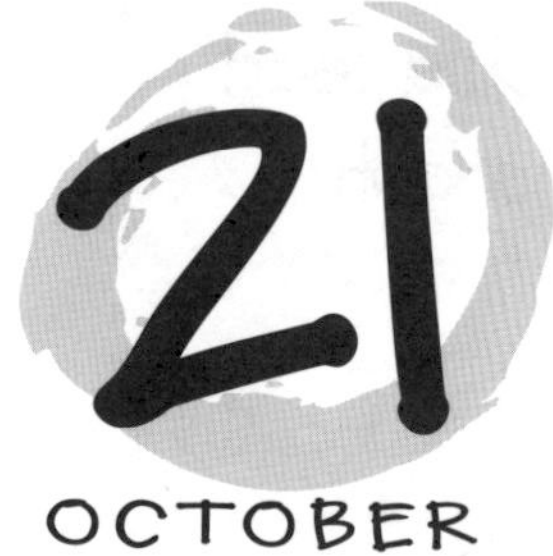

21 OCTOBER

In this picture of Jesus coming to the disciples across Galilee, the artist has deliberately got lots of things wrong.

Check your Bible and use your common sense to find out what's wrong. Read Matthew 14:22–33.

Puzzle

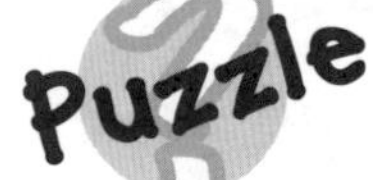

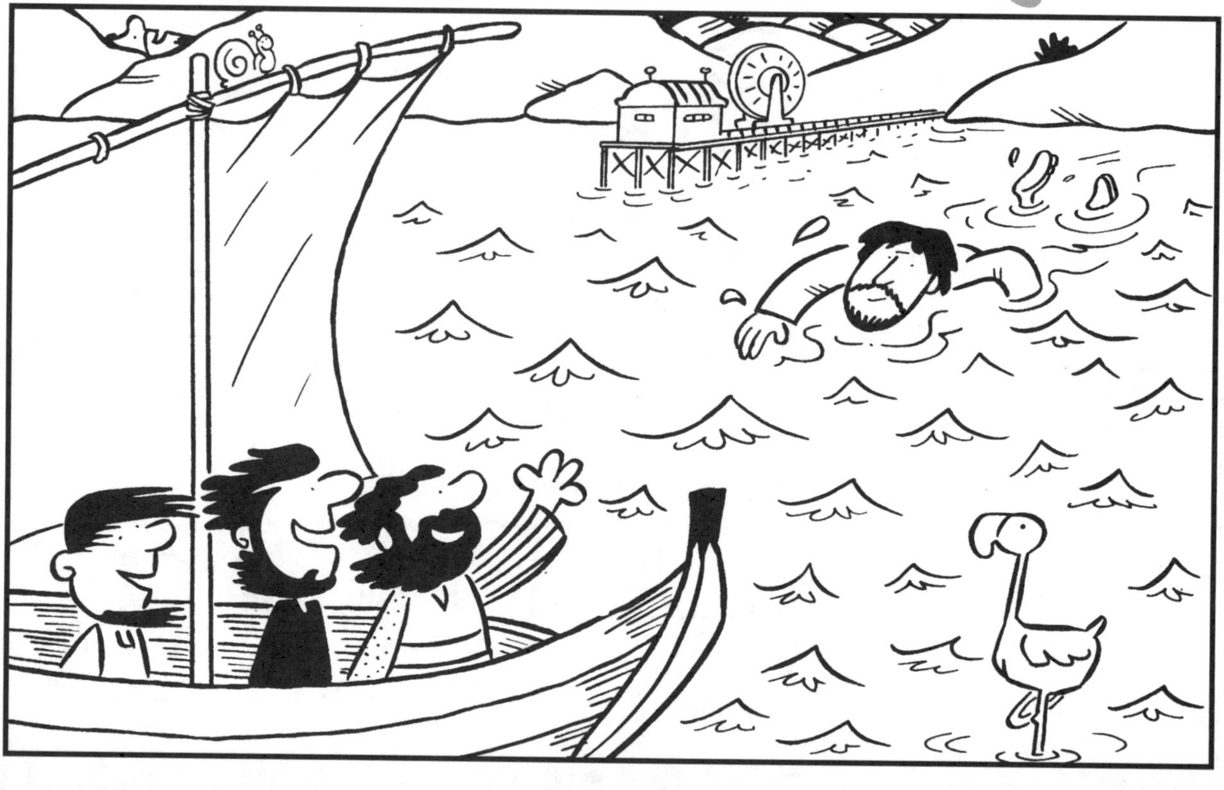

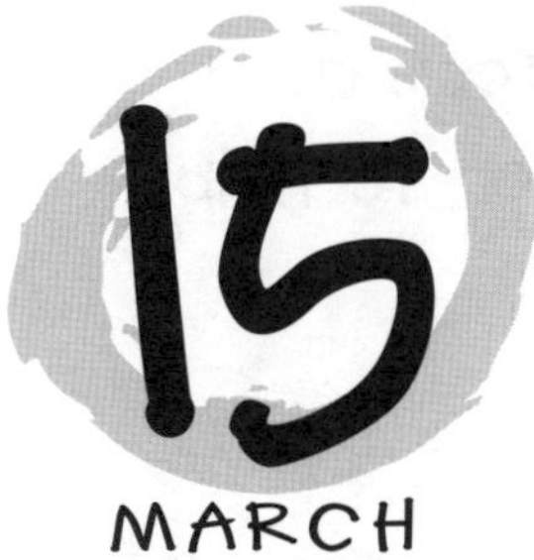

15 MARCH

After all the terrible things that happened in his kingdom, Pharaoh finally let Moses and his people leave Egypt.

Join up the dots to find what happened when they reached the Red Sea. See Exodus 14.

DOT-TO-DOT

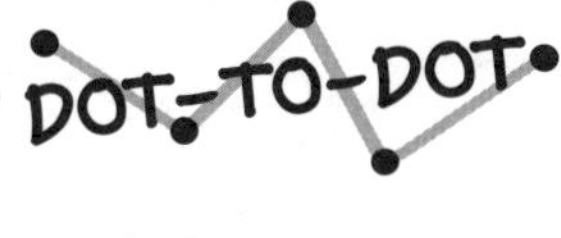

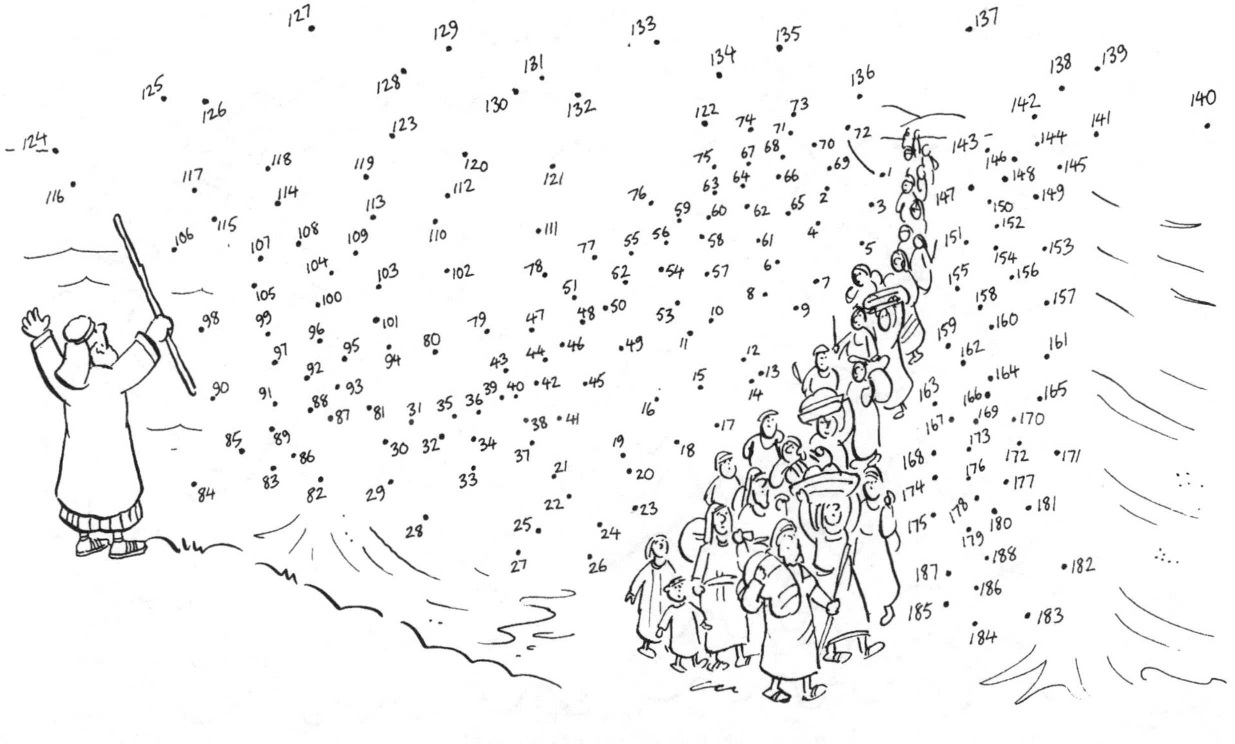

20

OCTOBER

Jesus' friends were caught in a storm at sea. Jesus walked across the water to help them.

Which route should Jesus take to the boat, without crossing the waves? See Matthew 14:22–33.

maze

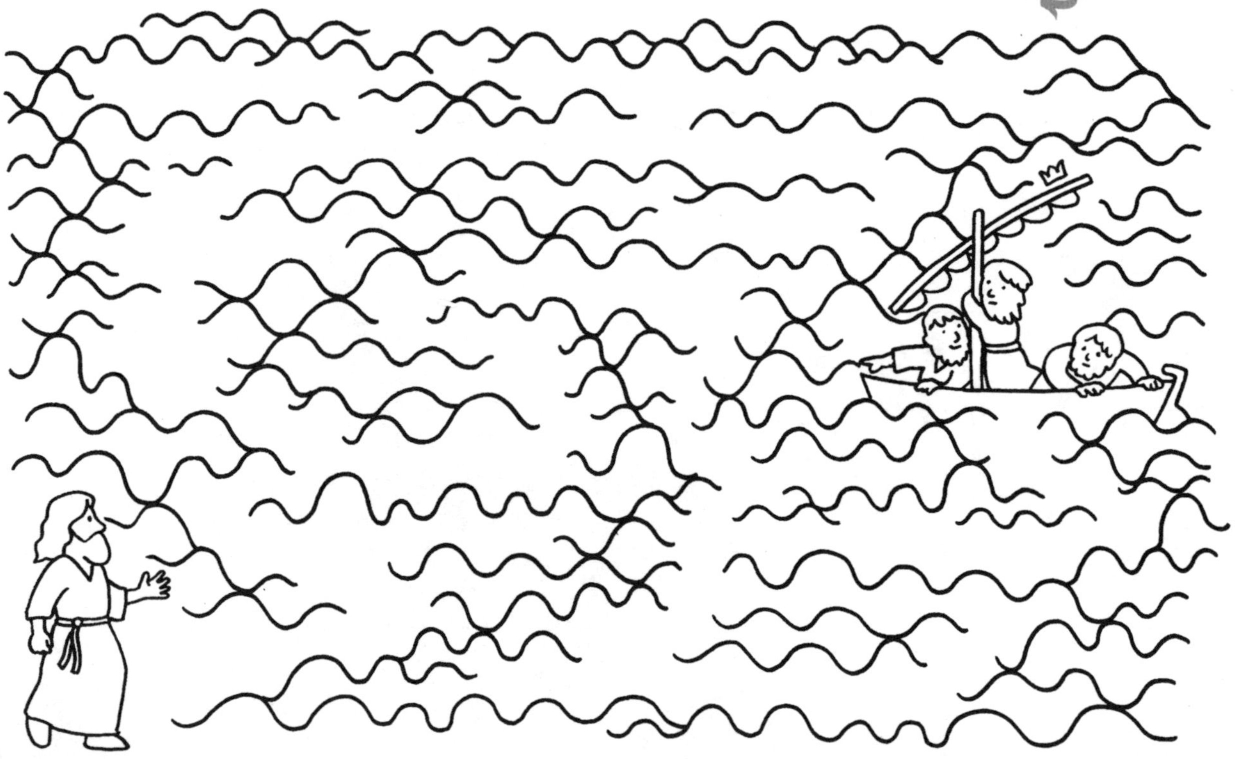

Put a circle around all the differences between these two pictures of Moses and the Israelites crossing the Red Sea.

Read this story in Exodus 14.

19

OCTOBER

Join the dots to find out where the tax-collector called Zacchaeus is sitting. Why did he climb up and what happened afterwards?

Read Luke 19:1–10 to see.
Who is calling to Zacchaeus?

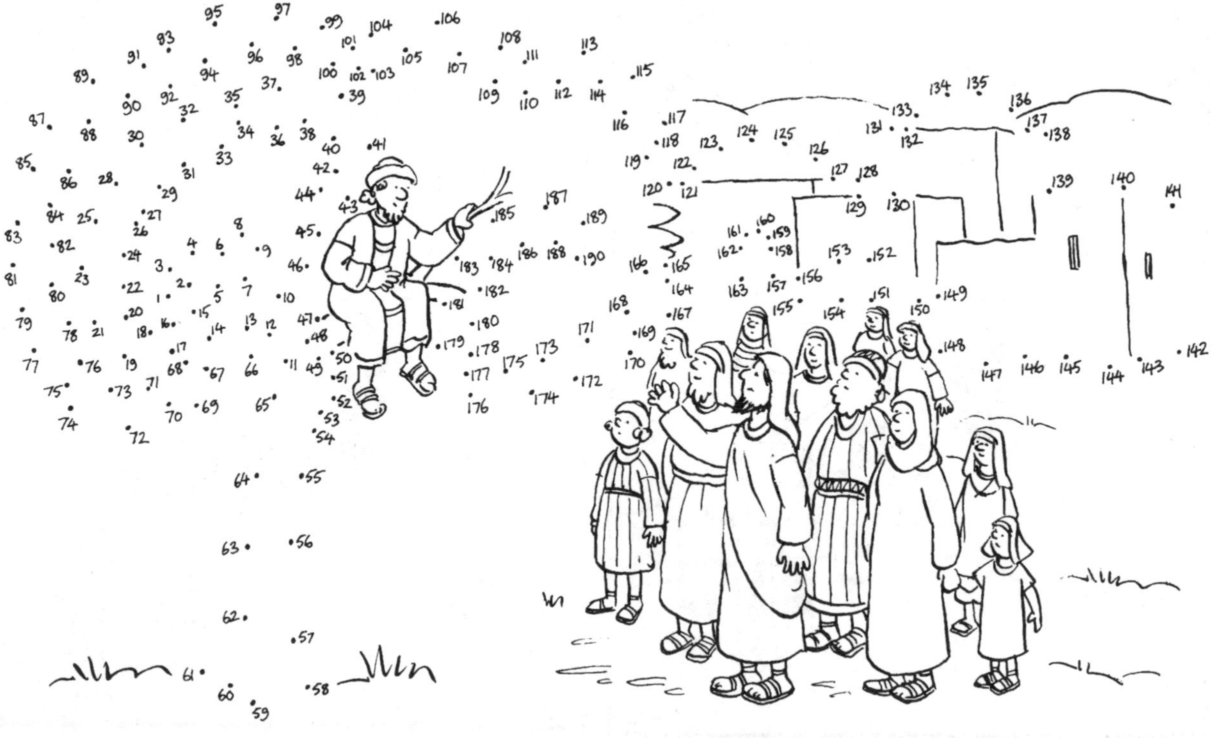

17

MARCH

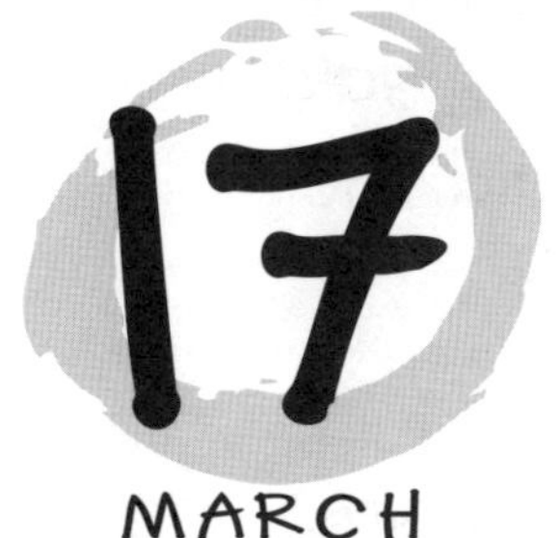

Can you find all the deliberate mistakes in this picture of the Israelites crossing the Red Sea?

You can read this story in your Bible in Exodus 14.

Color me!

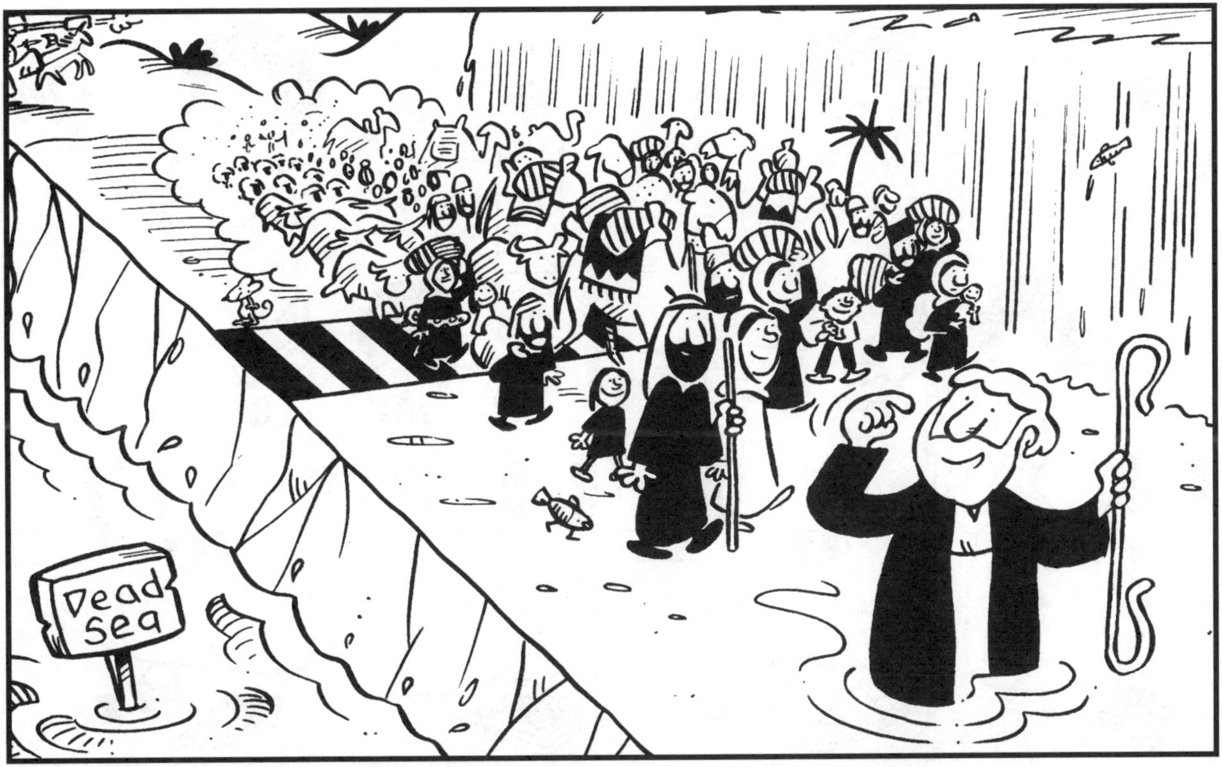

18 OCTOBER

Two men were praying. 'I'm so good,' said one. 'I'm sorry that I'm so bad,' said the other. Which prayer pleased God?

Read the story in Luke 18:9–14.
Find 10 differences between the two pictures.

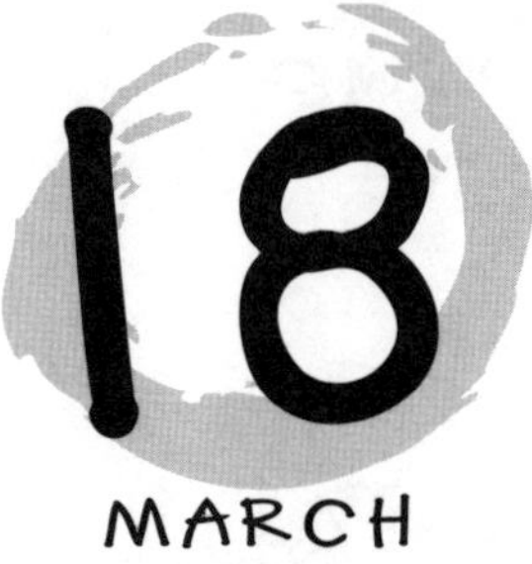

18

MARCH

The Israelites crossed the Red Sea in safety—but the Egyptians drowned. Draw some of the Egyptian soldiers.

Read this story in Exodus 14.

Draw me!

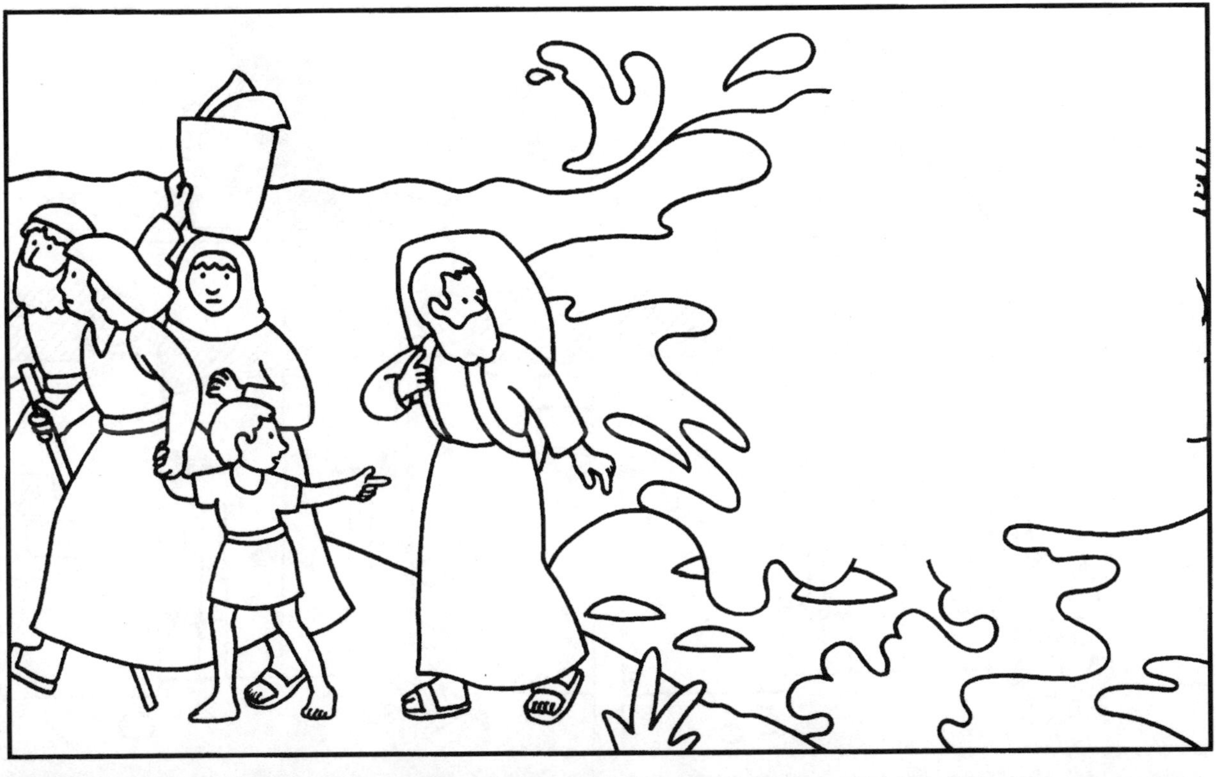

17

OCTOBER

Jesus told a story about a rich man who was so mean that he wouldn't help the poor man outside his front door.

Read the story in Luke 16:19–31.
Find 10 differences between these pictures.

19

MARCH

Miriam, Moses' sister, played her tambourine for joy when the Israelites escaped from the Egyptian Pharaoh.

Can you find 7 tambourines hidden in this picture?
Read Miriam's song in Exodus 15.

Color me!

16 OCTOBER

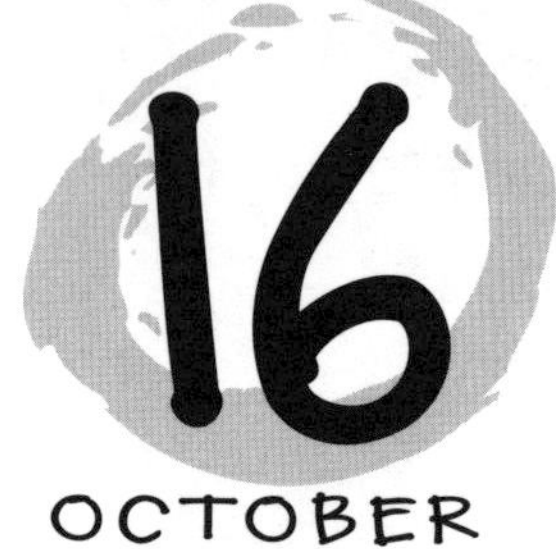

When the lost son returned home, his father was waiting for him. The artist has got lots of things wrong in this picture.

Check in your Bible if you're not sure if something is right. See Luke 15:11–32.

Puzzle

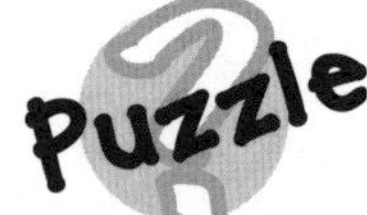

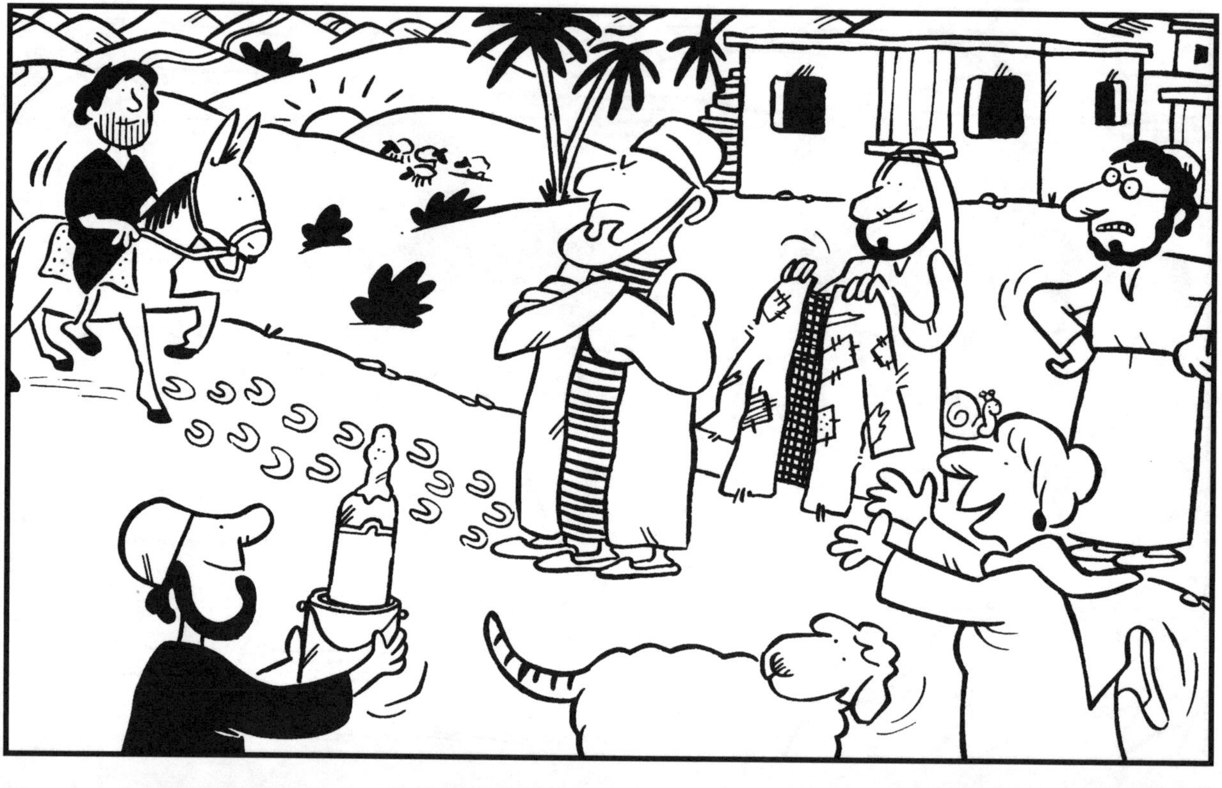

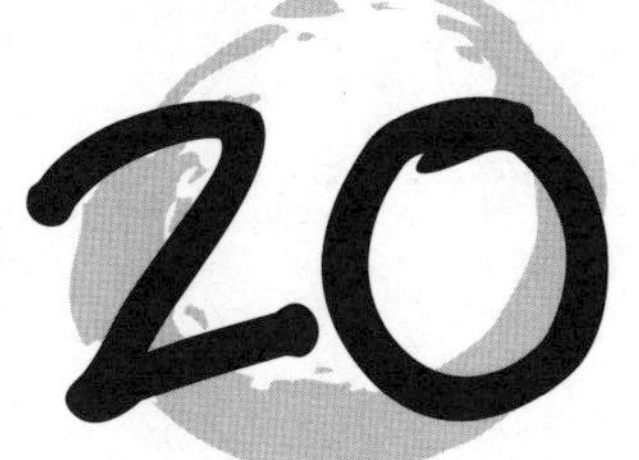

20

MARCH

God sent special food called manna for his people to eat in the desert.

Draw the manna on the ground then color the picture.
Read this story in Exodus 16.

Draw me!

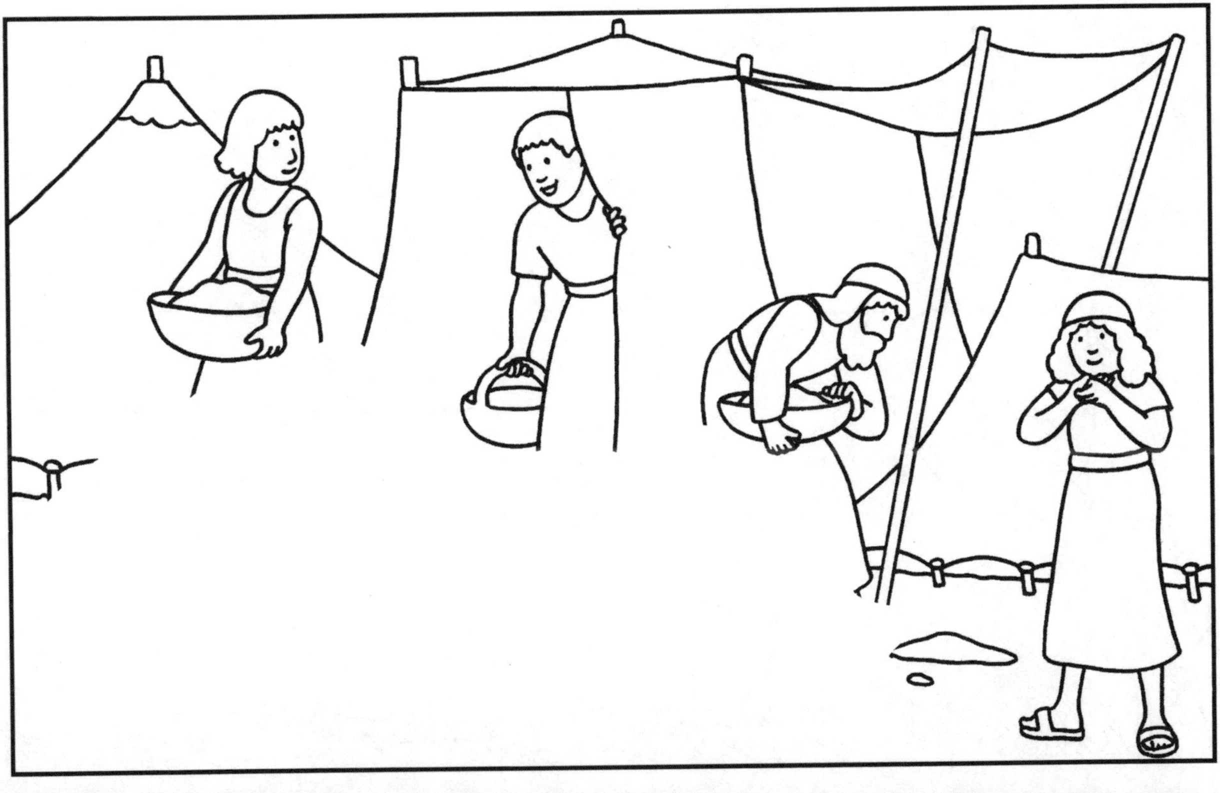

15
OCTOBER

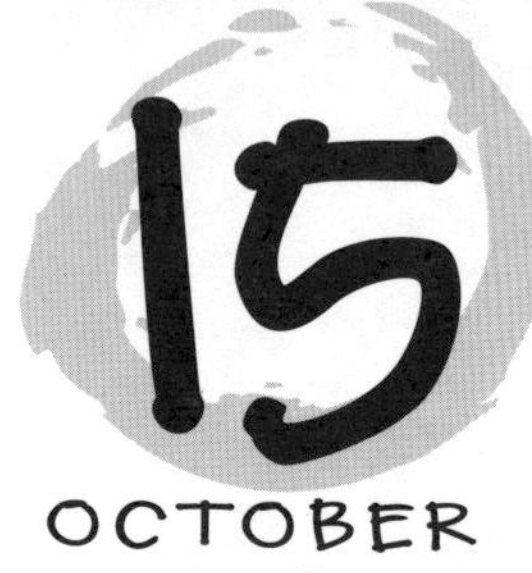

In this picture of the lost son, the artist hasn't finished drawing the pigs. Complete the pigs—and then color the picture.

Read the whole story in Luke 15:11–32.

Draw me!

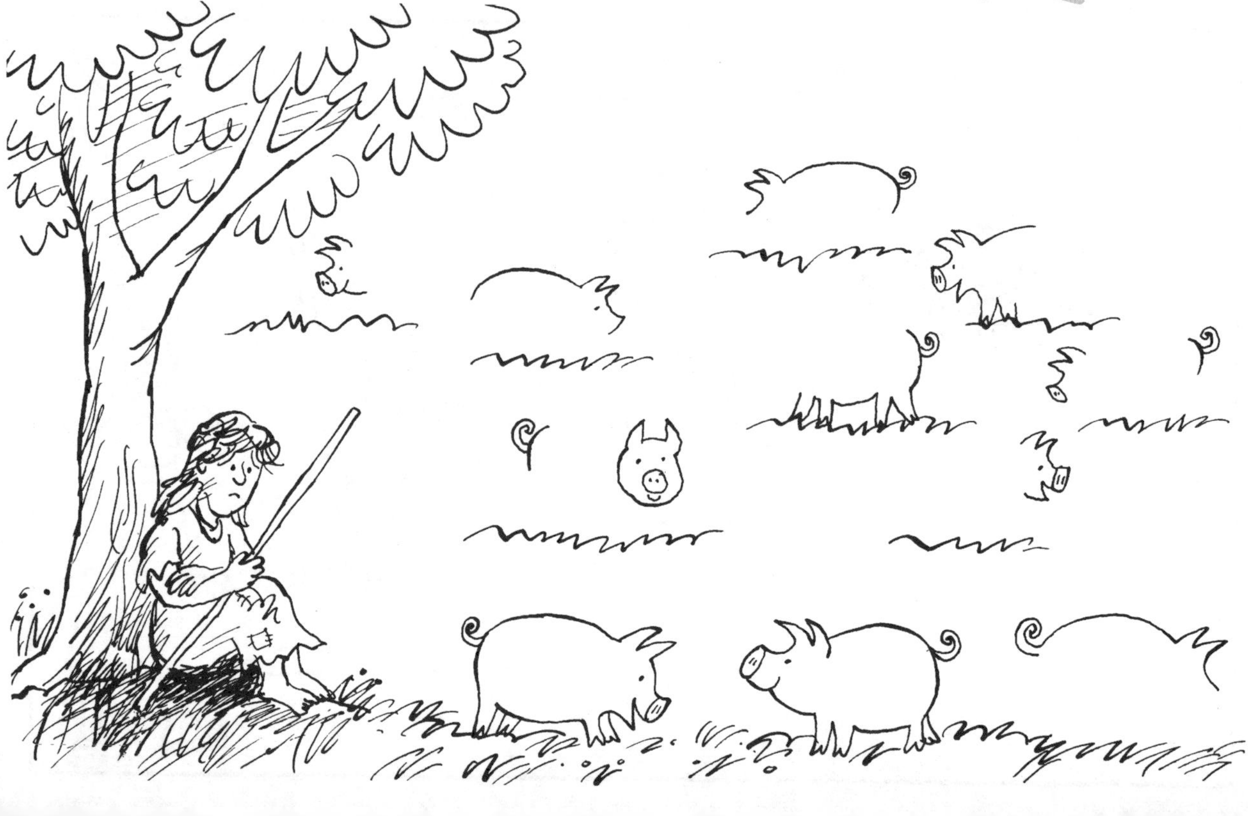

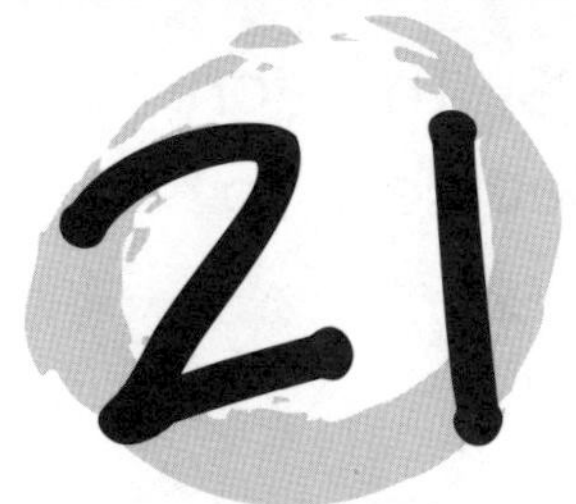

21 MARCH

Moses climbed Mount Sinai to meet God. Join up the lines to discover what he brought down the mountain.

Read about Moses' adventure in Exodus 20.

DOT-TO-DOT

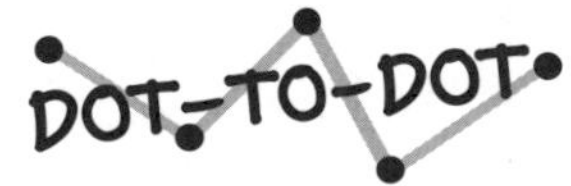

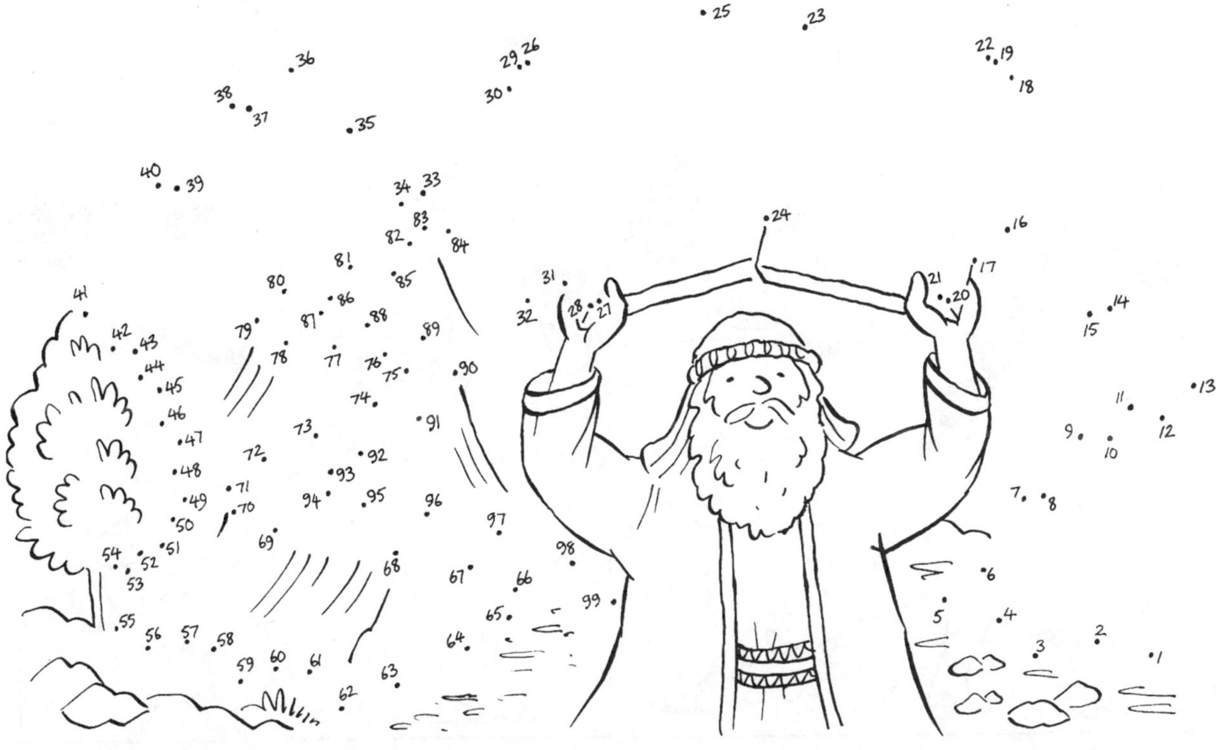

14

OCTOBER

While he was looking after the pigs, the son saw how stupid he had been. He decided to go home and say sorry to his father.

Find 10 differences between the pictures.
Read this story in Luke 15:11–32.

22
MARCH

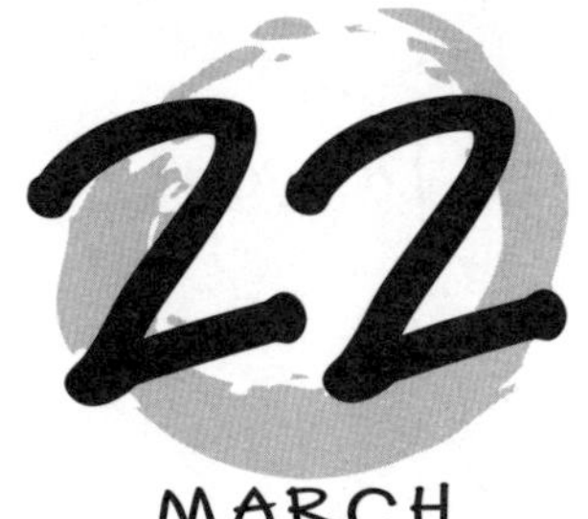

Moses is carrying two stones on which are written the Ten Commandments. Help Moses find the only way down Mount Sinai.

Now color the picture with felt-tips.
Read this story in Exodus 24:12–18.

maze

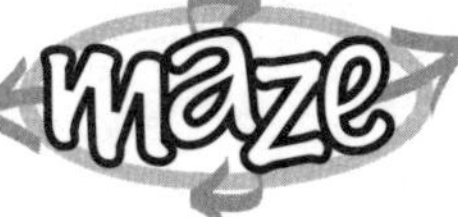

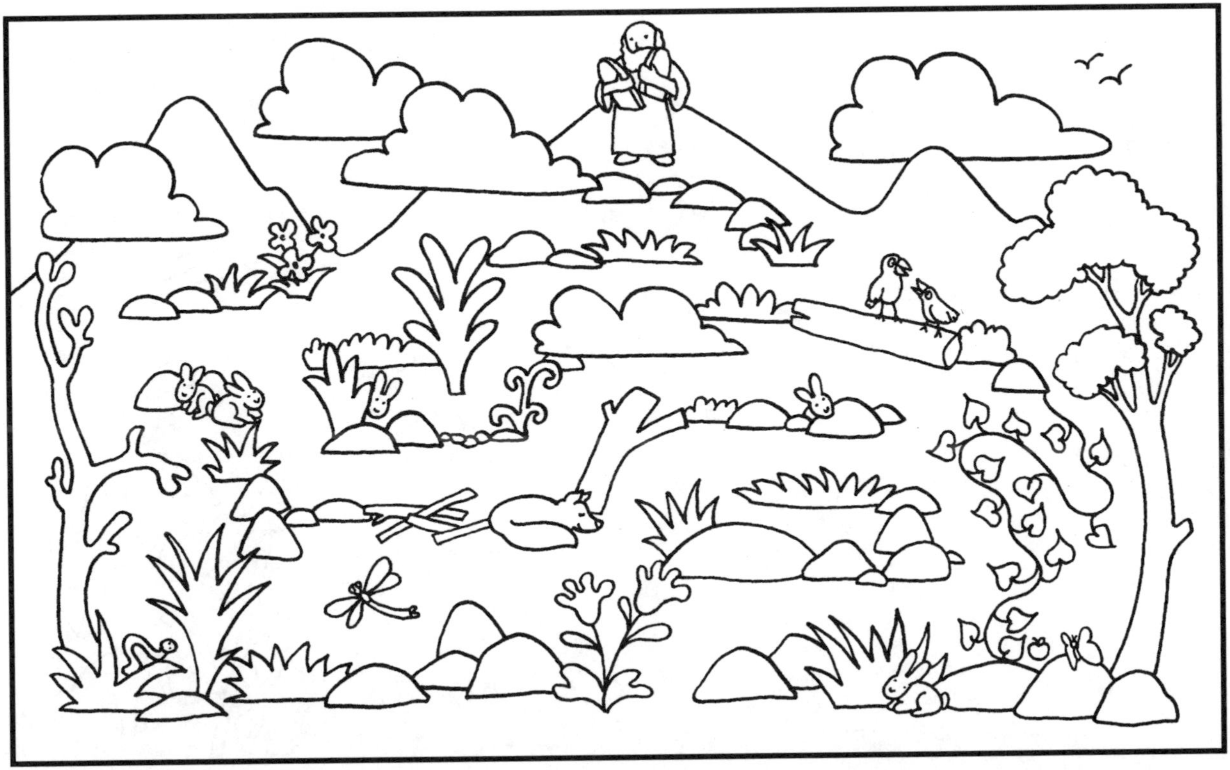

13

OCTOBER

Join up the dots to find out what the lost son did after he spent all his money. Do you think he is happy?

Do you know what he ate?
Read the story again from Luke 15:11-32 to find out.

DOT-TO-DOT

Put a circle around all the differences you can find between these two pictures.
Have you found 10?

You can read the story of Moses and the Ten Commandments in Exodus 20:1–21 and 24:12–18.

12
OCTOBER

Here is the lost son in a far country. He used up his money on parties and buying expensive presents.

Can you find 10 differences between these two pictures? Read this story in Luke 15:11–32.

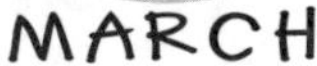

24

MARCH

The people of Israel gave their gold and jewels for a special tent of worship. Find 10 differences between these pictures of the treasures.

Read about the tent of worship in Exodus chapters 25—27.

OCTOBER 11

Jesus told a story about a boy who left home and became very sad. Help the boy get back to his loving father.

Read this story—often called the Prodigal Son—in Luke 15:11–32.

maze

25

MARCH

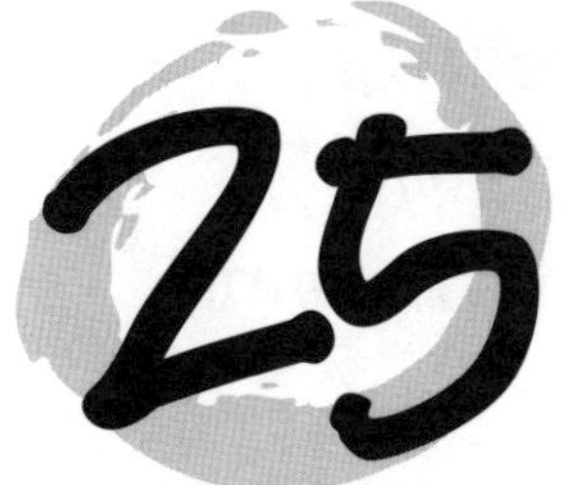

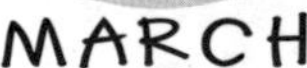

When the tent was finished, priests carried the ark of God inside. Draw the ark on the priests' shoulders.

You can read this story in Exodus 25:10–22.

Draw me!

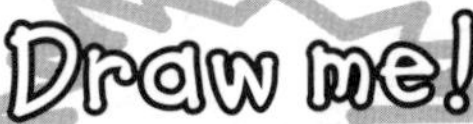

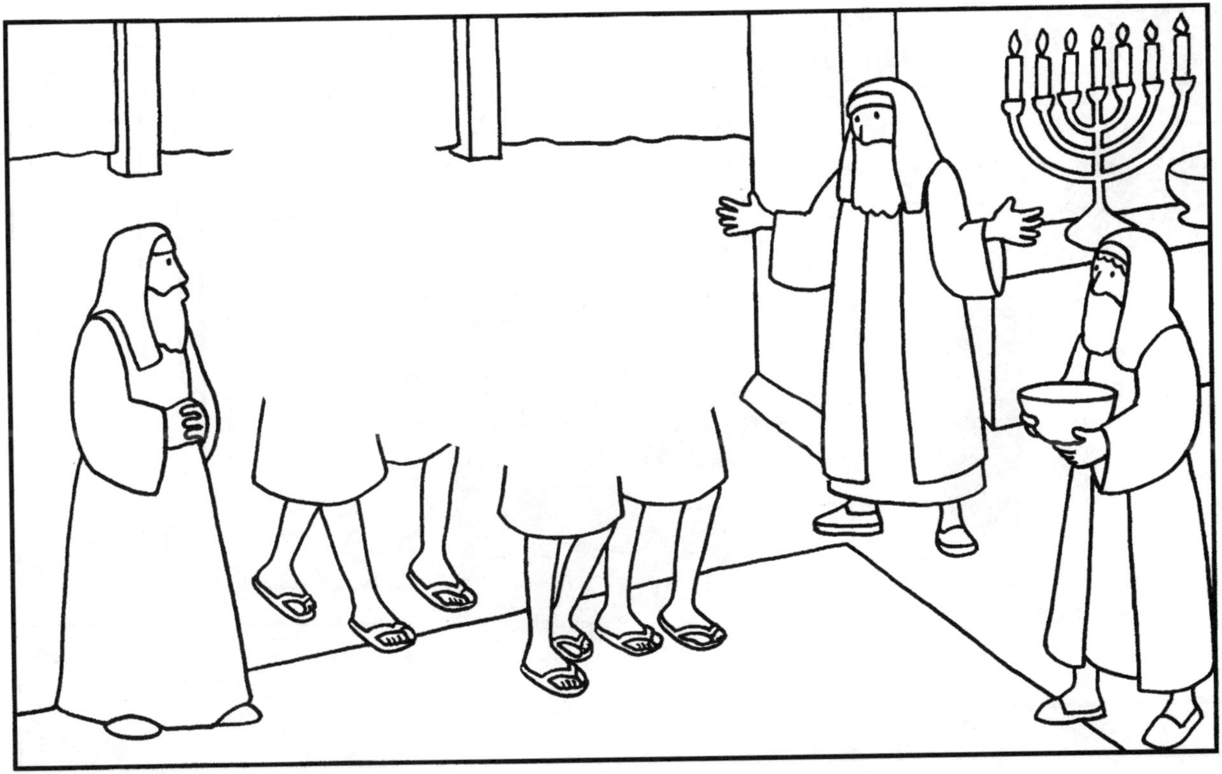

10
OCTOBER

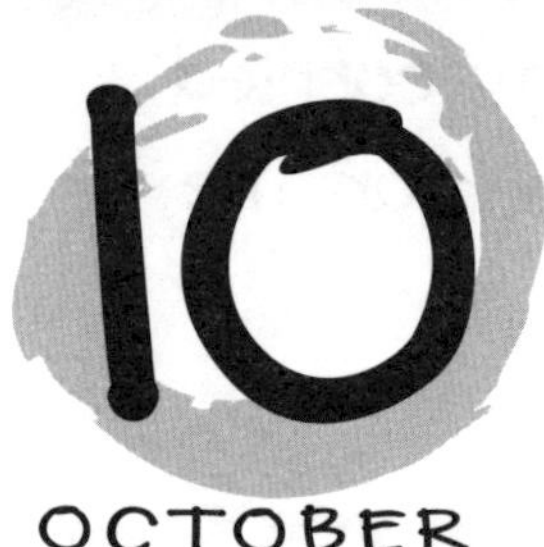

In this picture of the woman who lost her silver coin, the artist has made lots of funny mistakes. Put a circle around them all.

How many have you found?
Read the whole story in Luke 15:8–10.

Puzzle

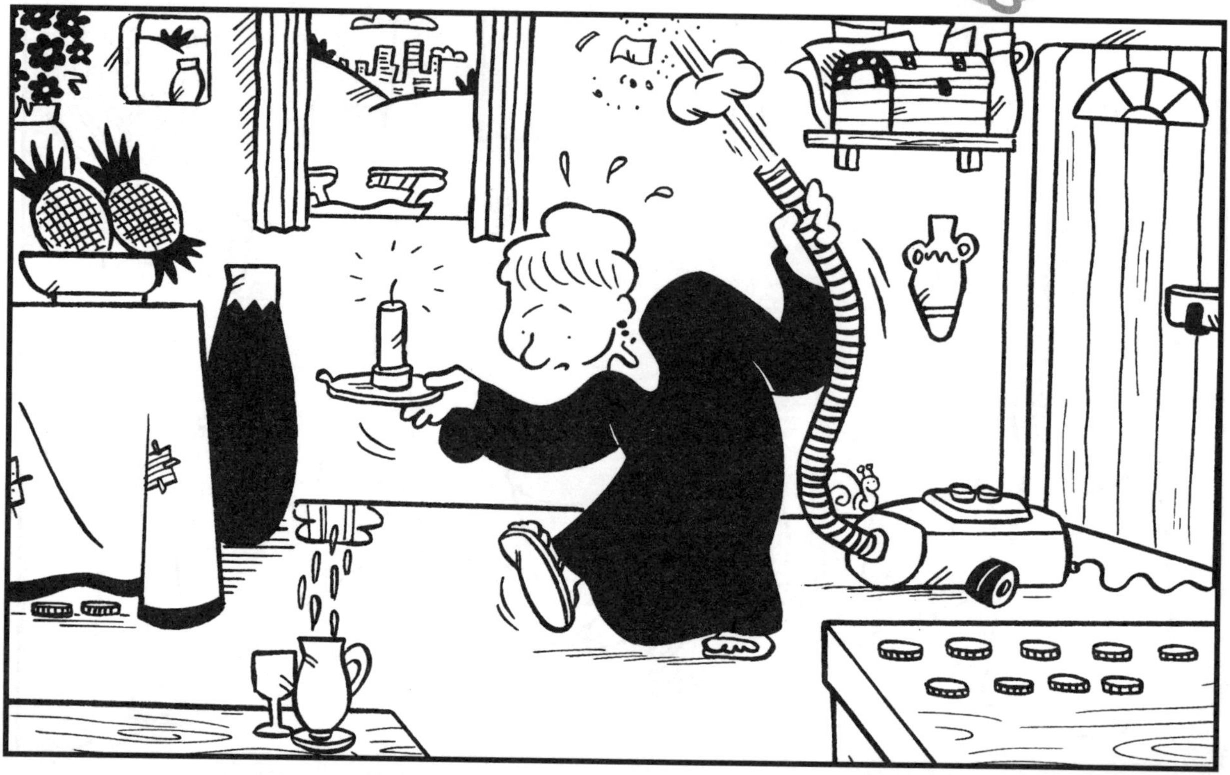

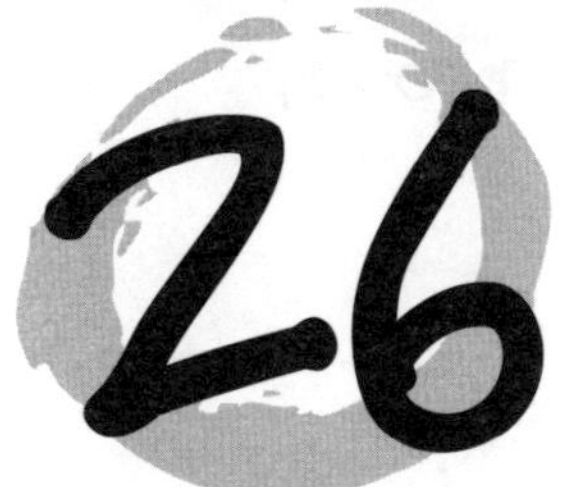

26

MARCH

When Moses came down Mount Sinai, he found the people worshiping a golden calf. Draw the idol in the empty space.

You can read this story in Exodus 32.

Draw me!

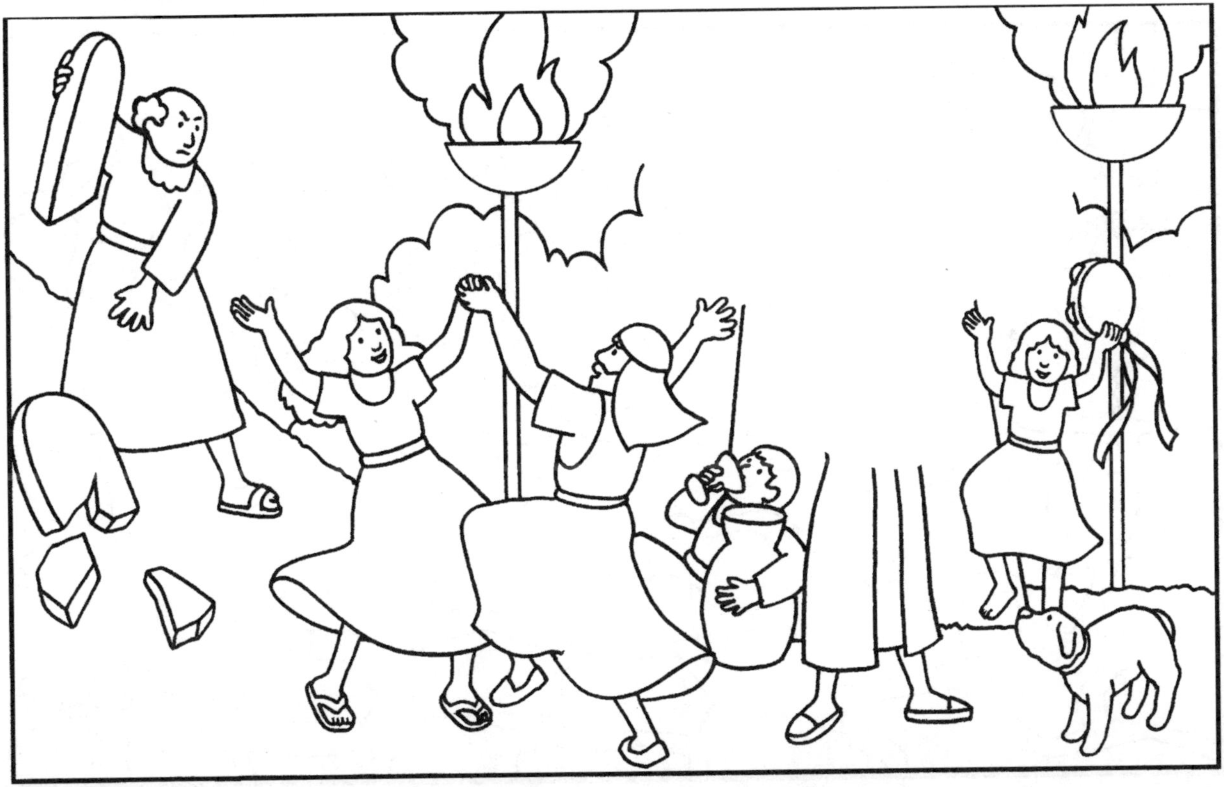

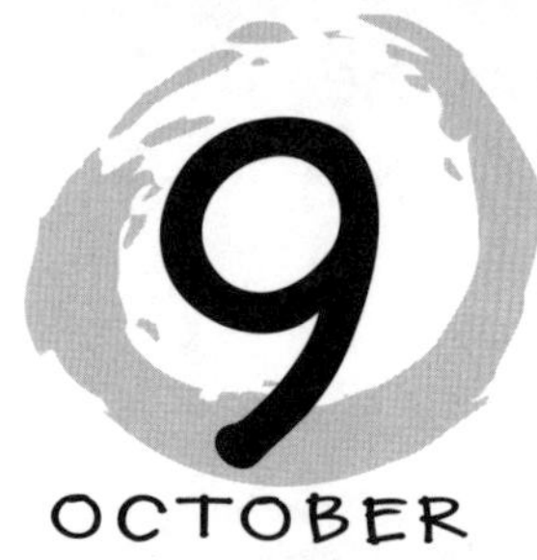

9 OCTOBER

Help the woman find her lost coin through the maze on the floor.
Don't cross any lines!

Read this story in Luke 15:8–10.

maze

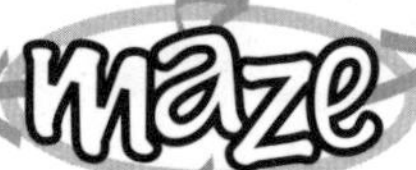

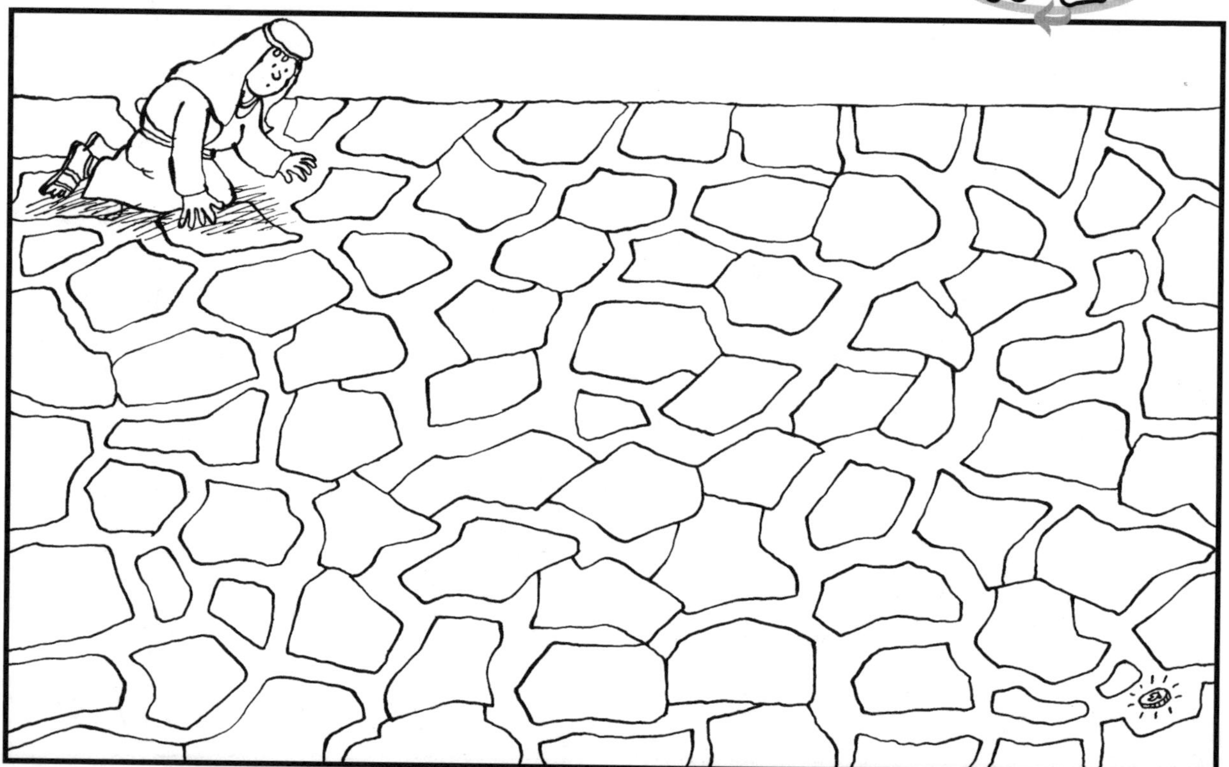

27

MARCH

Circle all the mistakes you can find in this picture of the Israelites worshiping the golden calf.

Check out the story in your Bible in Exodus 32:1–35.

Color me!

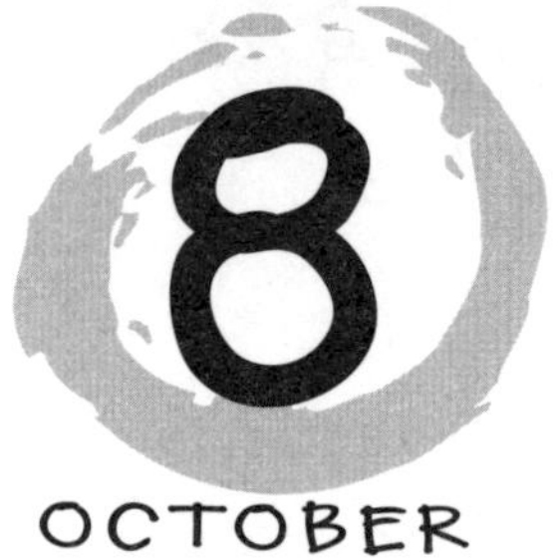

8 OCTOBER

The lady who lost her silver coin has finally found it! Can you find 10 differences between the pictures.

What is she using to see the coin?
Read the whole story in Luke 15:8–10.

SPOT THE DIFFERENCE

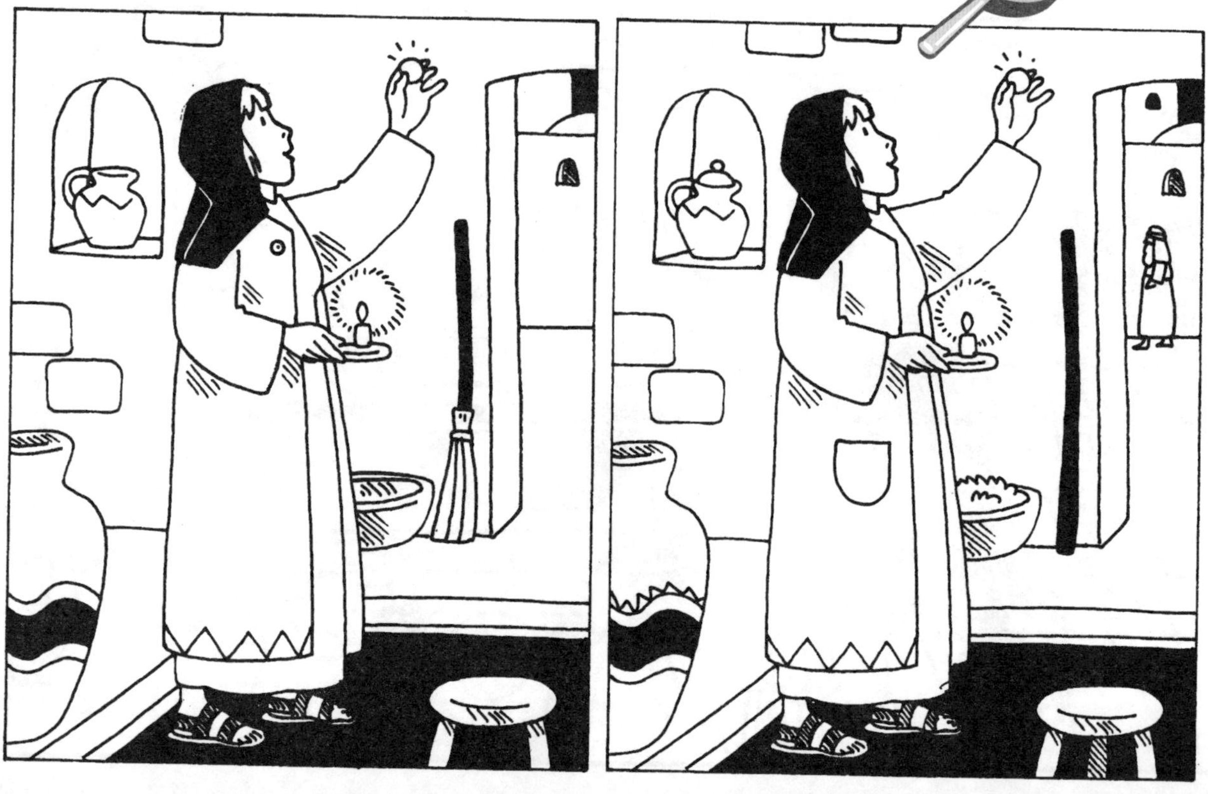

28

Moses led the Israelites through the desert. Which route will bring them to the oasis?

You can read this story in your Bible in Exodus 15:22–27.

7

OCTOBER

Jesus told a story of a woman who lost a silver coin. She swept her house until she found it. Which path has the most leaves to sweep?

Read the whole story in Luke 15:8–10.

Puzzle

29

MARCH

While they were traveling through the desert, the Israelites were bitten by snakes. Can you find more than 16 snakes?

You can read this story in Numbers 21:4–9.

Puzzle

6

OCTOBER

There are 10 differences between these two pictures of the shepherd searching for his lost sheep.

What can you see that might harm the sheep?
Read this story in Luke 15:4–7.

30

MARCH

When the Israelites were marching to the Promised Land, Moses sent spies ahead to find out what it was like.

Can you find at least 10 differences between these pictures of the spies' visit? See Numbers 13:1–33.

5

OCTOBER

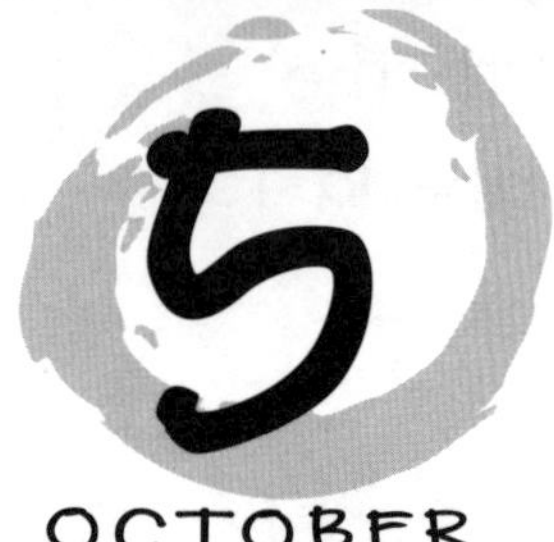

Join up the dots to find out where the shepherd has found his lost sheep. What is the shepherd holding in his left hand?

Was the shepherd happy when he found his lost sheep?
Read the story in Luke 15:4–7.

DOT-TO-DOT

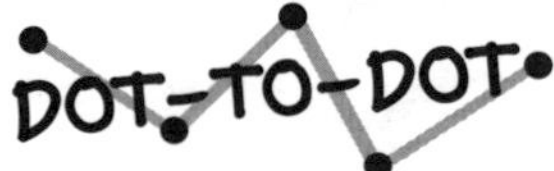

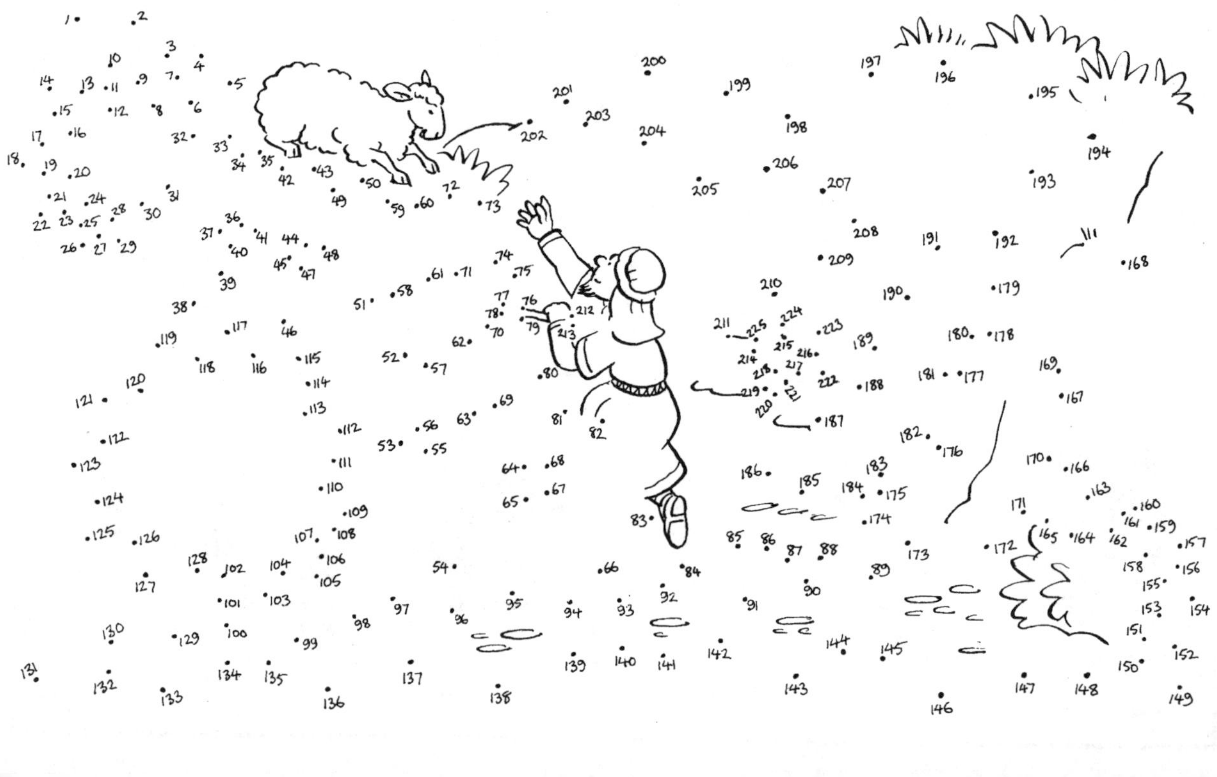

31

MARCH

Here are the spies returning from their trip to the Promised Land.

How many silly mistakes can you find in the picture?
You can read about the spies in Numbers 13:1–33.

Color me!

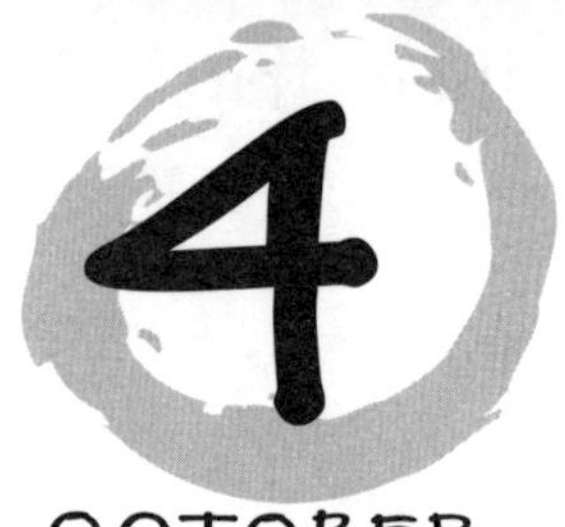

4

OCTOBER

Jesus told a story about a shepherd who lost one of his sheep. Help the shepherd to find the path to the lost sheep.

Read this story in Luke 15:4–7.

maze

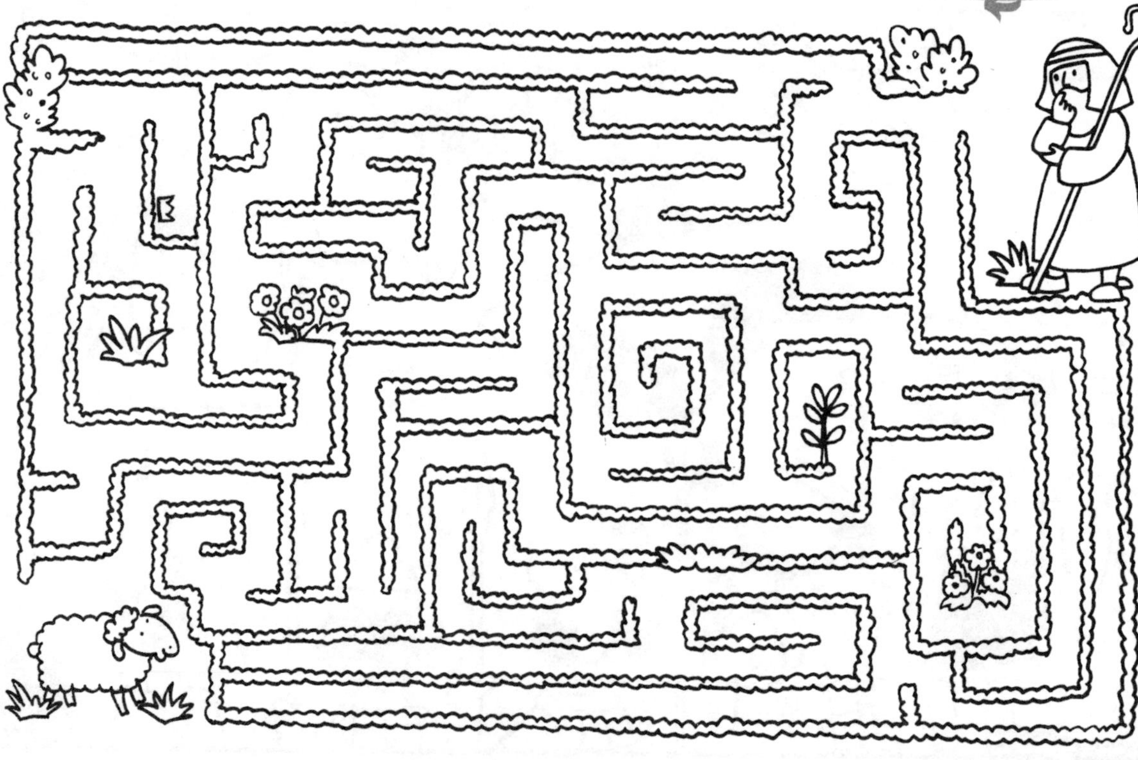

1

APRIL

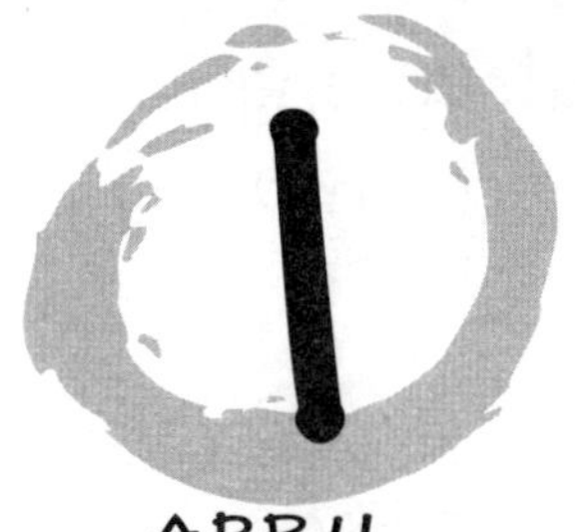

Old Moses died before the Israelites entered the Promised Land. Draw the land they were going to in the empty space.

You can read the story of the death of Moses in Deuteronomy 34.

Draw me!

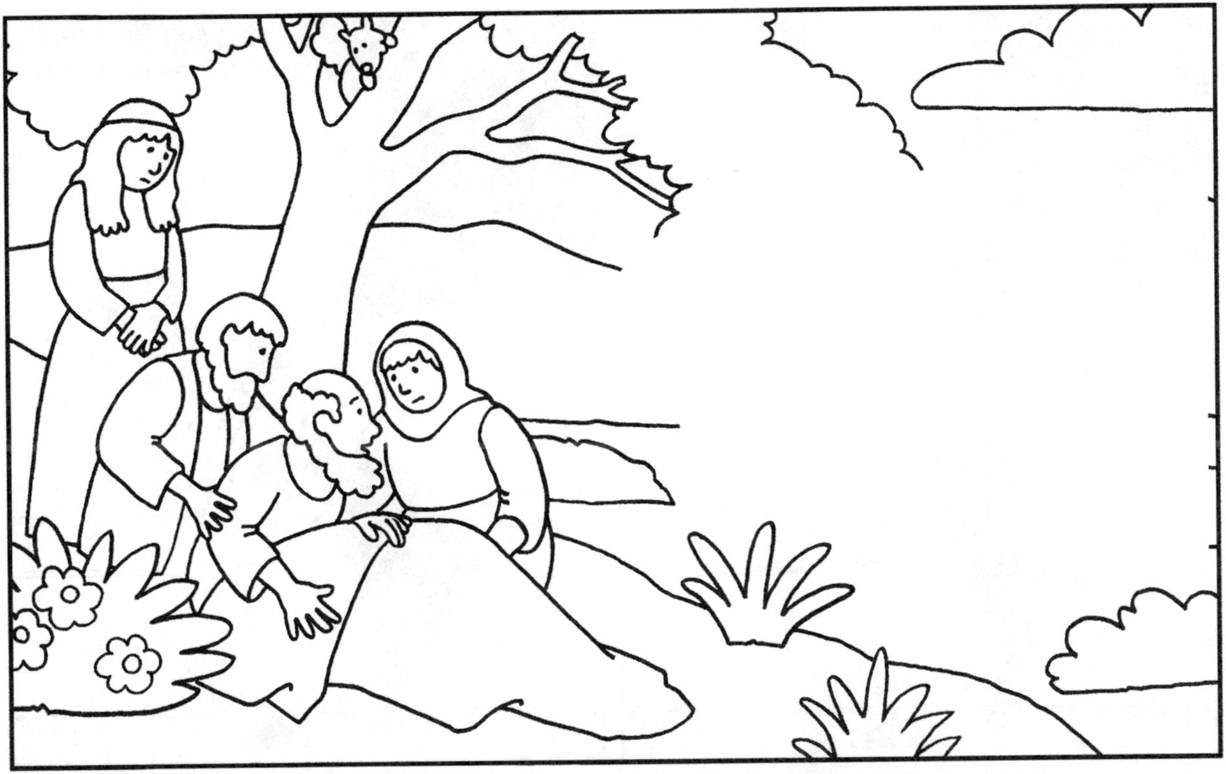

In another story, Jesus told about an enemy who came at night and planted weeds in a good farmer's cornfield.

Read this story in Matthew 13:24–30.
Find all 10 differences between these pictures.

2 APRIL

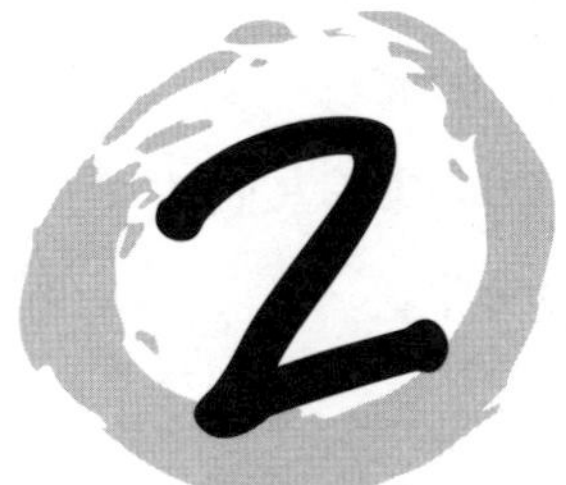

Join up the dots to find out why Balaam's donkey looks so frightened. Has it seen something?

You can read the story of Balaam and his donkey in Numbers 22:21–35.

DOT-TO-DOT

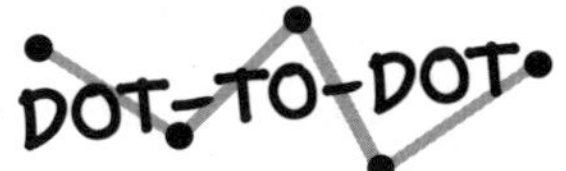

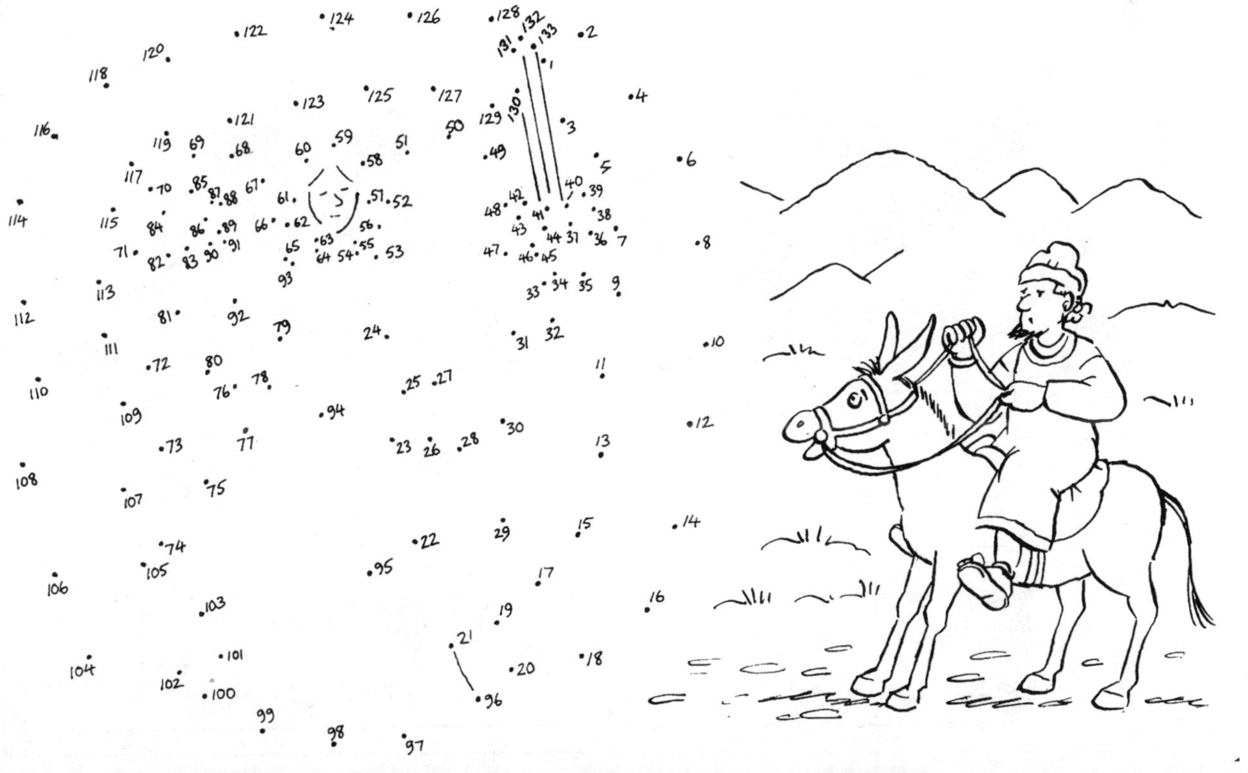

Jesus told a story about a rich king who invited all sorts of people—even beggars and blind people—to come to a great party.

Find 10 differences between these two pictures.
Read the complete story in Luke 14:15–24.

APRIL

Here is a picture of Balaam with his donkey. Which outline fits the finished picture?

**Practice drawing donkeys with the other outlines.
You can read this story in Numbers 22:21–35.**

Color me!

Jesus told a story about a tiny mustard seed that grew into a huge tree, where birds nested. Find 10 differences between these pictures.

Read this story in Luke 13:18-19.

Put a circle around all the differences you can find between these two pictures of Balaam and his donkey.

Can you find the deliberate mistake?
Read the story in Numbers 22:21–35.

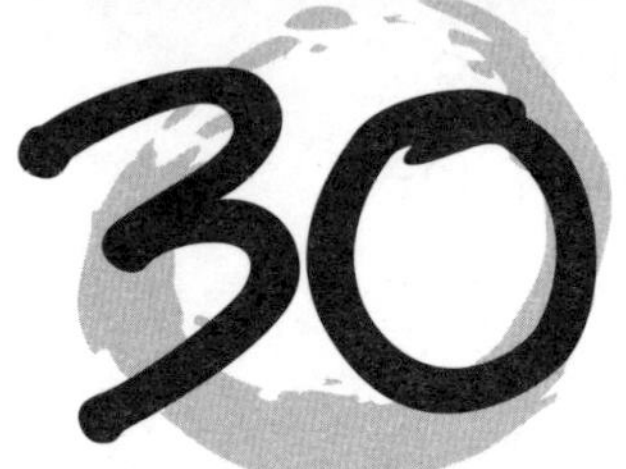

30
SEPTEMBER

Jesus told a story about a man who asked his neighbor for bread late at night. Find 10 differences between these two pictures.

You can read this story in Luke 11:5–10.

SPOT THE DIFFERENCE

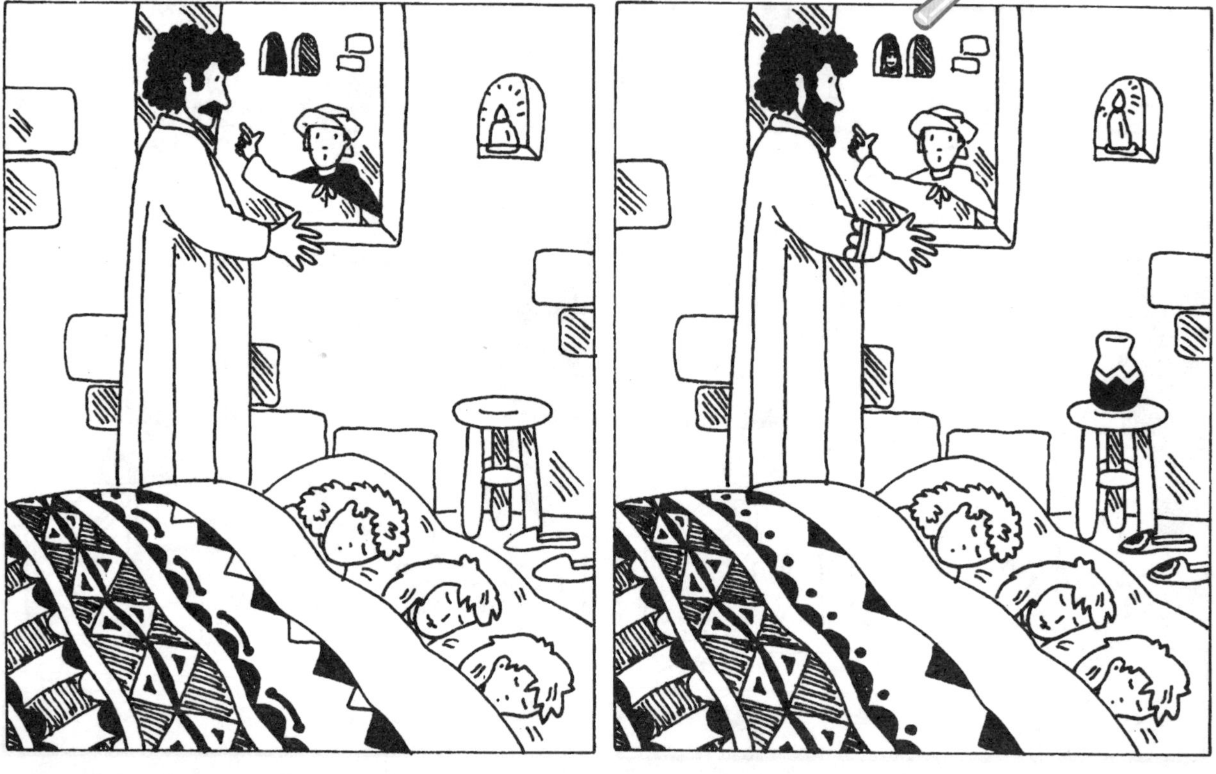

5

APRIL

At last Joshua led the Israelites out of the desert, across the river Jordan and into the Promised Land. The Jordan dried up.

Find 5 puddles in the picture.
Read this story in Joshua 3:1–17.

Color me!

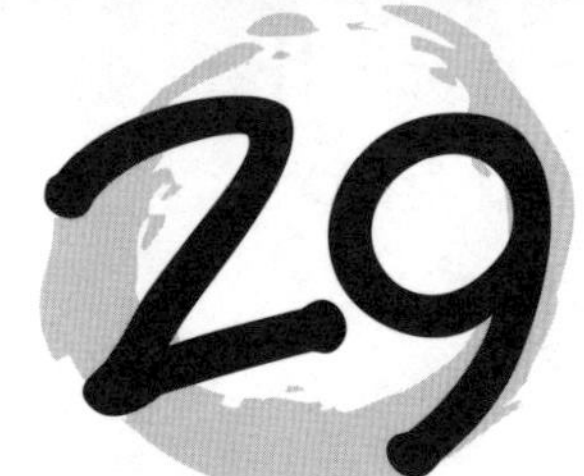

29 SEPTEMBER

Join up the dots to discover where the Good Samaritan is taking the injured man. Who pays for him to stay there?

You can read this story in Luke 10:25–37.

DOT-TO-DOT

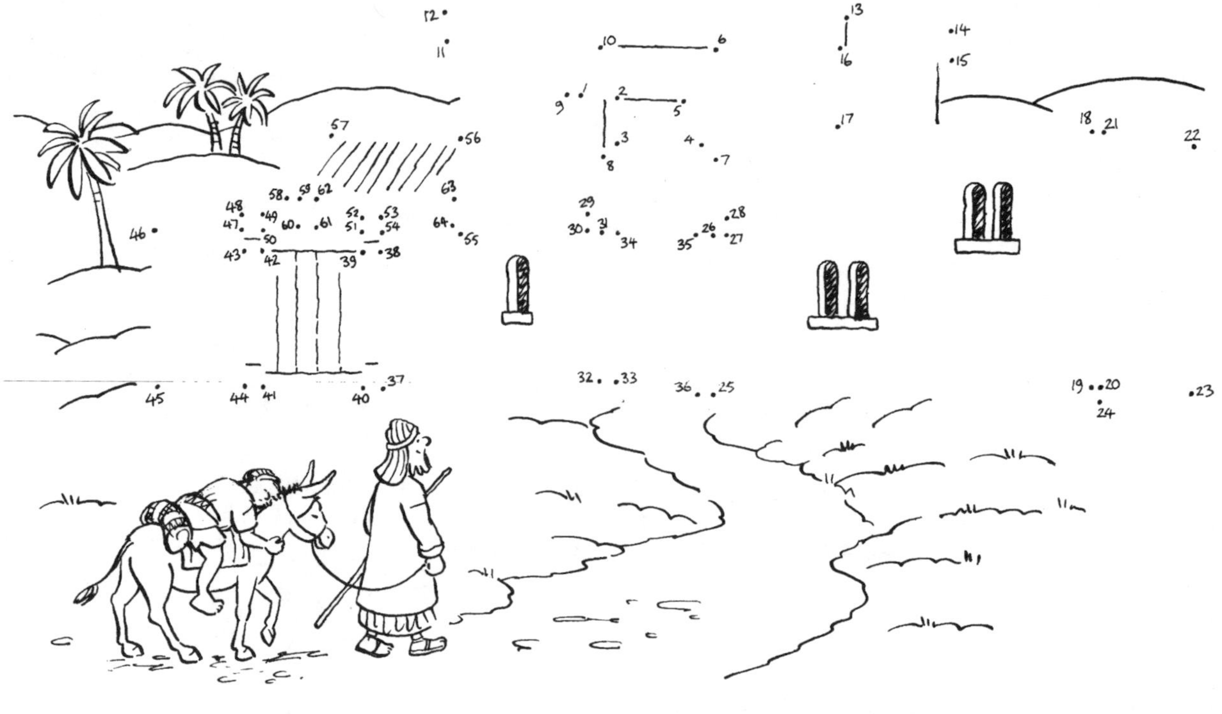

6 APRIL

Here is one of the Israelite spies in Jericho.
How can he reach Rahab's house?

Read this spy story in Joshua chapter 2.
What happened to Rahab after Jericho fell?

Color me!

28 SEPTEMBER

The kind stranger who helped the man who had been robbed is often called the Good Samaritan.

Follow the line to find out to which inn he takes the injured man. You can read this story in Luke 10:25–37.

maze

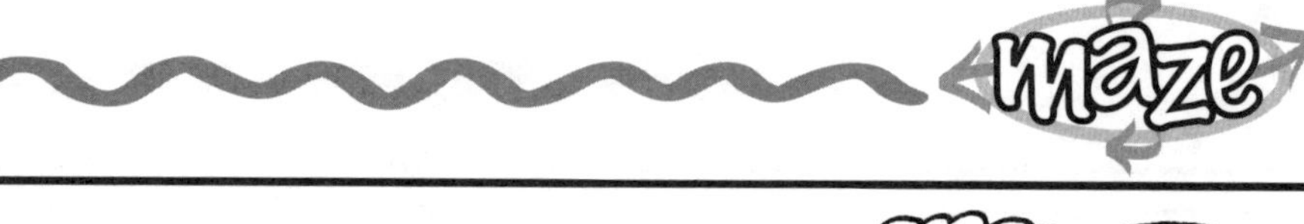

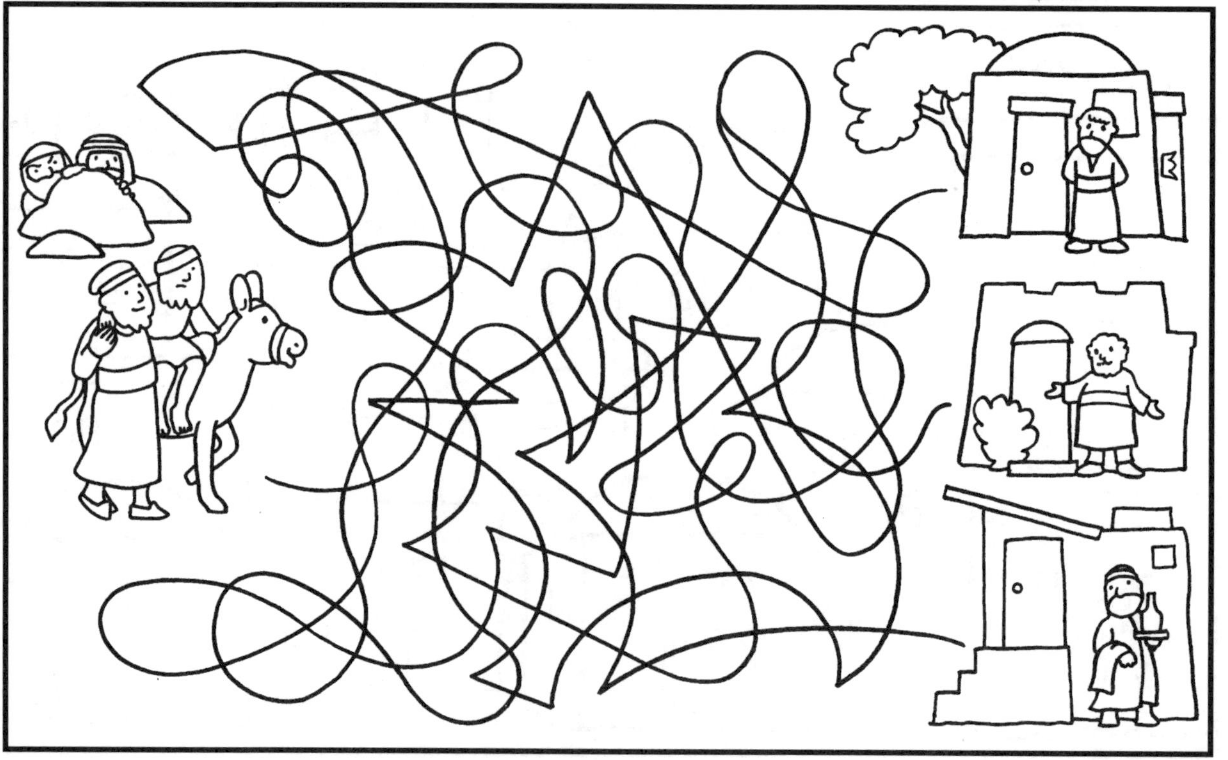

7 APRIL

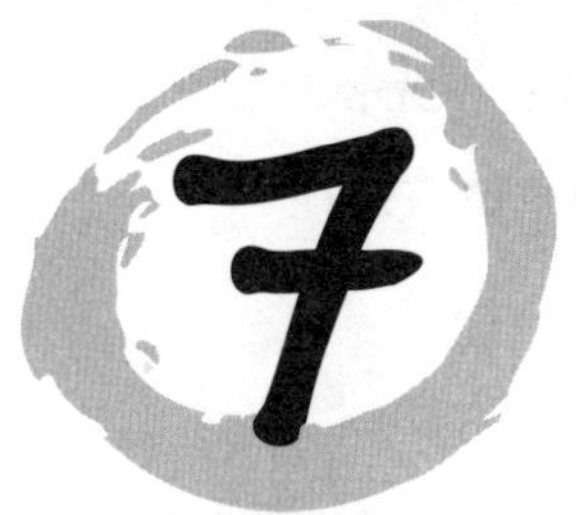

Joshua and the Israelites attack the city of Jericho. Join up the dots to find out what happened when the trumpets sounded.

Read this story in Joshua 6.

DOT-TO-DOT

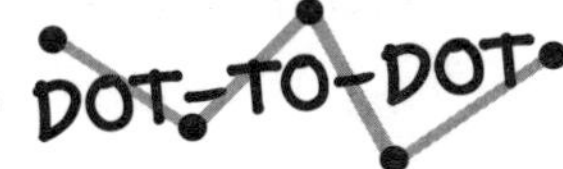

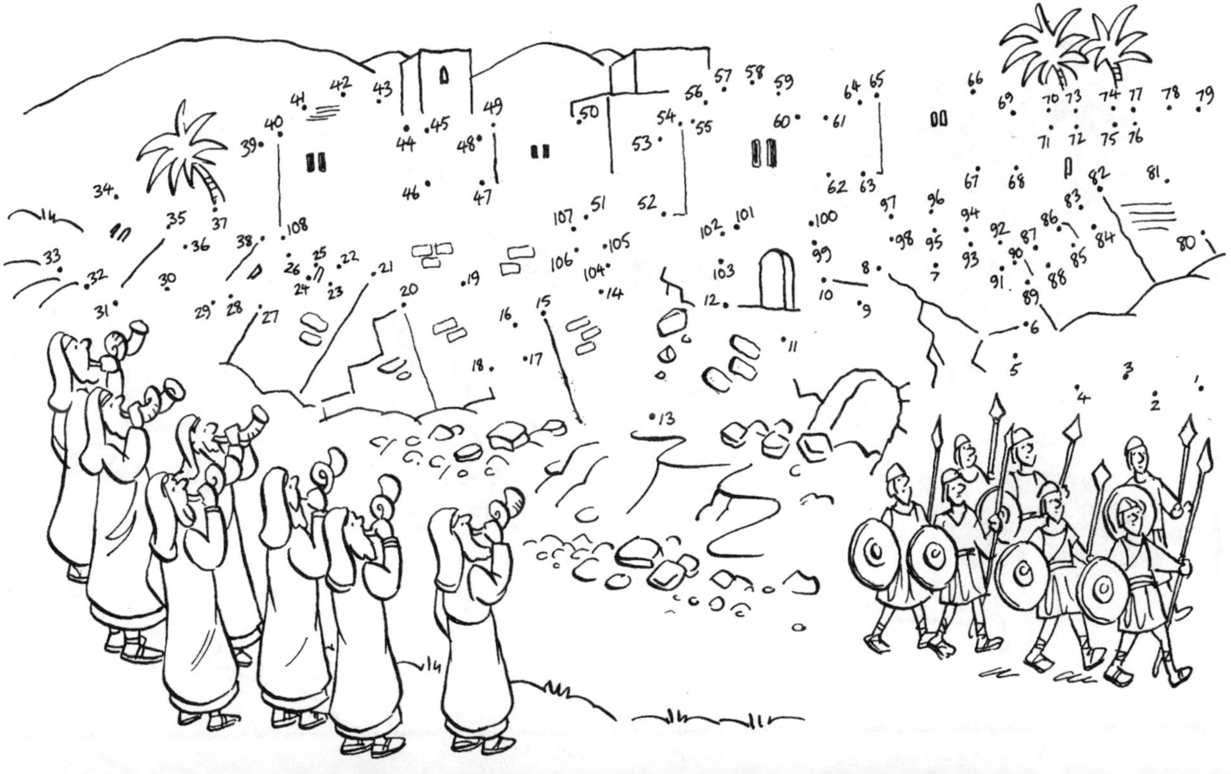

27

SEPTEMBER

In this picture of the man who was robbed on the road, the artist has deliberately made lots of mistakes.

Circle all the mistakes you can find. Which is the funniest? Read what really happened in Luke 10:25–37.

Puzzle

Spot 10 differences between these two pictures of a priest blowing his horn at the battle of Jericho.

Read this story in Joshua 6.

26

SEPTEMBER

Here are 4 pictures of the good Samaritan and his donkey. Which two pictures are exactly the same?

You can read the story of the good Samaritan in Luke 10:25–37.

Puzzle

9

APRIL

The priests of Israel carried the Ark of the Covenant around the walls of Jericho before the city finally collapsed.

List all the deliberate mistakes you can find in this picture.
Read Joshua 6:15–21.

Color me!

25
SEPTEMBER

The man who was a foreigner stopped to help the man who had been robbed. He bandaged him and took him to a hotel.

Can you find 10 differences between these two pictures? You can read this story in Luke 10:25–37.

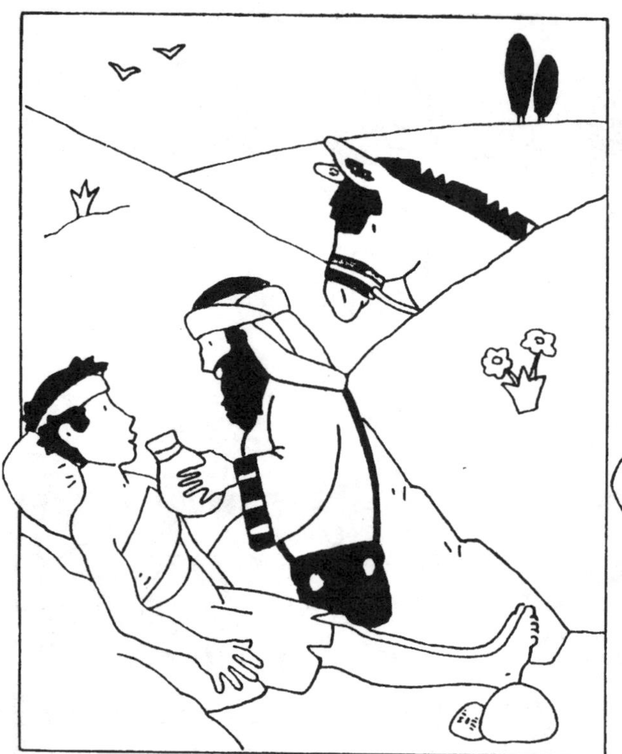

Can you find 10 differences between these two pictures of the broken down walls and houses of Jericho?

You can read the complete story of the defeat of Jericho in Joshua 5:13—6:27.

24
SEPTEMBER

Jesus told a story about this man, who was robbed while he was walking to Jericho. Follow the lines to see which person helps him.

You can read this story in Luke 10:25–37.
Where did the man who helped come from?

Puzzle

Deborah was a leader of the Israelites. She sat under a palm tree and gave advice.

You can read about her in Judges 4. Can you find 8 hats in this picture?

Color me!

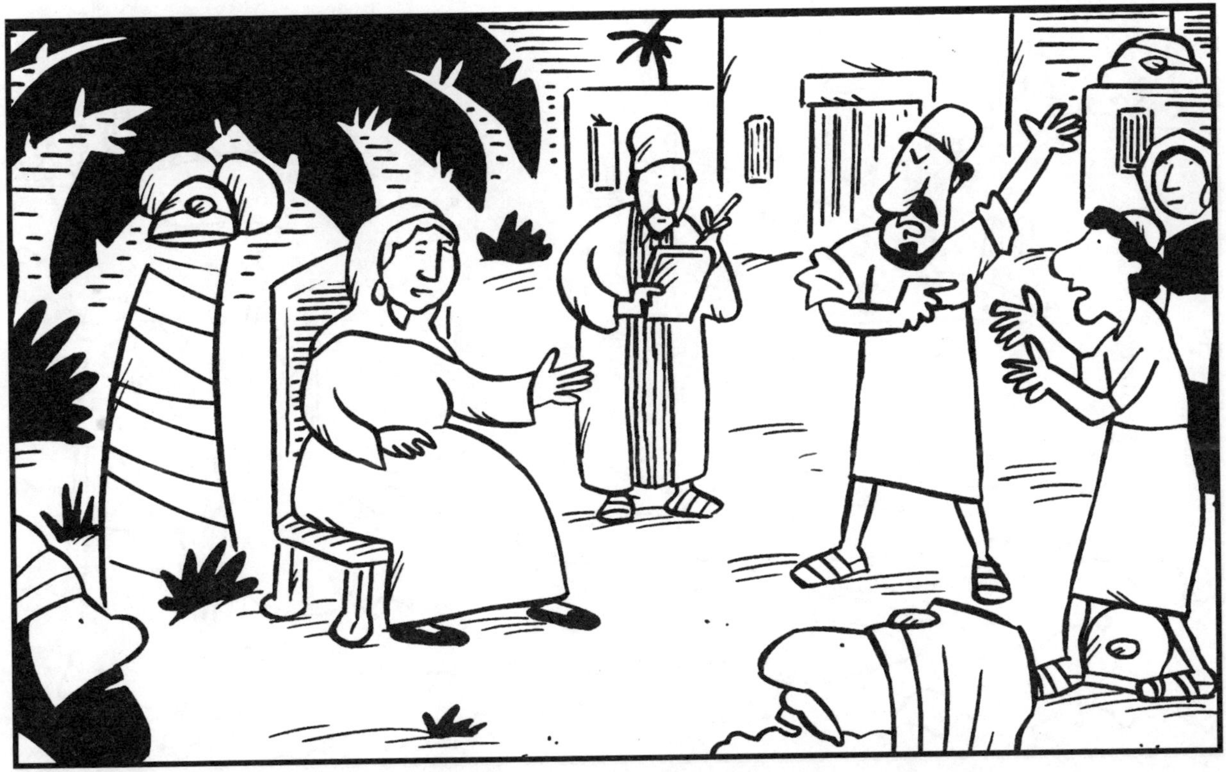

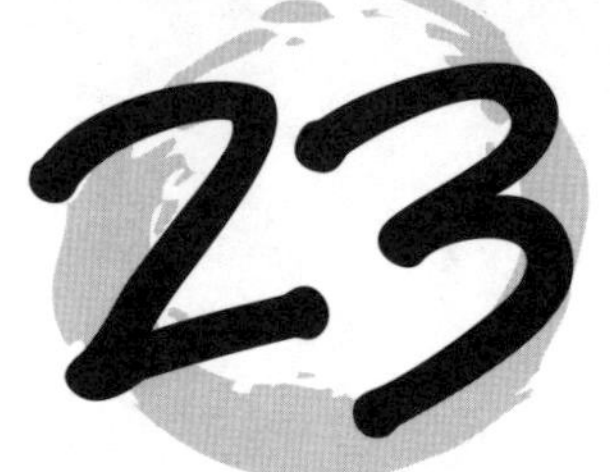

23 SEPTEMBER

Here is a man setting out on a journey from Jerusalem to Jericho. Join up the dots to complete the picture.

You can read this story in Luke 10:25–37.

DOT-TO-DOT

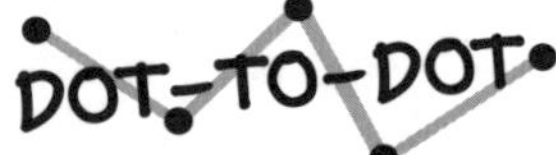

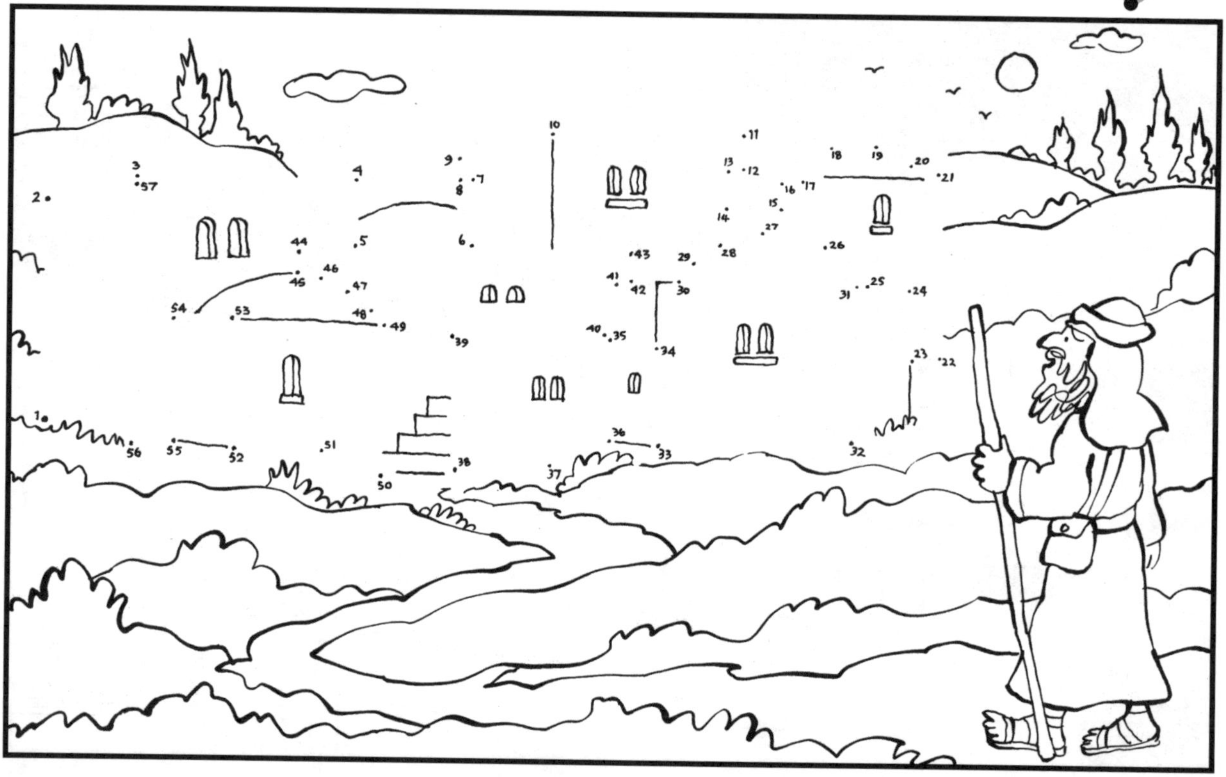

12

APRIL

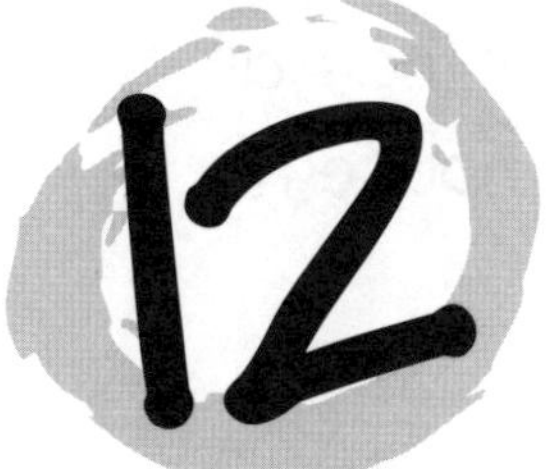

Gideon was another brave leader of the Israelites. He attacked the enemy using trumpets and torches!

Can you find 3 pairs of pictures that are exactly the same?
Read all about it in Judges 7:1–22.

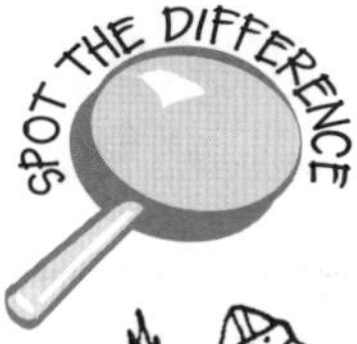

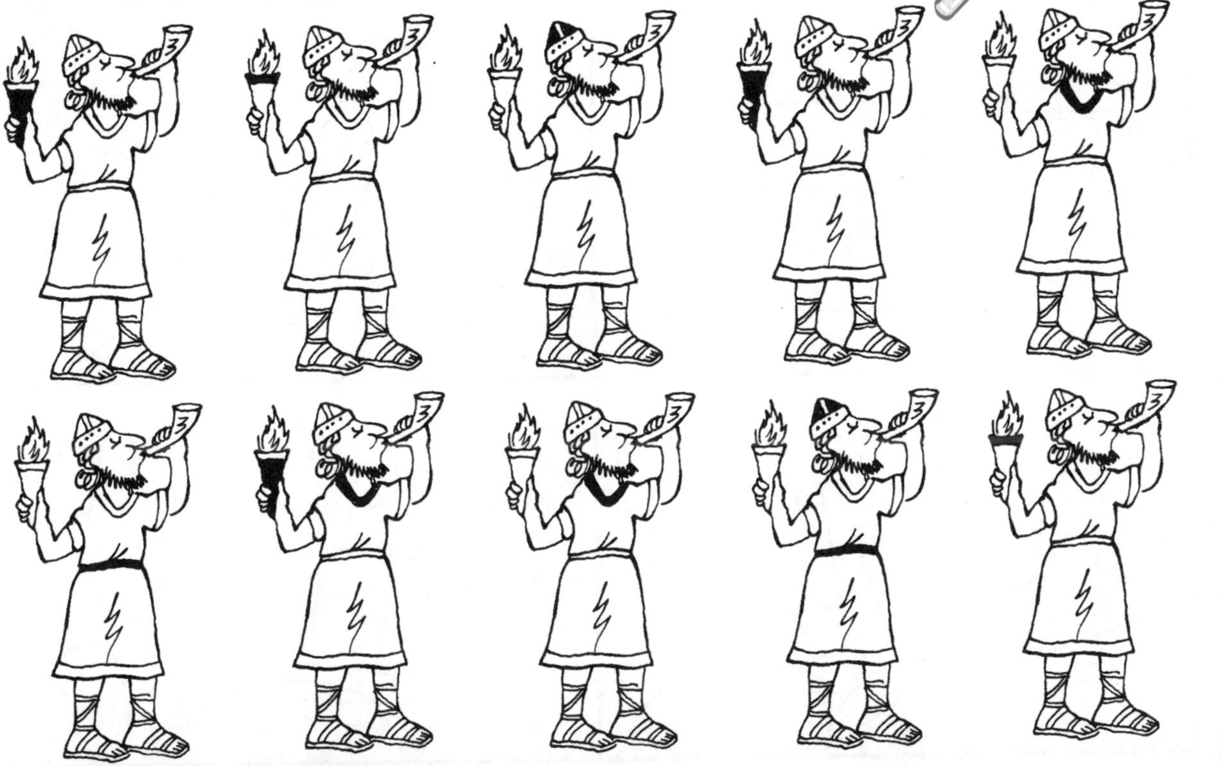

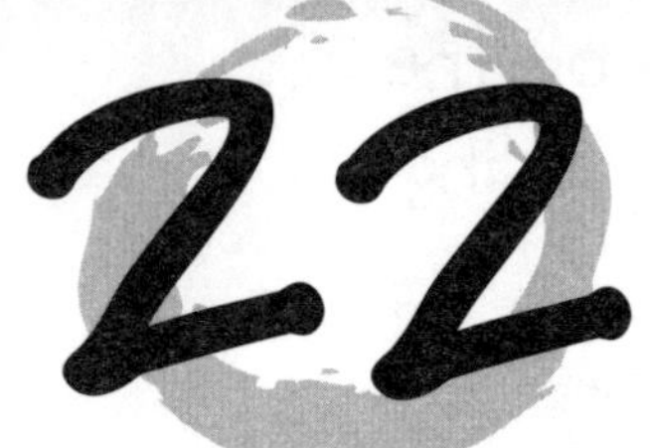

22
SEPTEMBER

Here are two houses. Which picture has all the pieces to make up both these houses?

Read the story of two houses in Luke 6:46–49. What happened to them both?

Puzzle

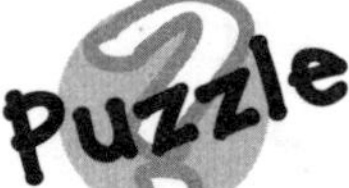

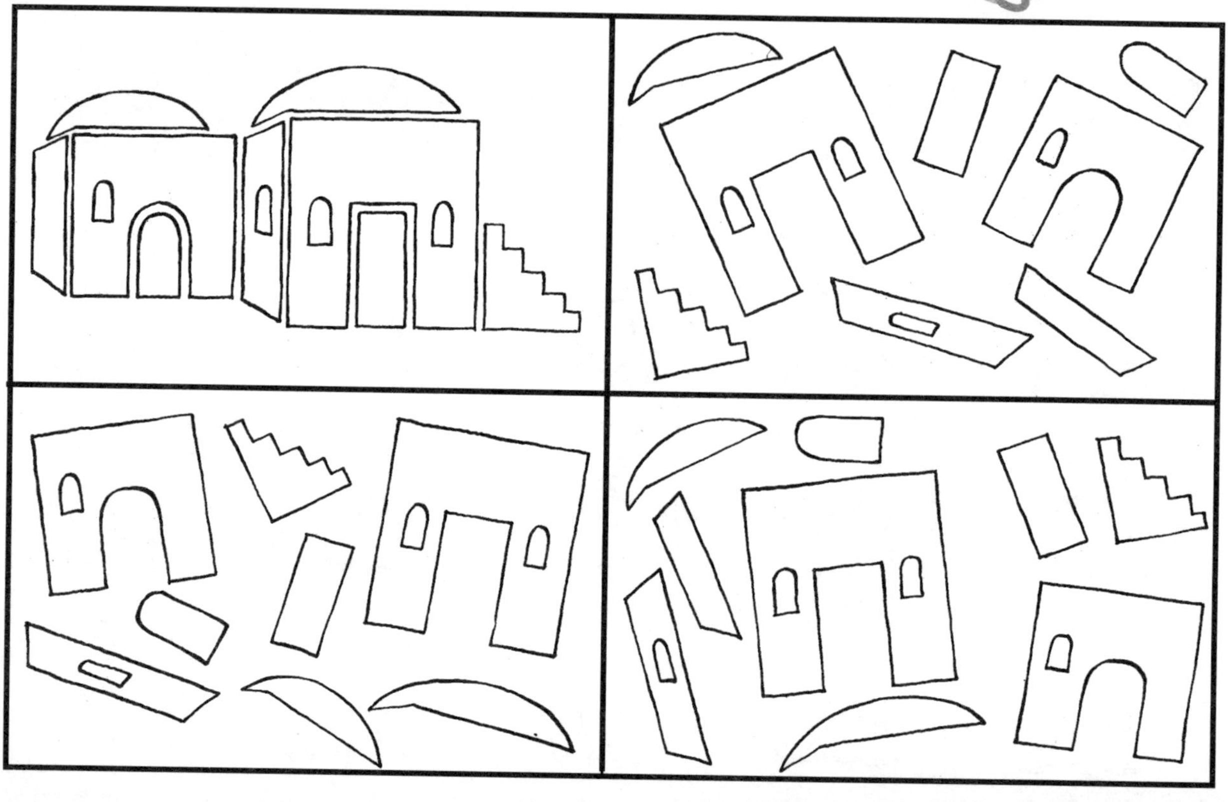

Samson was strong and brave.
He killed a lion that attacked him.

Find 10 differences between these two pictures.
Read this story in your Bible in Judges 14:1–9.

21 SEPTEMBER

Jesus told a story about a man who built a house on rock and another who built on sand. When storms came, the house on sand collapsed.

Read Luke 6:46–49. Can you find 10 differences?

SPOT THE DIFFERENCE

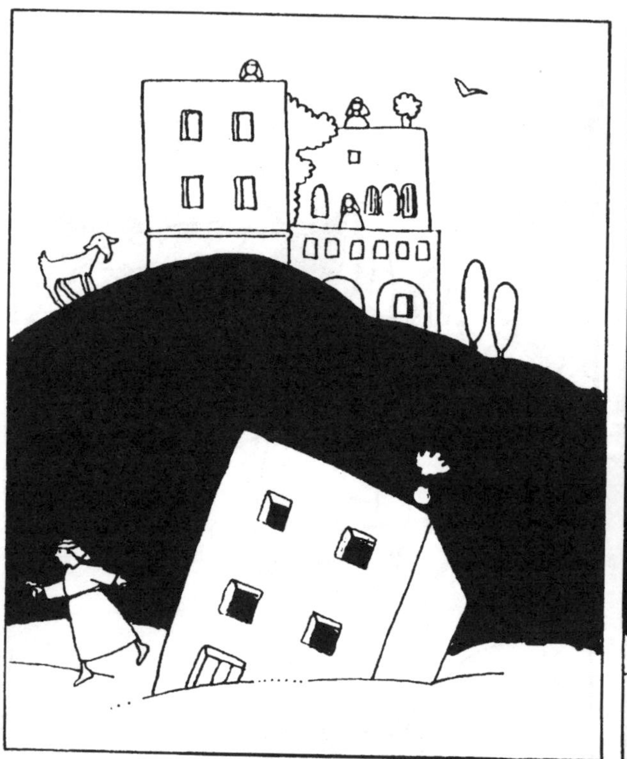

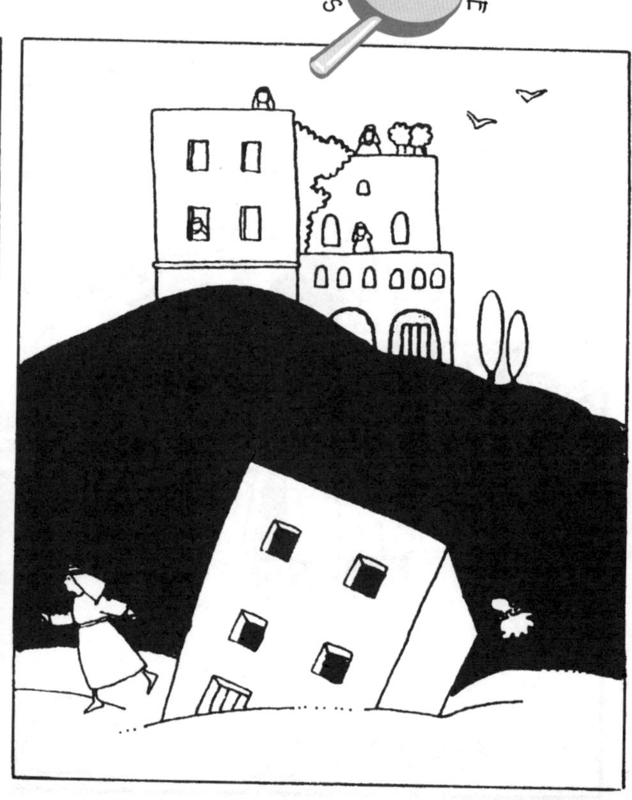

14

APRIL

After Samson killed the lion, he found that bees had made a nest in its body.

Write down all the deliberate mistakes the artist has made in this picture of Samson and the lion.

Read Judges 14:1–9.

Color me!

20

These 6 drawings of a house in Jesus' time all look the same. But only 2 are <u>exactly</u> the same.

Can you spot them?
Why did houses have very small windows?

15
APRIL

Samson told Delilah that if she wove his hair with her loom he would lose his strength. Find 10 differences between these pictures

You can read this story in Judges 16:13–14.

19

SEPTEMBER

Jesus is at the front of the boat. Circle all the mistakes the artist has deliberately made in this picture.

Read Mark 4:35–41 and find out what Jesus said to the wind and the waves.

Puzzle

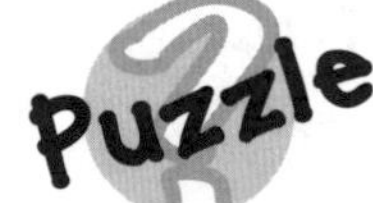

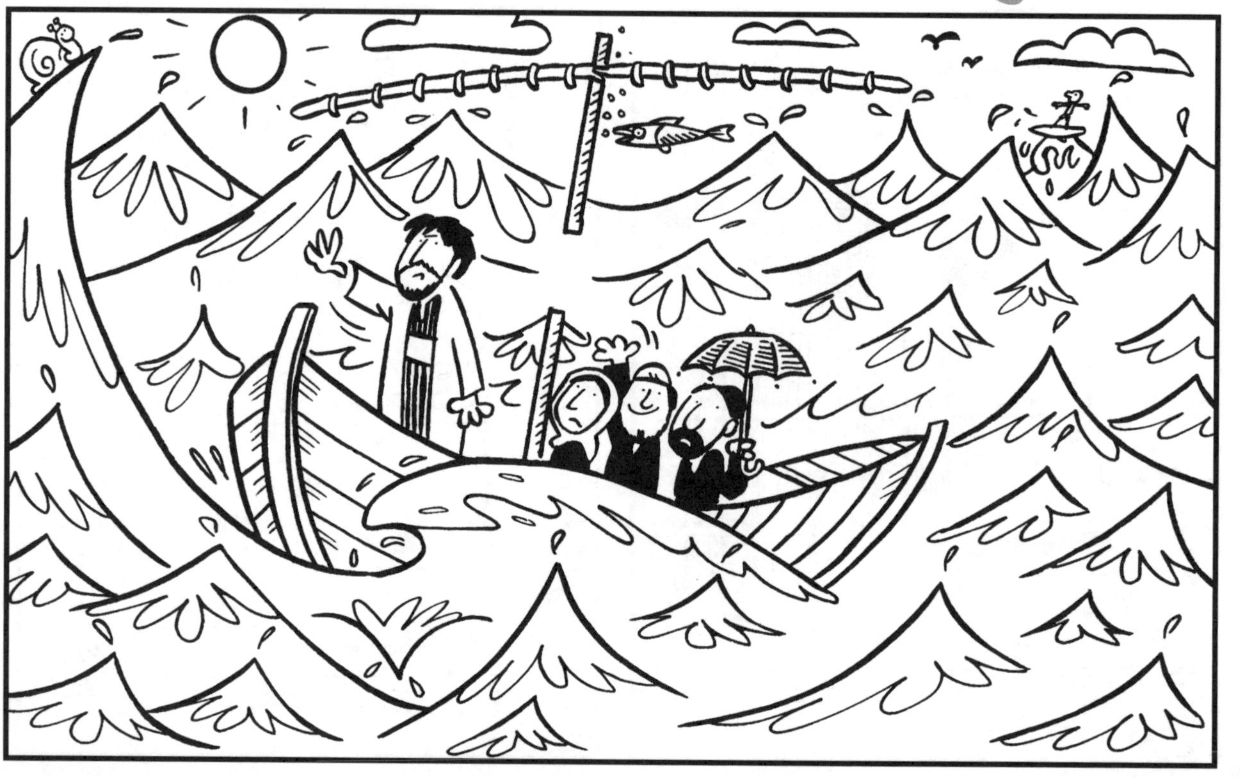

16

APRIL

Delilah discovered that Samson was only strong while his hair grew long. So she cut it short while he was asleep.

Can you find 8 pairs of scissors here?
Read the story in Judges 16:1–21.

Color me!

18

SEPTEMBER

Here are two pictures of Jesus stilling the storm. Can you find 10 differences between the two pictures?

You can read the whole story in Matthew 8:23–27.

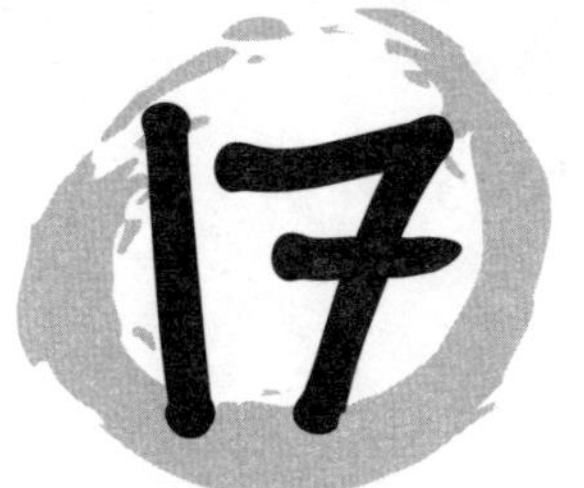

17 APRIL

Samson was captured by his enemies. When his strength returned, he pulled down a building where they were having a party.

Join up the dots to see what Samson is doing.
Read Judges 16:23–30.

DOT-TO-DOT

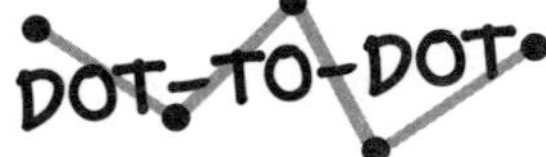

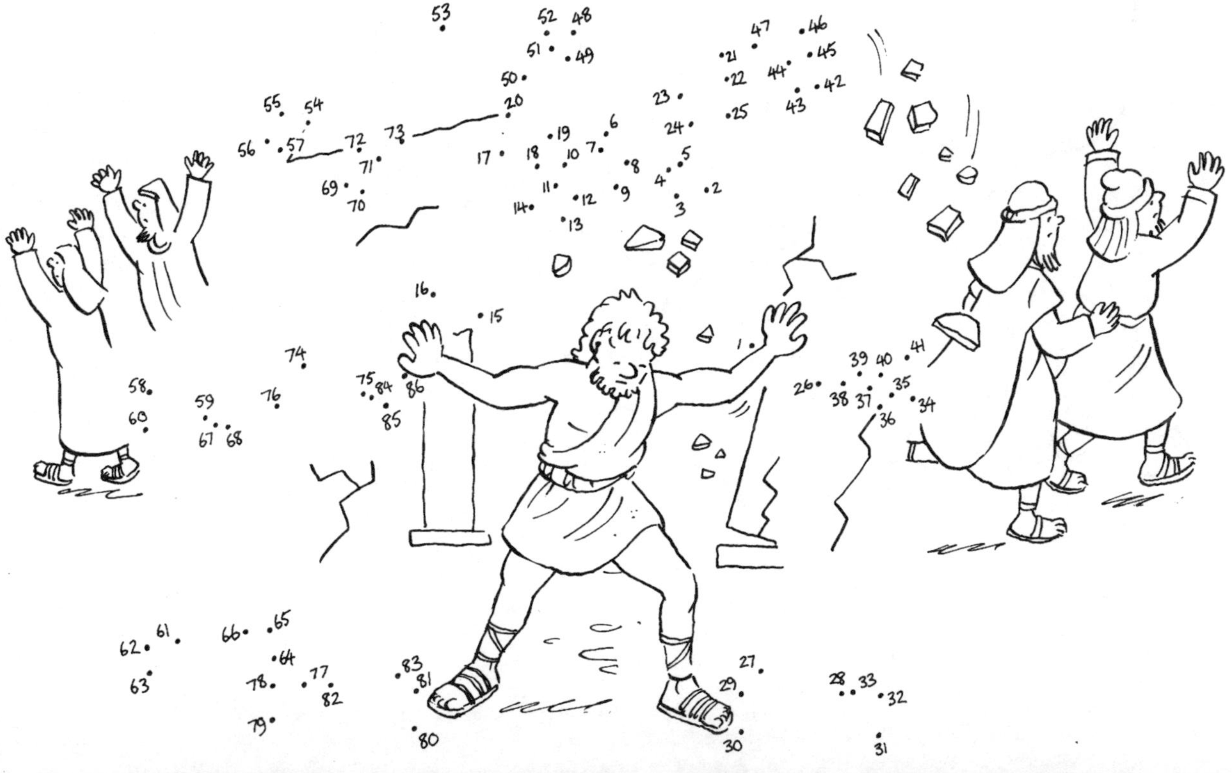

17 SEPTEMBER

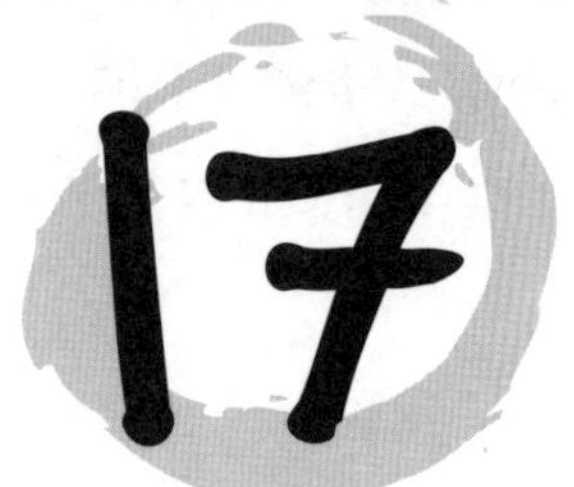

What is happening here? Join up the dots to find out why Jesus' disciples look so frightened.

You can read what happened next in Matthew 8:23–27.

DOT-TO-DOT

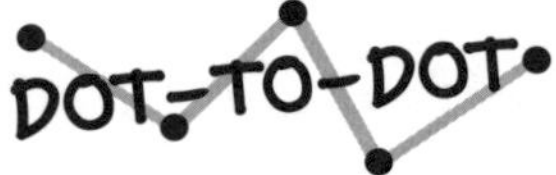

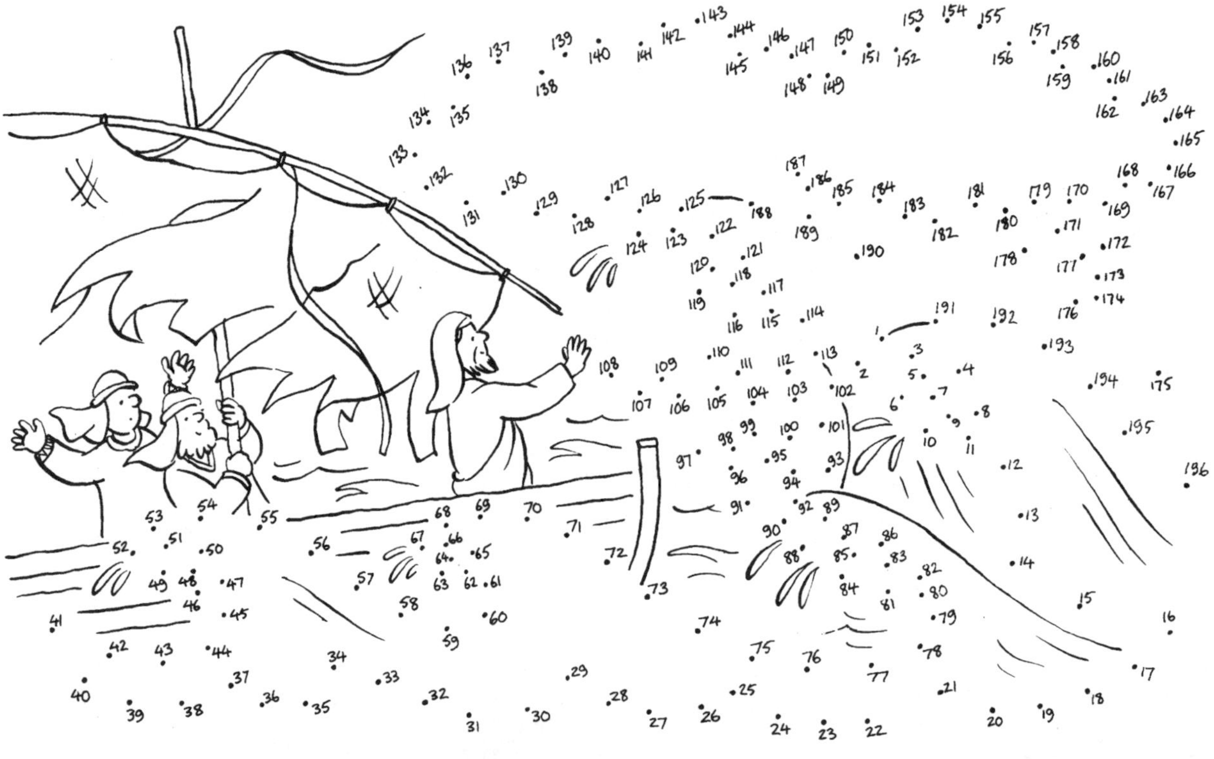

18

APRIL

When her husband died, Ruth looked after her mother-in-law, Naomi, and went back to Bethlehem with her.

Can you find the road that will bring them to her town of Bethlehem. Read this story in Ruth 1:1–22.

16

SEPTEMBER

When everybody had eaten enough loaves and fishes, the disciples collected all the leftovers. There were twelve baskets full!

Finish this picture of the baskets, and then color it in.
Read the story in John 6:1–15.

Color me!

 **APRIL**

While she was living in Bethlehem, Ruth went to gather wheat in fields belonging to a man called Boaz.

Find 20 harvest mice hidden here.
Read about Ruth in the wheatfields in Ruth chapter 2.

Color me!

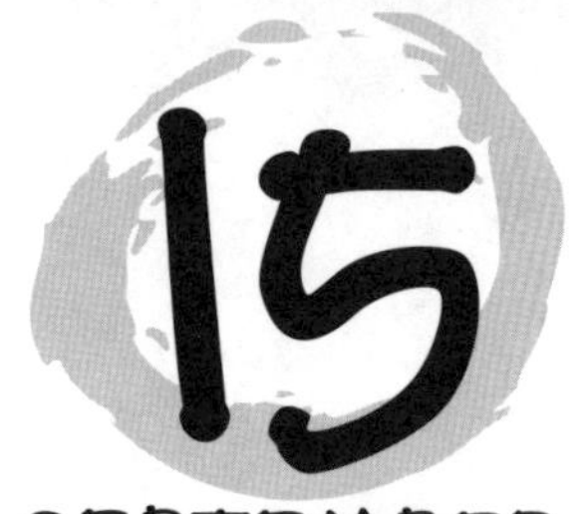

15
SEPTEMBER

The artist has drawn 6 pictures of Jesus and the boy with loaves and fishes. Which two pictures are exactly the same?

Read the story in John 6:1–15.

SPOT THE DIFFERENCE

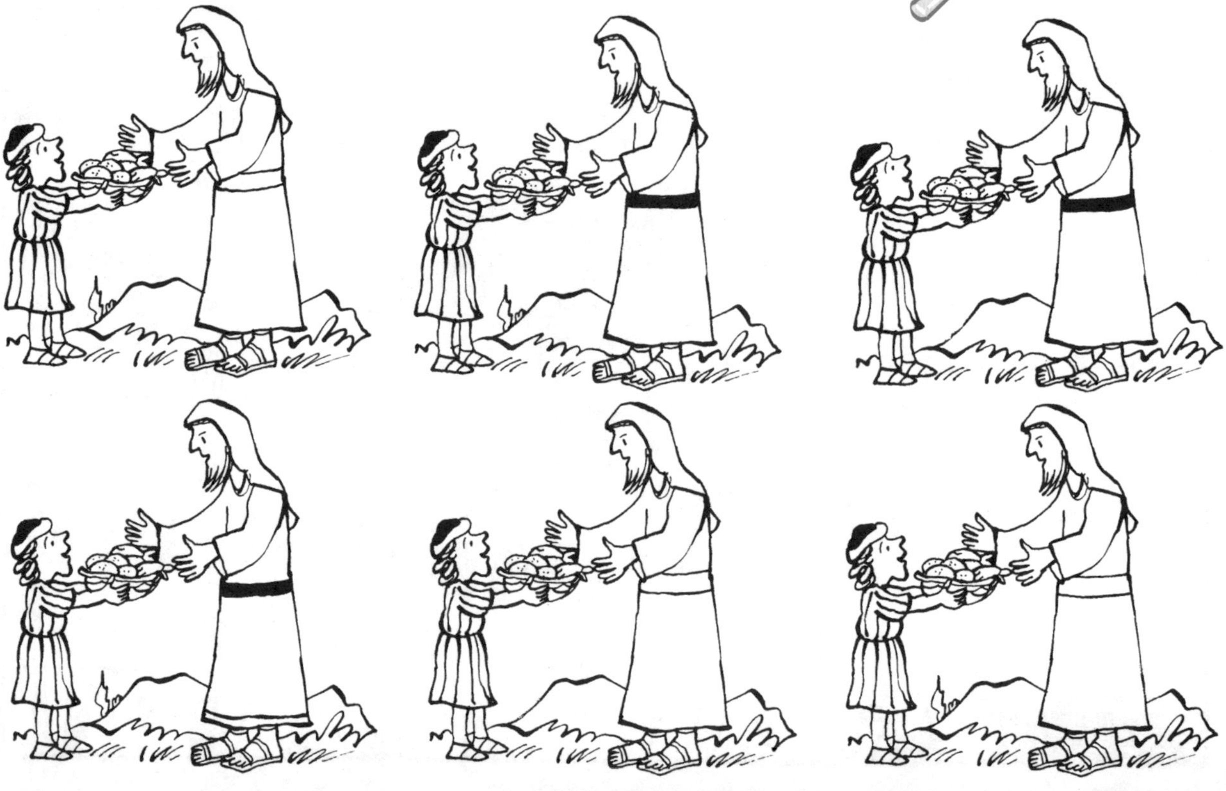

Find at least 10 differences between these two pictures of Ruth collecting fallen wheat in the fields.

Can you see Boaz watching her?
Read this story in Ruth chapter 2.

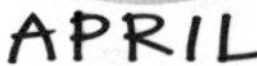

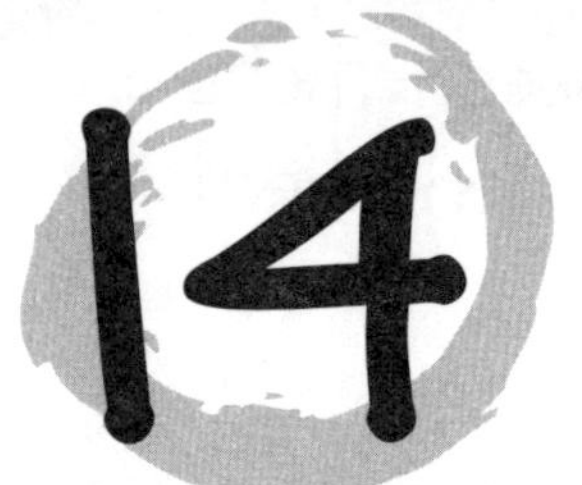

14 SEPTEMBER

In this picture of the story of the loaves and fishes, the artist has deliberately made a lot of mistakes. How many can you find?

Do you think the people sat at tables to eat?
Read John 6:1–15.

Puzzle

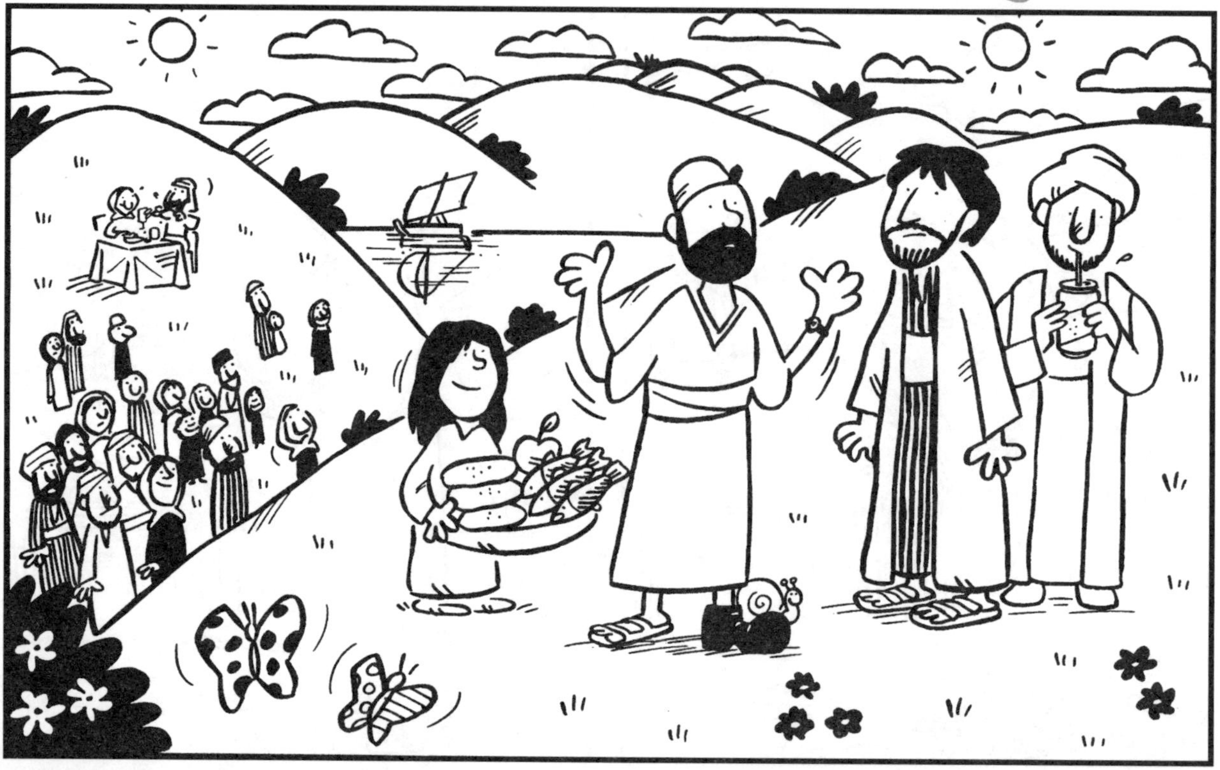

APRIL

21

Ruth can collect any wheat that is left in the fields when the reapers have finished.

Which route must she take to collect the most wheat to feed Naomi and herself?
See Ruth 2.

Puzzle

13

SEPTEMBER

Here is another picture of the boy with loaves and fishes. Can you find 10 differences between these reflected pictures?

Read this story in John 6:1–15.
Was any food left after the picnic?

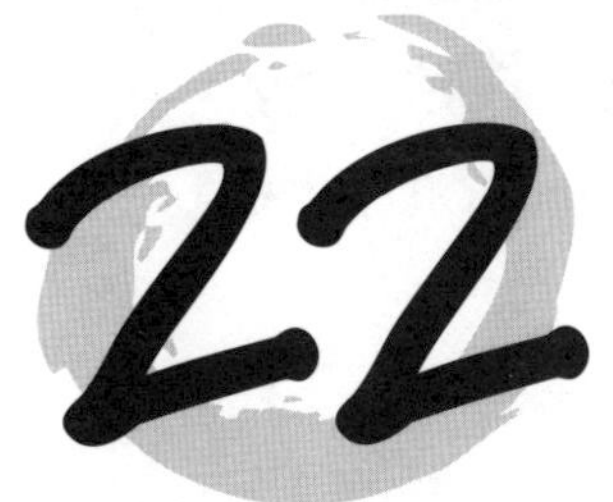

22
APRIL

All these pictures of Ruth gathering wheat are exactly the same—except one.

Which is the odd one out? Color in the odd one.
Read Ruth 2.

SPOT THE DIFFERENCE

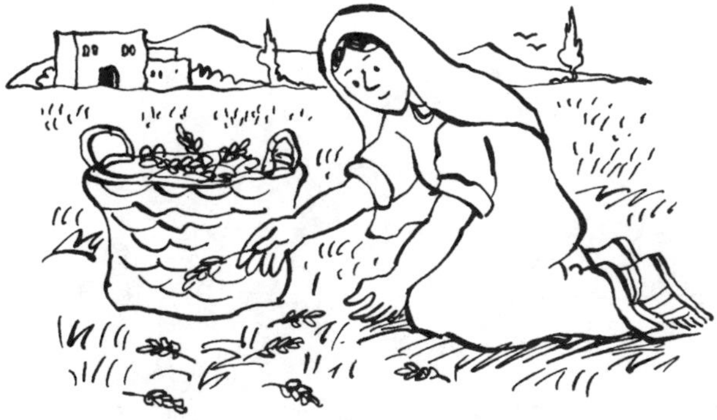

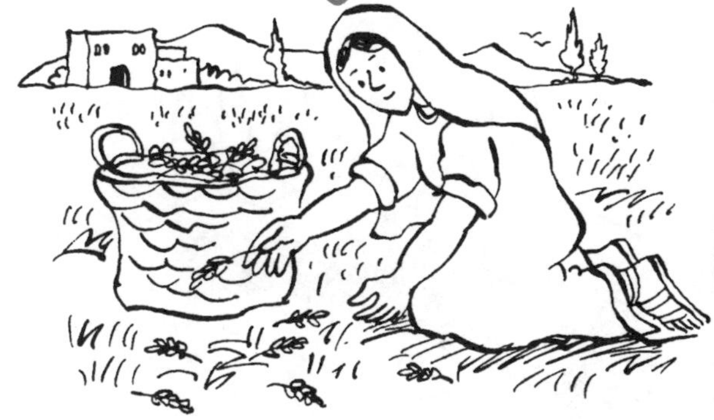

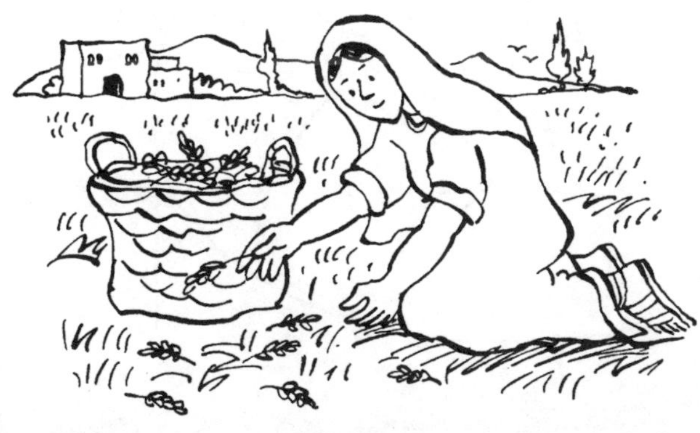

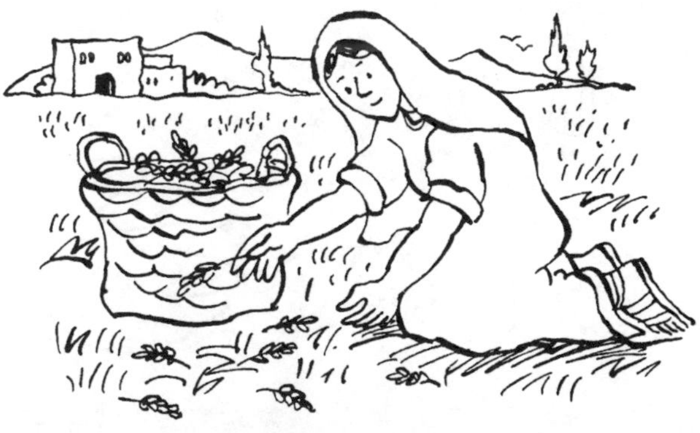

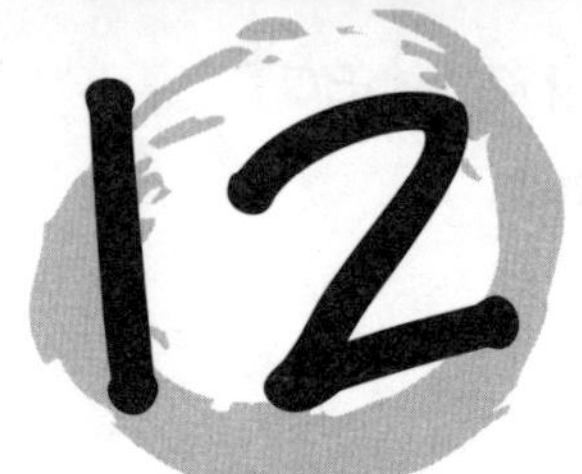

12 SEPTEMBER

Join up the dots to find out what this boy is holding. Why are so many people gathered here?

Read John 6:1–15 to find out what Jesus did with what the boy gave him.

DOT-TO-DOT

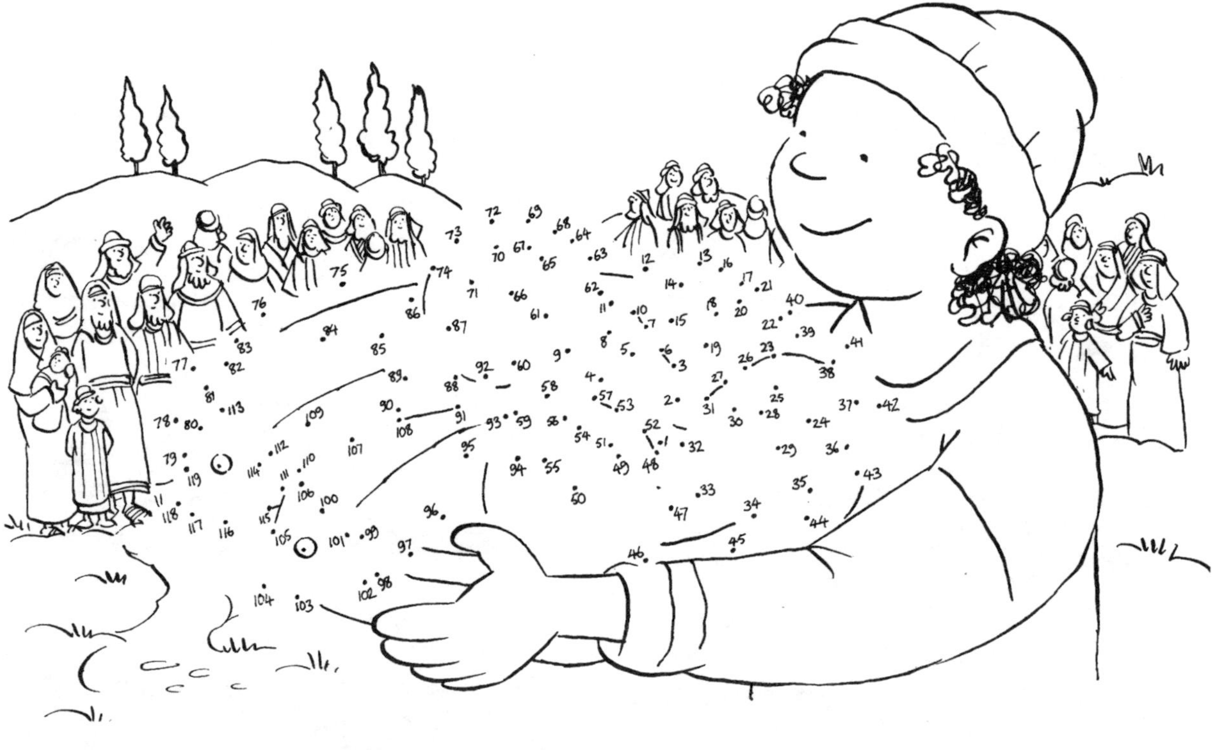

23
APRIL

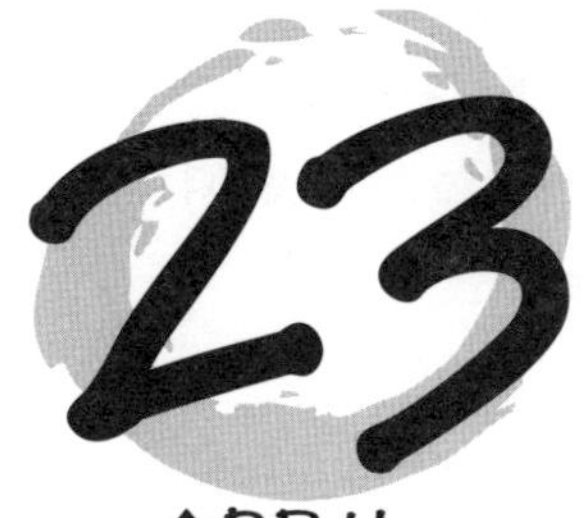

Put a circle around every deliberate mistake you can find in this picture of Ruth gathering wheat near Bethlehem.

Check the story in Ruth chapter 2.

Puzzle

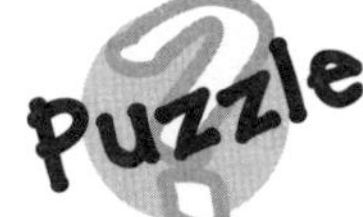

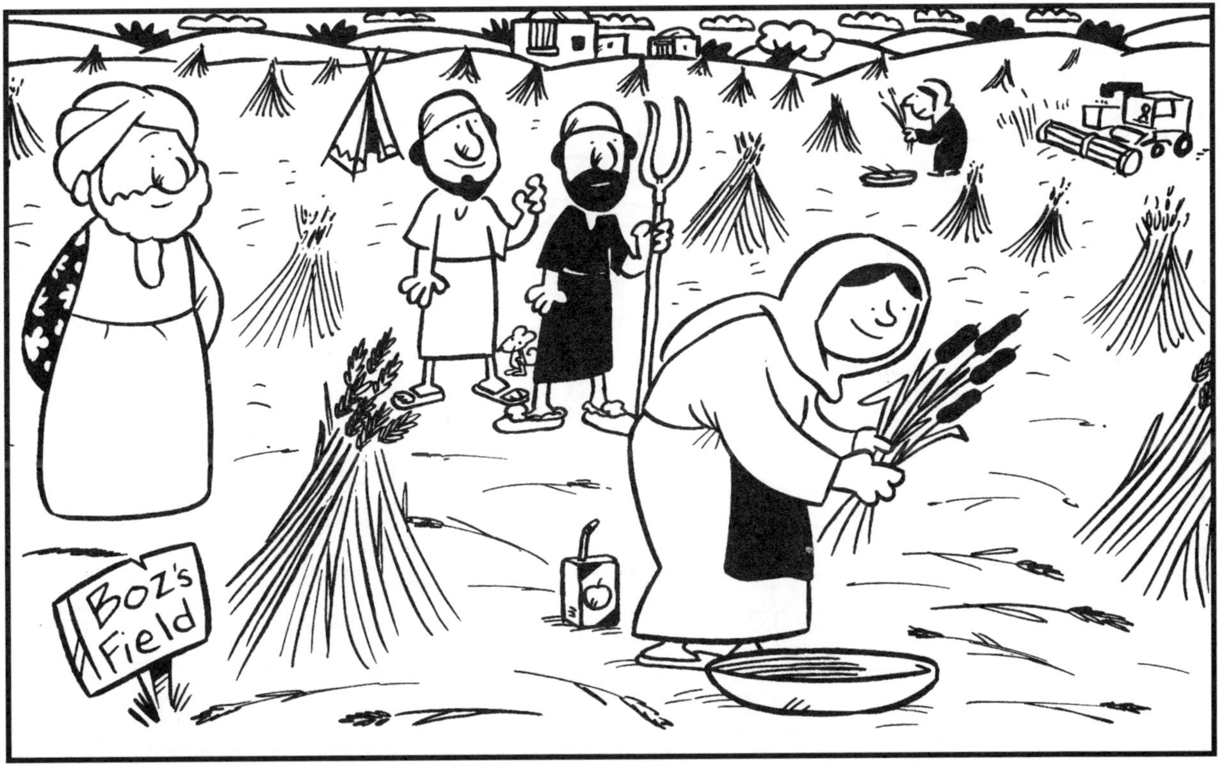

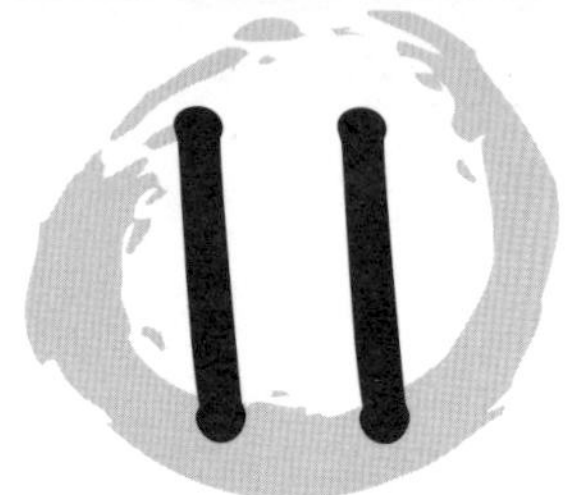

11 SEPTEMBER

Jesus had been teaching all day and people were hungry. The only person with food was a boy with five loaves and two fish.

Which path will take the boy to Jesus?
Read the whole story in John 6:1–15.

maze

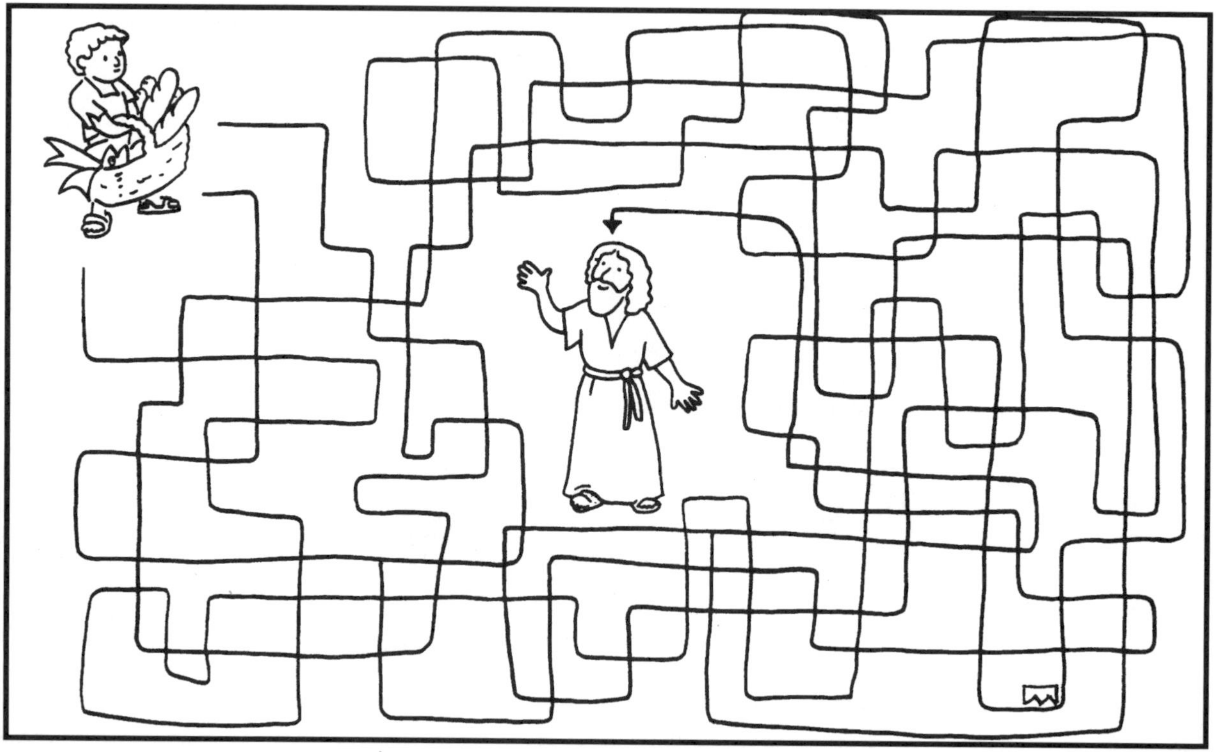

24 APRIL

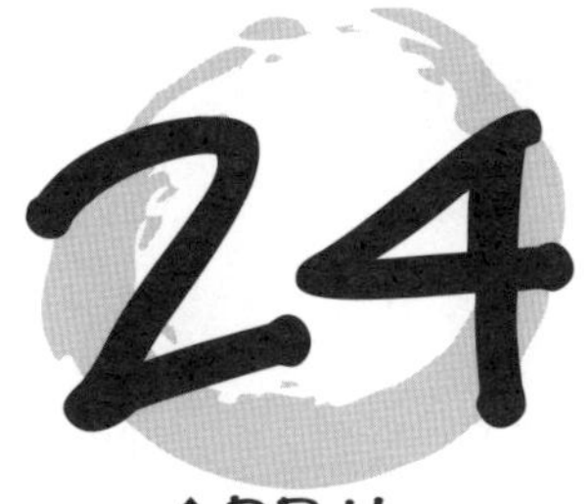

One day a woman called Hannah came to the Temple. She was sad because she had no children.

Find 20 tears hidden in the picture.
Read what Hannah prayed for in 1 Samuel 1:1–20.

Puzzle

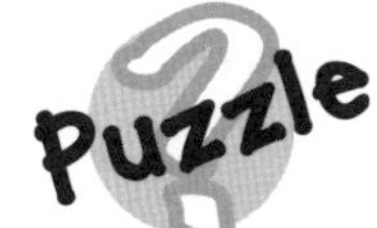

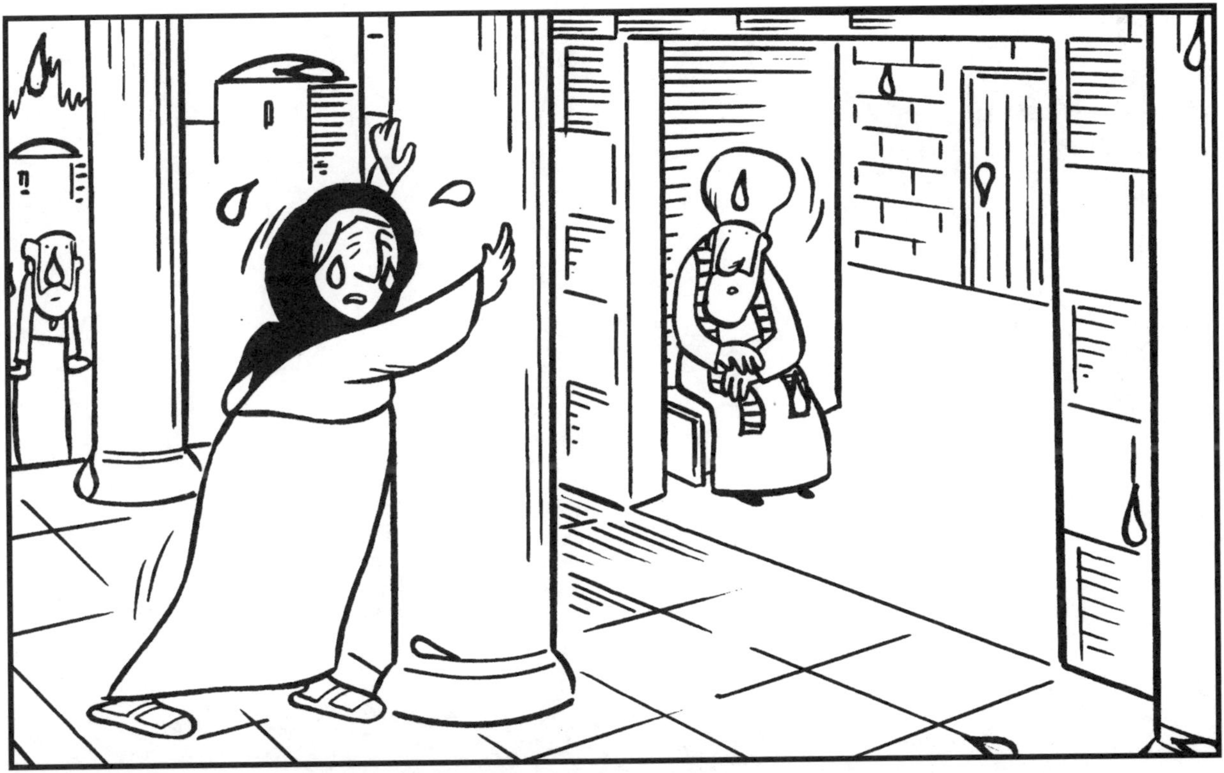

10

SEPTEMBER

Here is a picture of Jesus healing a man.
One outline fits the picture exactly.
Which one?

Now complete the other pictures.
Read this story in Luke 17:11–19.

Color me!

25
APRIL

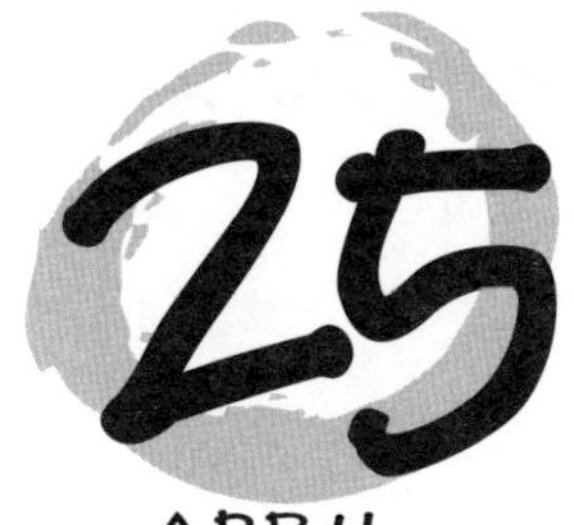

Hannah had a son called Samuel. She gave him to serve God in the Temple. Circle all the deliberate mistakes in this picture.

Read about Hannah's promise in 1 Samuel 1:21—2:11.

Puzzle

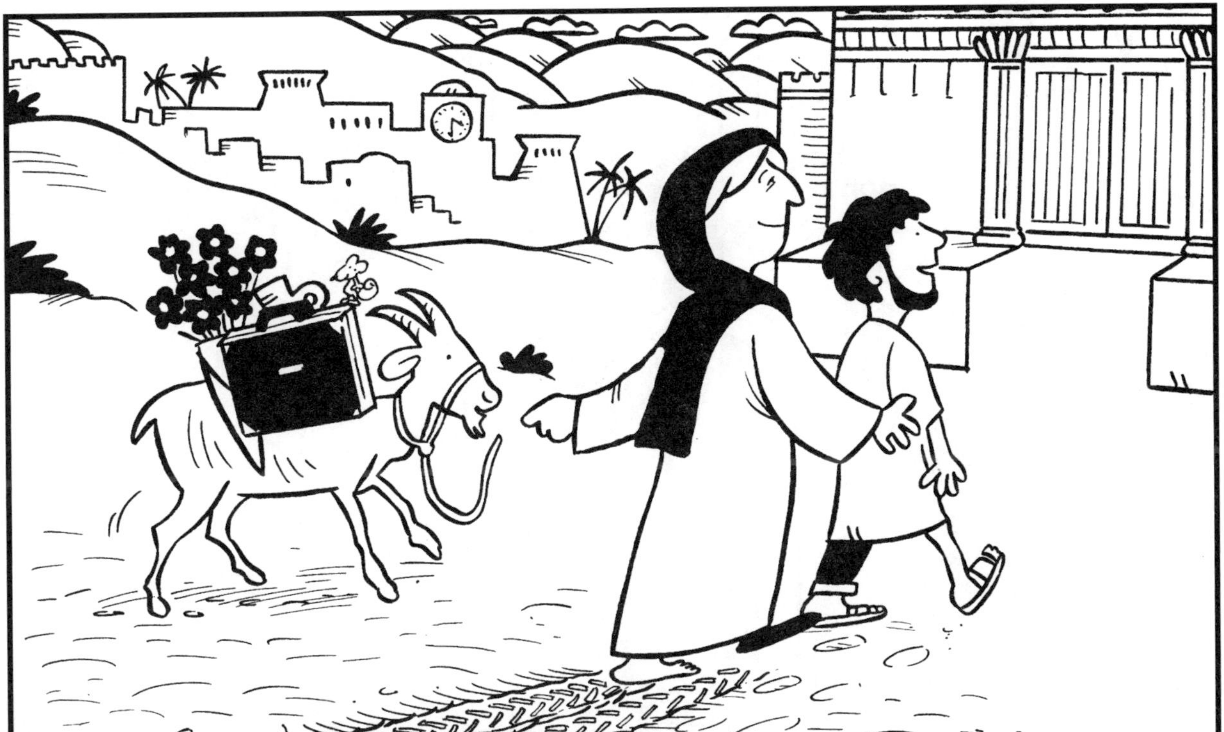

9

SEPTEMBER

Jesus healed a woman who had a very bad back. Can you find all the deliberate mistakes in this picture?

Read this story in Luke 13:10–17.
How long had this woman been ill?

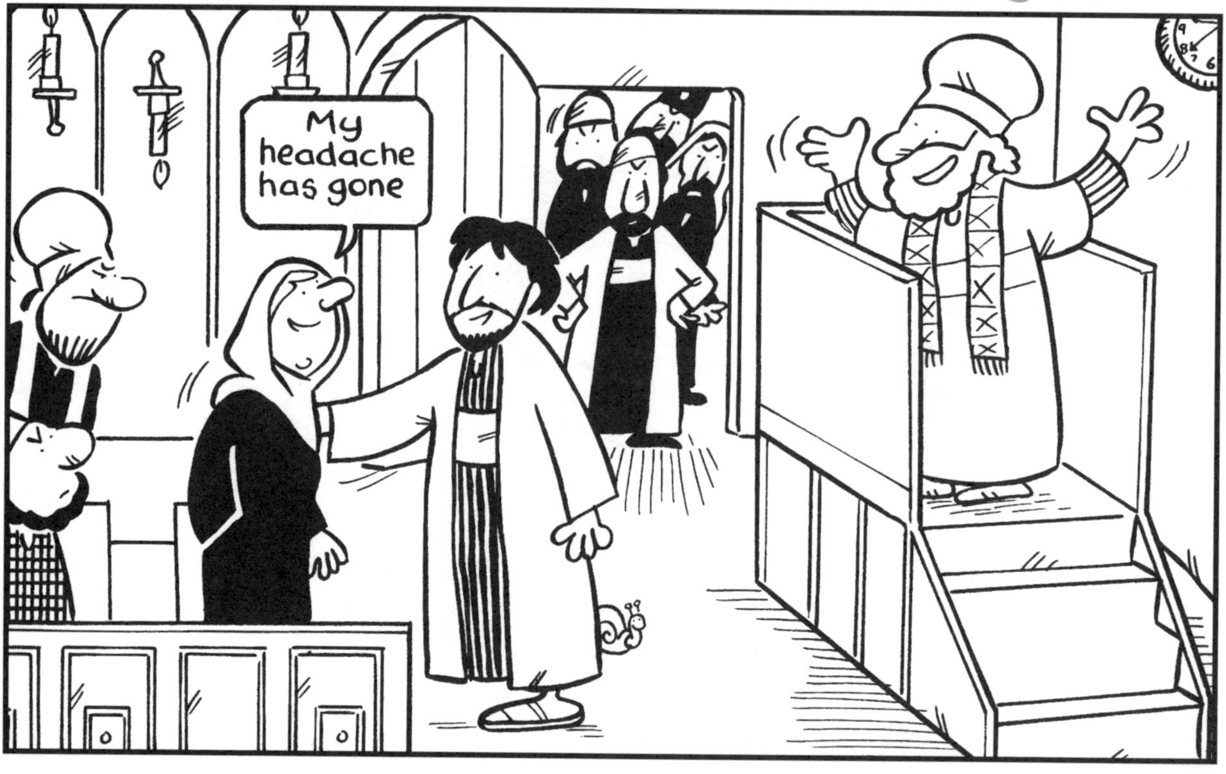

26

APRIL

Find at least 10 differences between these two pictures of Hannah bringing Samuel to serve God in the Temple.

See 1 Samuel 1:24–28.

8

SEPTEMBER

Here is another picture of the sower.
Can you find 12 corn stalks hidden
in this picture?

Read the story of the sower in Matthew 13:1–23.

Color me!

27
APRIL

The artist has drawn the high priest Eli, and given 3 more outlines of priests. Draw 3 more priests and color them in neatly.

What is Eli holding?
Read about Samuel and Eli in 1 Samuel 2:18–20.

Color me!

7 SEPTEMBER

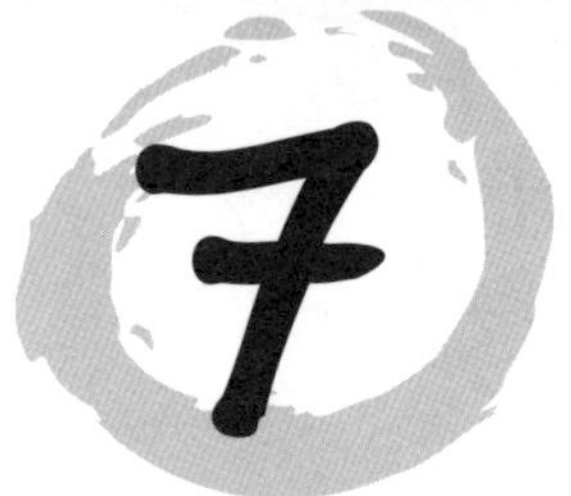

Jesus told a story about a farmer scattering his seeds. Now find all the mistakes in the picture.

Read this story in Matthew 13:1–23.
How many different places did the seed land on?

Puzzle

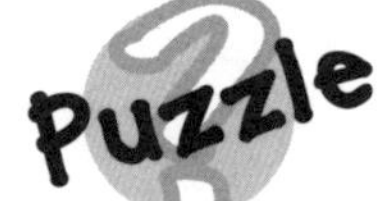

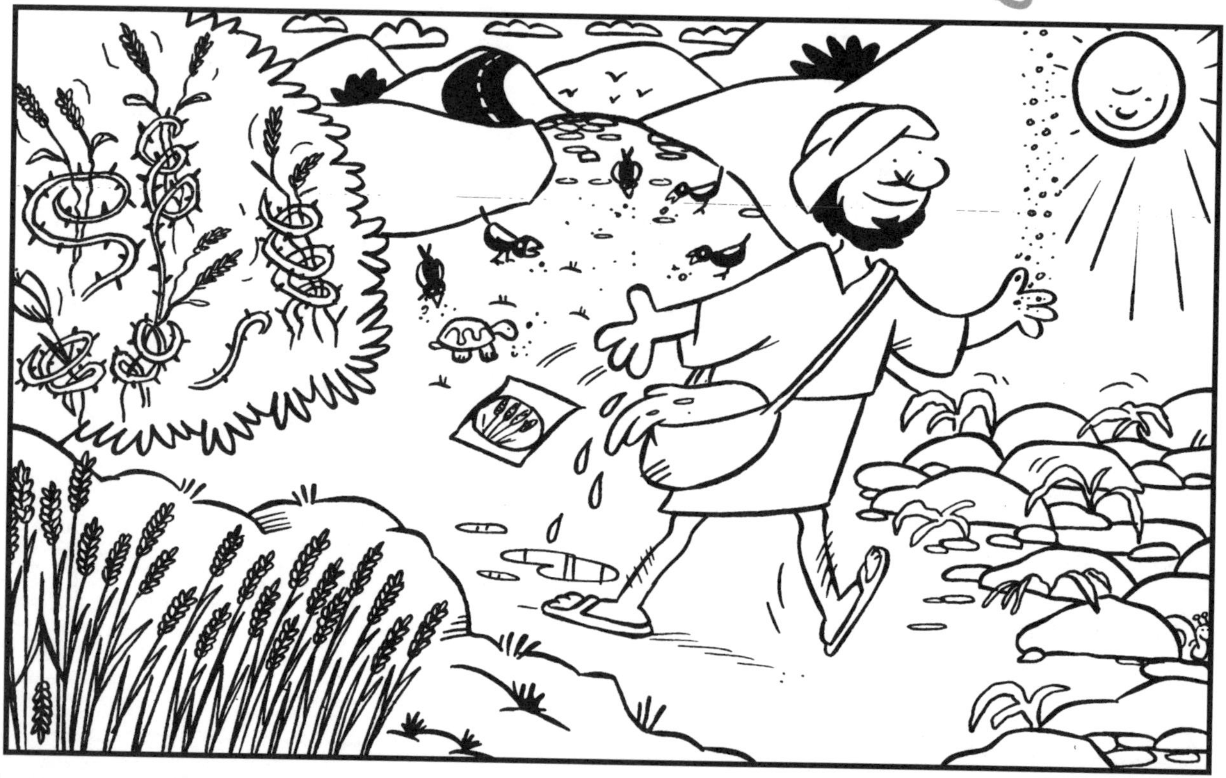

28 APRIL

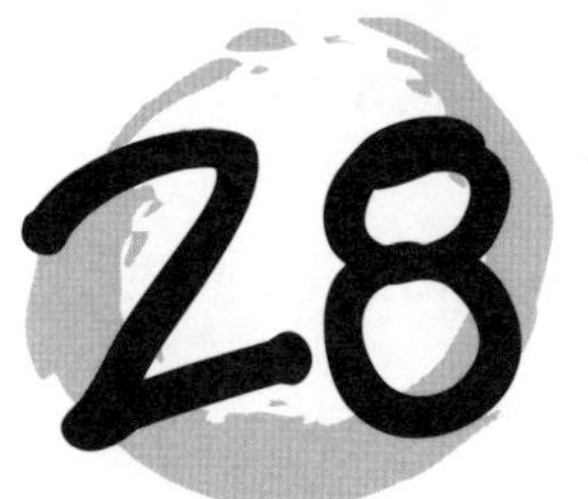

Samuel heard God call his name one night. Join up the dots to find out where Samuel was when he heard God's voice.

Read this story in 1 Samuel 3:1–21.

DOT-TO-DOT

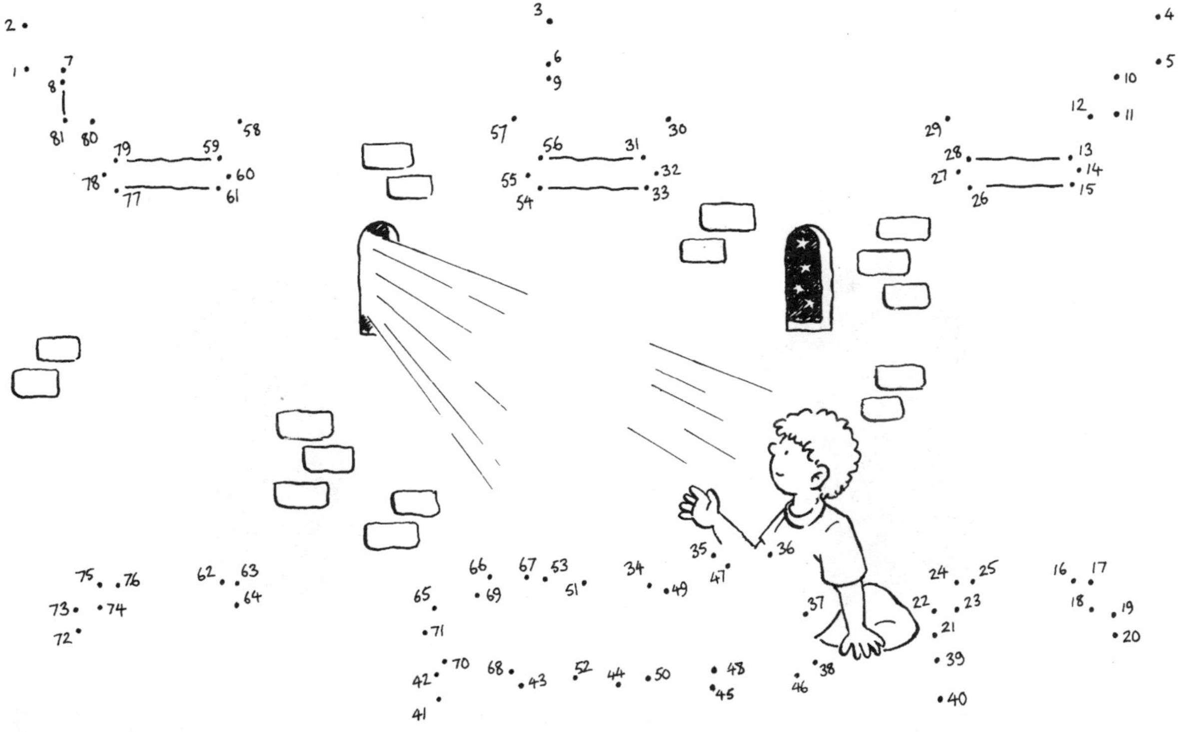

6

SEPTEMBER

Jesus told a story about a farmer sowing seed in his field. Can you find 10 differences between these two pictures of the sower?

Read about the sower in Luke 8:4–8.

29
APRIL

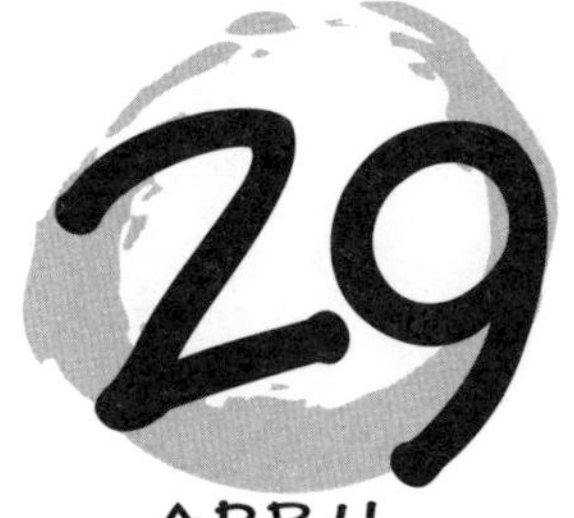

All these pictures of Samuel in bed in the Temple look the same. But look carefully, and you will discover one is slightly different. Which one?

Read this story in 1 Samuel 3:1–21.

SPOT THE DIFFERENCE

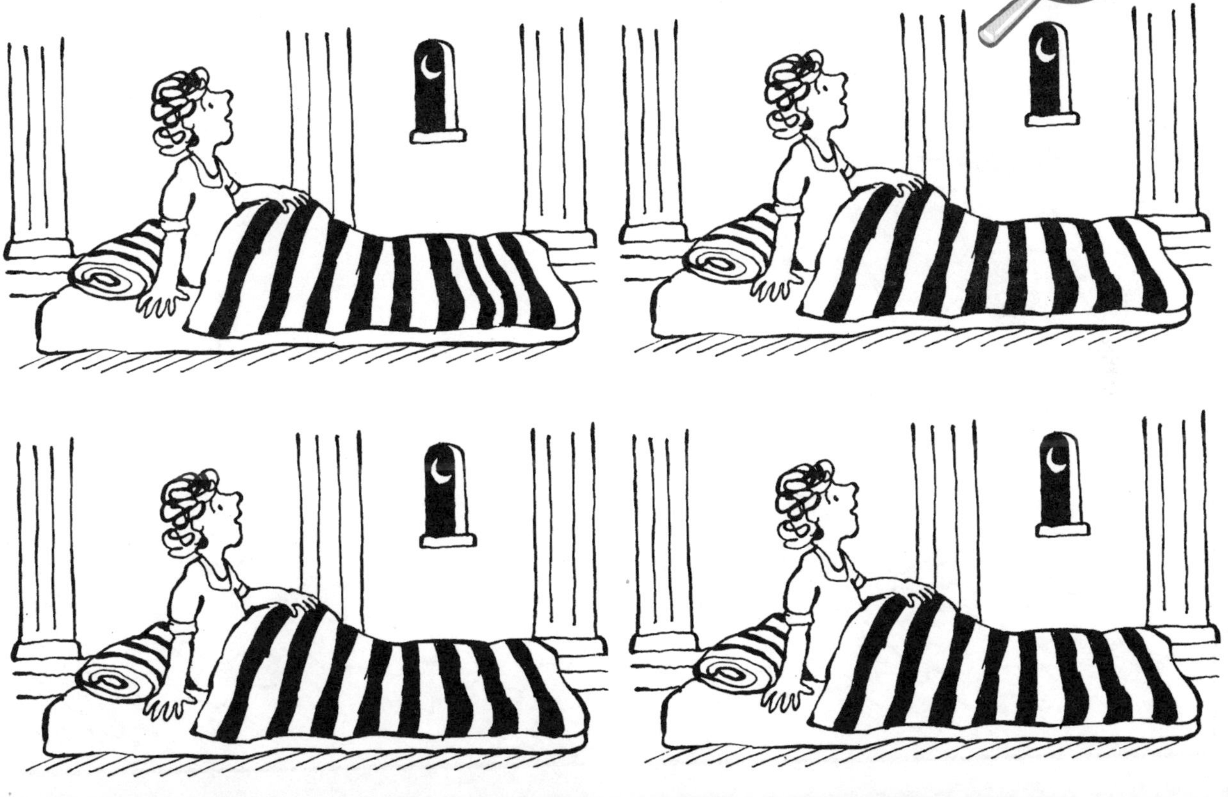

5

SEPTEMBER

What is this farmer doing in his field?
Join up the dots to find out.
Why is he doing this?

Read a story that Jesus told about a farmer in his field in Matthew 13:44.

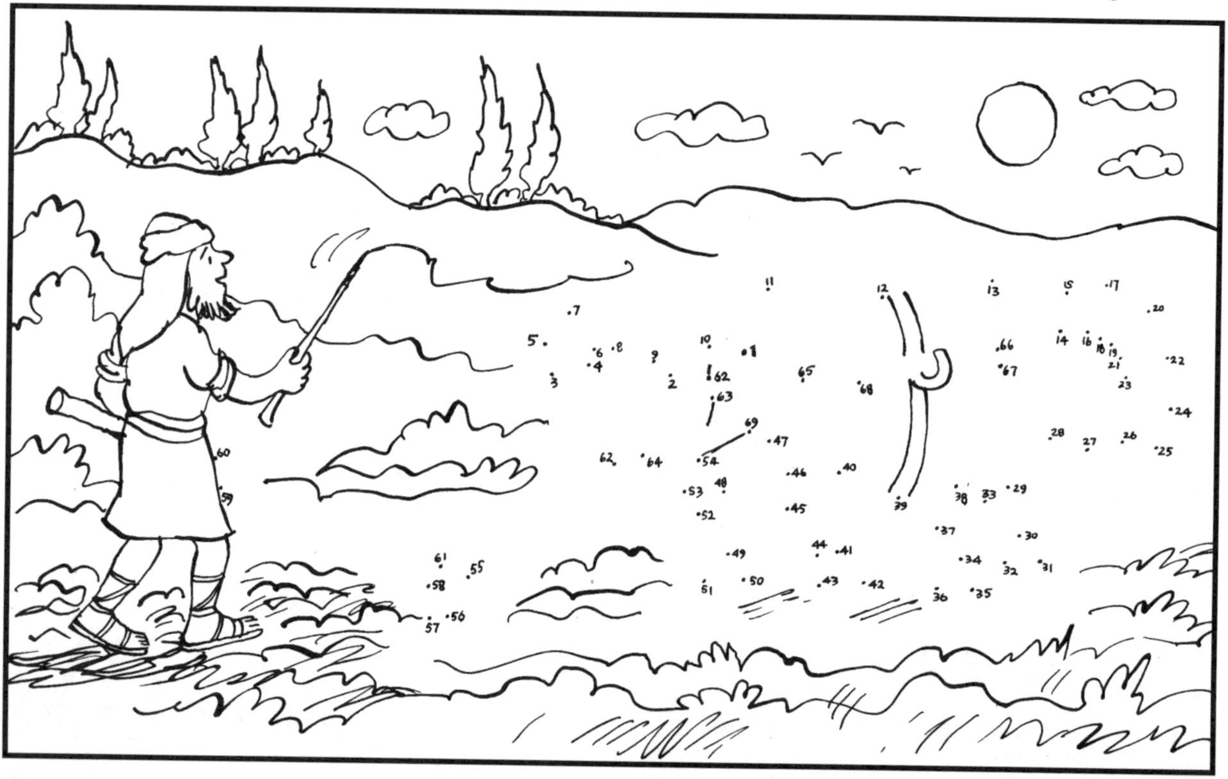

30

APRIL

When Samuel heard God's voice, at first he thought it was Eli. He ran in to ask what he wanted. Can you find 9 moons hidden in this picture.

Read this story in 1 Samuel 3:1–21.

Puzzle

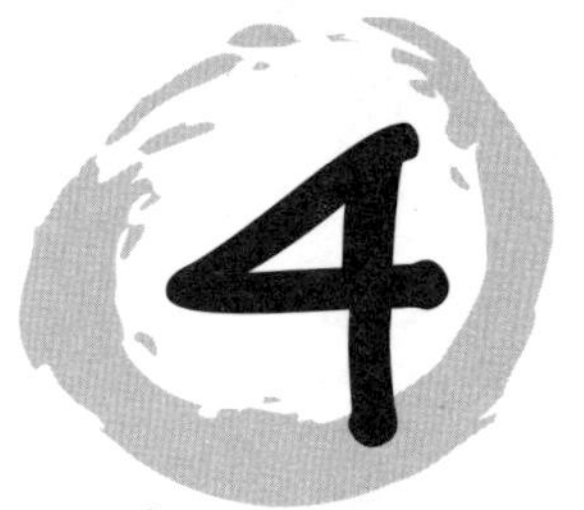

4

SEPTEMBER

Here is another picture of Jesus healing the little girl. Can you find 12 doves hidden in the picture?

Read the story about the little girl in Luke 8:40–56.

Puzzle

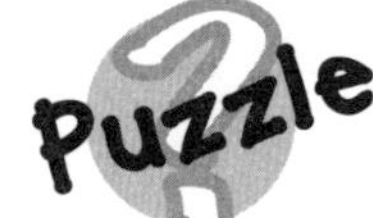

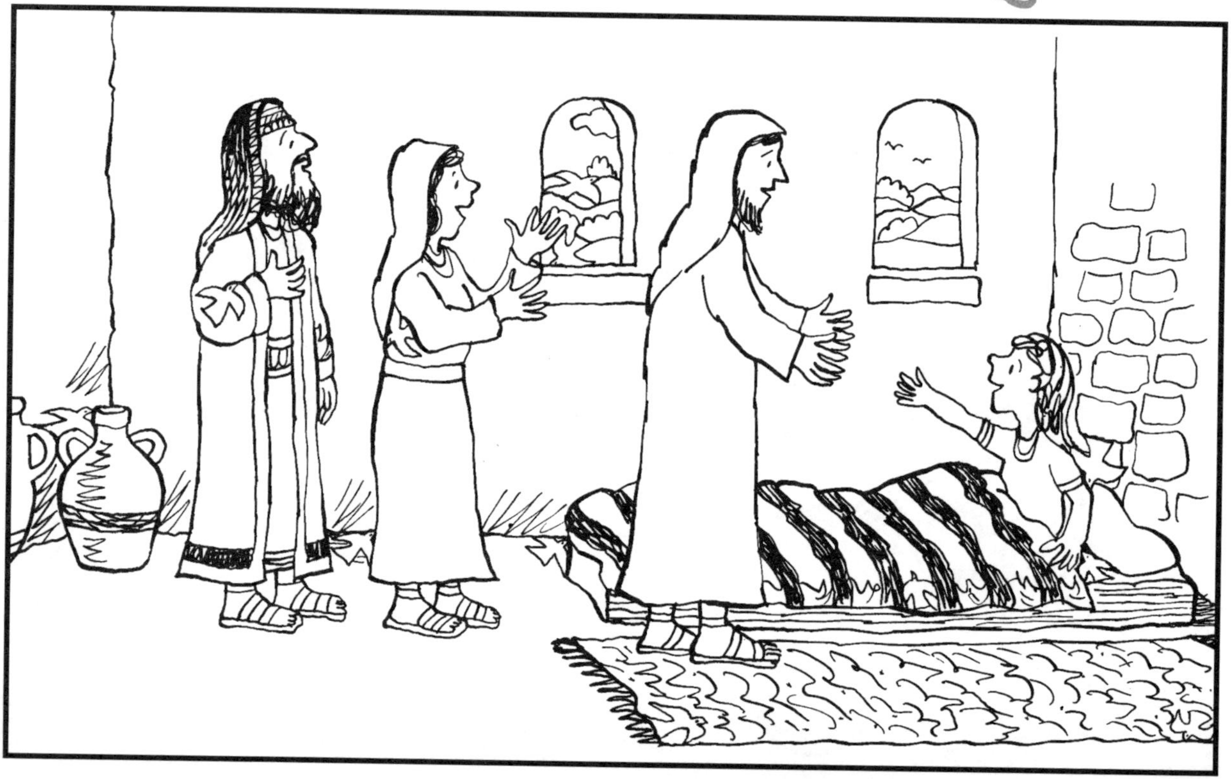

MAY

When Samuel grew up he became a prophet. He poured oil on David's head to show that one day he would be king of Israel.

Find 8 horns in this picture.
Read this story in 1 Samuel 16:1–13.

Puzzle

3

SEPTEMBER

Jesus brought this little girl back to life. How many funny mistakes has the artist made in this picture?

Read about the girl in Luke 8:40–56.
Where did she live?

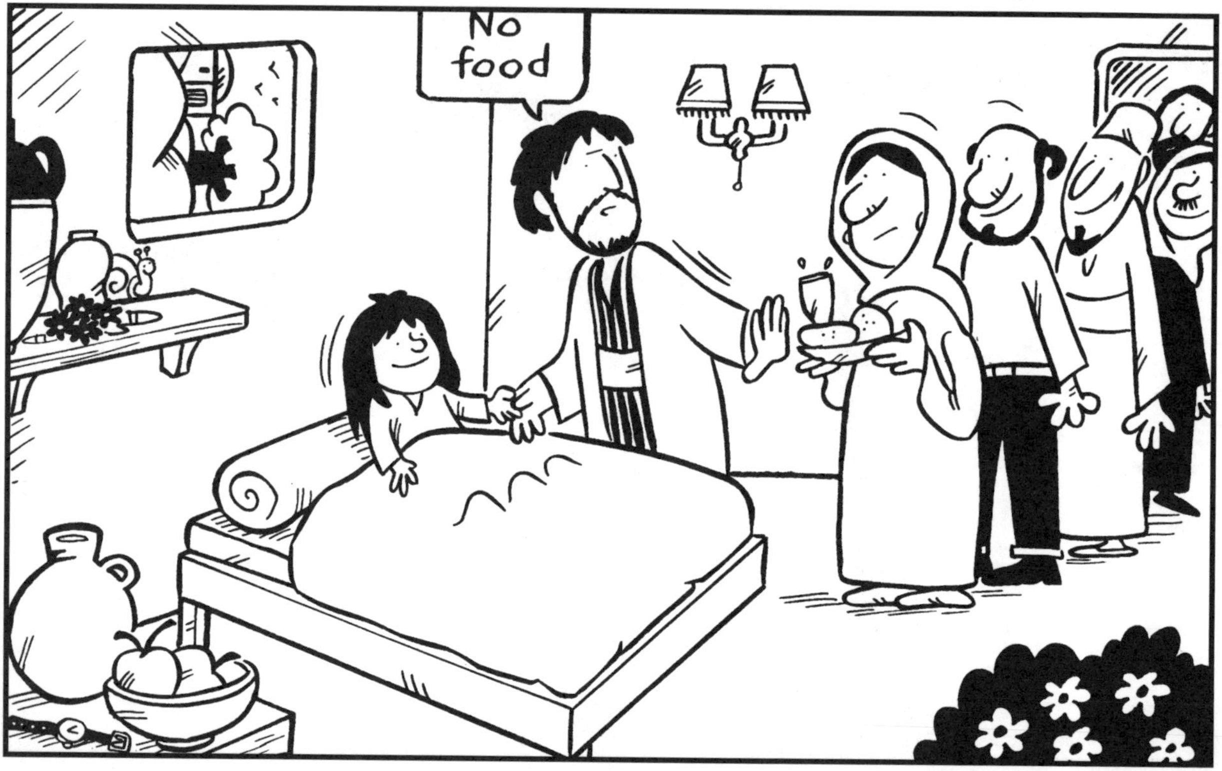

David was a shepherd before he became king of Israel. The artist hasn't finished drawing these sheep: can you help?

Then color in the whole picture with felt-tips or colored pencils. Read the "shepherd psalm", Psalm 23.

Color me!

2

SEPTEMBER

This servant owed the king a lot of money.
Why do you think he is kneeling down?

Find out what happened to him by reading Matthew 18:21–35.
Can you find all 10 differences between these two pictures?

What is this picture? To find out, shade in all the areas which have a dot in them.

Read Psalm 23 for a clue!

Color me!

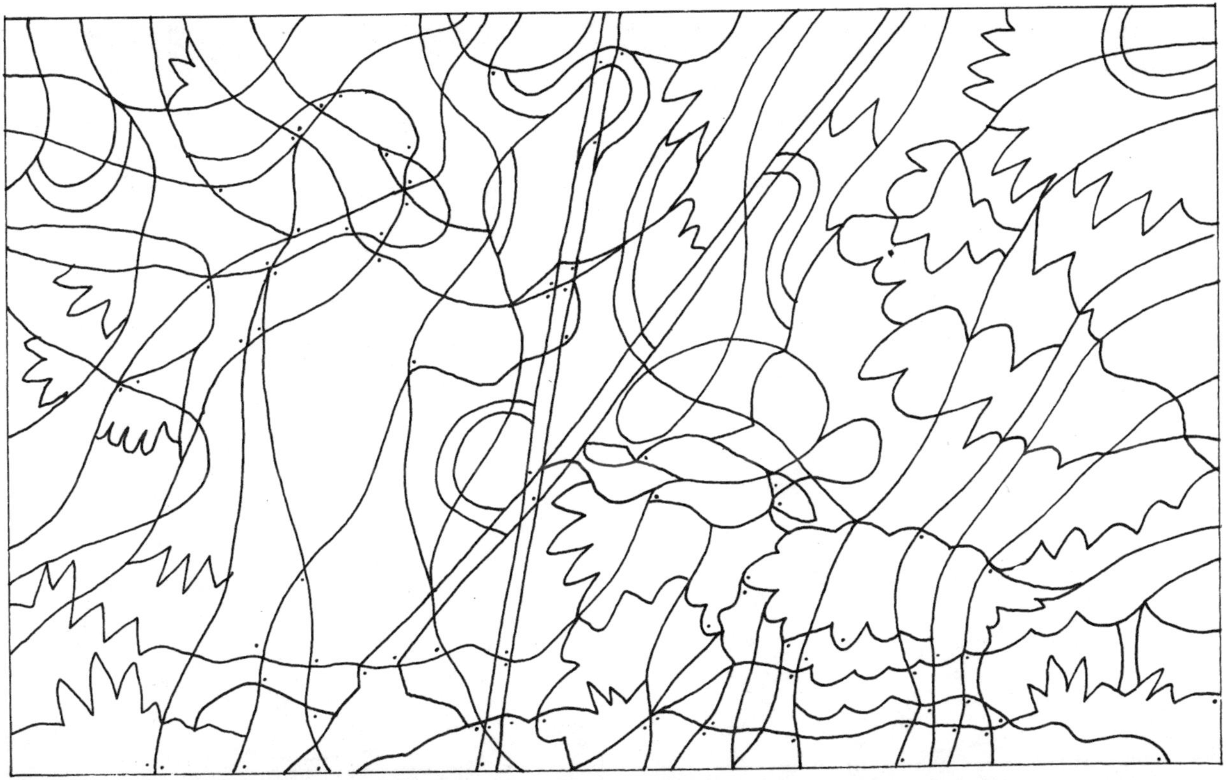

1

SEPTEMBER

These fishermen are using a dragnet to catch all sorts of fish in the Sea of Galilee.

Read what Jesus said about the dragnet in Matthew 13:47–50.
Now find 10 differences between the two pictures.

4
MAY

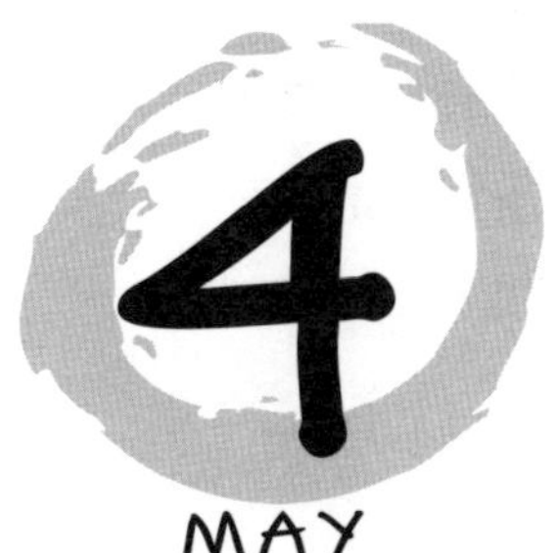

Which outline fits the shape of the picture of the shepherd? Now finish all the shepherd drawings.

Read about David the shepherd boy in 1 Samuel 16:11.

Color me!

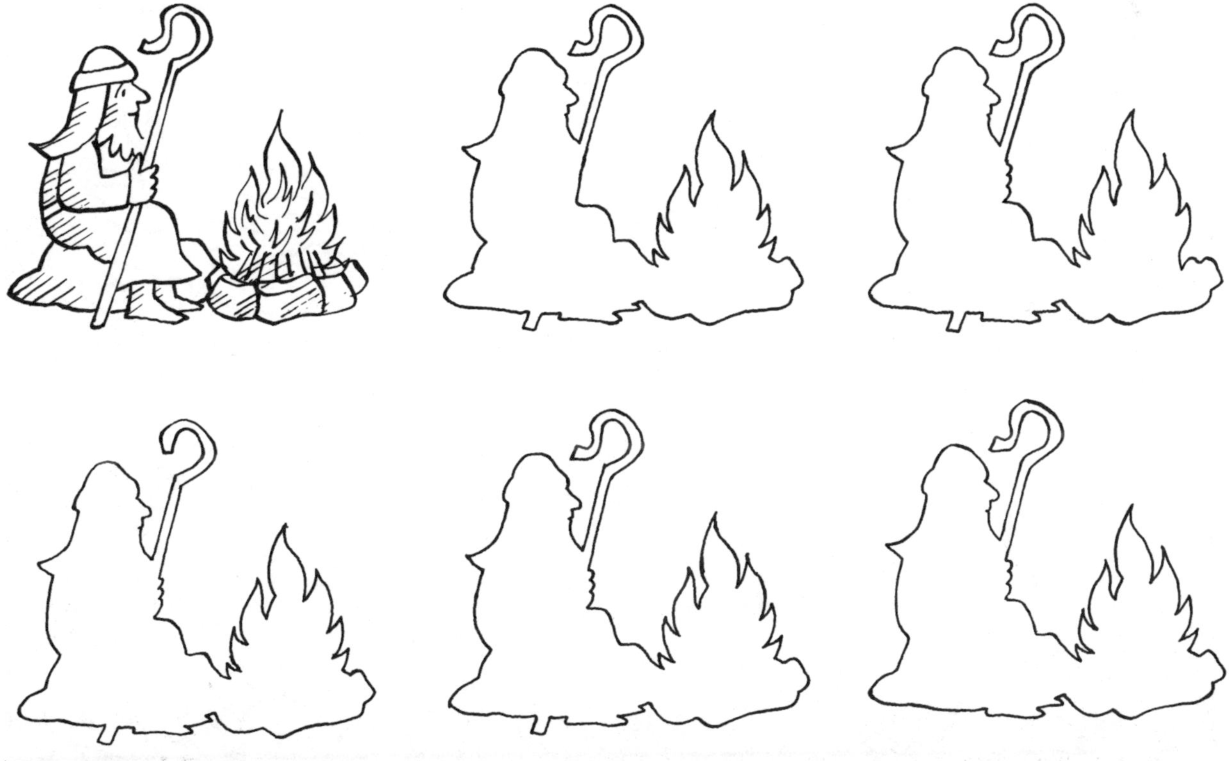

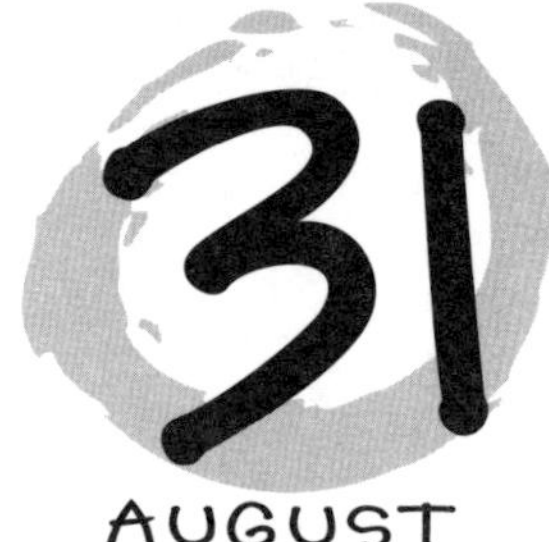

31 AUGUST

A pot of treasure, 10 coins and a sheep are all hidden in this picture. Can you find them for the farmer who is plowing his field?

Read this story that Jesus told in Matthew 13:44.

Puzzle

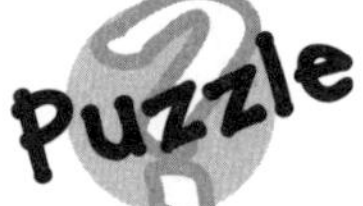

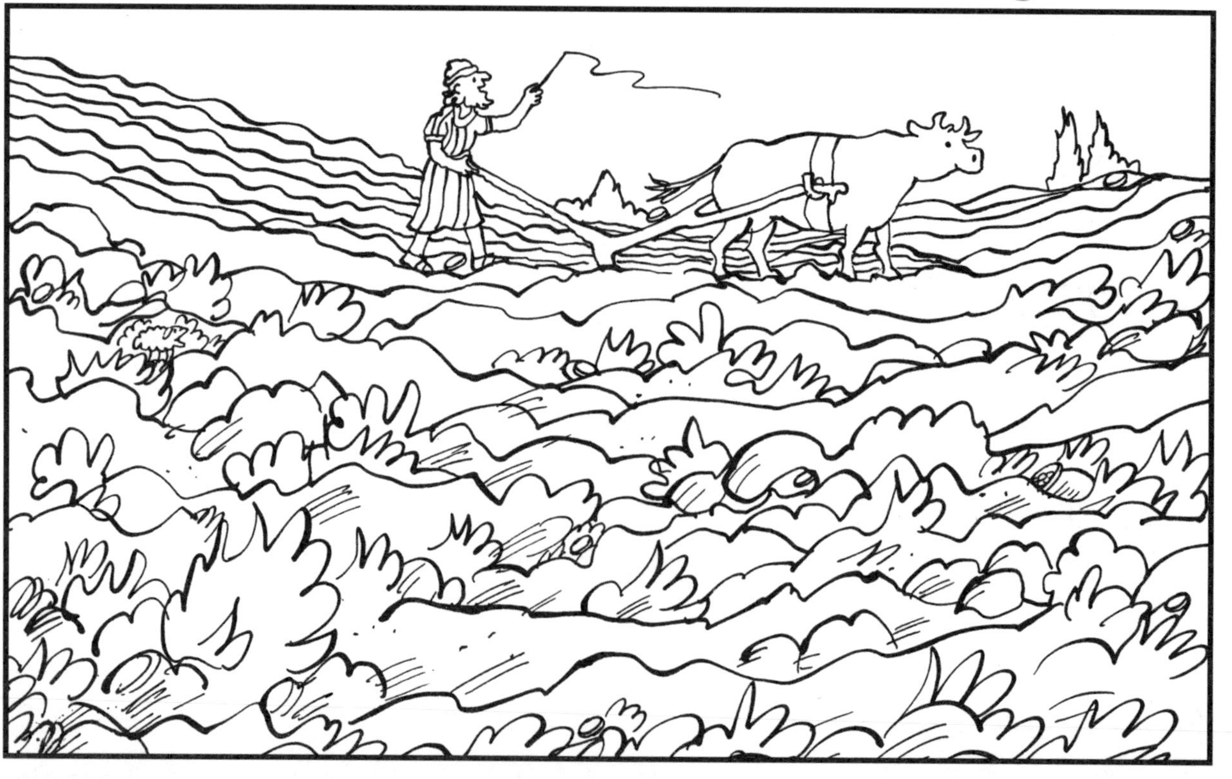

Complete this picture of David looking after his sheep. Have you given him a shepherd's crook?

Read Isaiah 40:11.

MAY

Draw me!

What has this man just found?
Where has he found it? Is he happy?

Read the whole story Jesus told in Matthew 13:44.
Now find at least 10 differences between the two pictures.

6
MAY

How many overlapping shepherd's crooks can you find here?

Read about the shepherd's crook, or staff, in Psalm 23.

Color me!

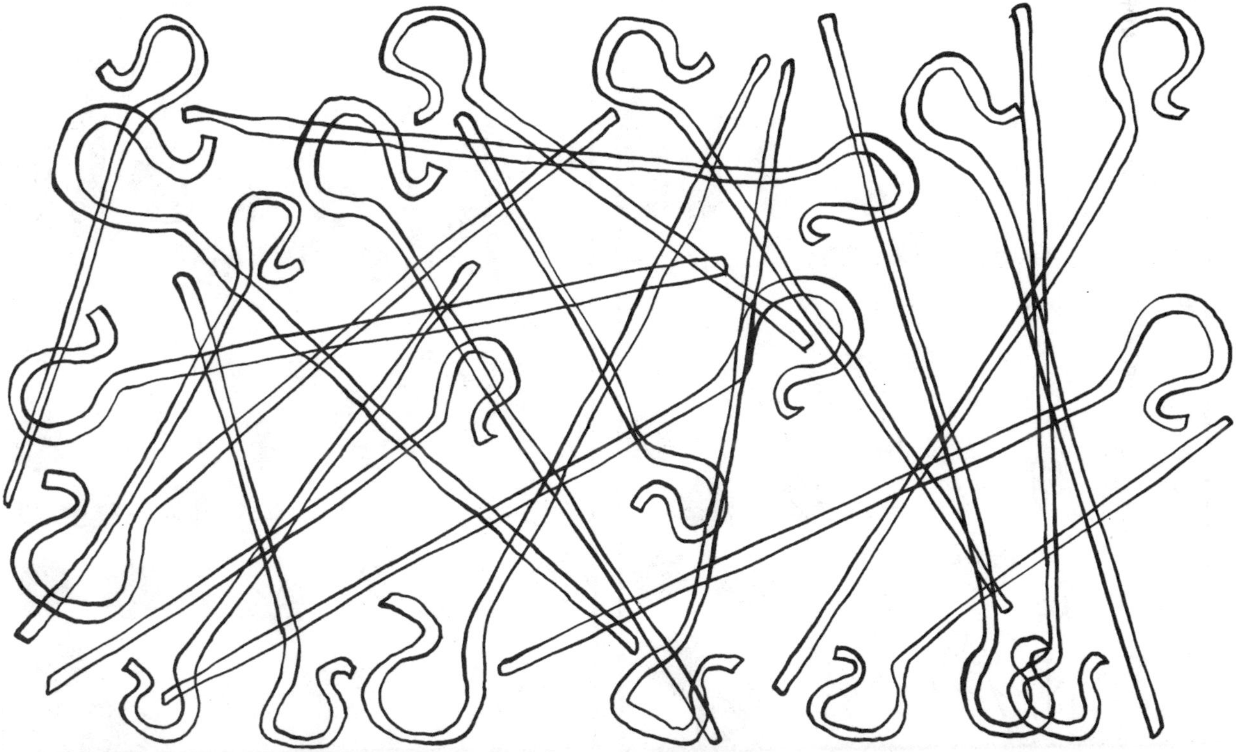

Jesus taught the people outside.
He said that God made the flowers look
more beautiful than even the richest king.

Find 10 differences between these pictures.
Read this story in Matthew 6:25–34.

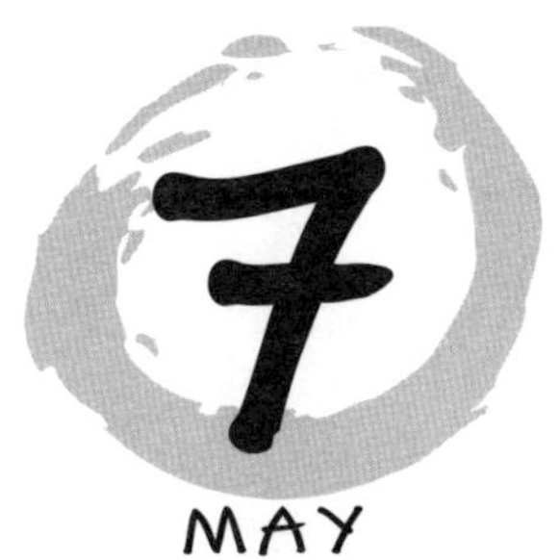

7
MAY

David is beating a lion that tried to attack his flock of sheep. Can you draw in the lion?

You can read this story in 1 Samuel 17:34–37

Draw me!

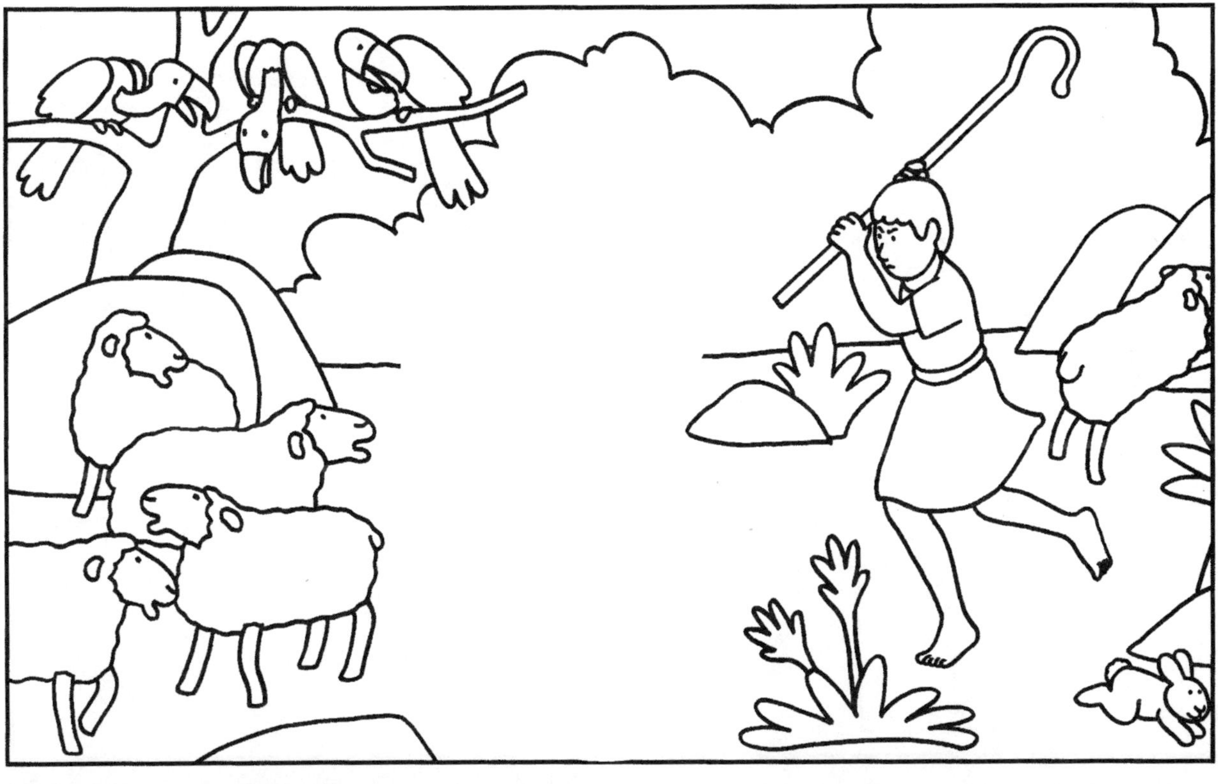

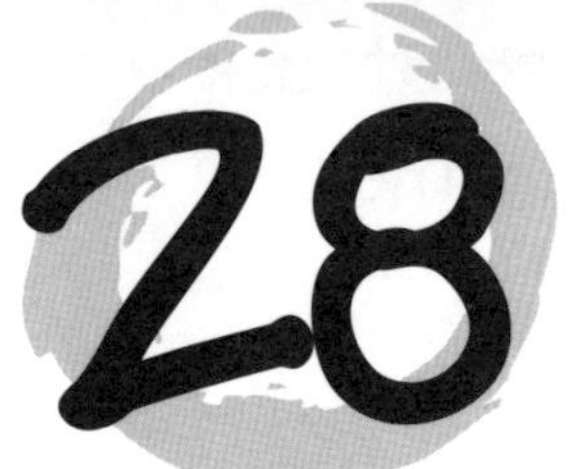

28
AUGUST

One of these lamps is hidden under a table! Jesus said we shouldn't hide our light. Find 10 differences between the two pictures?

Read this story in Matthew 5:14–16.

SPOT THE DIFFERENCE

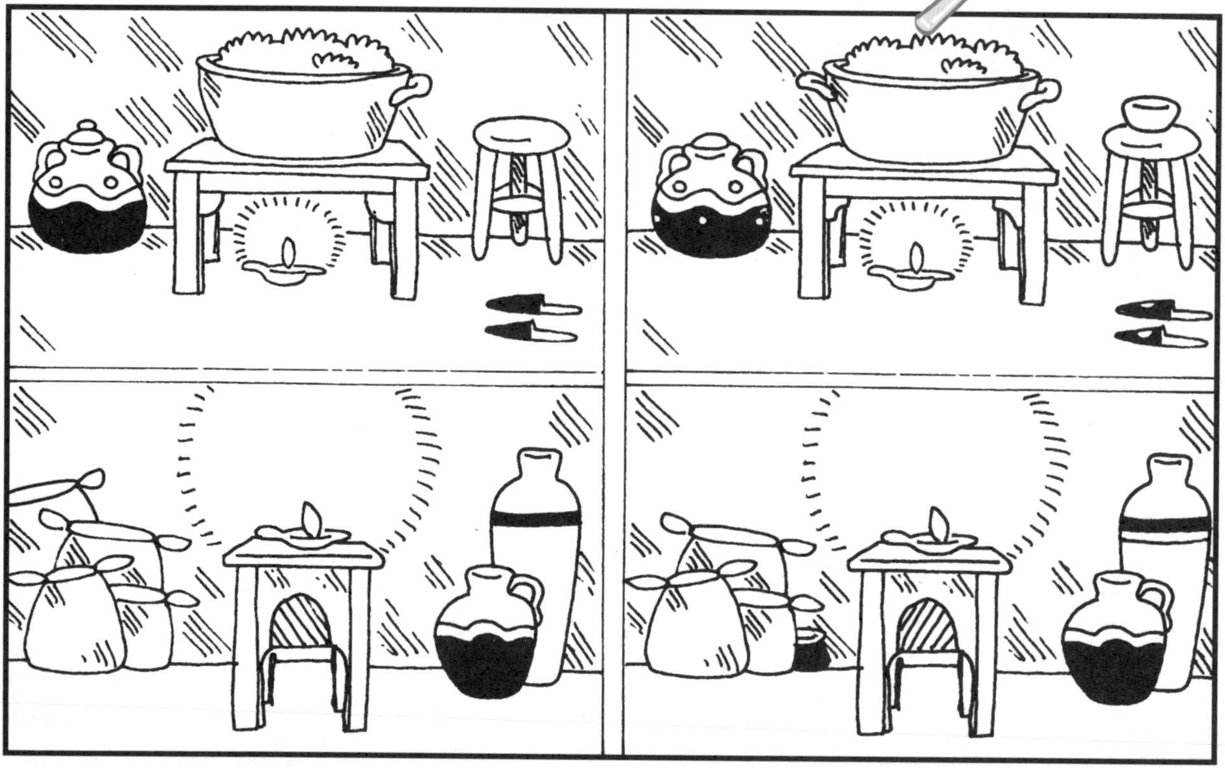

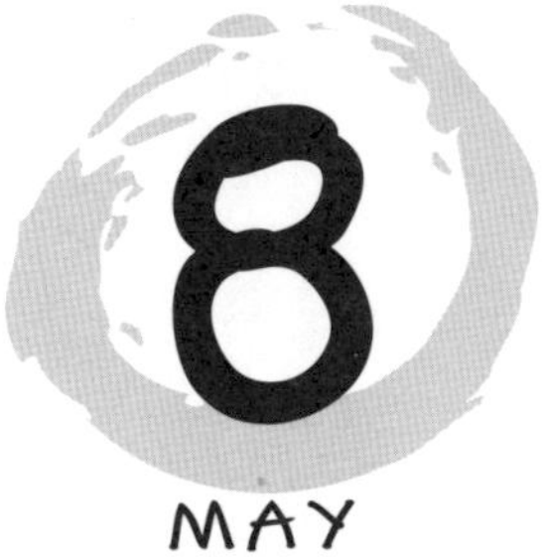

8

MAY

David used to play his harp to make King Saul happy. How can he reach his harp? David must walk only where the floor tiles touch.

Read the story of Saul's sadness in 1 Samuel 16:14–23.

maze

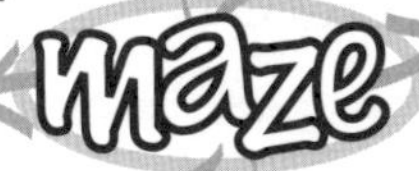

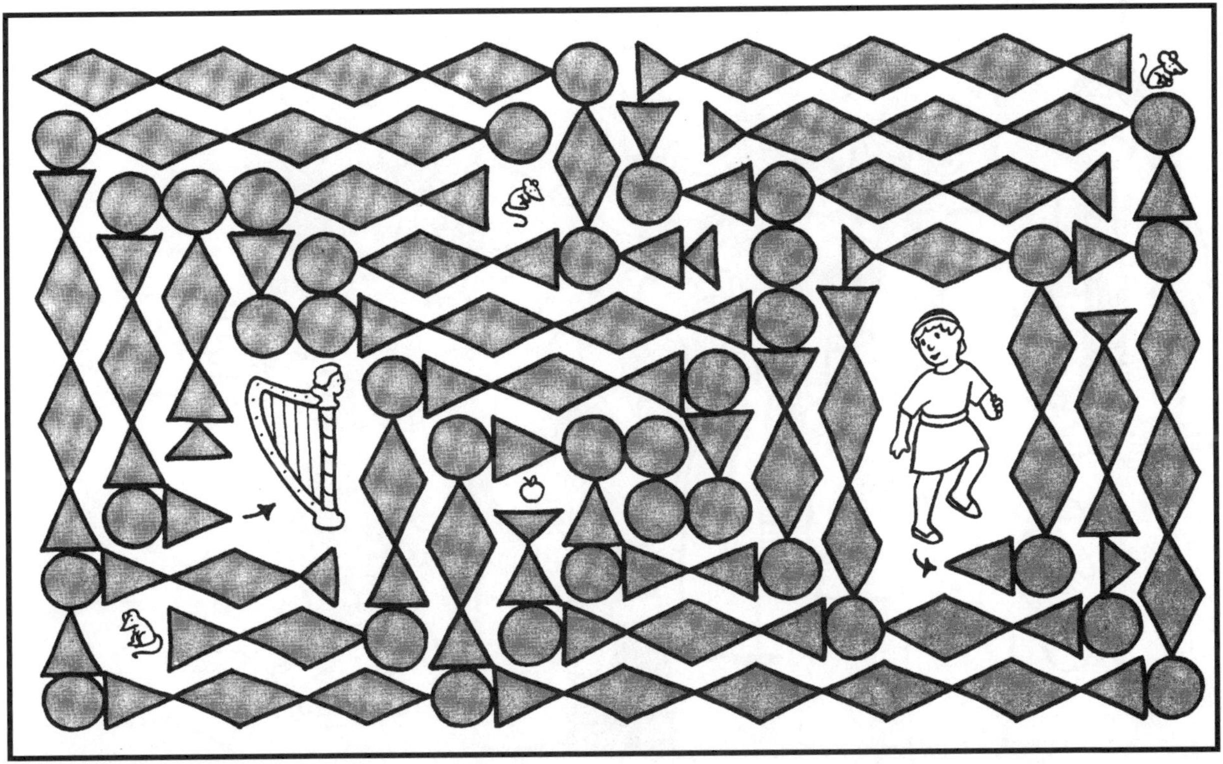

27
AUGUST

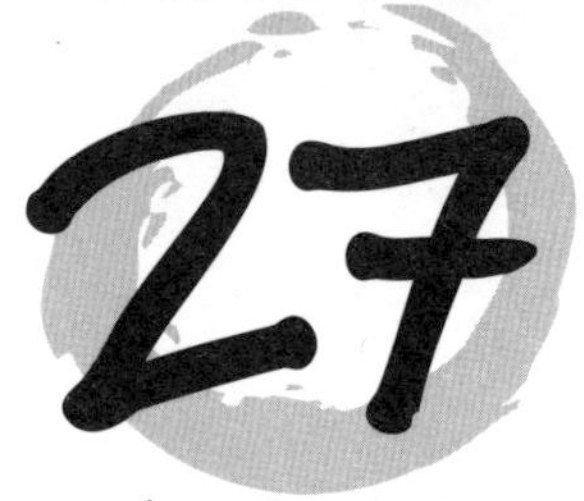

Jesus is preaching to the people. Circle all the funny mistakes in the picture. How many have you found?

Read Matthew 4:12–17 to find out what Jesus is telling the people to do.

Puzzle

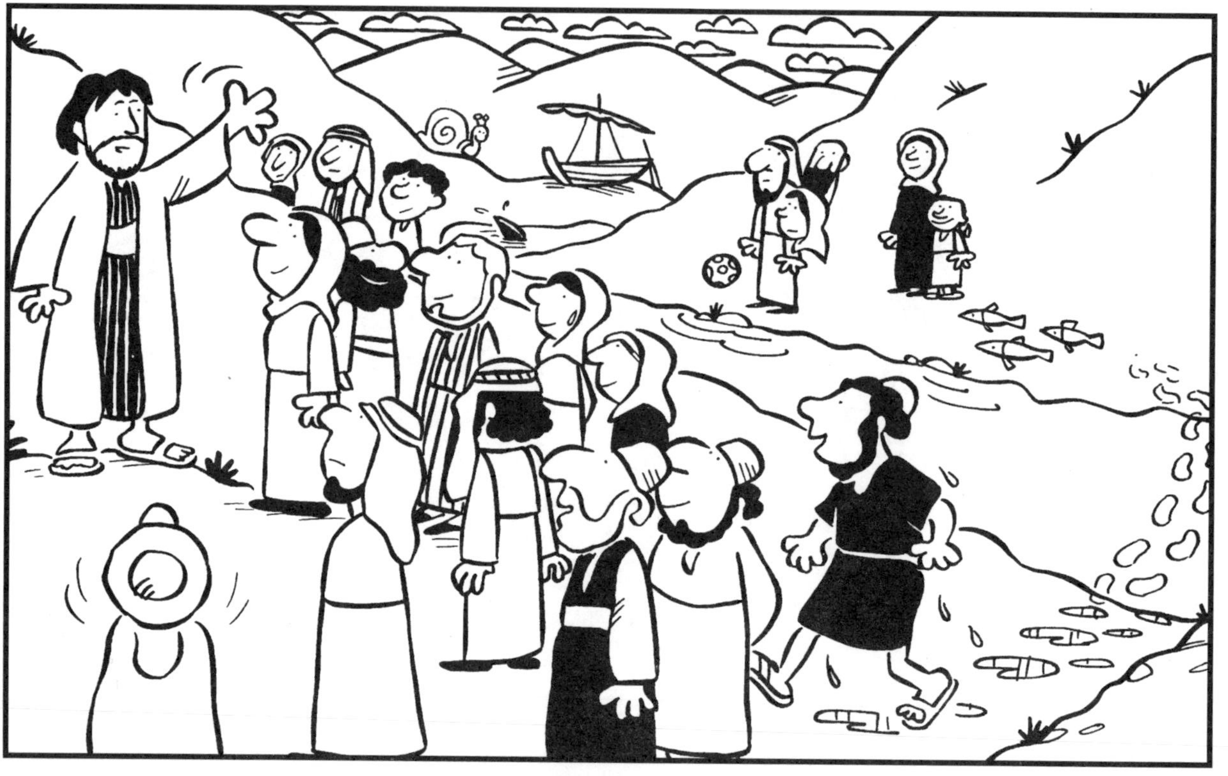

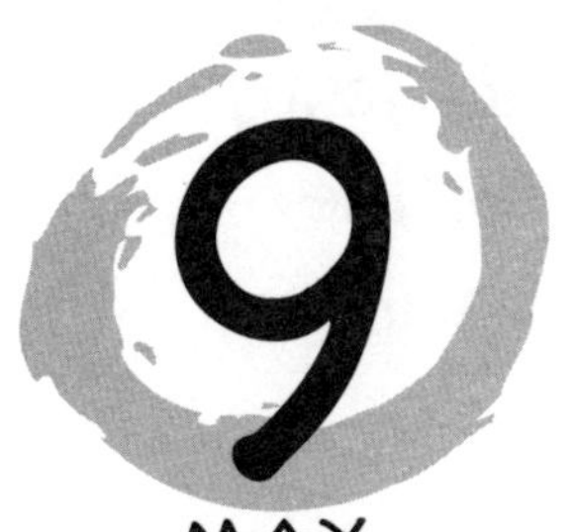

9 MAY

David played the harp, or lyre, to King Saul. Two of these harps are exactly the same. Which two?

You can read about David's harp in 1 Samuel 16:23.

SPOT THE DIFFERENCE

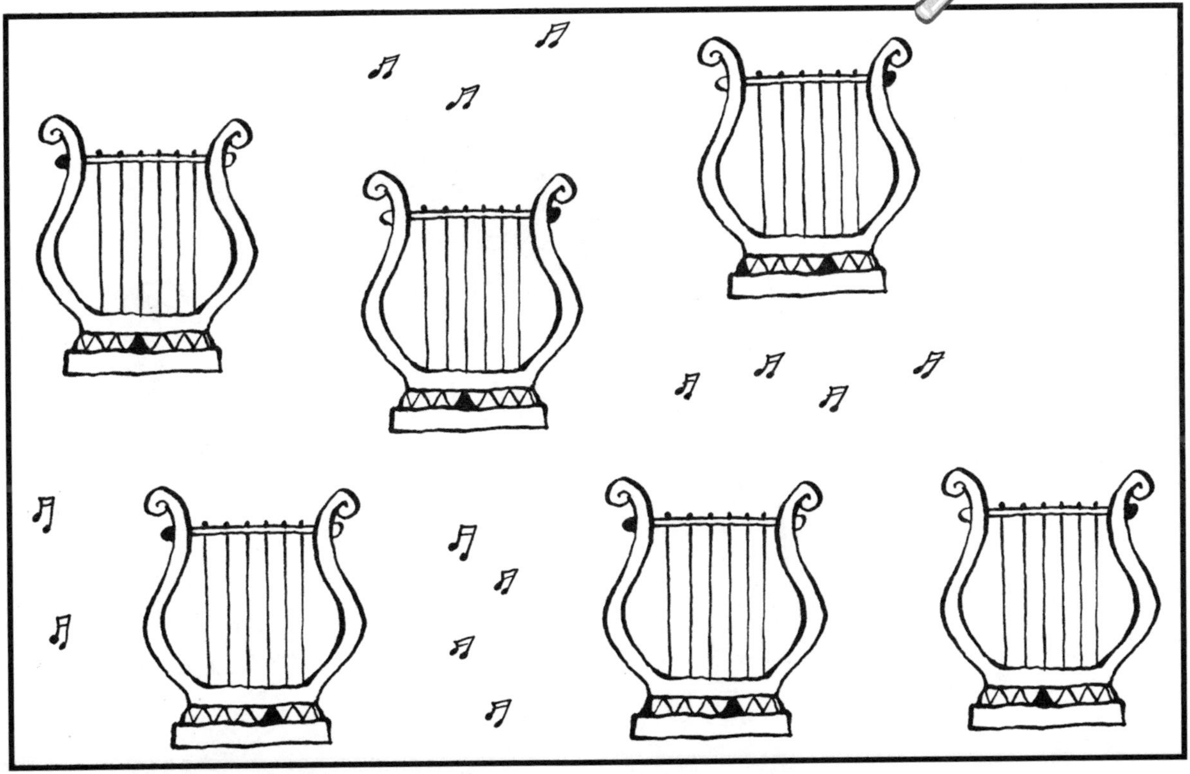

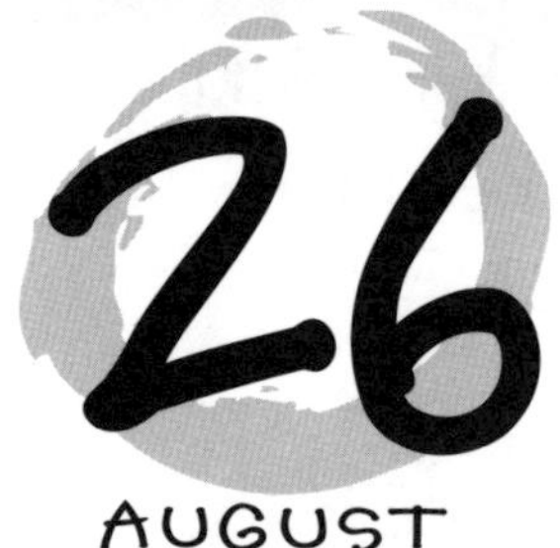

26
AUGUST

Here are 4 pictures of the man who Jesus healed after he'd been lowered from the roof. Now he can stand and walk again.

One picture is different from all the others. Which one?
Read this story in Luke 5:17–26.

SPOT THE DIFFERENCE

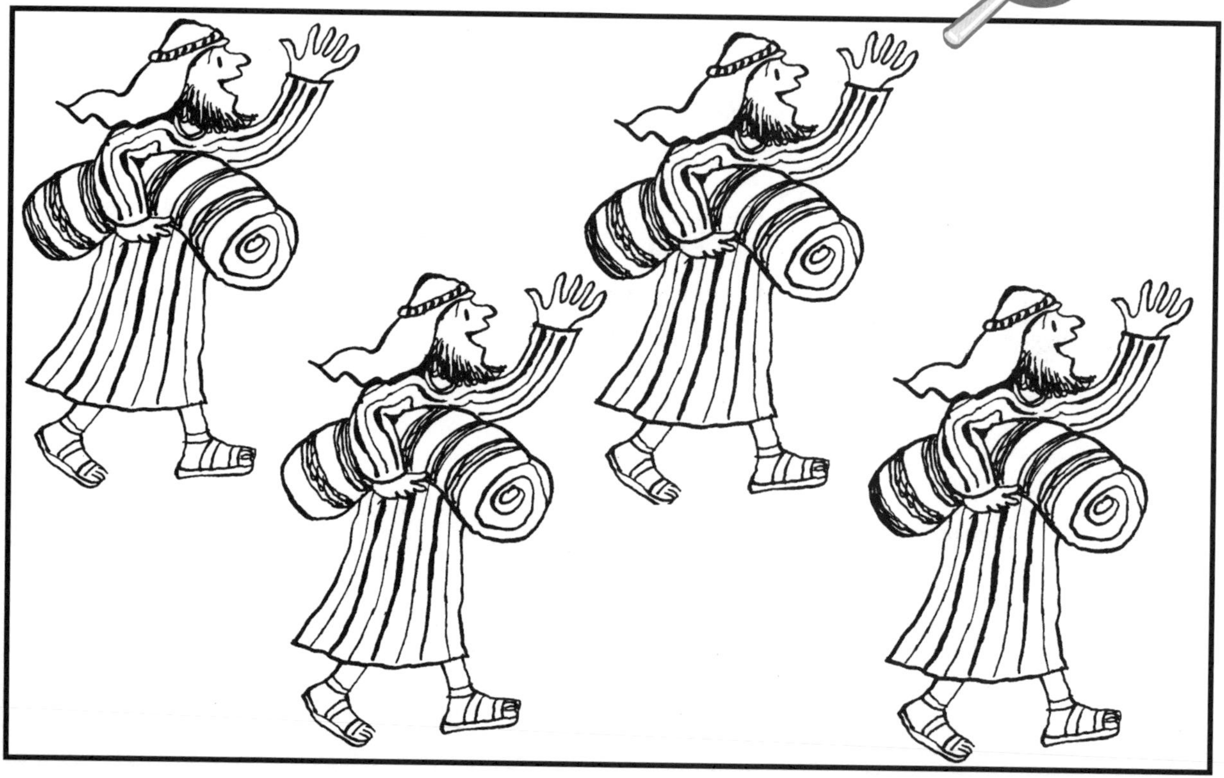

10 MAY

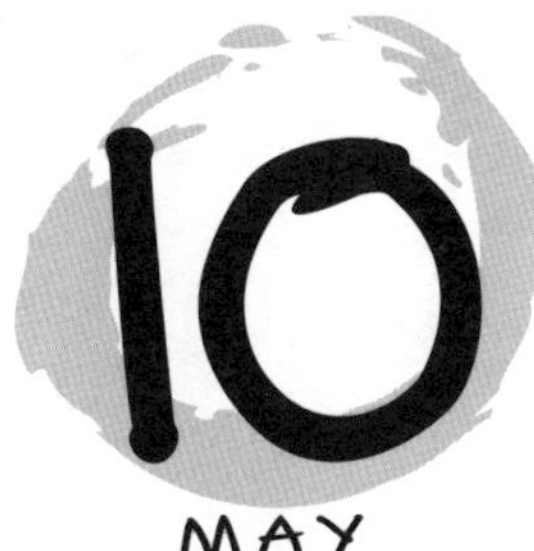

Join up the dots to find out who is listening to David playing his harp.

You can read this story in 1 Samuel 16:14–22.

DOT-TO-DOT

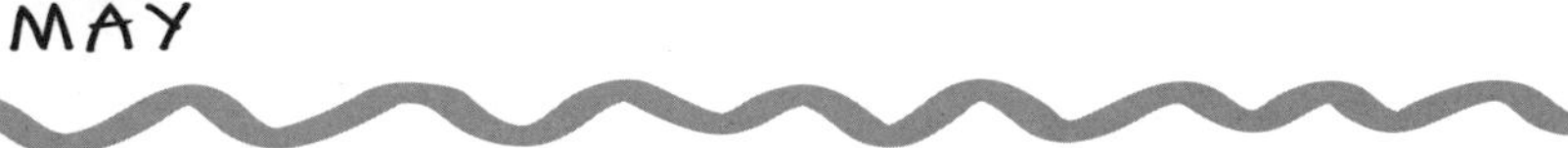

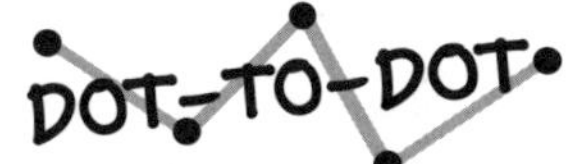

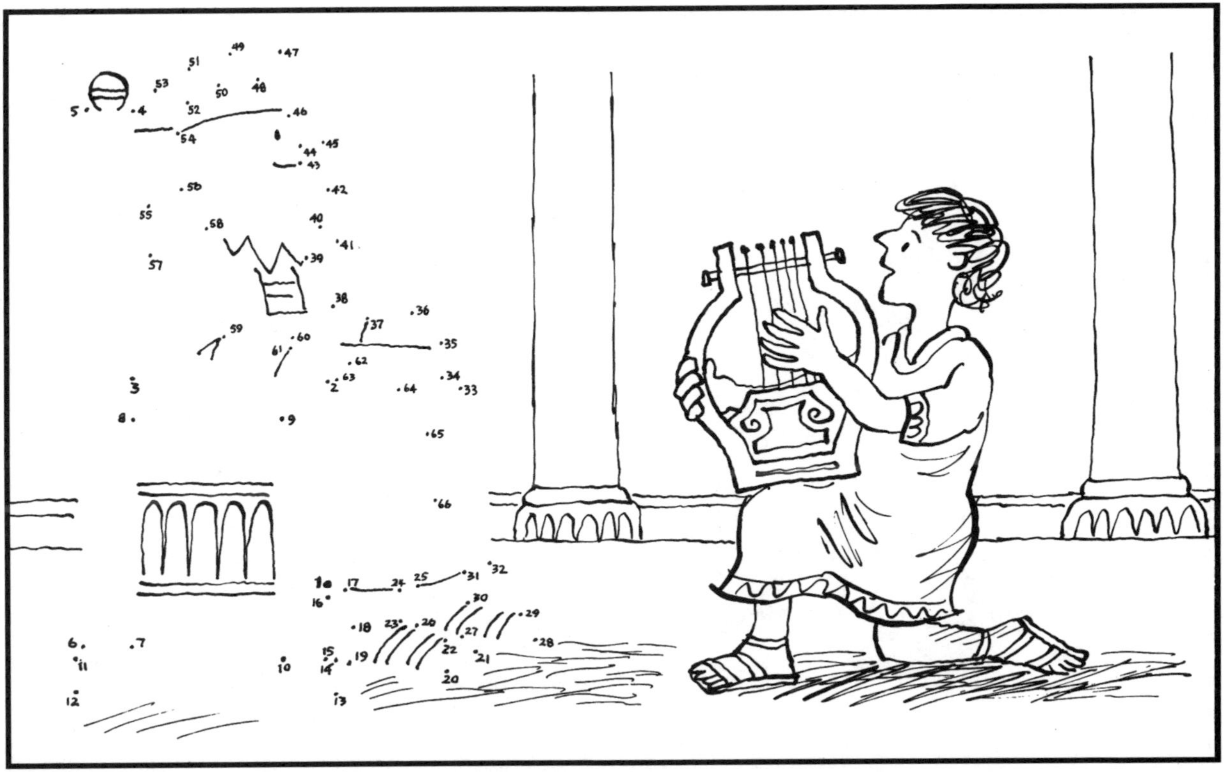

25 AUGUST

What are the men on the roof doing?
Join up the dots to find out.

Read this story in Luke 5:17–26.
What happened to the man on the mattress?

DOT-TO-DOT

11

MAY

Saul became very jealous of David and hurled a spear at him when he was playing his harp one day.

Draw Saul throwing the spear.
This story is in 1 Samuel 18:6–11

Draw me!

24 AUGUST

Here is another picture of the man who Jesus healed after he'd been let down through the roof.

There are a whole lot of mistakes. Can you find them all? Read this story in Luke 5:17–26.

Puzzle

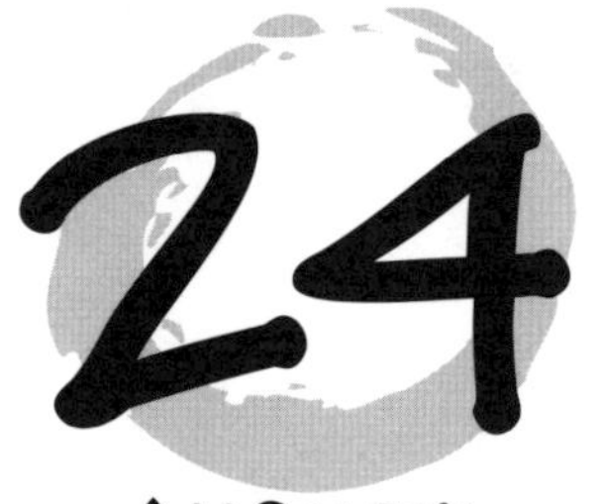

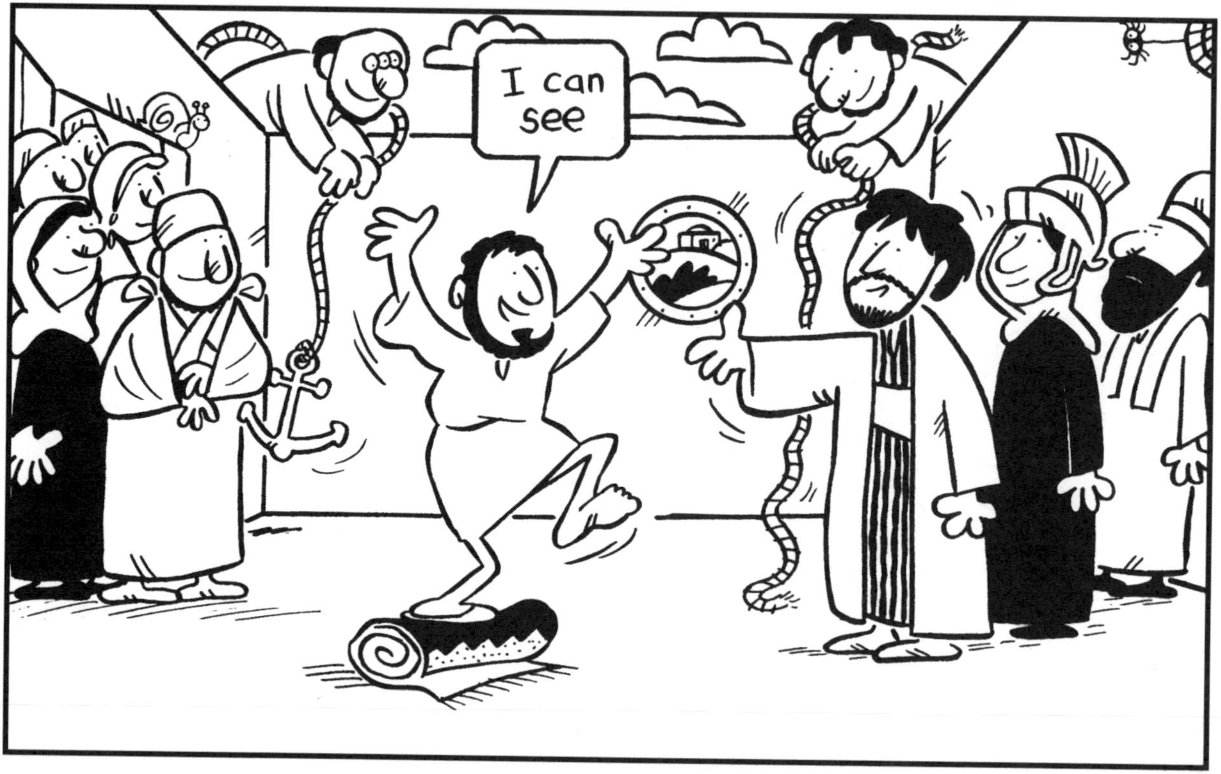

12

MAY

Here is another picture of David playing to King Saul. Make a list of all the silly mistakes that the artist has made here.

Do you know the name of Saul's son, David's friend?
Look at 1 Samuel 19:1–3

**Puzzle

23

AUGUST

Join up the dots to find out what the men on the roof are doing.
What happened to the sick man?

Find out by reading Luke 5:17–26.
Then color in the picture with felt-tips.

DOT-TO-DOT

13
MAY

Draw in David playing his harp.
Do you think he might be singing a psalm?

Read Psalm 8.

Color me!

22
AUGUST

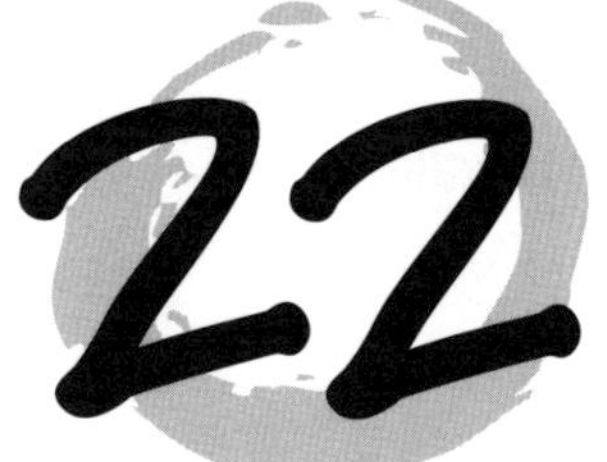

These people want to sail across the Sea of Galilee to meet Jesus. Which way must they take to get there without crossing any waves?

maze

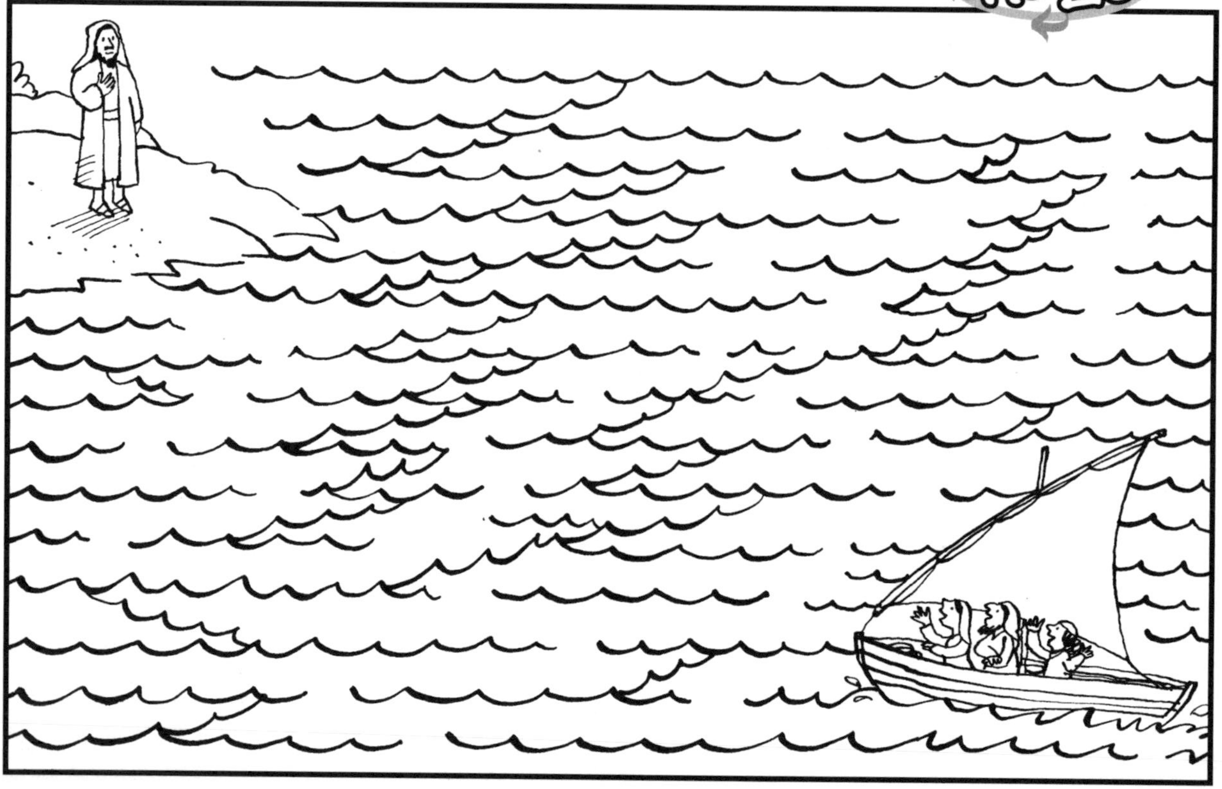

14

MAY

David said he wanted to fight the giant Goliath, and Saul offered to lend him his armor. Find 6 helmets hidden in this picture.

Did David use the armor?
Read about David and Goliath in 1 Samuel 17:38–51.

Puzzle

21

AUGUST

Here is another picture showing Jesus telling his friends how to catch more fish. Who does the boat belong to?

List all the deliberate mistakes the artist has made. Read this story in Luke 5:1–11.

Puzzle

15

MAY

David collected 5 stones from the stream to use in his sling to fight Goliath.

Which line must he follow to find exactly 5 stones? Read 1 Samuel 17:50.

Puzzle

20

AUGUST

Join up the dots to find out what these three men are doing.
What happened after this?

Find out the answer in Luke 5:1–11.

DOT-TO-DOT

16 MAY

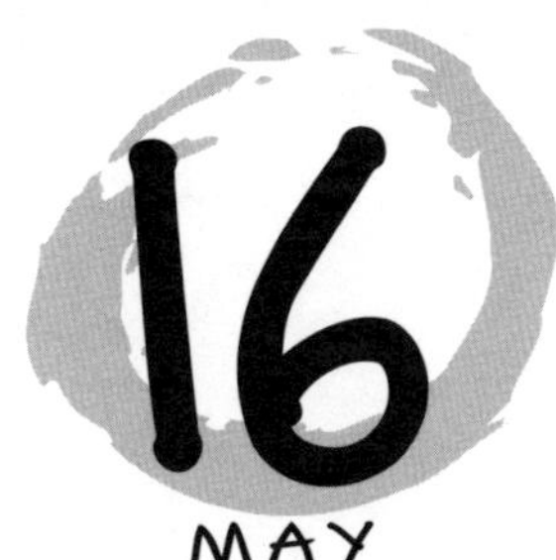

David is throwing a stone from his sling. Join up the dots to find his target.

Read this story in 1 Samuel 17:38–51.

DOT-TO-DOT

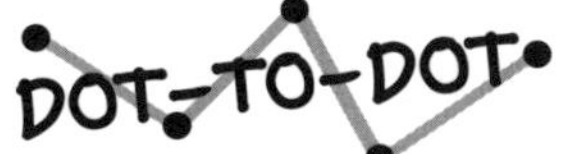

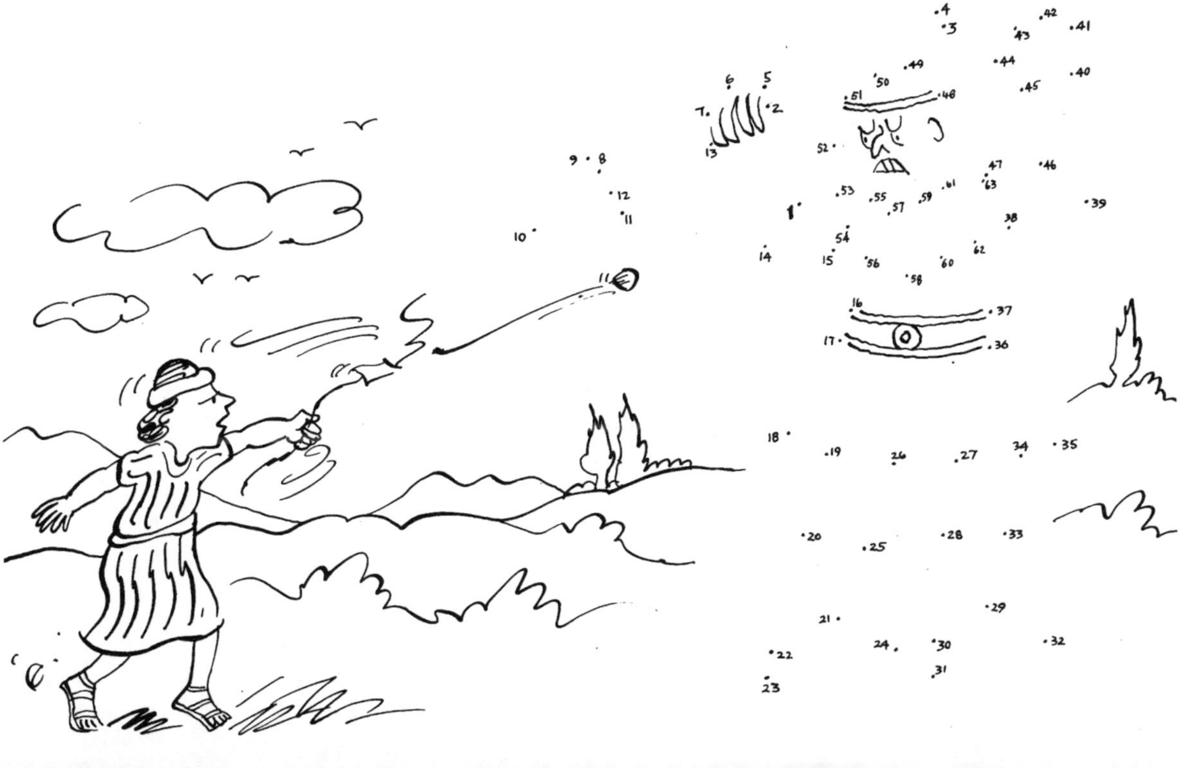

Here are 5 people from Jesus' time. Can you match them with the things needed for their job? Draw a line to join them up.

17

MAY

The Philistine giant Goliath has fallen. Draw in David and his sling.

How did Goliath lose his head?
Read 1 Samuel 17:48–51.

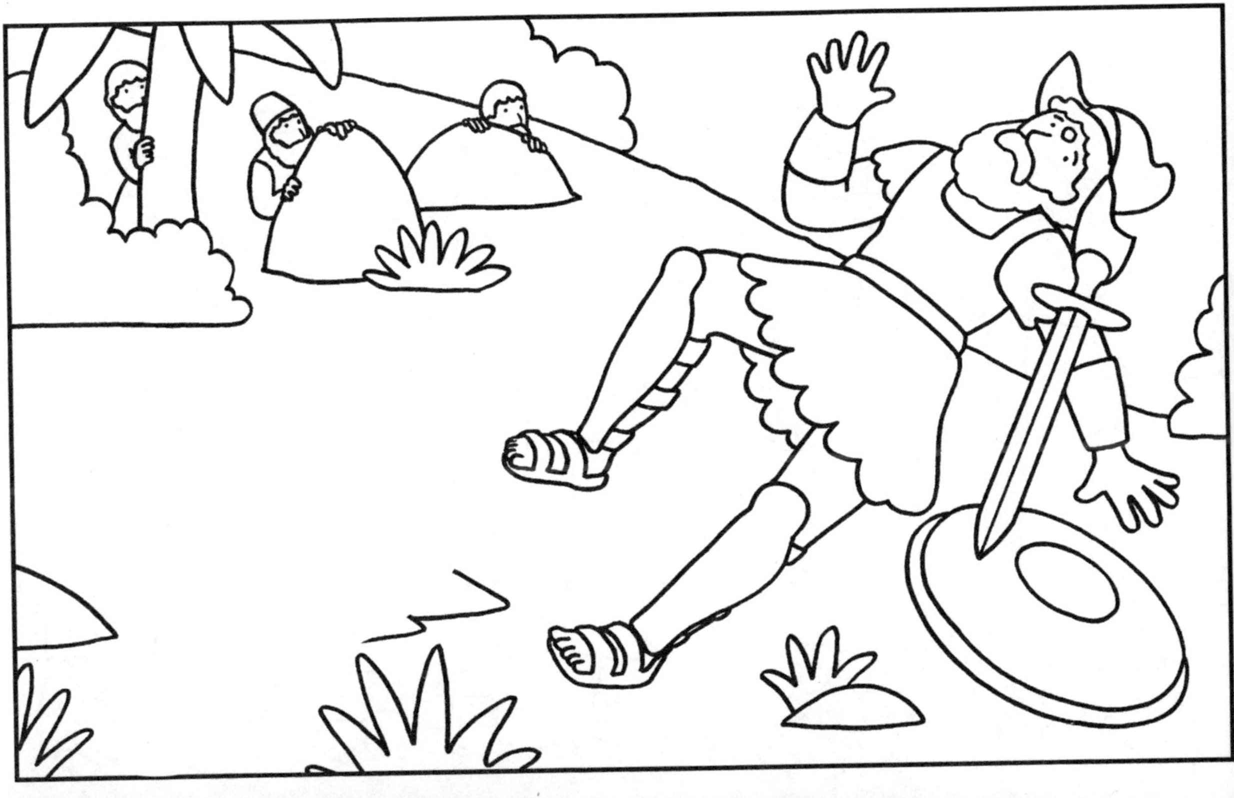

18

AUGUST

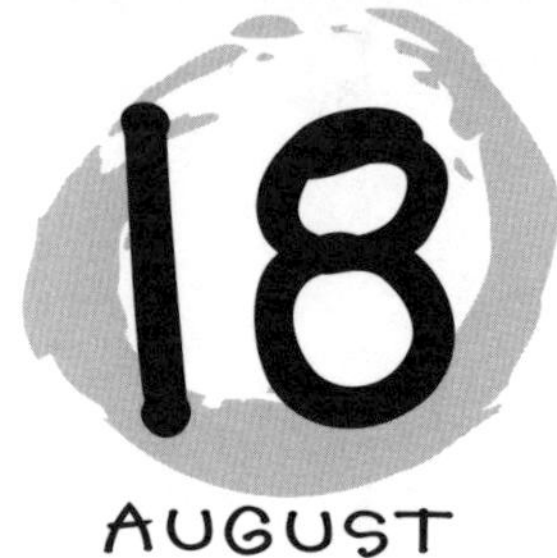

Jesus called 12 disciples altogether. One appears twice here. Which one?

Find the names of all Jesus' disciples in Matthew 10:1–4.

Color me!

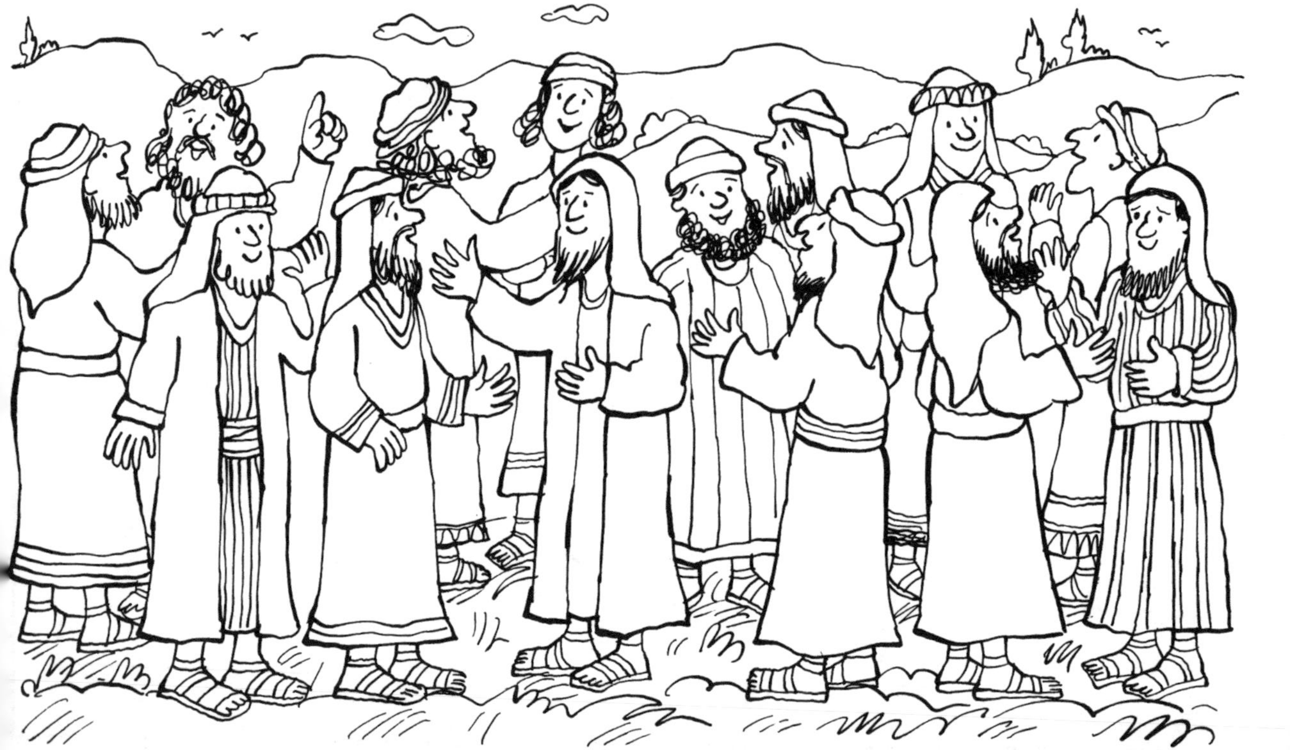

18 MAY

Join up the dots to find out how David beat the giant Goliath. What did the Philistine soldiers do after their giant was killed?

See 1 Samuel 17:51–52.

DOT-TO-DOT

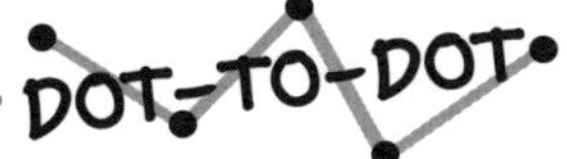

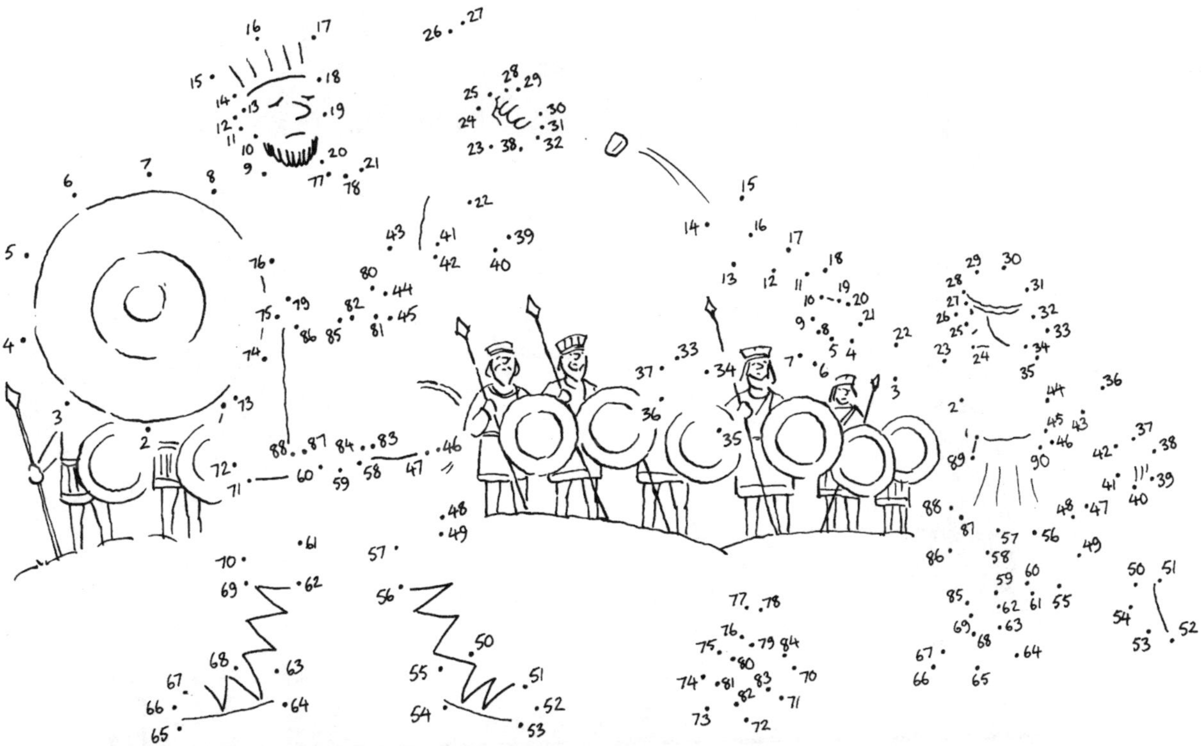

17
AUGUST

The artist has made lots of mistakes in this picture of Jesus calling Matthew. Circle all the mistakes you can find. How many do you have?

Did Matthew really say 'No'?
Read about the call of Matthew in Matthew 9:9.

Puzzle

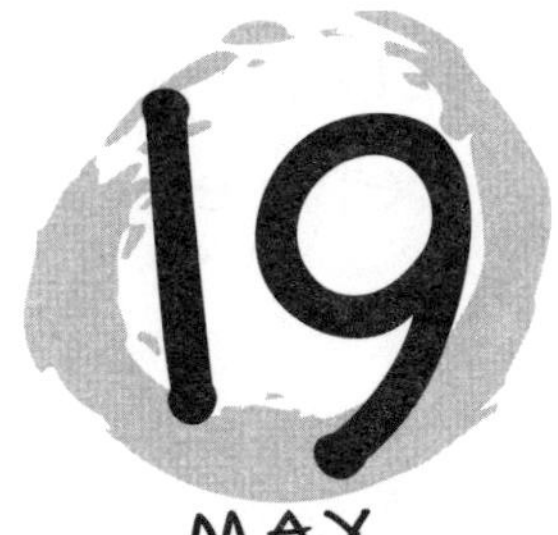

19
MAY

Draw a red circle around the 10 black stones in this picture. Whose sword did David use to cut off Goliath's head?

See 1 Samuel 17:51.

Puzzle

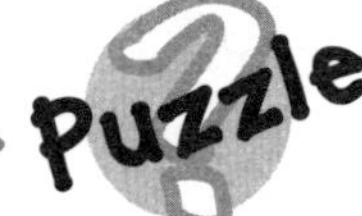

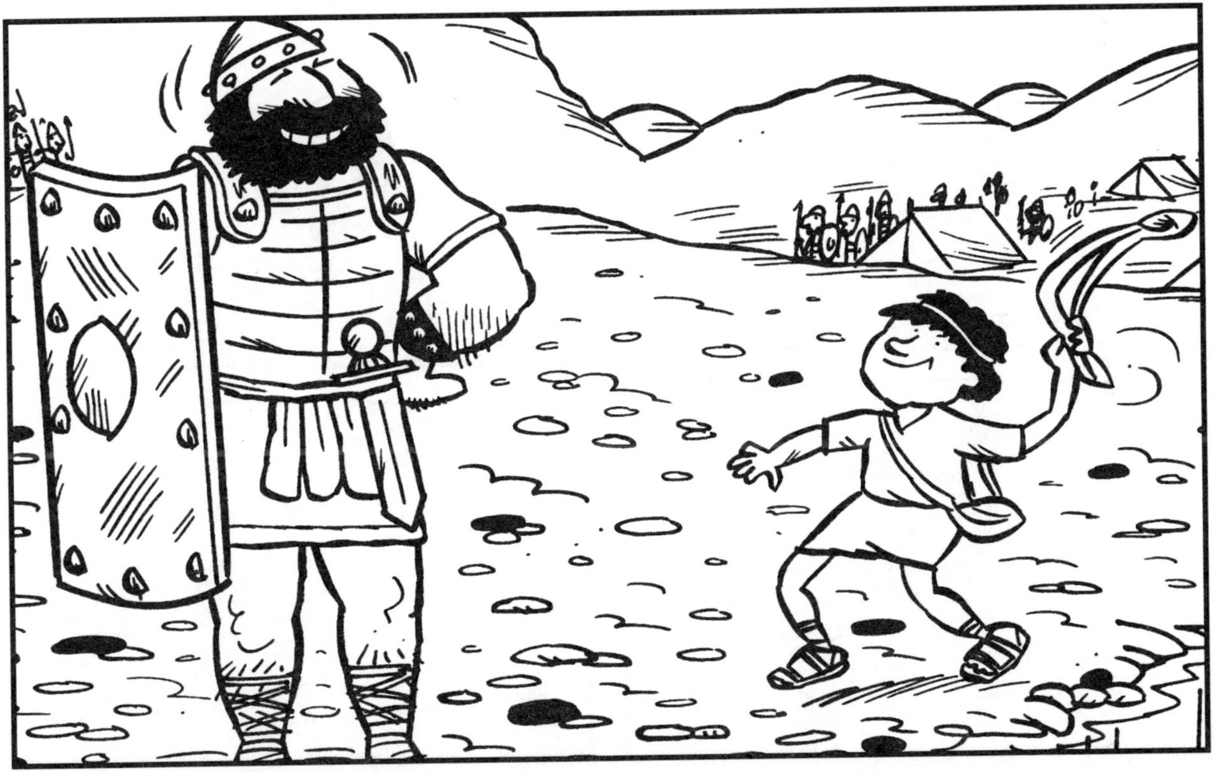

16
AUGUST

Here are two pictures of Matthew collecting taxes. Can you find 10 differences between them?

Read about the call of Matthew in Matthew 9:9.

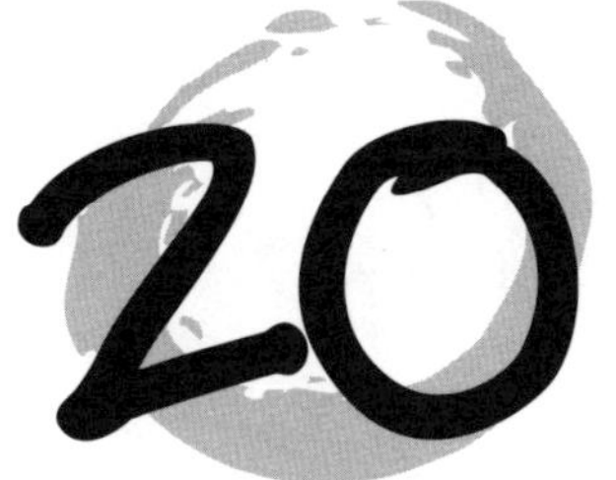

20 MAY

The artist has made lots of silly mistakes in this picture of David and Goliath.
Make a list of them.

Check the story in 1 Samuel 17 if you're not sure.

Puzzle

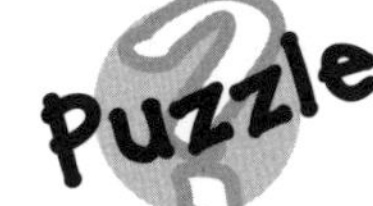

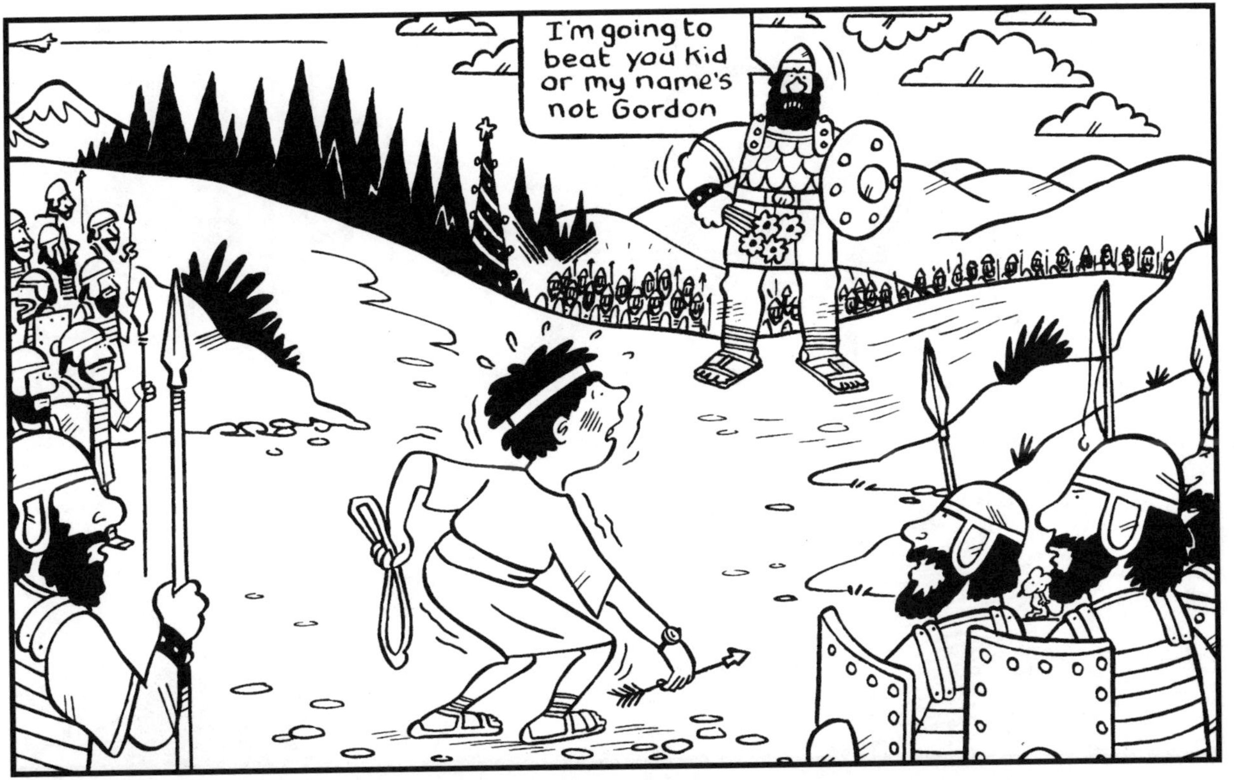

15

AUGUST

Matthew was a greedy tax-collector, but Jesus told him to follow him too. Can you find 12 money-bags hidden in this picture?

Read about the call of Matthew in Matthew 9:9.

Puzzle

21

MAY

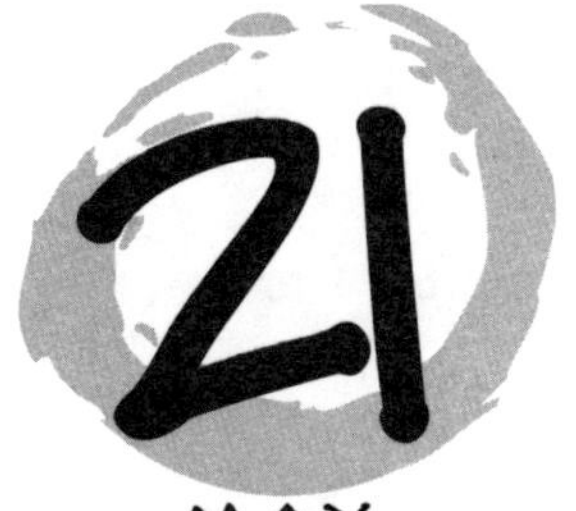

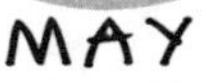

David wants to cross the River Jordan. Can you find the way he needs to go to cross to the other side?

Read about David crossing the River Jordan in 2 Samuel 19:15–18.

maze

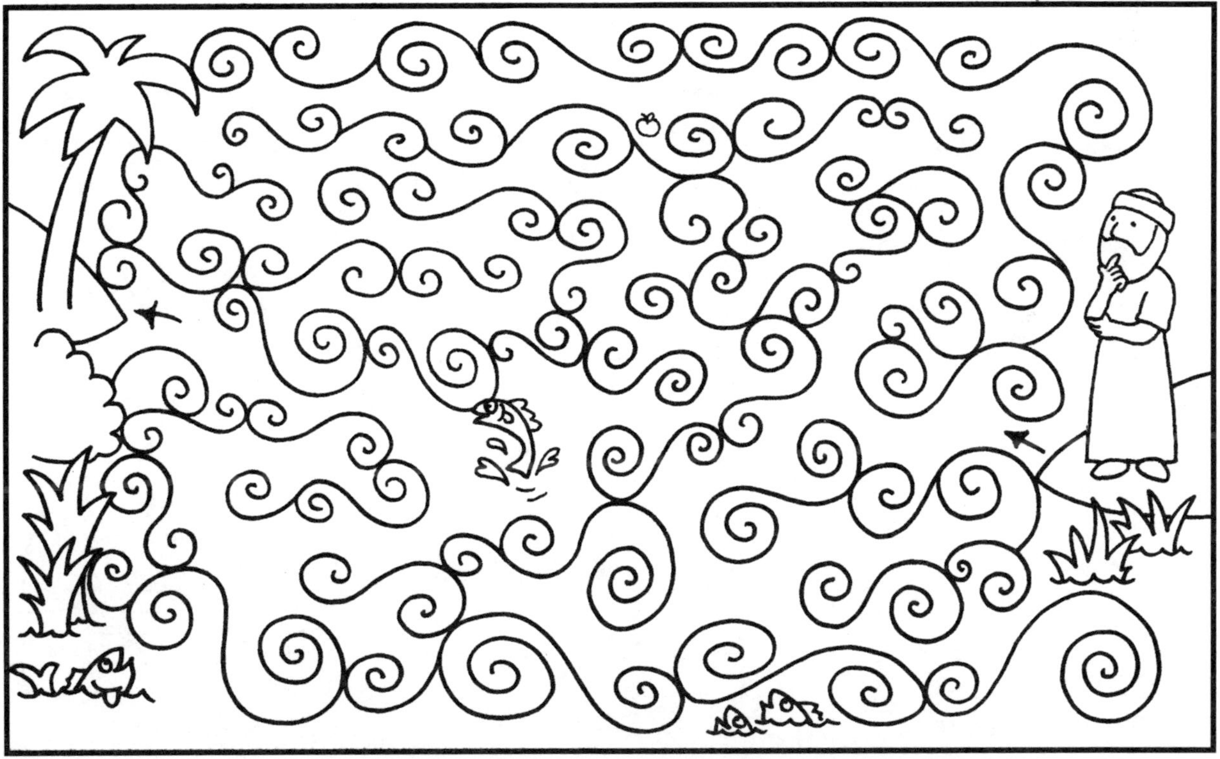

14

AUGUST

These pictures of Andrew and Peter on a fishing trip are in the wrong order.

Put them in the right order by numbering the little boxes from 1 to 6. Read Matthew 4:18–20.

Puzzle

22
MAY

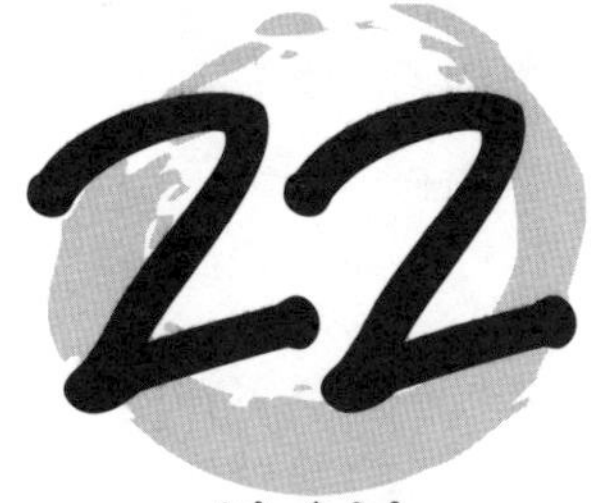

One day, David discovered King Saul asleep in a cave. Which path must David take to escape from Saul before he wakes up?

Read this story in 1 Samuel 24:1–22.

maze

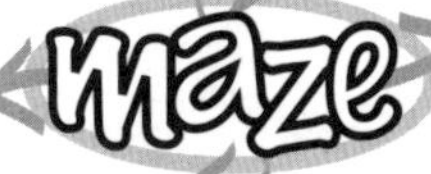

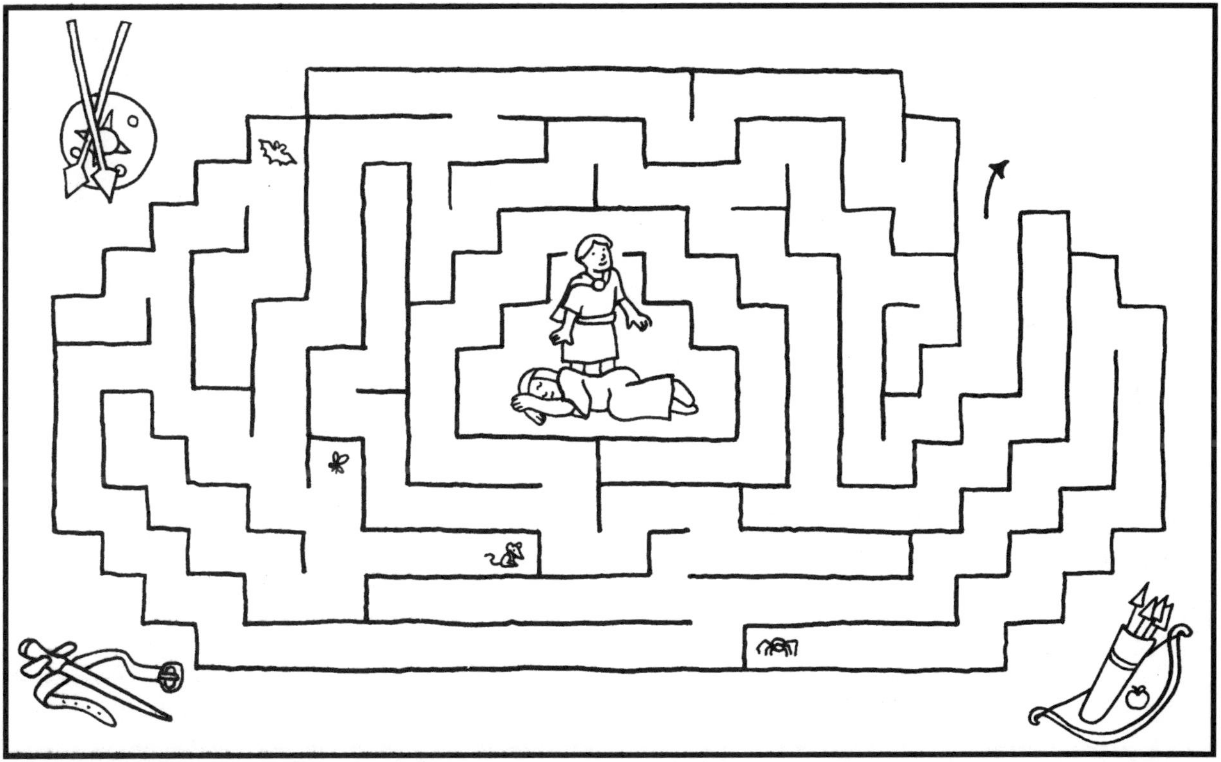

13

AUGUST

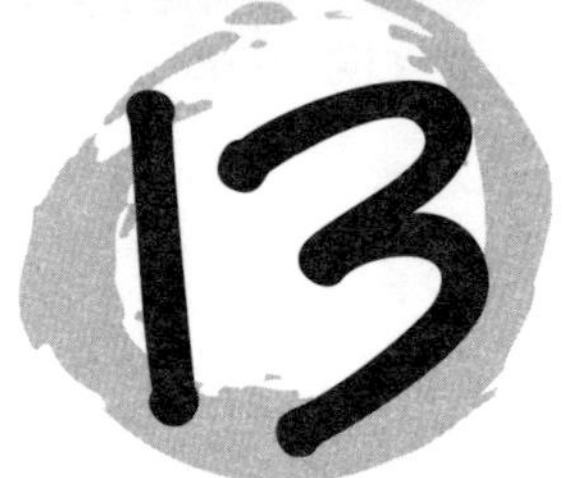

Here is a mystery picture. Shade the areas with dots in to find the hidden picture. What is it?

Read about Jesus' friends, who used one of these, in Matthew 4:18–20.

Puzzle

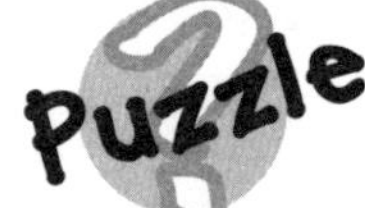

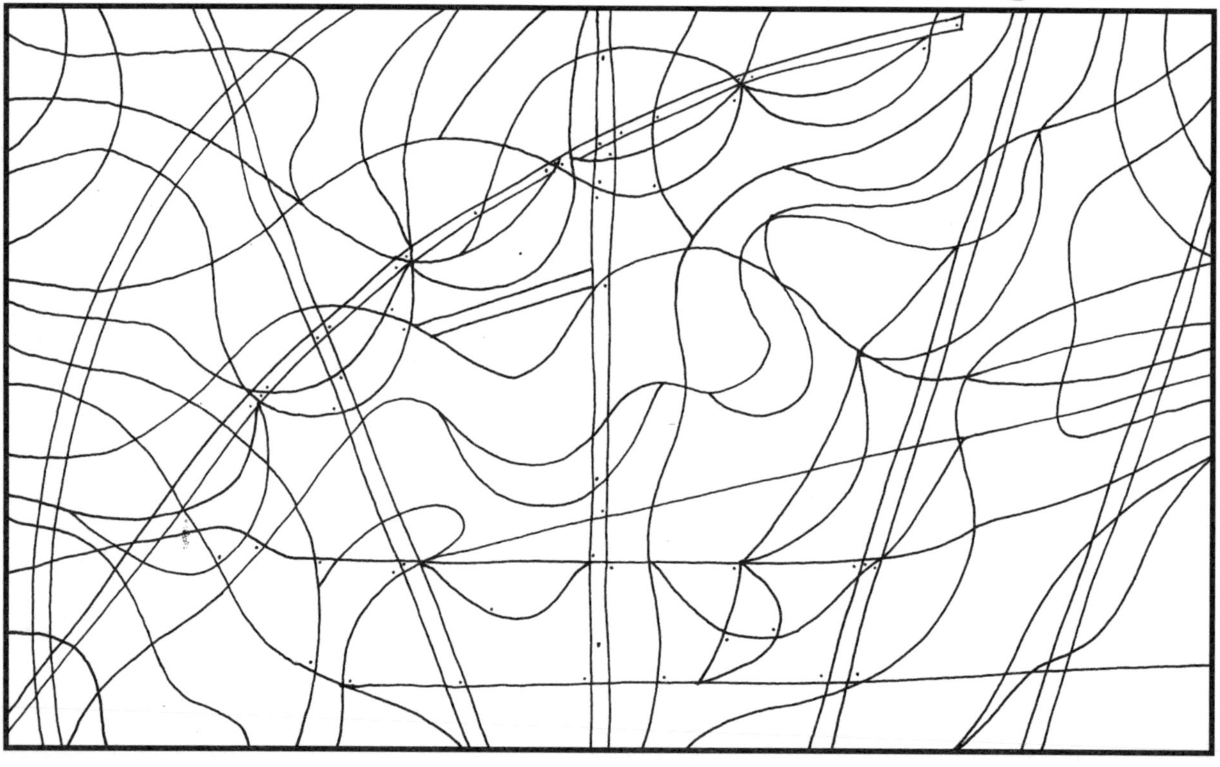

23 MAY

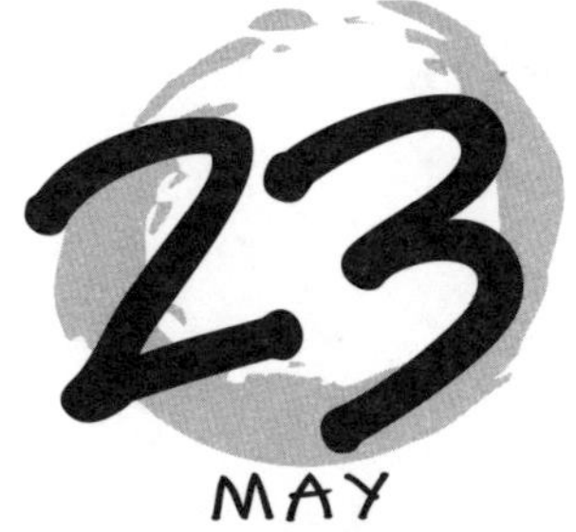

David has found King Saul asleep in a cave. Draw in the sleeping king, then color the picture.

You can read this story in 1 Samuel 24:1–7.

Draw me!

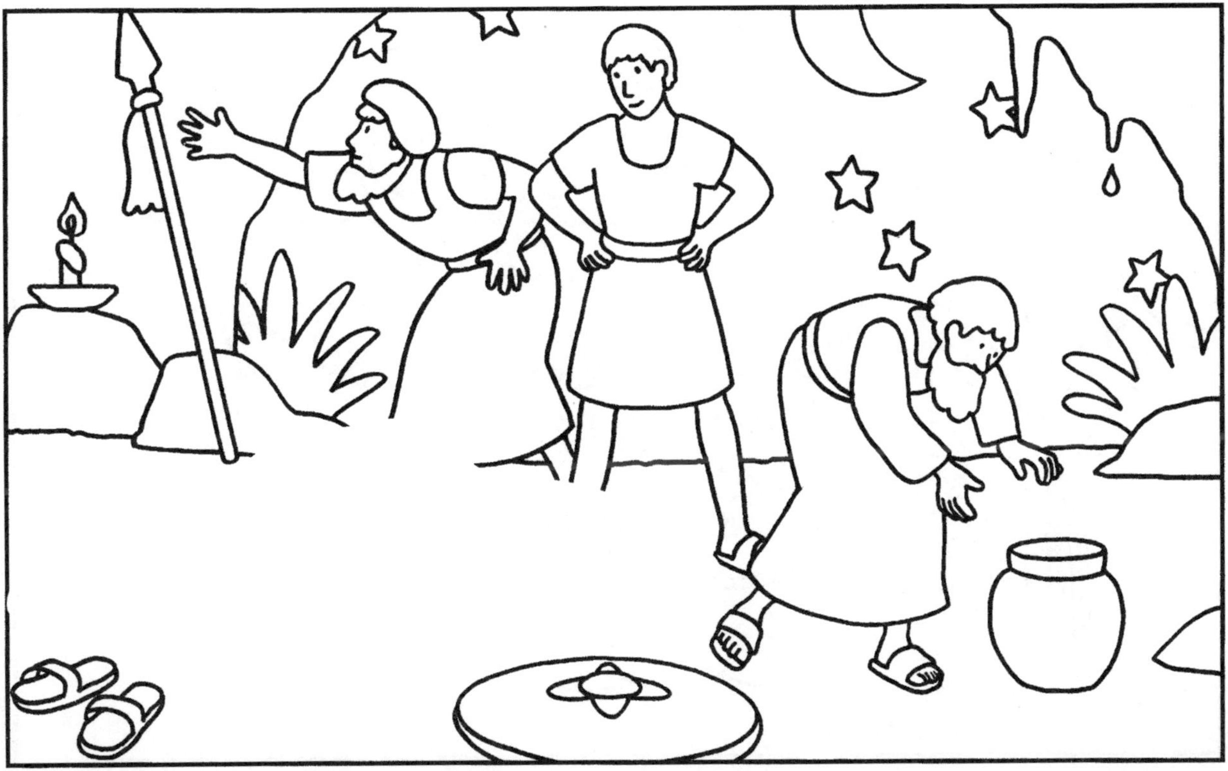

12

AUGUST

In this picture of Jesus calling fishermen to follow him, the artist has made lots of mistakes. List them.

Read this story in Matthew 4:18–20.
Did they have radios in Jesus' time?

Puzzle

24

MAY

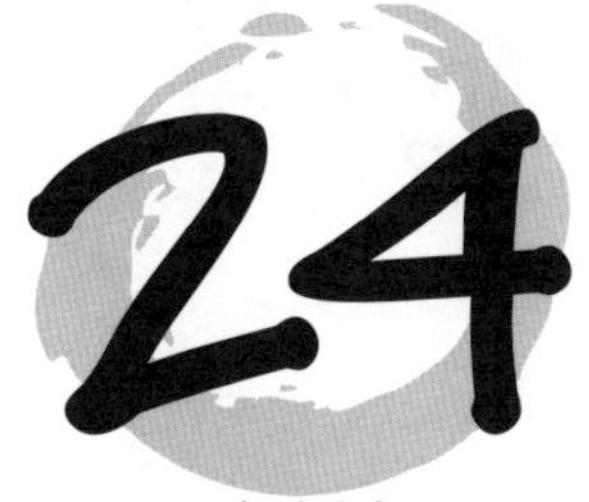

When David became king, he ordered the priests to bring something special to Jerusalem. Join up the dots to find out what it was.

Now read this story in 2 Samuel 6:12–15.

DOT-TO-DOT

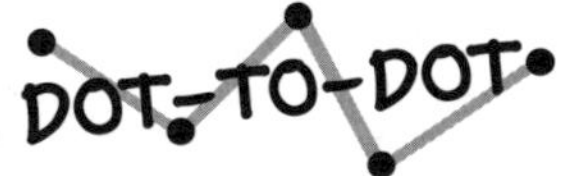

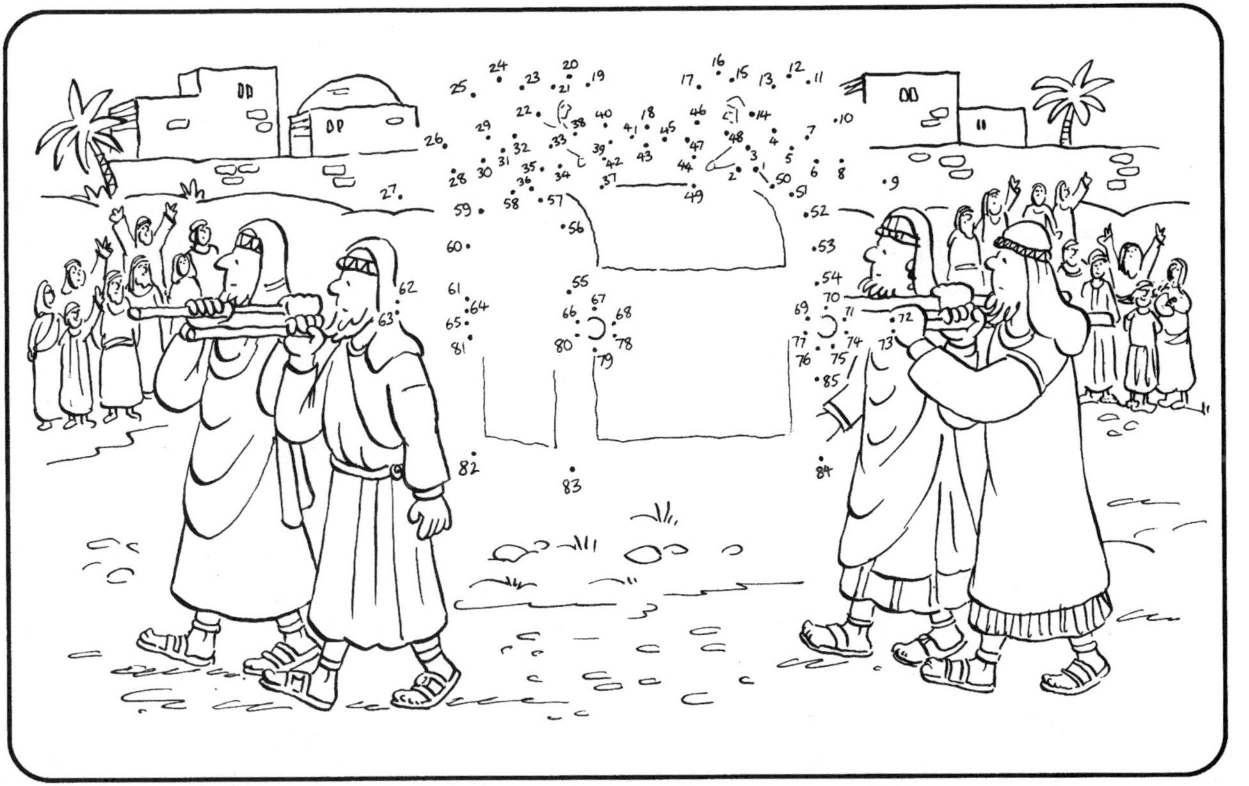

11

AUGUST

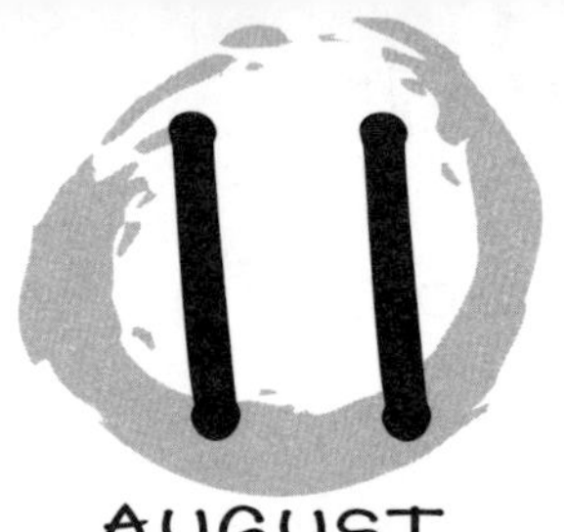

Here are some of Jesus' fisherman friends.
Which fisherman caught the most fish?
Follow the lines to the nets.

Read about Jesus' fisherman friends in Matthew 4:18–20.

Puzzle

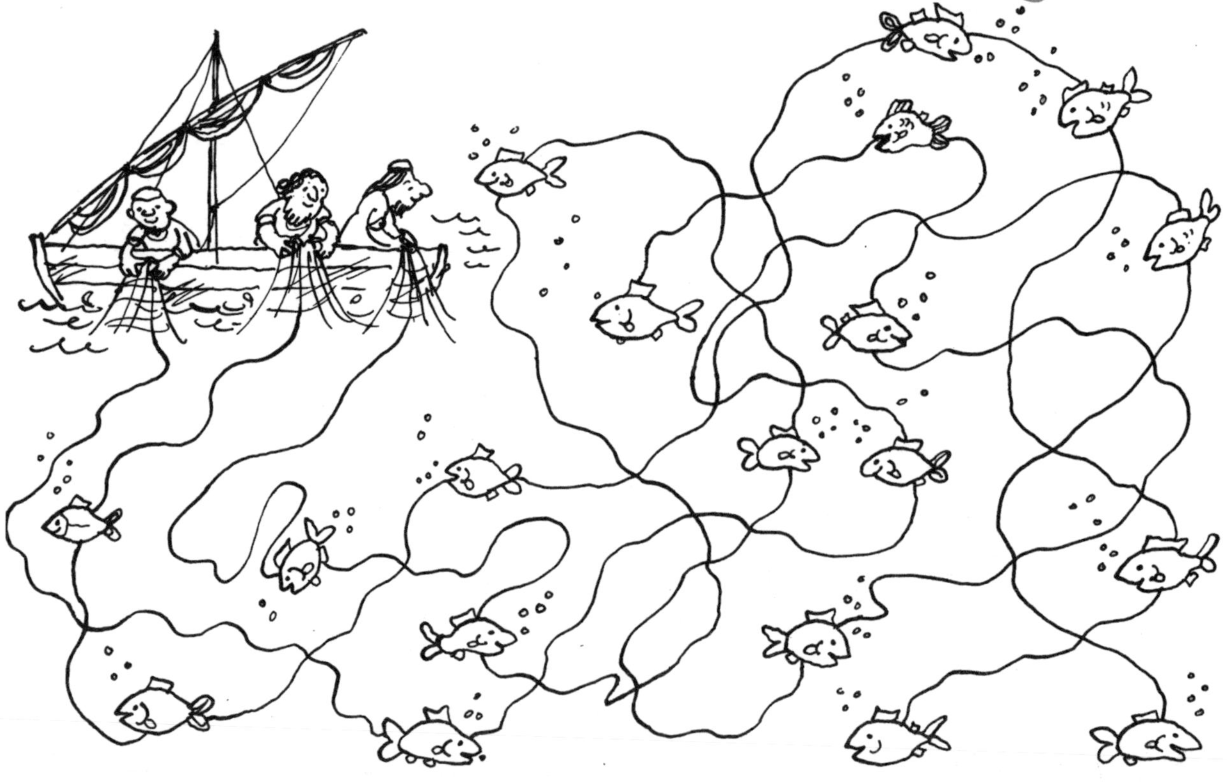

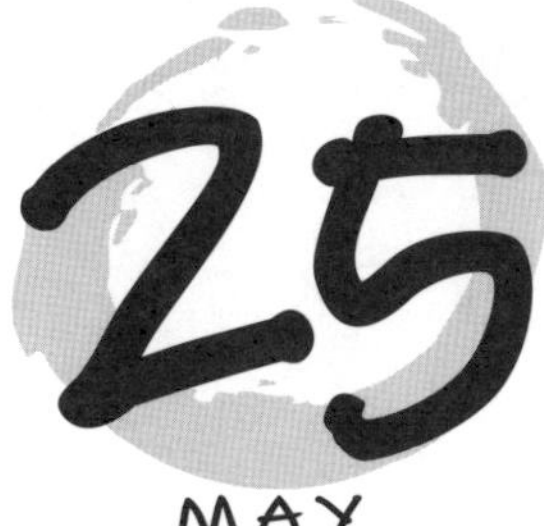

25

MAY

Princess Michal was very cross when she saw David dancing wildly in front of the Ark of the Covenant. Find 6 raisin cakes hidden in the picture.

Read this story in 2 Samuel 6:16–22.

Puzzle

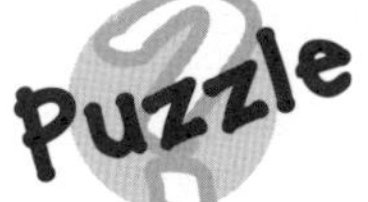

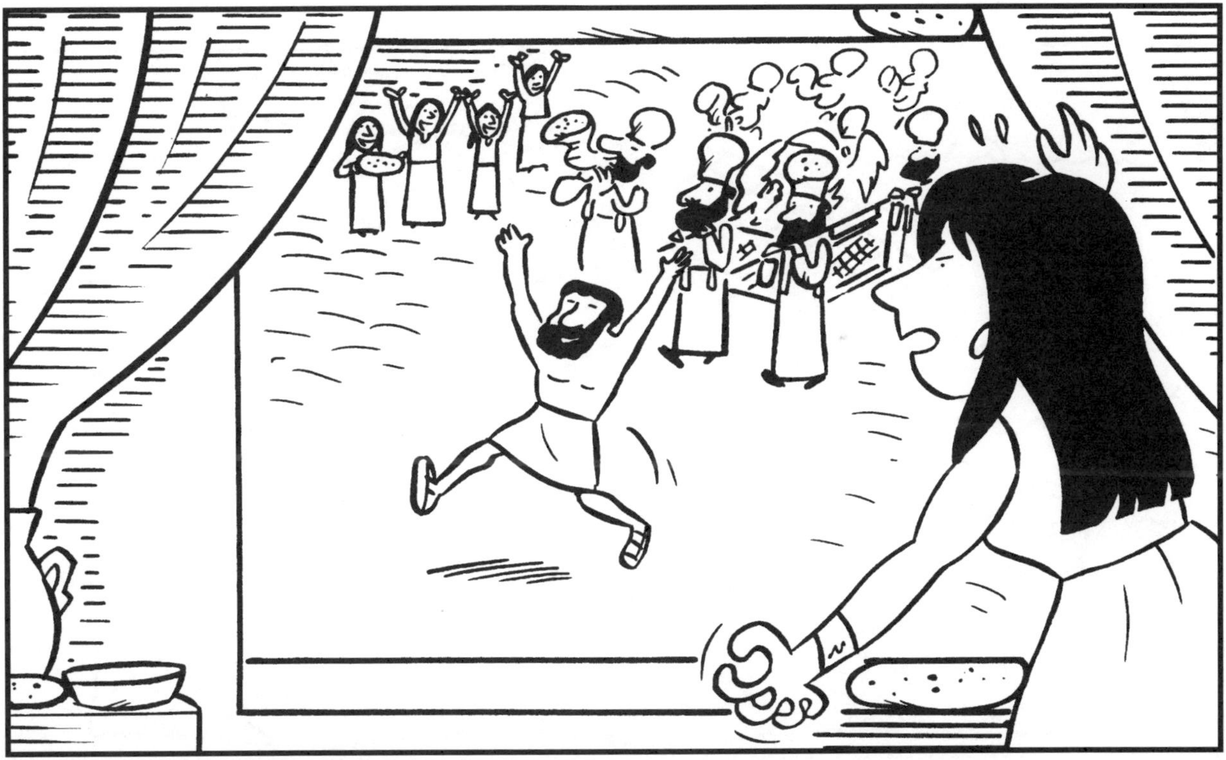

10 AUGUST

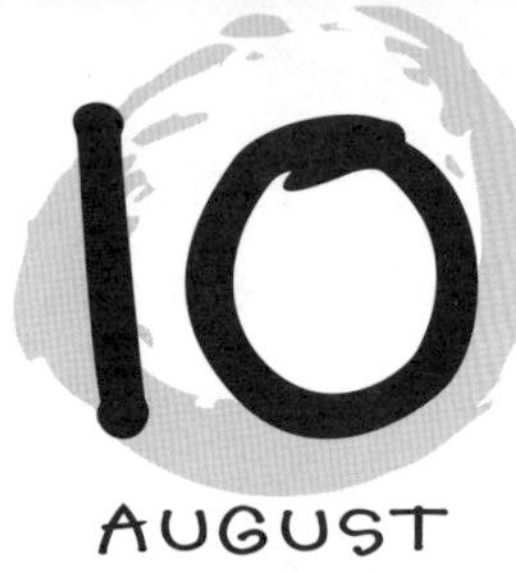

Jesus' special friends, James and John, were fishermen, as well as Peter and Andrew. Can you find the fishes' way through the broken net to the other side?

See Luke 5:1–11.

maze

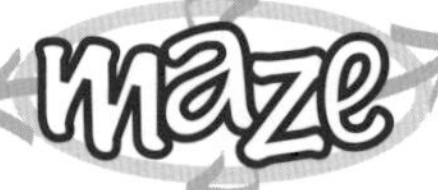

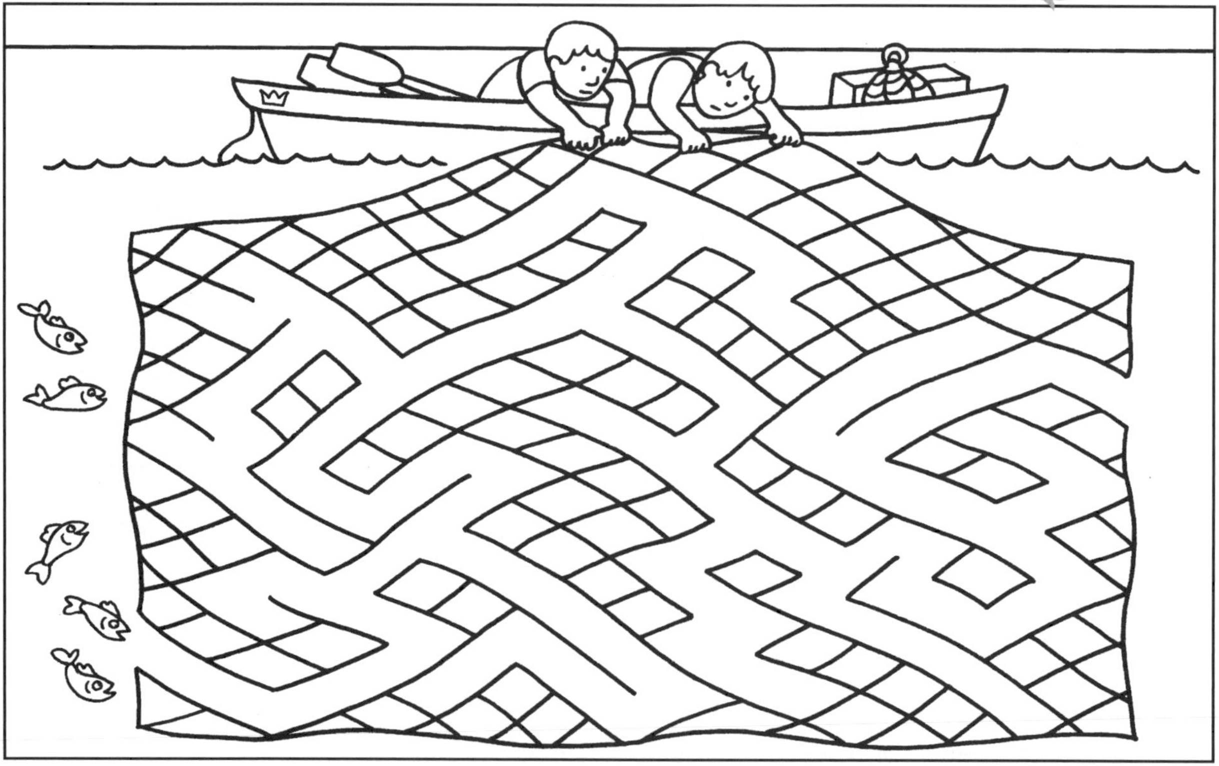

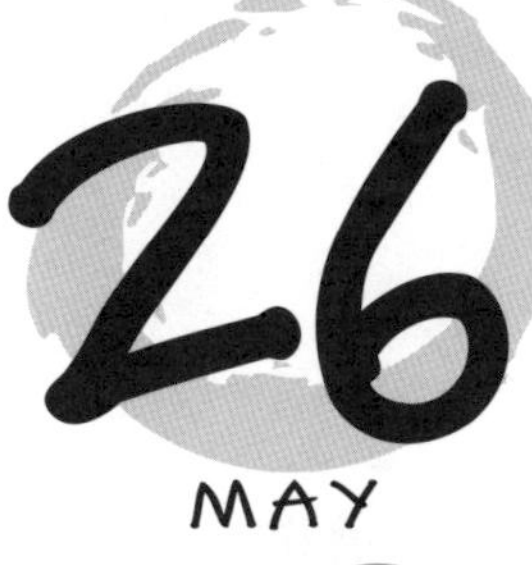

26
MAY

David's son Absalom rebeled against his father. He caught his hair in a tree while he was running away.

You can read this story in 2 Samuel 18:1–17.
Draw two soldiers in the empty space.

Draw me!

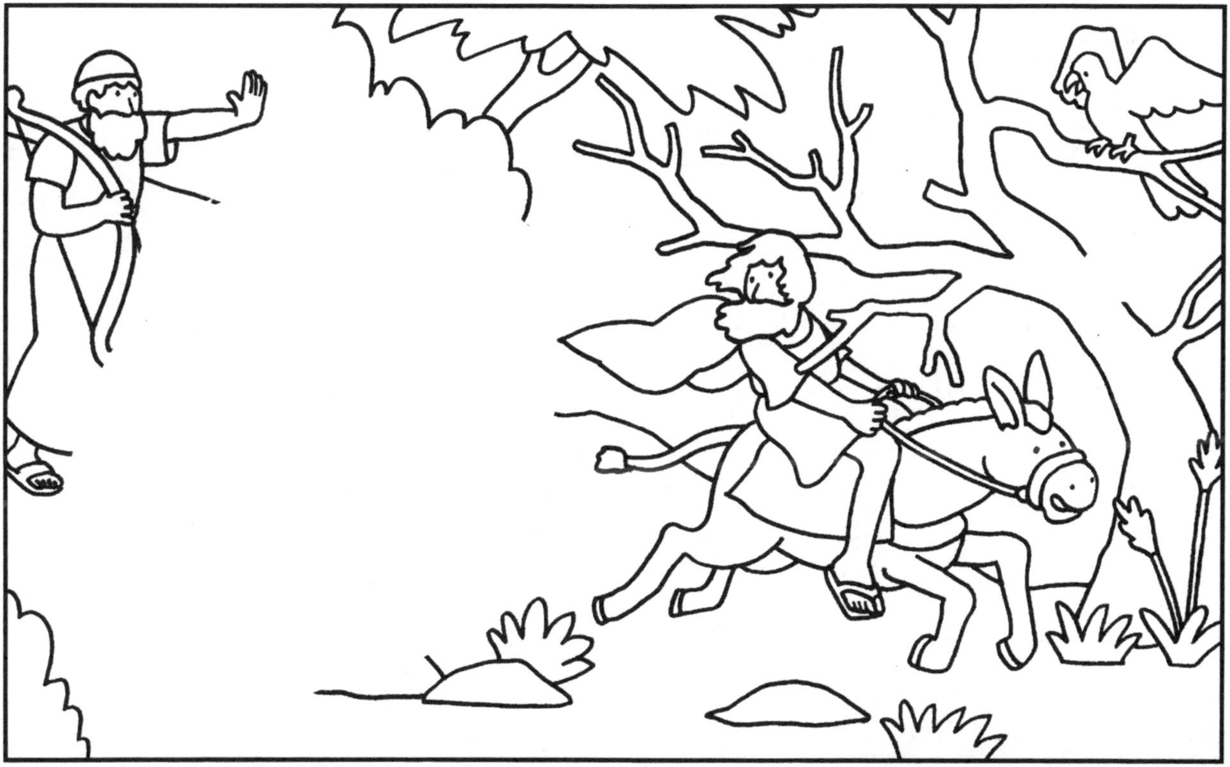

9

AUGUST

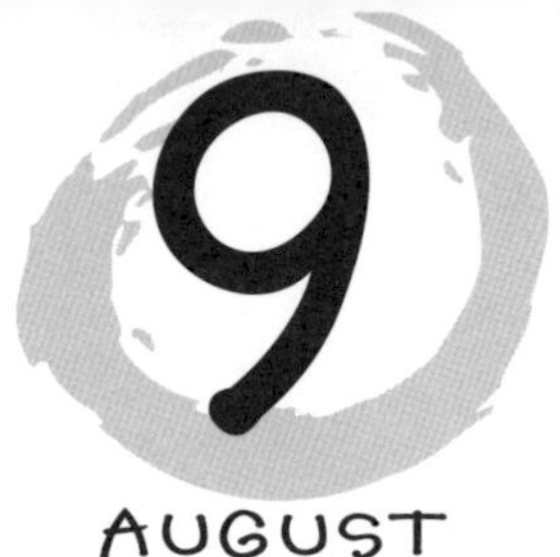

Peter and Andrew were fishermen when Jesus called them to follow him. They fished in the Sea of Galilee.

Can you find 10 striped fish in this picture?
Read this story in Matthew 4:18–20.

Puzzle

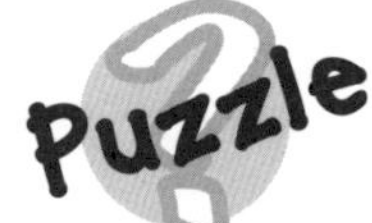

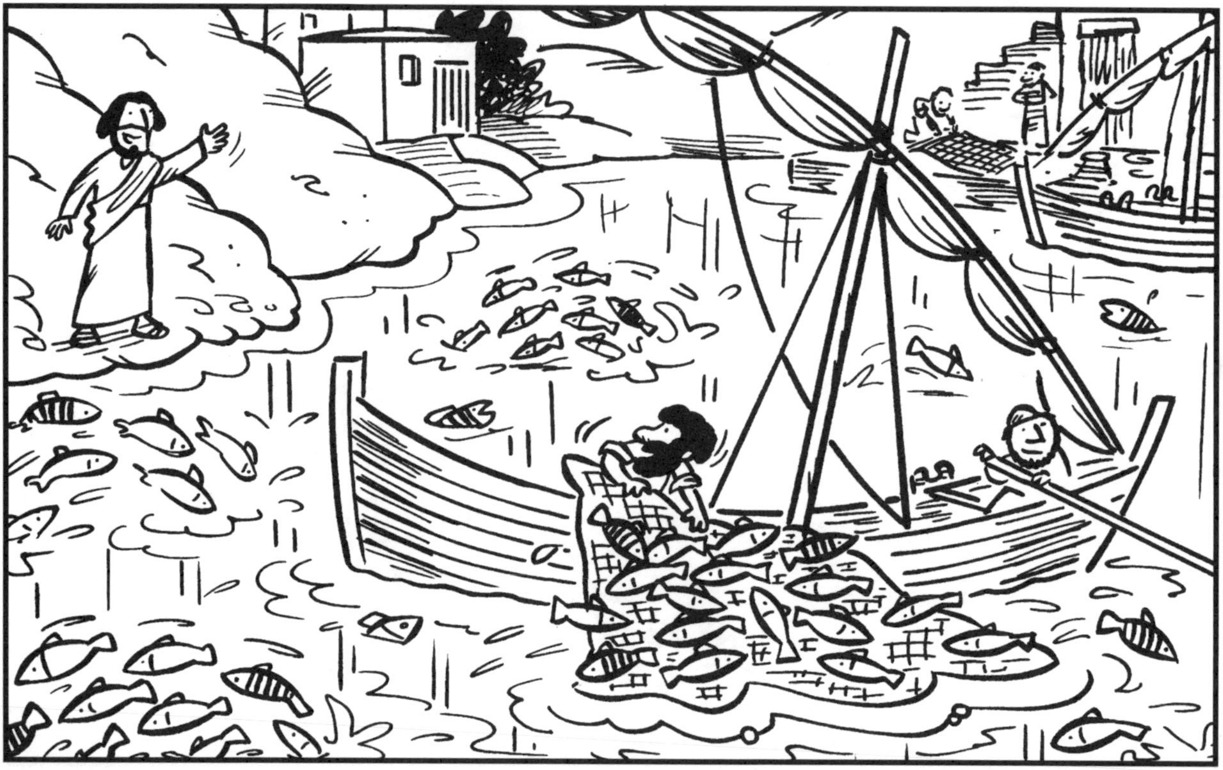

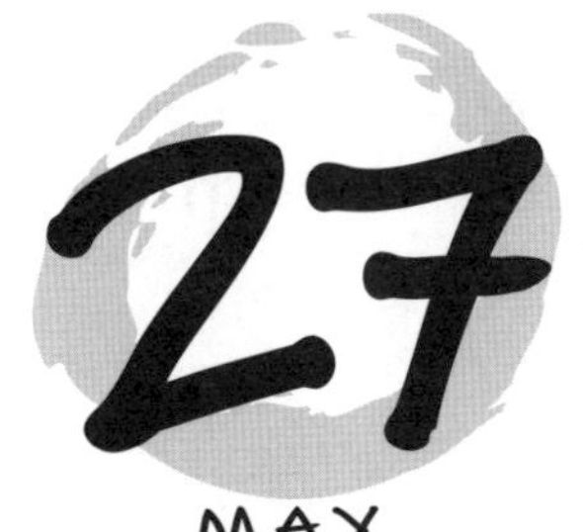

27 MAY

David's son Solomon built a magnificent Temple in Jerusalem. Can you find 10 cats hiding in this picture of the building of the Temple?

Read about the building of the Temple in 1 Kings 6.

Puzzle

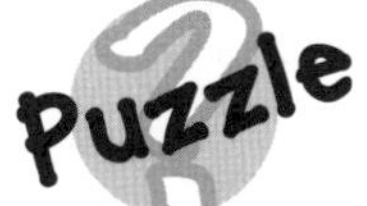

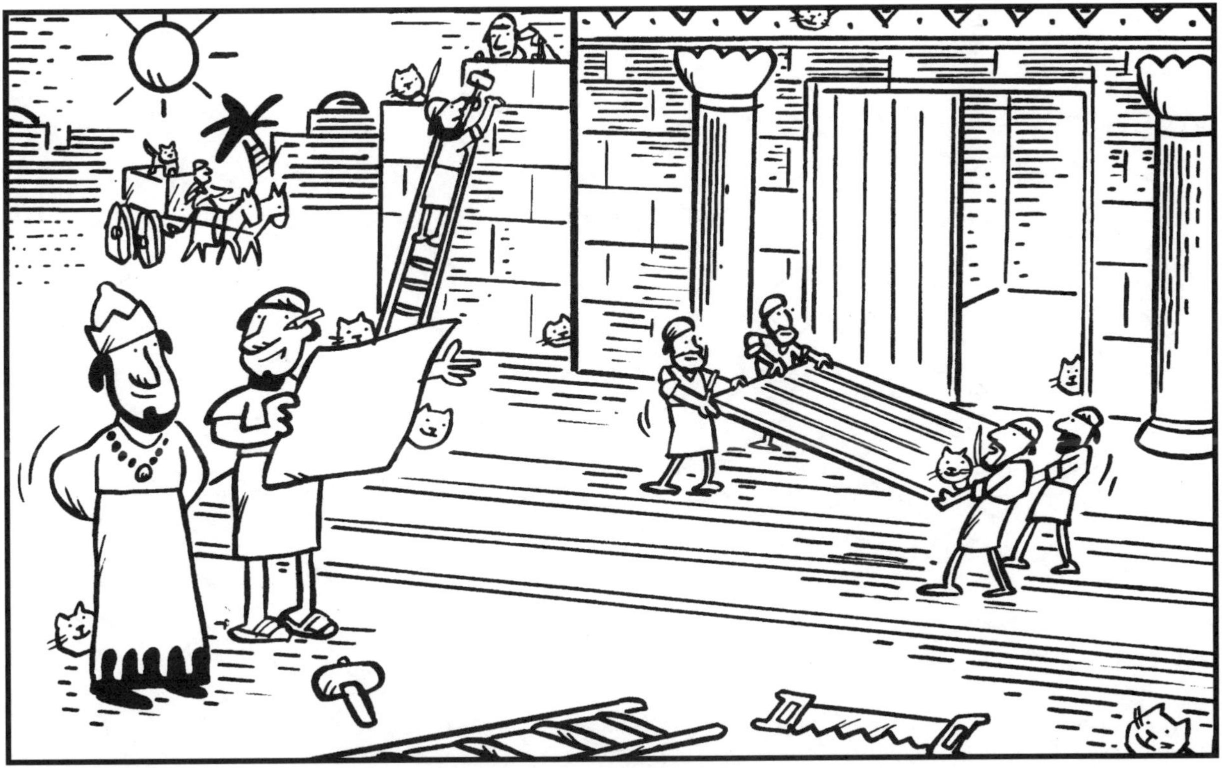

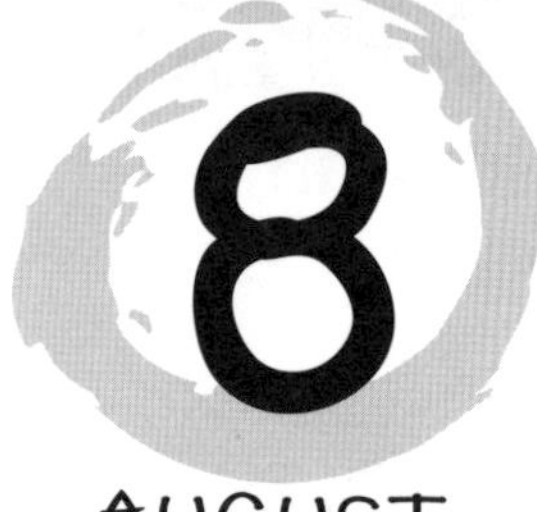

8
AUGUST

Jesus said to Peter and Andrew, 'Come with me and I will teach you to catch men.' Which path does Jesus need to take to bring him to Peter and Andrew?

Read this story in Matthew 4:18–20.

maze

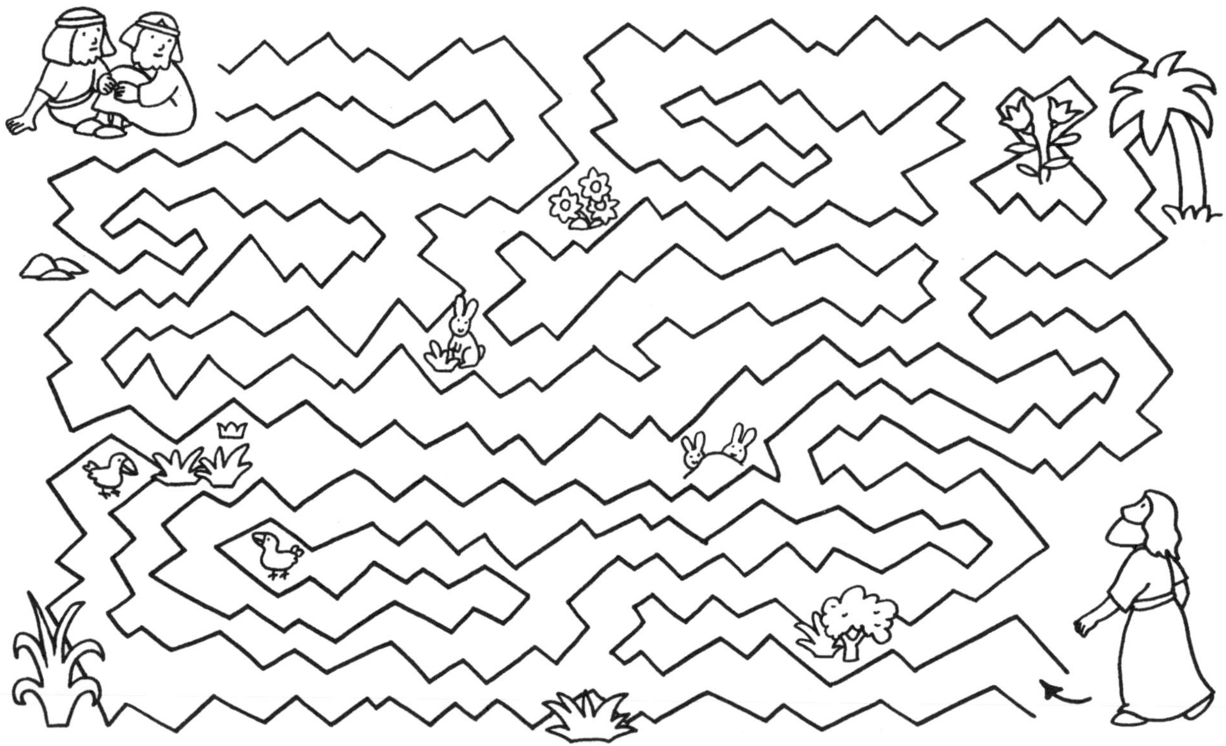

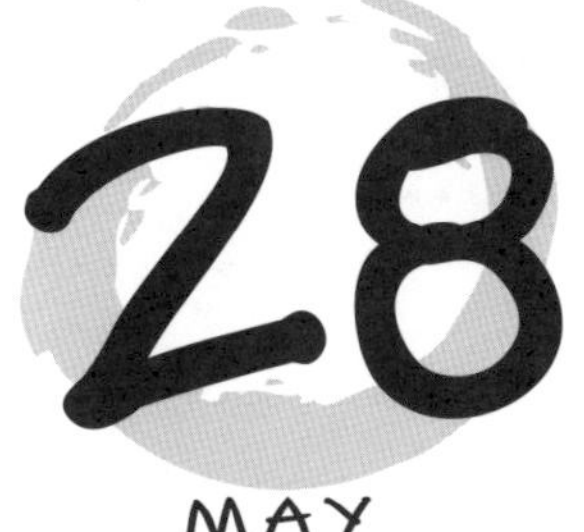

28
MAY

The Queen of Sheba came a long way to visit King Solomon, because she had heard that he was very wise. Find the path that will lead her to Solomon.

Read this story in 1 Kings 10:1–13.

maze

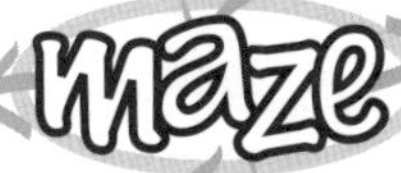

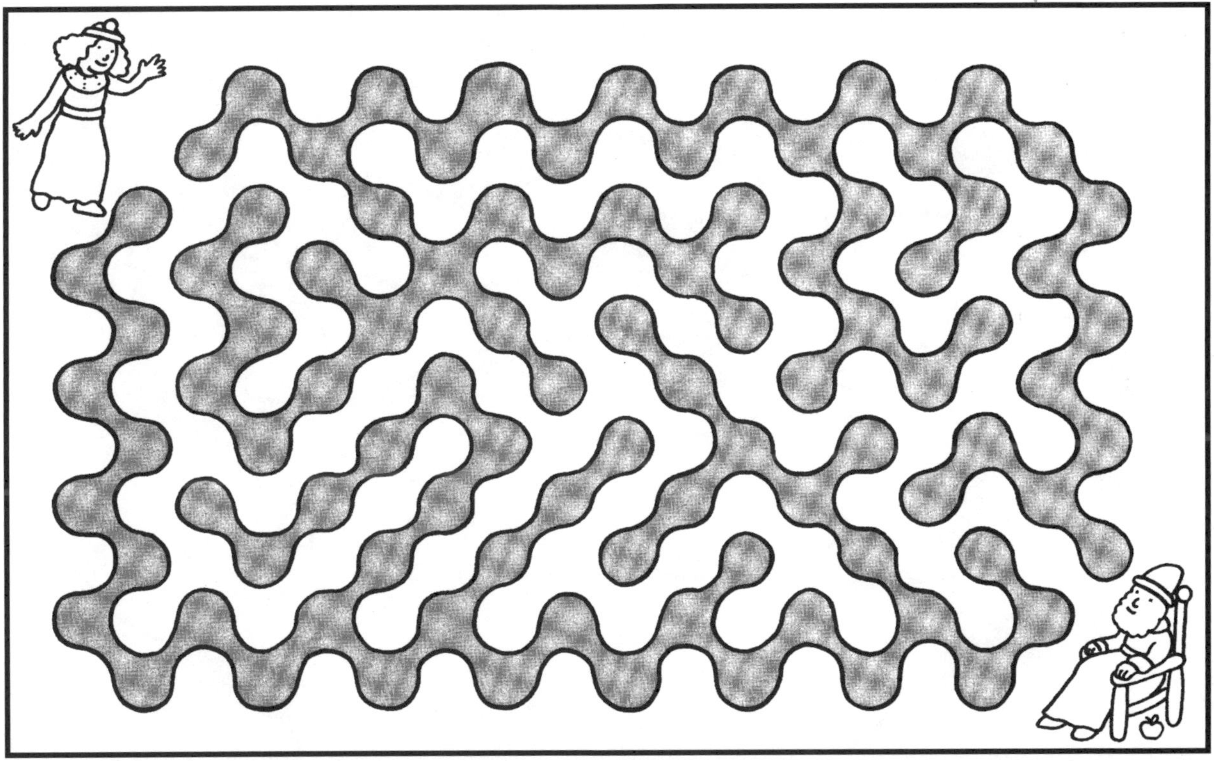

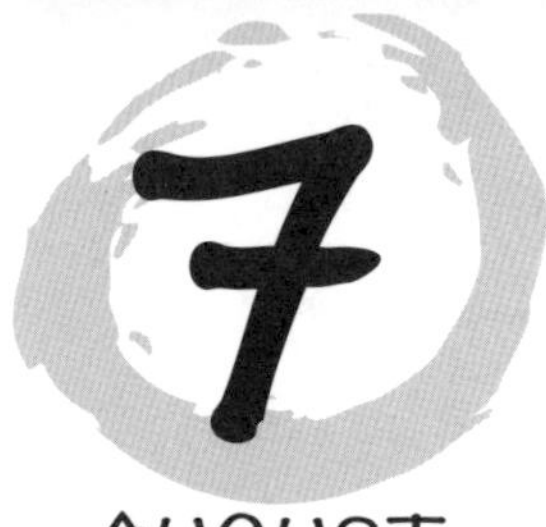

7
AUGUST

In this picture of Jesus and the woman at the well, the artist has made lots of mistakes.

Some are easy.
For others, you will need to check the story in John 4:1–26.

Puzzle

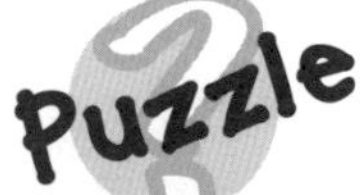

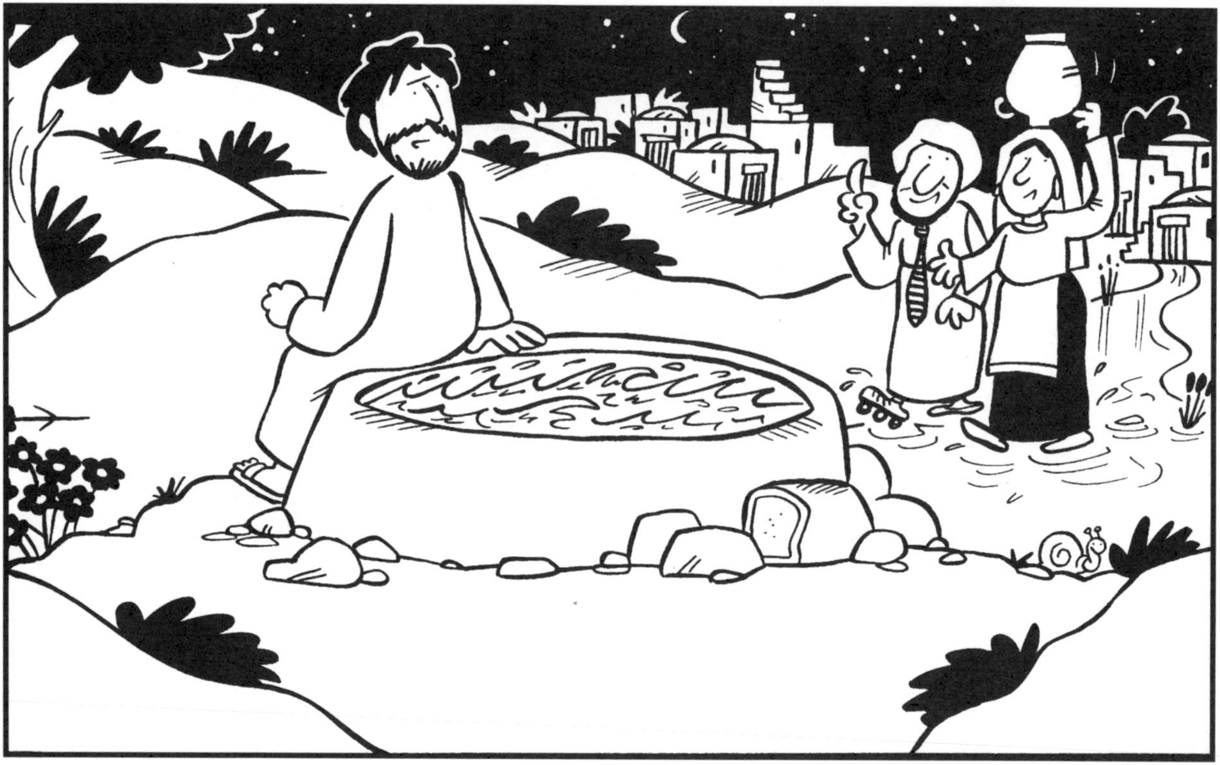

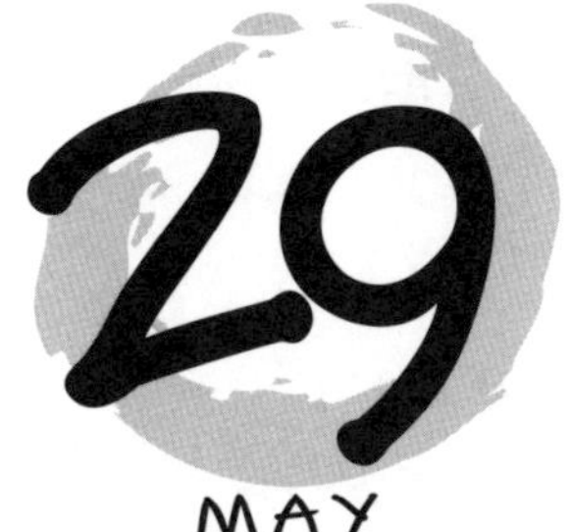

29
MAY

The Queen of Sheba wanted to discover if Solomon was as wise as people claimed.

Can you find 6 crowns hidden in this picture?
Read this story in 1 Kings 10:1–13.

Puzzle

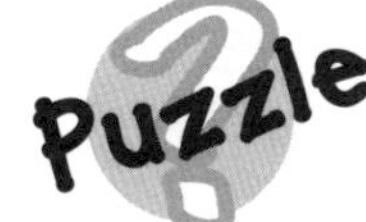

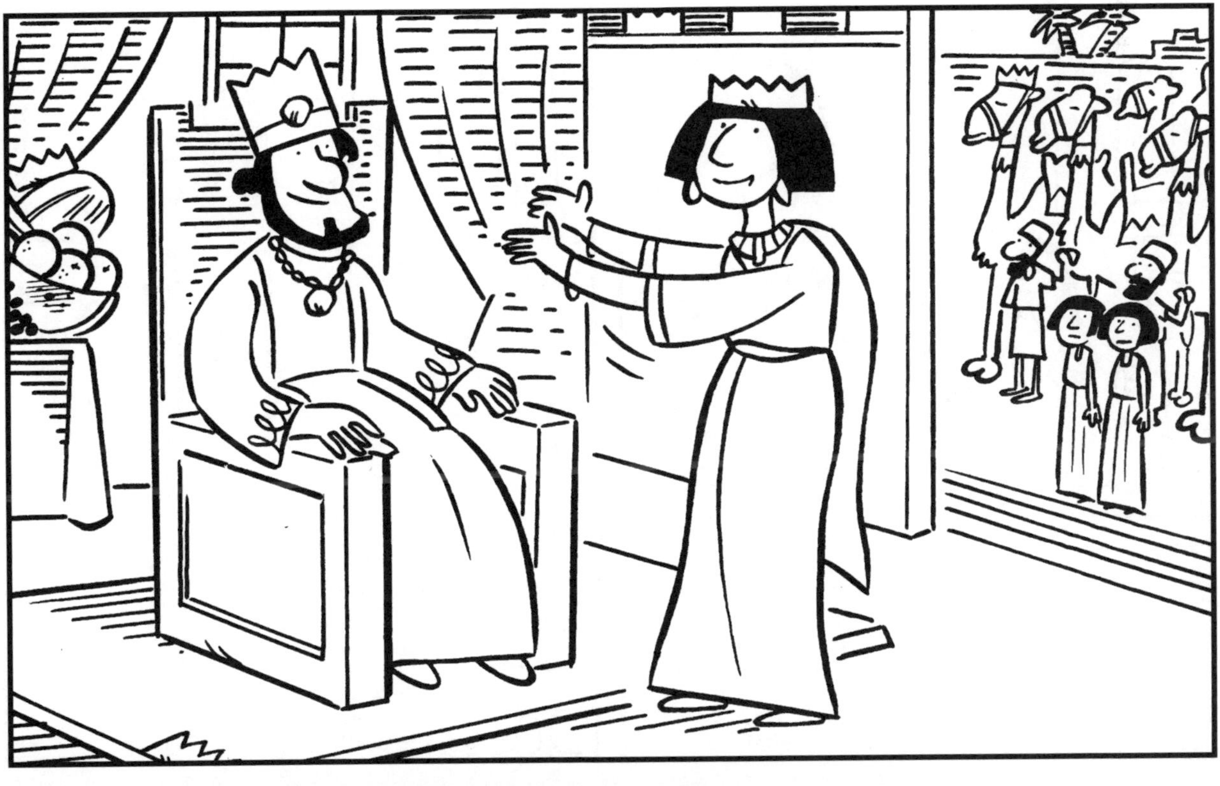

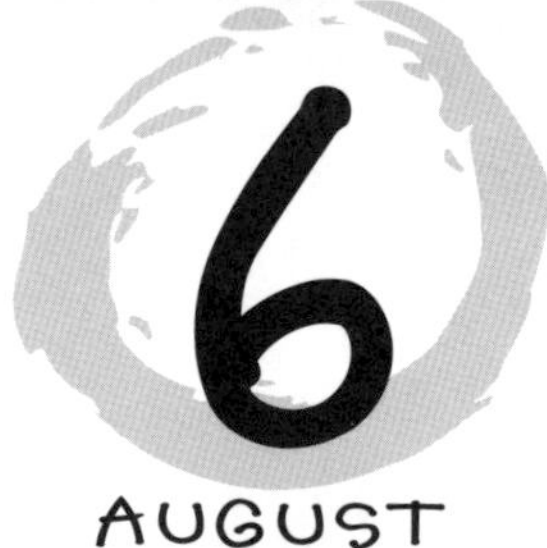

6
AUGUST

There are 10 differences between these two pictures of Jesus talking to the woman at the well.

Circle all the differences you can find. Have you got all 10? Read this story in John 4:1–26.

SPOT THE DIFFERENCE

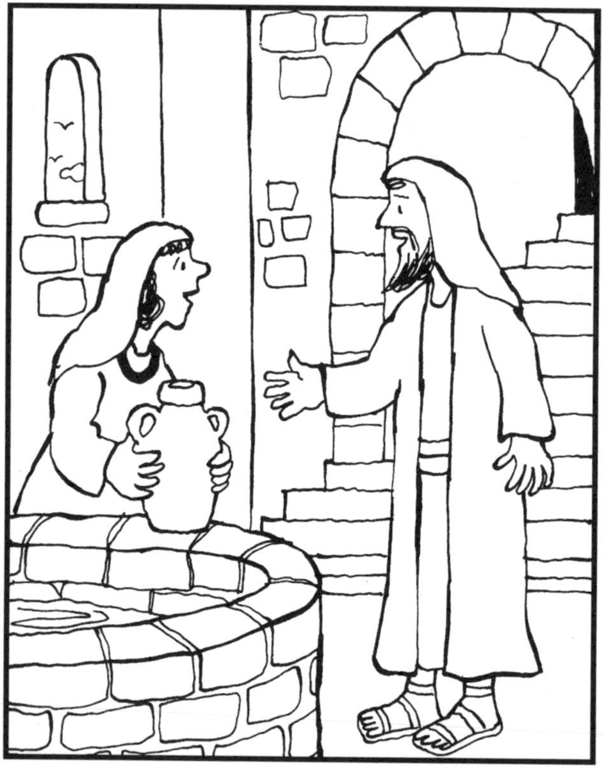

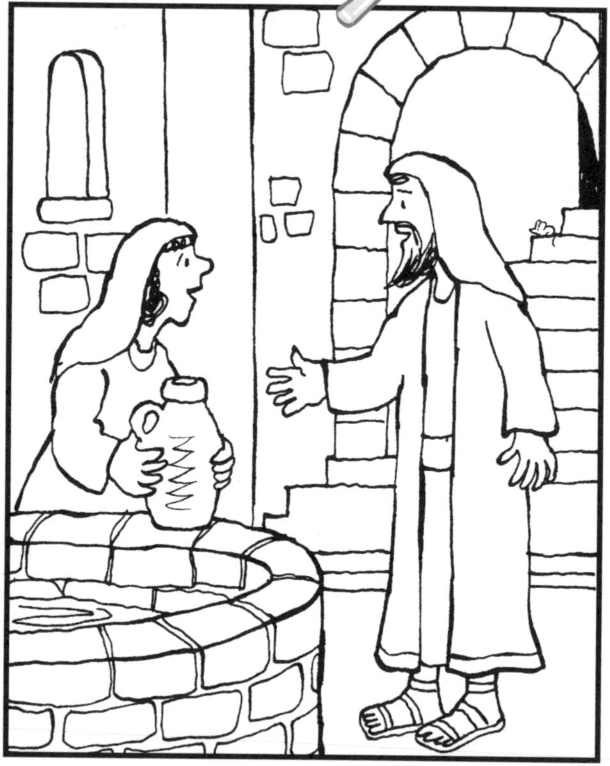

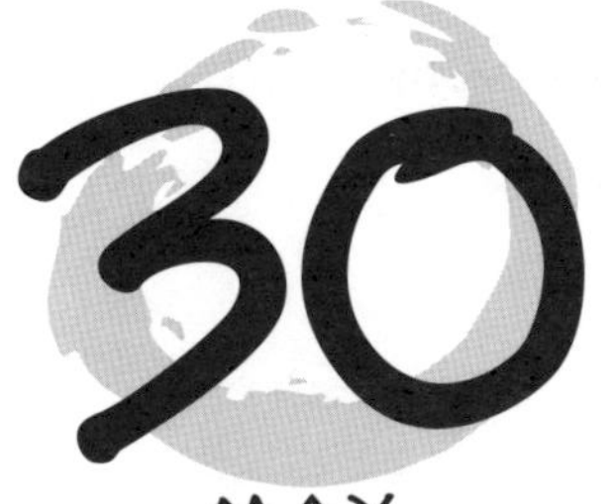

30 MAY

When she visited Solomon, the Queen of Sheba brought wonderful presents for him.

Find at least 10 deliberate mistakes in this picture of her visit.
Read this story in 1 Kings 10:1–13.

Puzzle

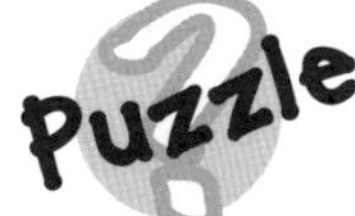

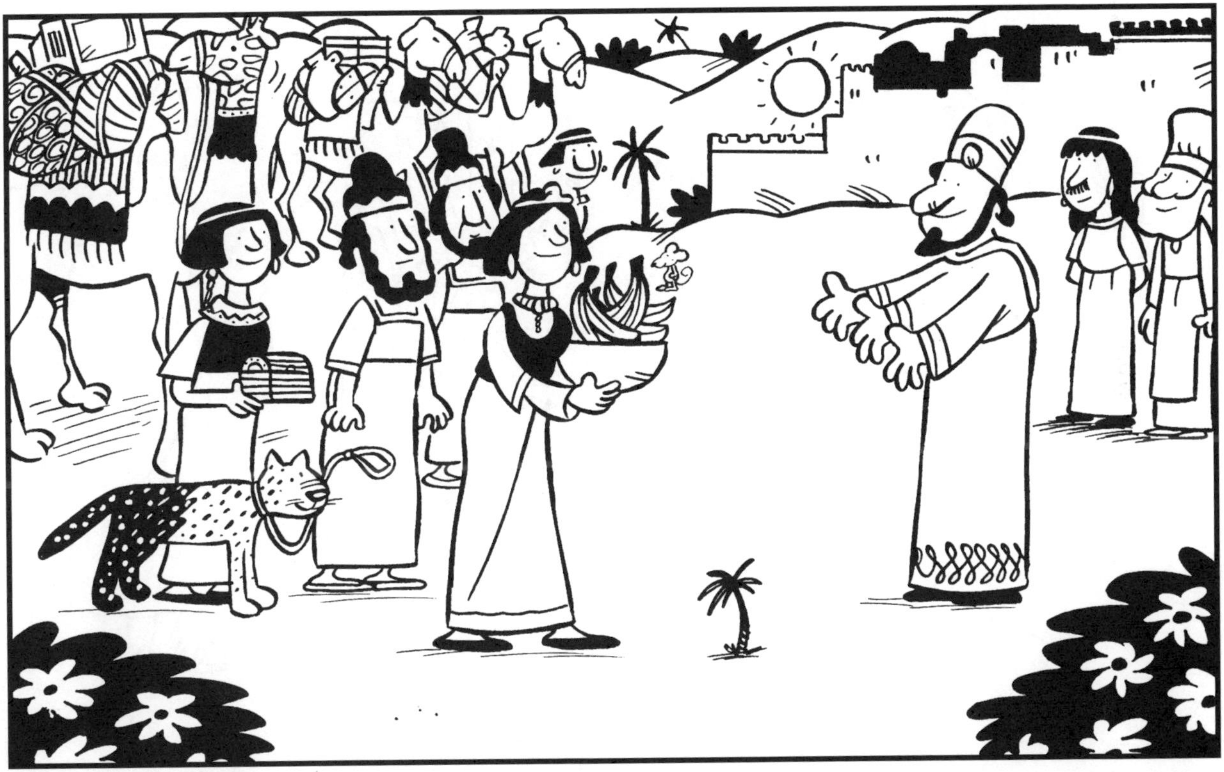

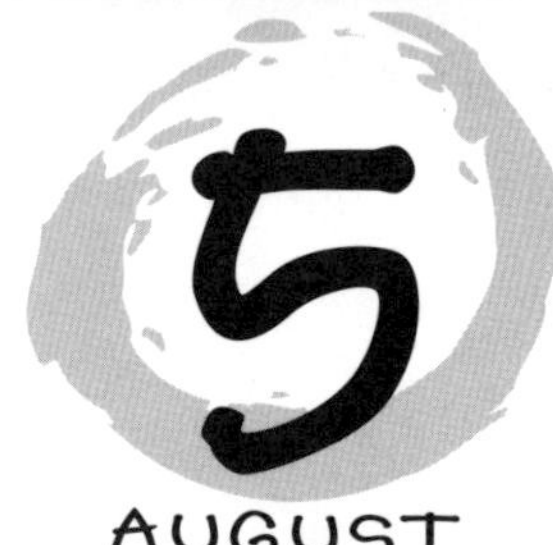

5 AUGUST

Join up the dots to find what the woman is holding and where she is standing.

Find out what Jesus said to her in John 4:1–26.
Where did this woman live?

DOT-TO-DOT

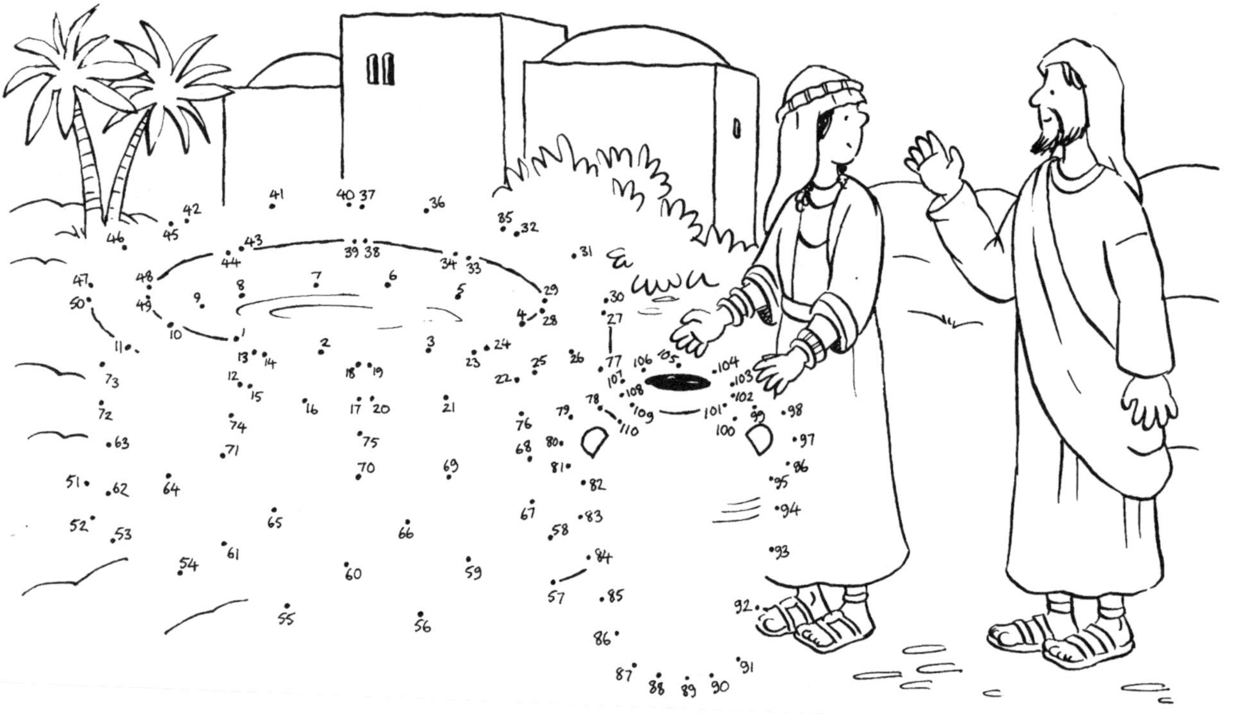

31 MAY

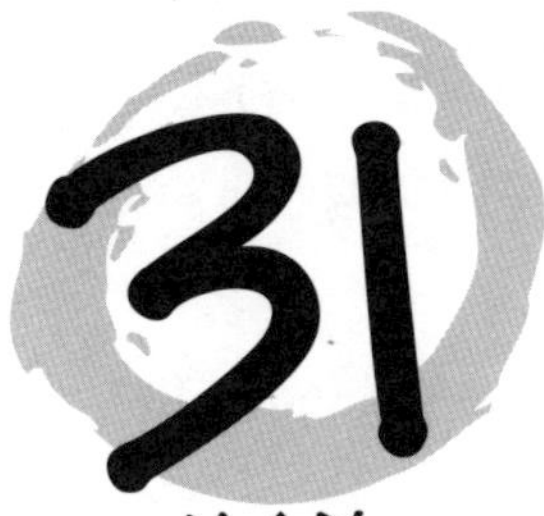

The prophet Elijah was alone in the desert, and was very hungry. Join up the dots to find out how he received food.

Read this story in 1 Kings 17:1–6

DOT-TO-DOT

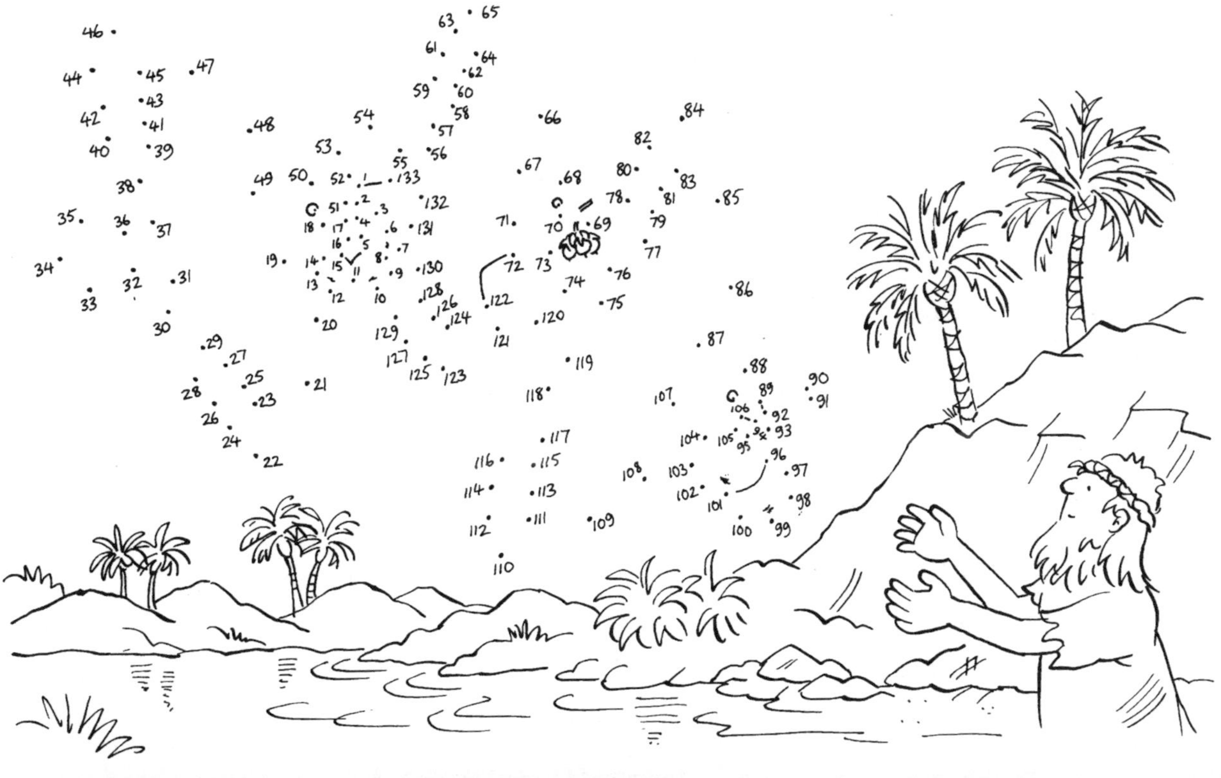

4

AUGUST

Jesus met a woman at a well in Samaria and asked her for water. He said he could give her everlasting water.

Can you find the path that will lead the woman with the pot to the well? Read this story in John 4:1–26.

maze

JUNE 1

The artist has made lots of deliberate mistakes in this picture of Elijah being fed in the desert.

Put a circle around all the mistakes you can find. How many did you discover? Read the story in 1 Kings 17:1–6.

Puzzle

3

AUGUST

One night a man called Nicodemus visited Jesus to ask him how to love God. Help Nicodemus find the path to bring him to Jesus.

Read what they talked about in John 3:1–16.

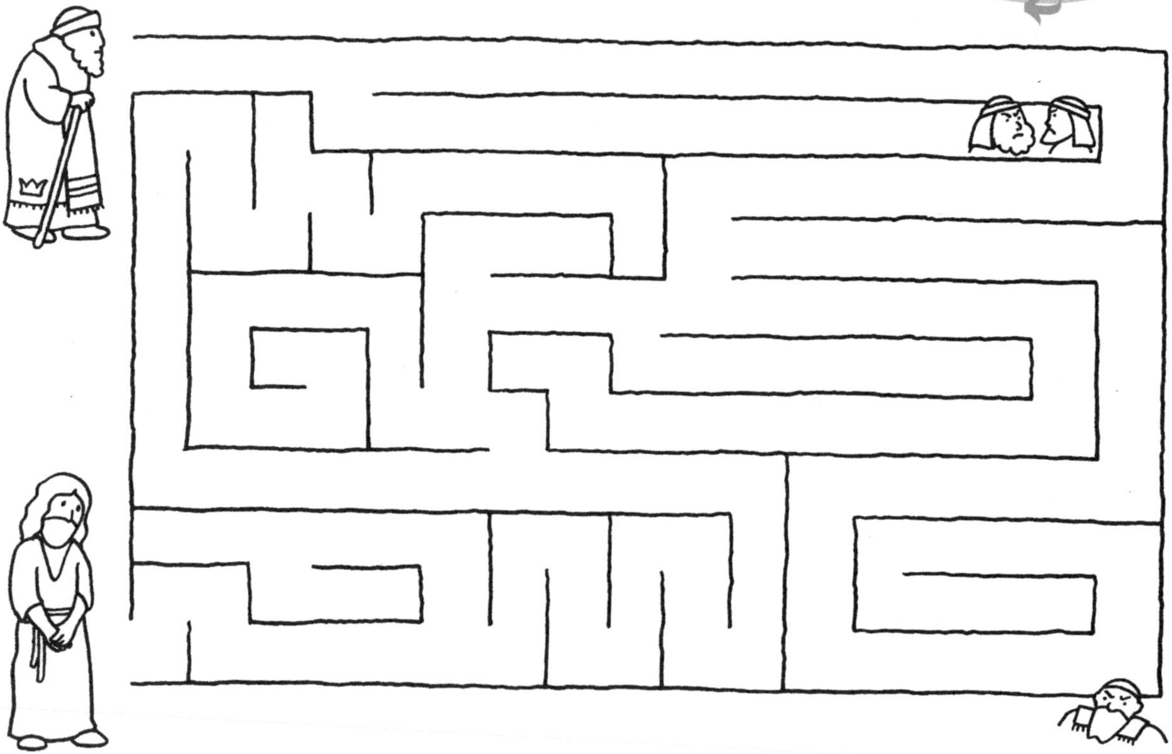

maze

2

JUNE

Elijah built a stone altar and put an ox on it to sacrifice. Join the dots and you'll discover what Elijah asked God to send down on the altar.

See 1 Kings 18:16–39.

DOT-TO-DOT

2
AUGUST

In this picture of Jesus' miracle at Cana, the artist has deliberately made some silly mistakes.

Circle all the mistakes you can find. How many have you spotted? Read this story in John 2:1–11.

Puzzle

3
JUNE

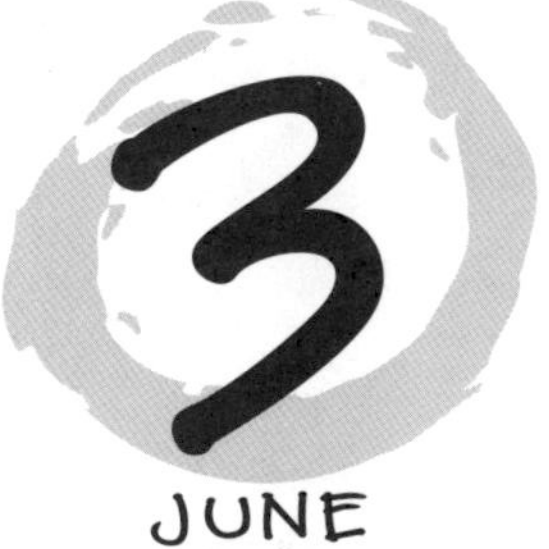

During the time of the prophet Elijah, King Ahab ruled Israel. His wife was the wicked Queen Jezebel. Find 9 hairbrushes hidden in this picture.

You can read about Ahab and Jezebel in 1 Kings 21.

Puzzle

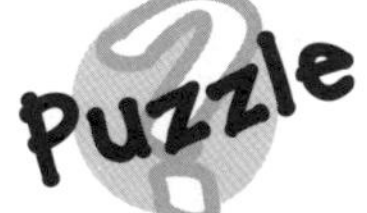

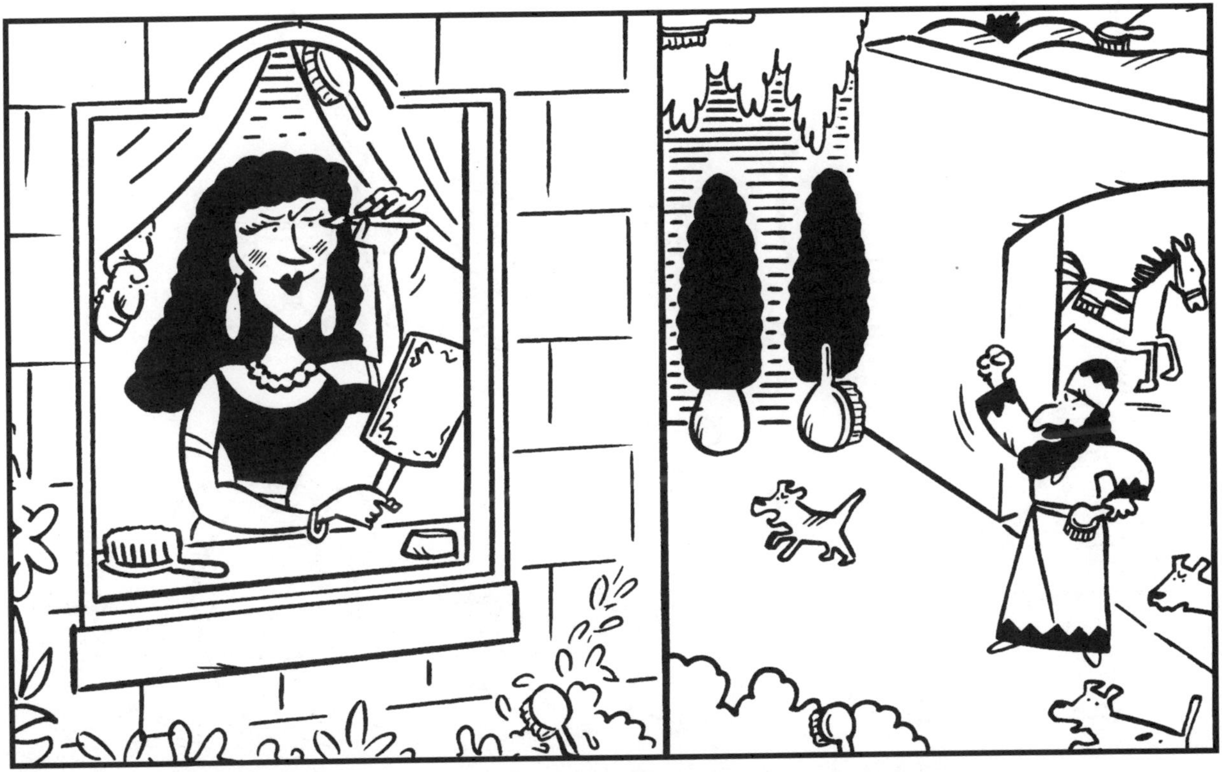

1

AUGUST

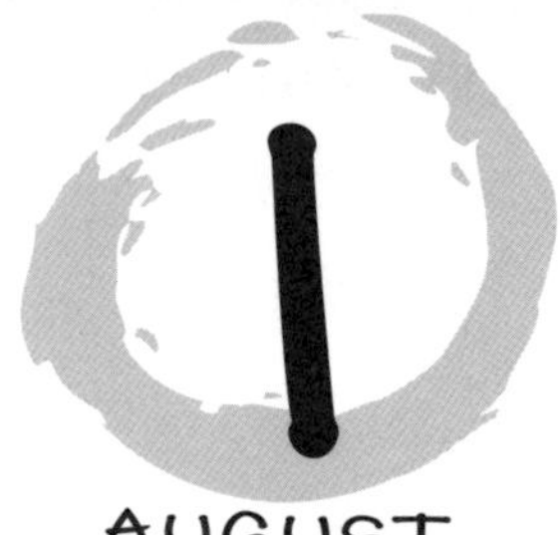

Here are five drawings of wine cups and a jar. Which ones are just the same?

Read the story of Jesus turning water into wine in John 2:1–11.

Puzzle

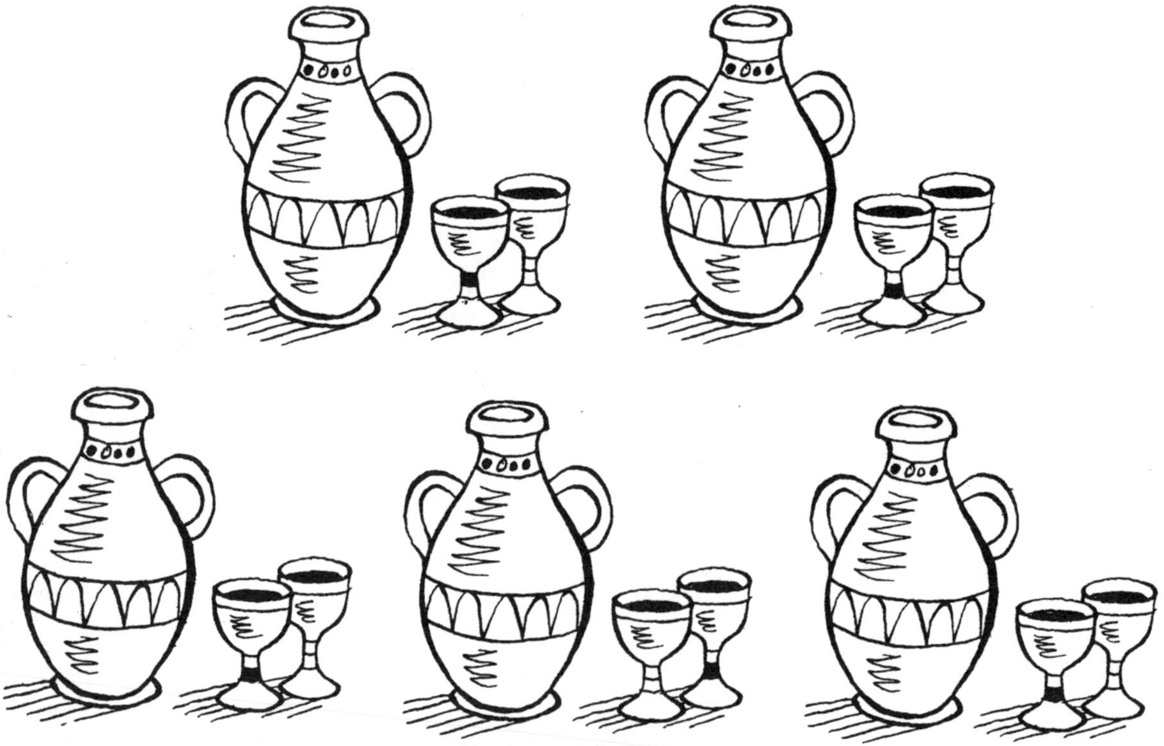

4 JUNE

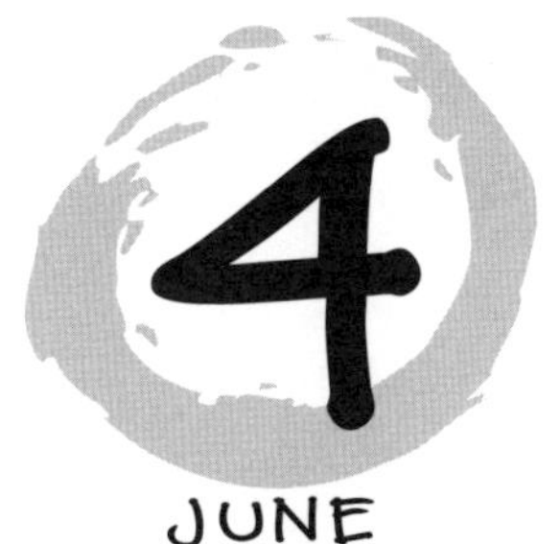

King Ahab decided that he wanted to have a vineyard that belonged to a man called Naboth.

Find 9 bunches of grapes in this picture.
Read this story in 1 Kings 21.

Puzzle

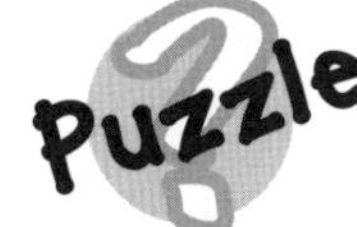

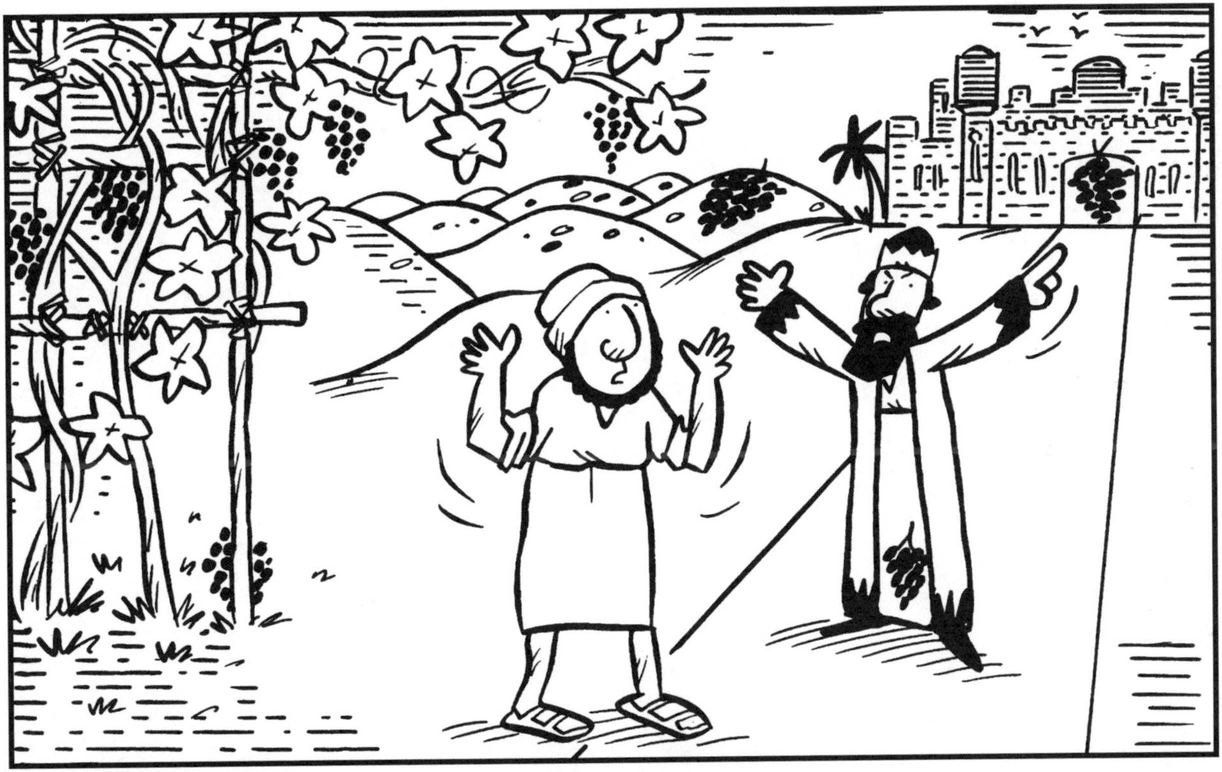

31

JULY

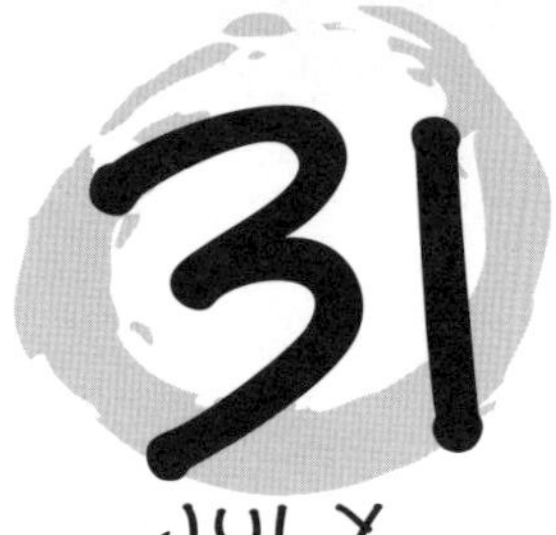

The servants are pouring water into the pots; Jesus turned it into wine. Can you find 10 hidden wine cups?

Read this story in John 2:1–11.

Puzzle

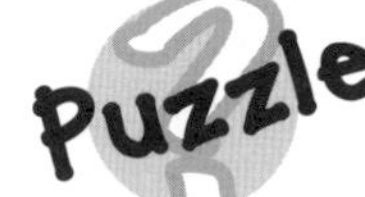

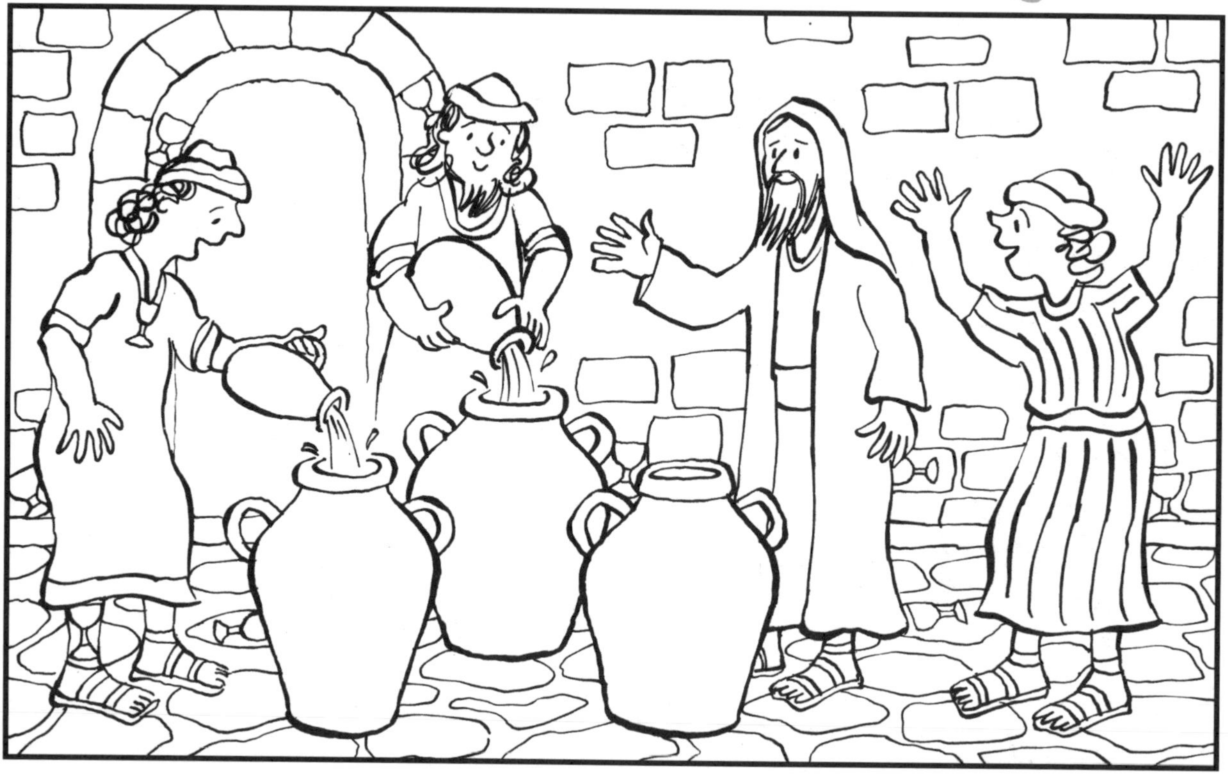

5
JUNE

Join up the dots and discover what happened to Elijah when he finished his life on earth.

Read about Elijah and Elisha in 2 Kings 2:1–13.
What is Elijah giving to Elisha?

DOT-TO-DOT

30
JULY

Jesus did his very first miracle at a wedding in the village of Cana. Join up the dots to complete the picture.

Read John 2:1–11.
What happened to the water in these big pots?

DOT-TO-DOT

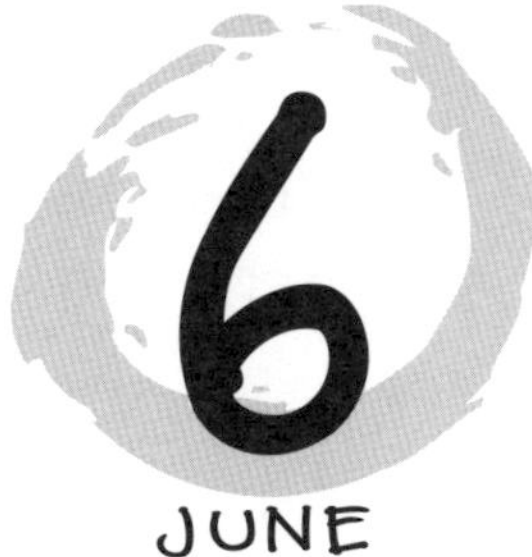

6

JUNE

Naaman had a terrible skin disease. The prophet Elisha told him to wash in the river Jordan. Help Naaman find the best path to the river.

Read about Naaman in 2 Kings 5:1–15.

maze

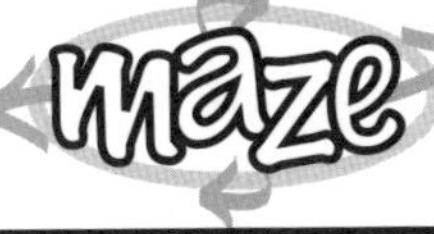

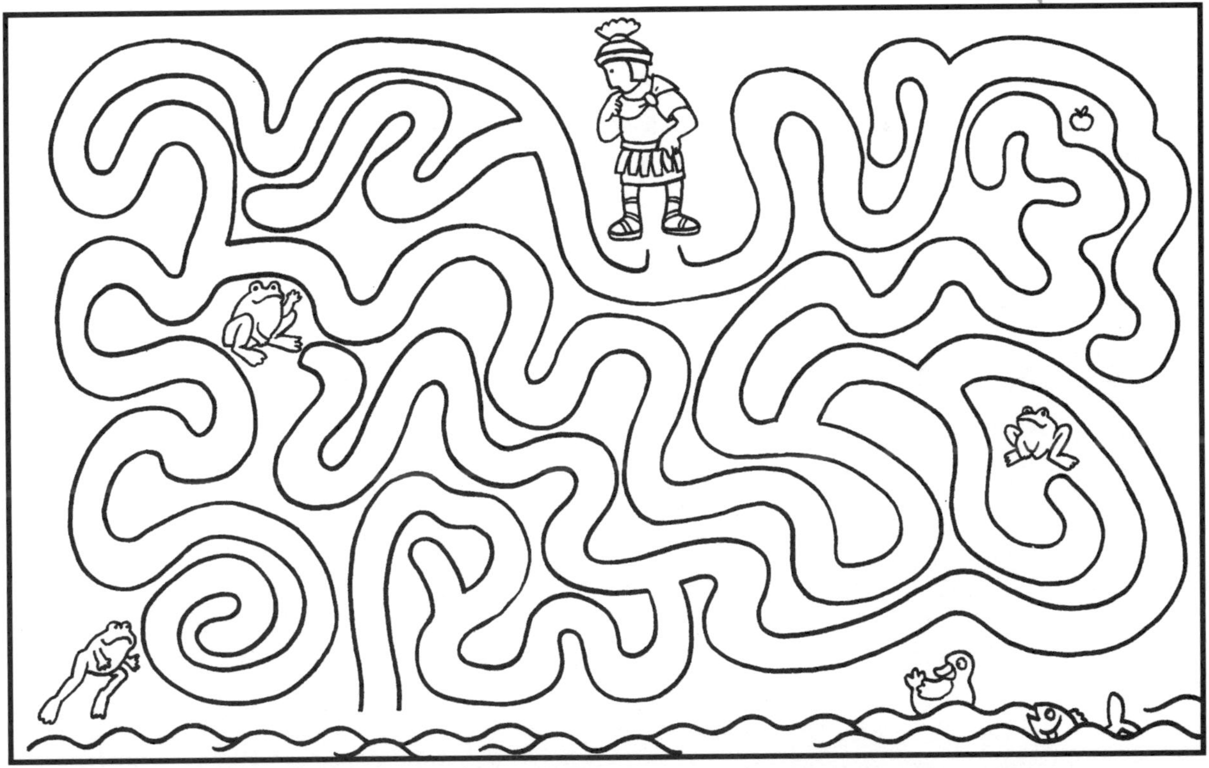

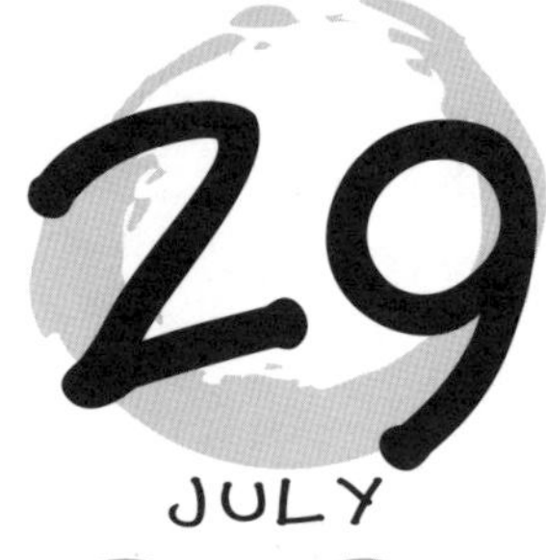

29 JULY

Jesus went to see John the Baptist. He asked John to baptize him in the river Jordan. Join up the dots to find what appeared over Jesus' head after he had been baptized.

Read Matthew 3:13–17.

DOT-TO-DOT

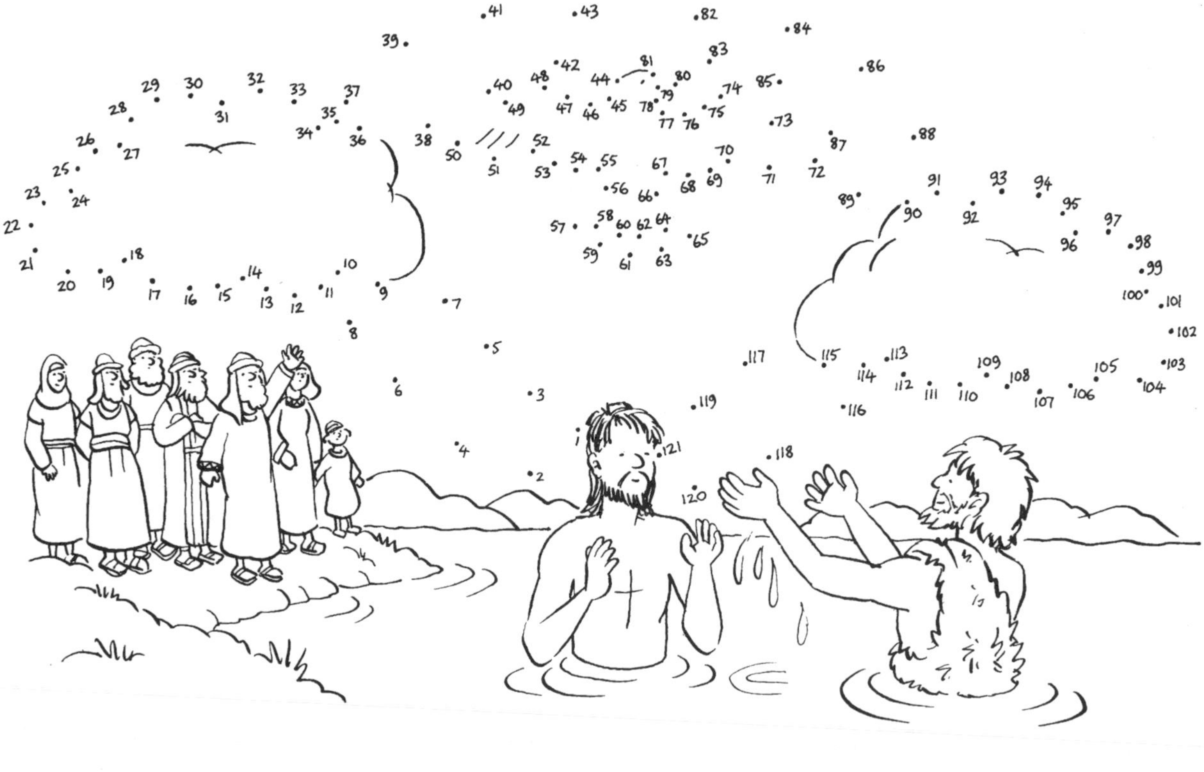

7

JUNE

What is this man making? Join the dots up to find out.

You can read about a potter in Jeremiah 18:3–6.

DOT-TO-DOT

28
JULY

In the Temple in Jerusalem stood great golden candlesticks. Can you find 3 pairs of candlesticks here?

Read about Jesus in the Temple in Luke 2:41–52.

Puzzle

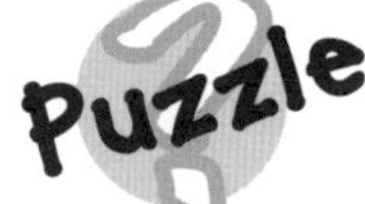

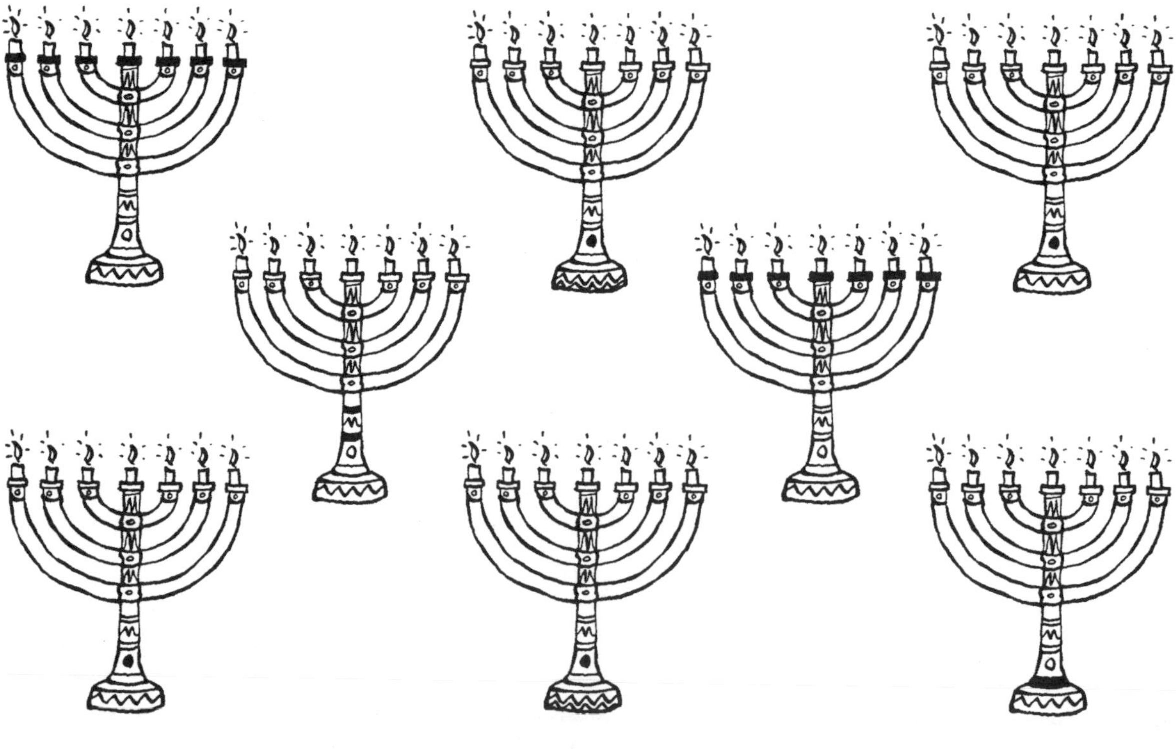

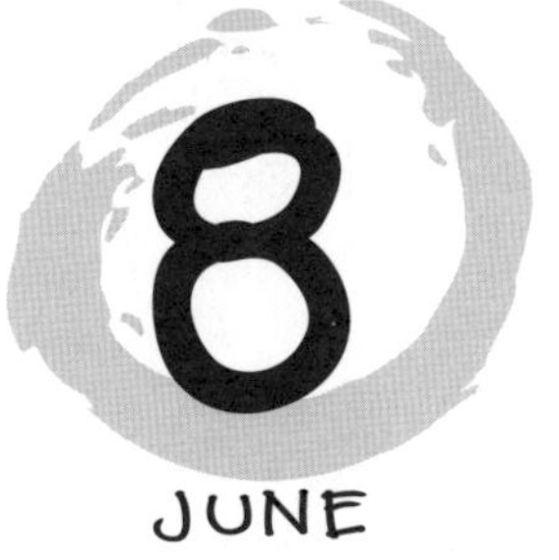

8
JUNE

The Israelites disobeyed God, and were taken captive. After 70 years, they were allowed to return to Jerusalem. Which path will take them to Jerusalem?

Read this story in Ezra 1:1–11.

maze

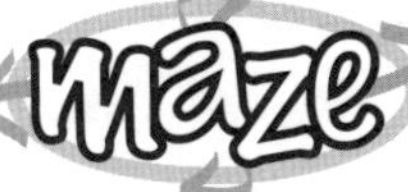

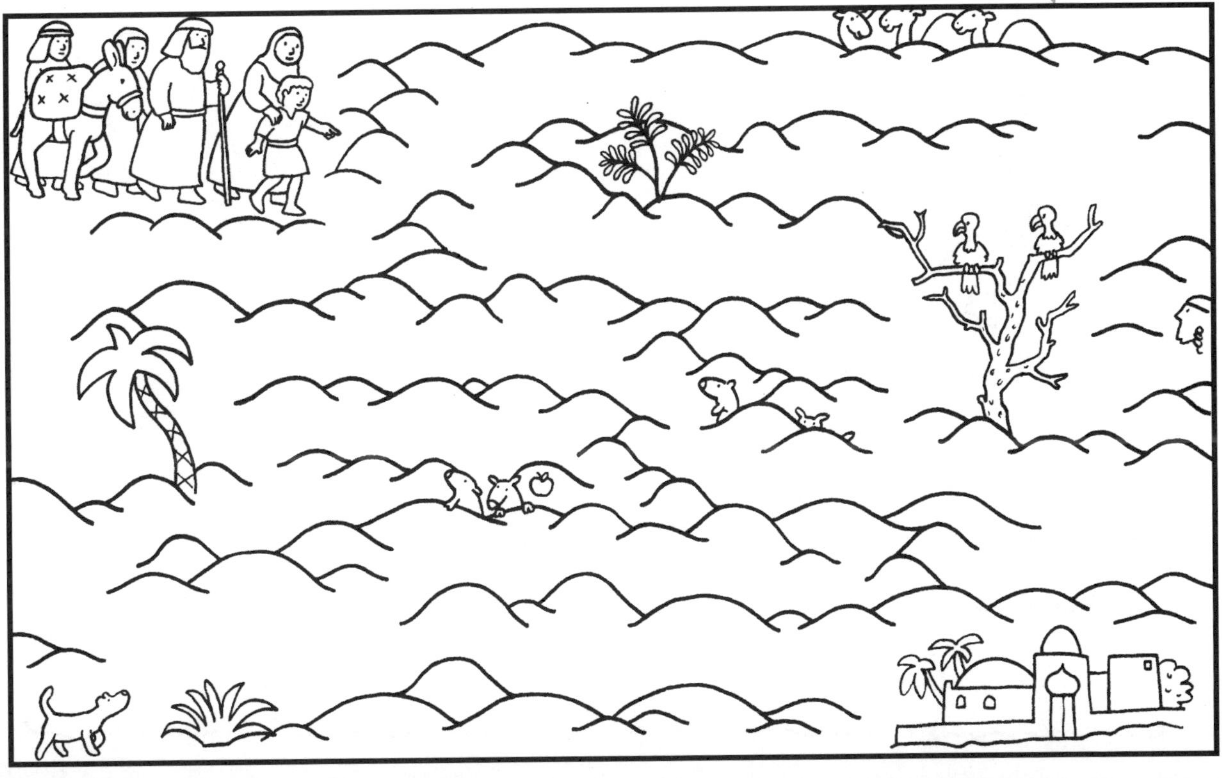

27
JULY

Here are 3 unfinished pictures of a priest. Finish them off, using the complete picture as a guide.

Read this story in Luke 2:41–52.

Puzzle

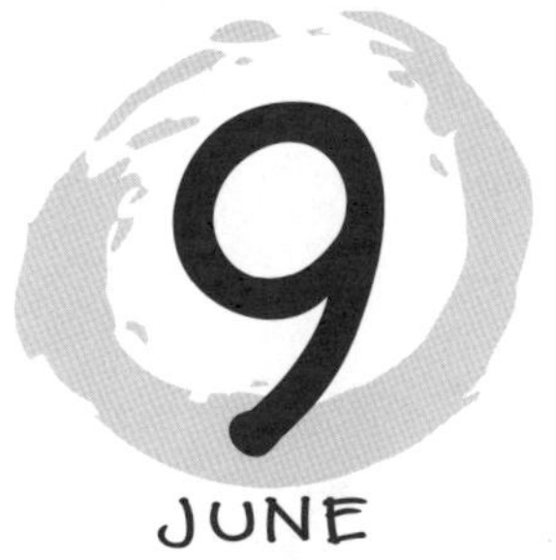

9 JUNE

Vashti was Queen of Persia—but her husband grew tired of her. Can you find 9 ear-rings hidden in this picture?

Read about Queen Vashti in the book of Esther chapter 1.

Puzzle

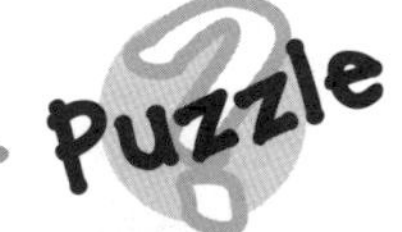

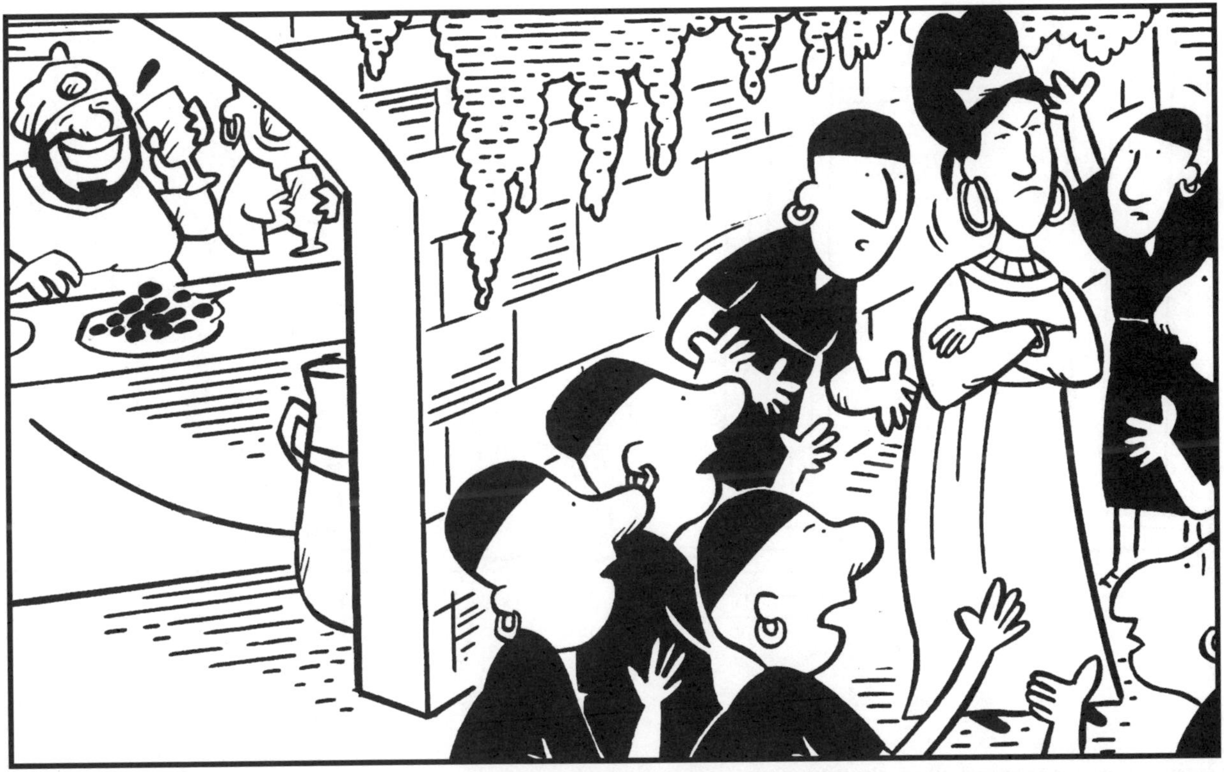

26 JULY

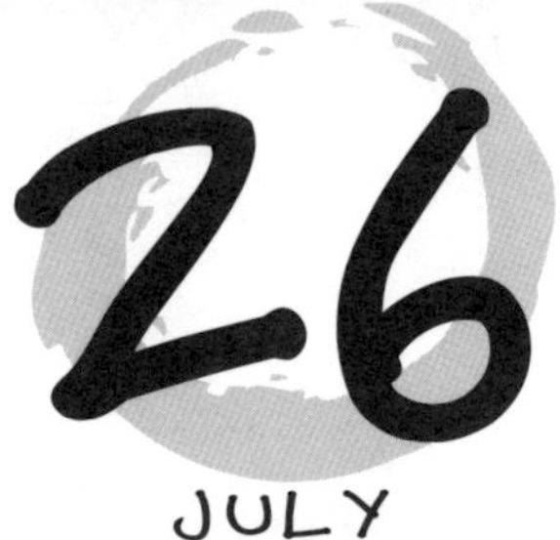

Jesus spent time in the Temple talking to the priests. 10 scrolls are hidden in this picture of the Temple.

Can you find them all? Now color the picture with felt-tips. Read this story in Luke 2:41–52.

Puzzle

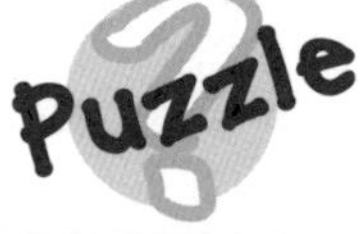

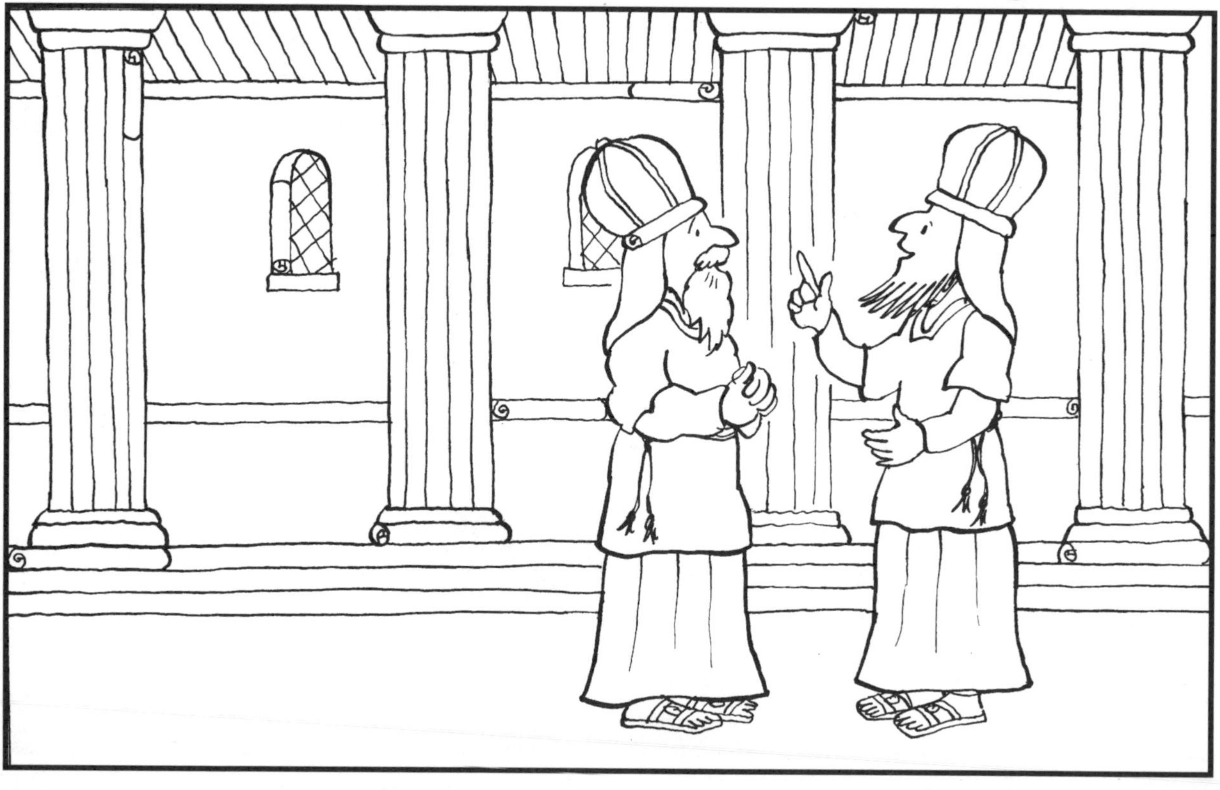

Queen Esther invited the king to a banquet with a wicked man named Haman. Put a circle around the 10 mistakes the artist has made in this picture.

Read the story in Esther 5—7.

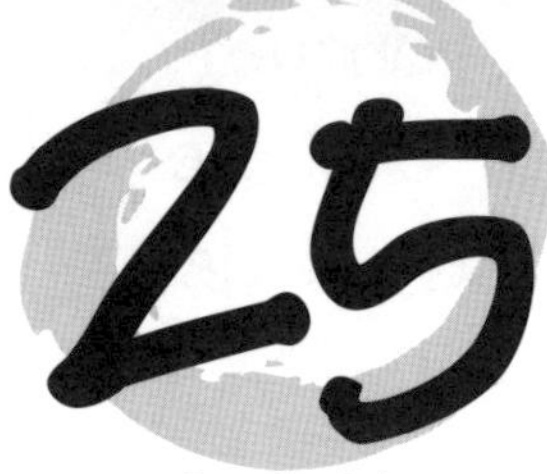

25
JULY

When Jesus was twelve, he visited Jerusalem with Joseph and Mary. They lost him. Help Mary follow the tiles on the temple floor to find Jesus.

Read this story in Luke 2:41–52.

maze

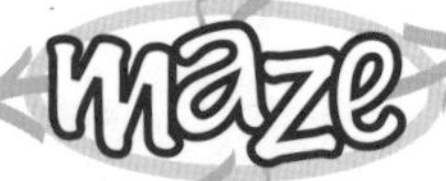

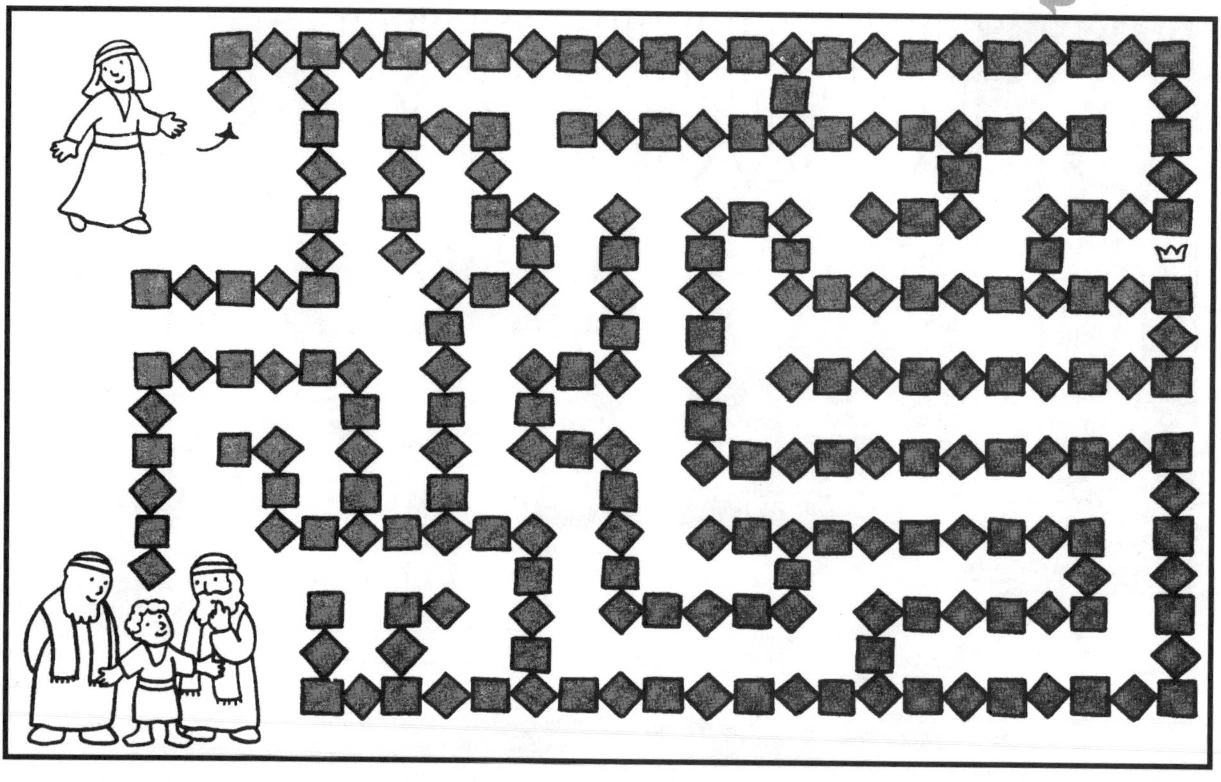

11

JUNE

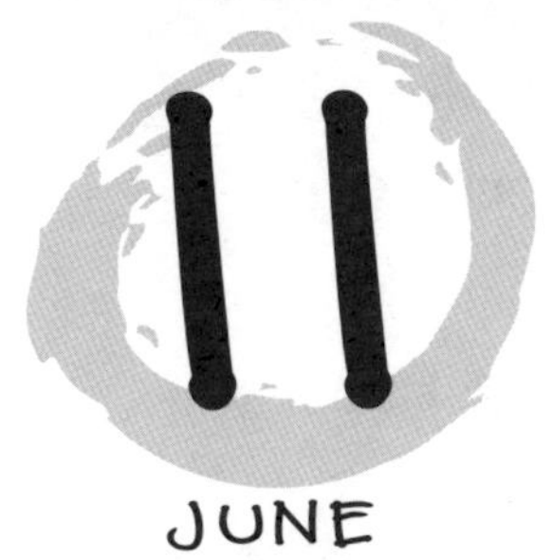

When Queen Esther had dinner with the king, she said, 'Haman is trying to kill my people, the Jews.'

Can you find 10 spiders hidden in the picture? Now color the picture with felt-tips. Read the story in Esther 5—7.

Color me!

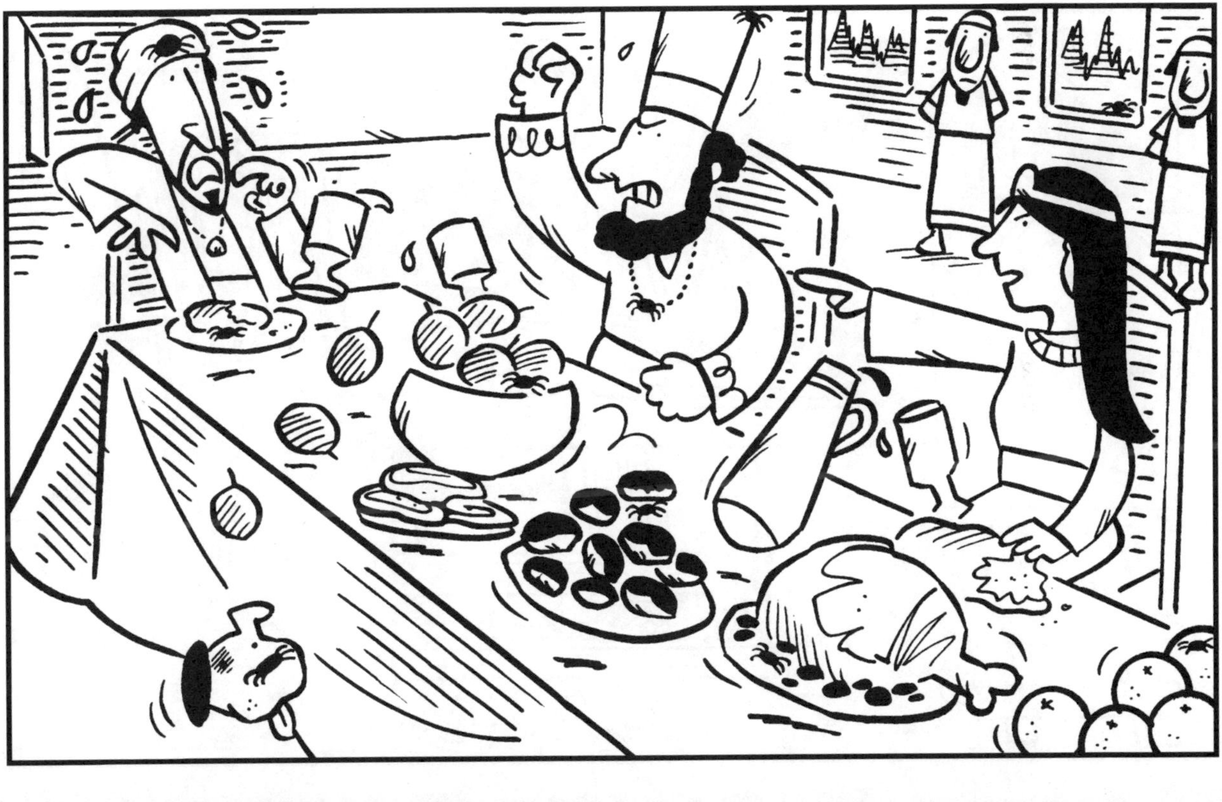

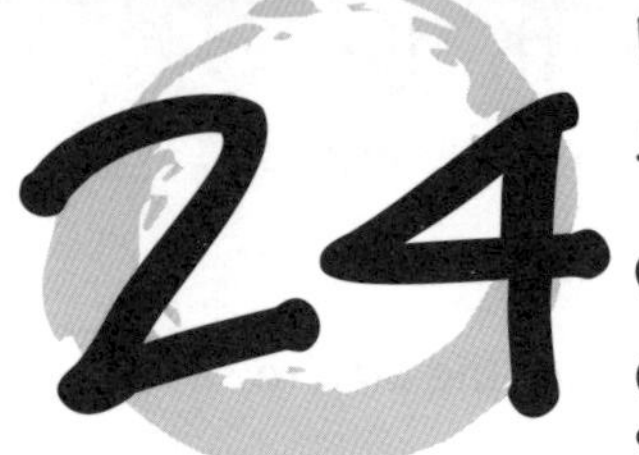

24
JULY

When it was safe again, Joseph took his family back to Nazareth. He worked as a carpenter.

Can you find any mistakes in this picture of Joseph's workshop? See Matthew 2:19–23.

Puzzle

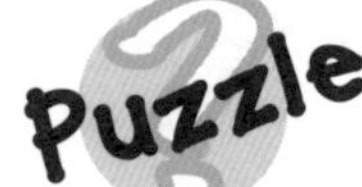

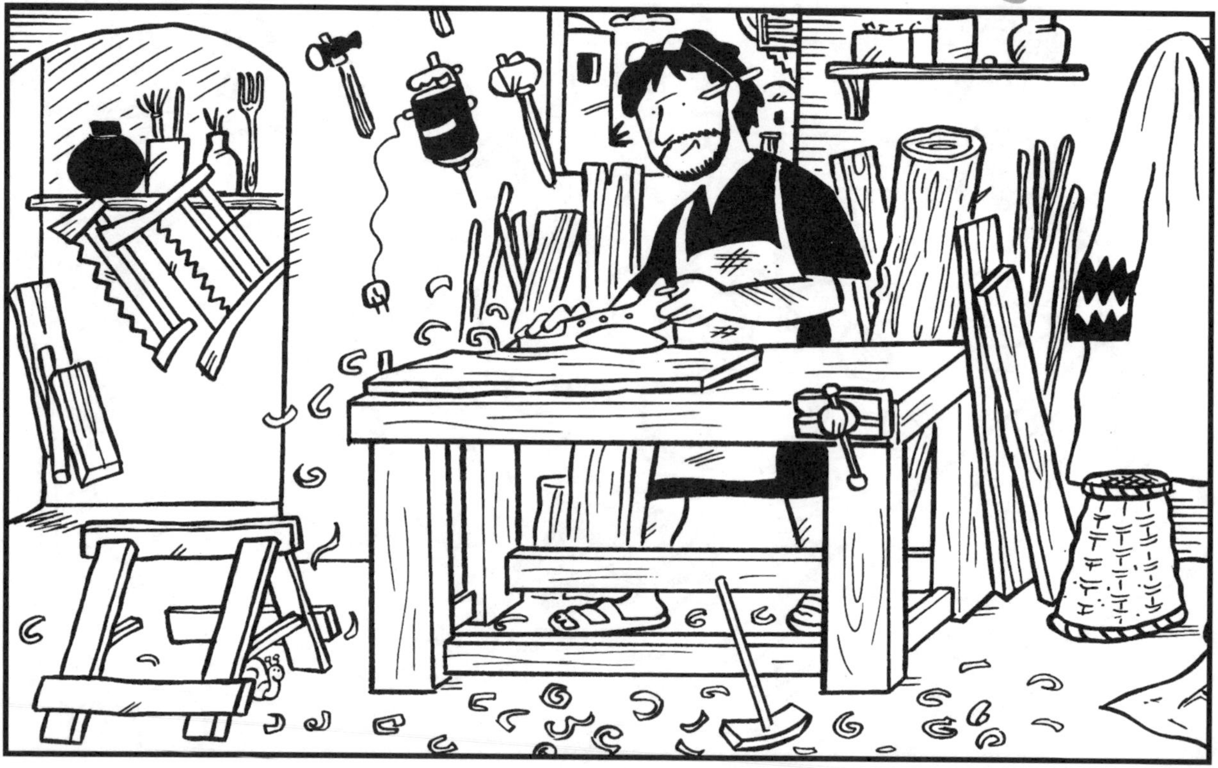

12

JUNE

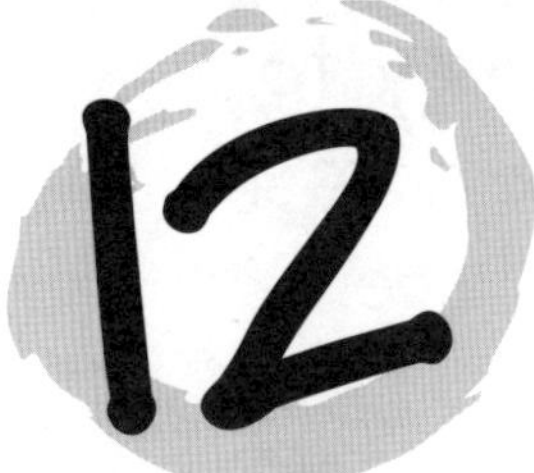

Before tractors were invented, farmers plowed their fields using oxen. Can you find a path that will lead the farmer to his lunch basket?

Read about plowing in Isaiah 28:23–29.

maze

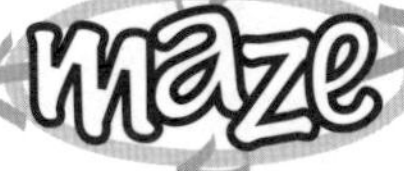

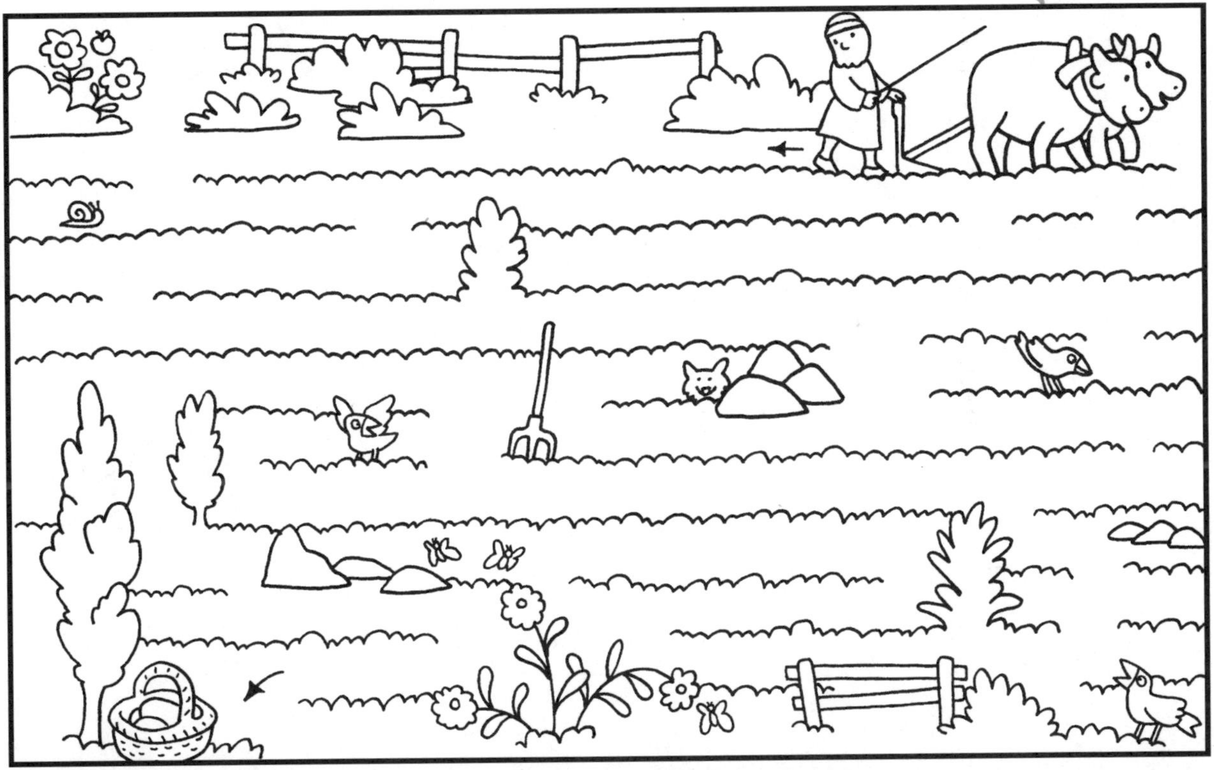

23 JULY

Mary and Joseph made a long journey to reach safety in Egypt. Join up the dots to find what sort of tree they saw there.

Read this story in Matthew 2:13–15.

DOT-TO-DOT

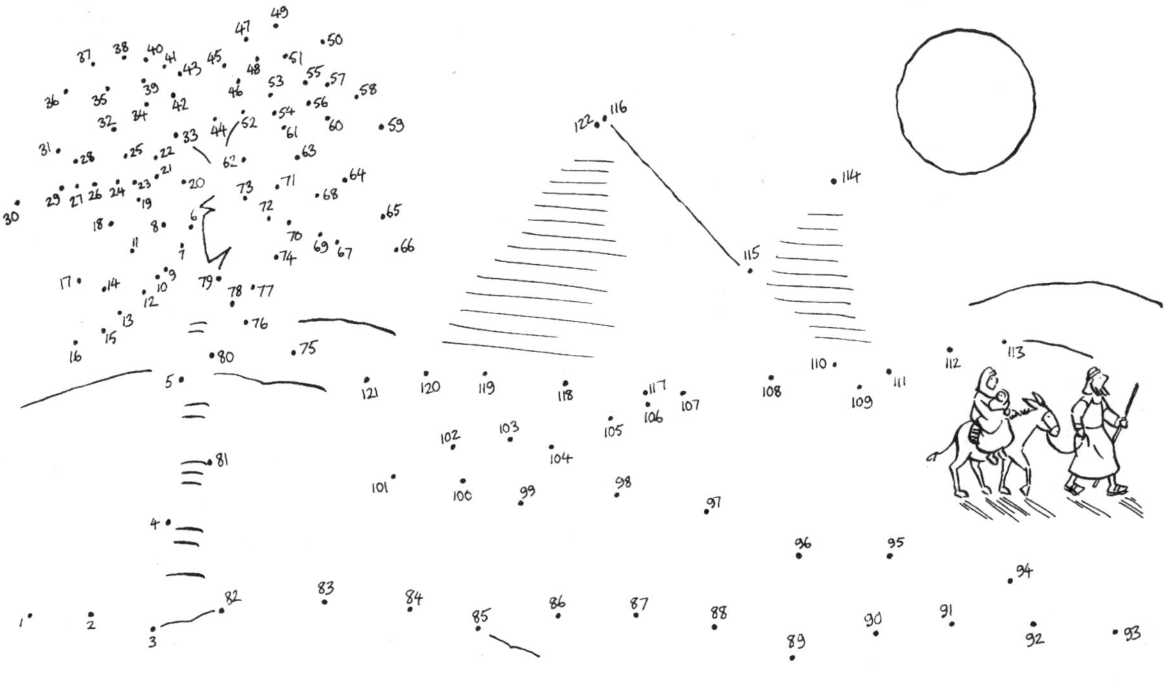

13
JUNE

The people grew very angry with the prophet Jeremiah because he brought them bad news. Join up the dots to find out why he can't move.

Read the whole story in Jeremiah 20:1–6.

DOT-TO-DOT

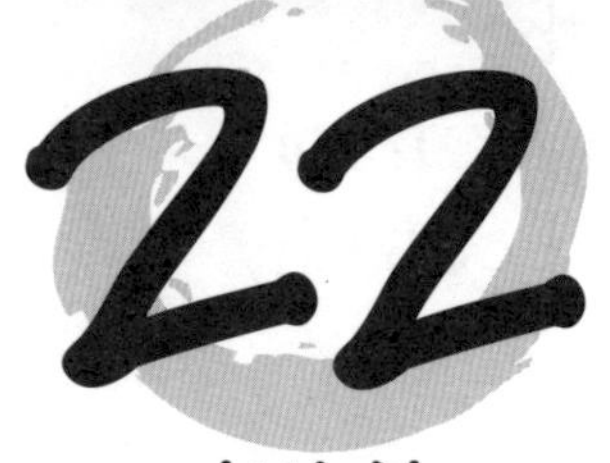

22
JULY

An angel told Joseph it wasn't safe to stay in Bethlehem, so he took Mary and baby Jesus to Egypt.

Which path must they take to arrive safely in Egypt? Matthew 2:13–15.

maze

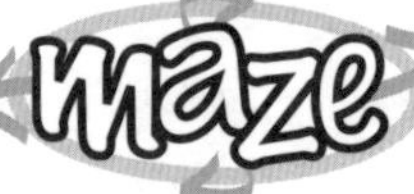

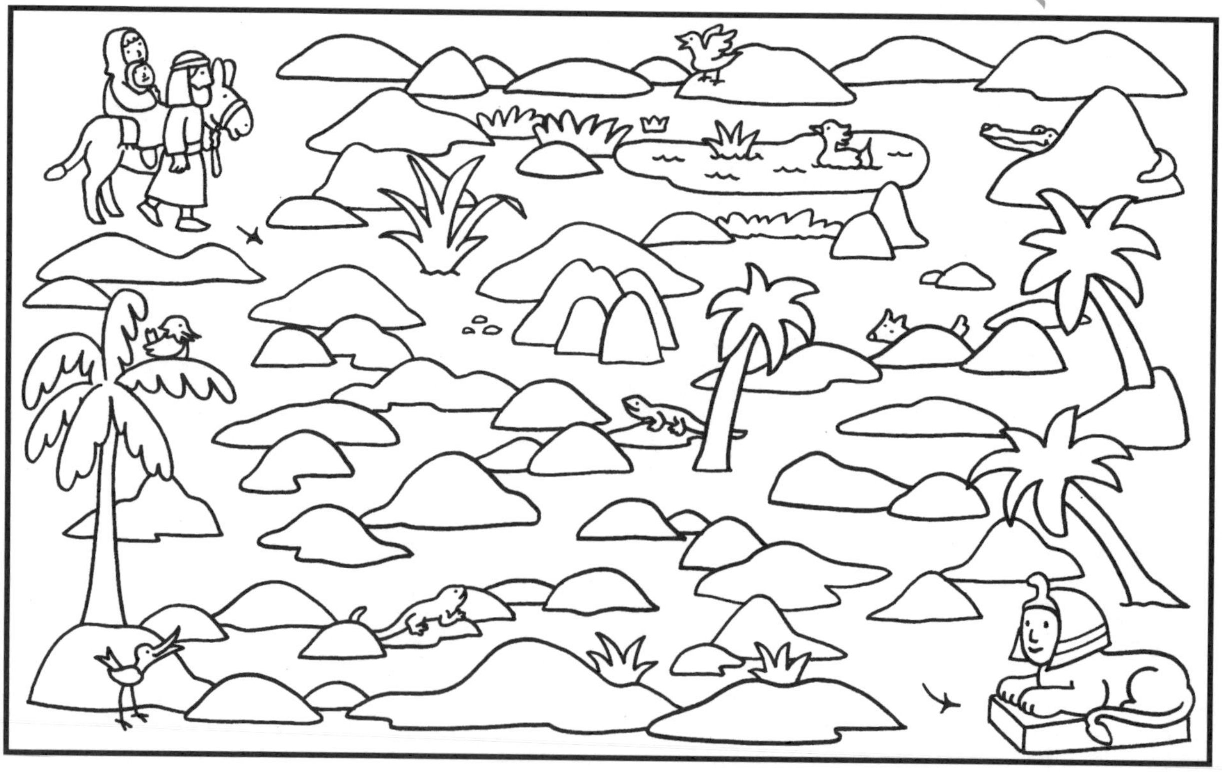

14

JUNE

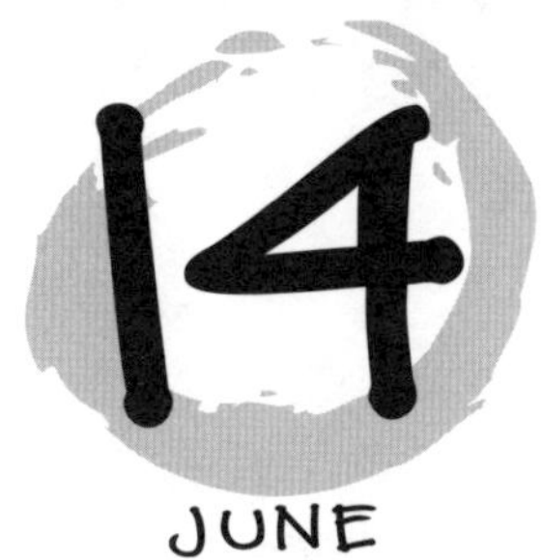

Jonah was thrown into the sea after the ship he was in hit a terrible storm. A great fish swallowed him.

How does the fish reach Jonah?
Read this story in Jonah 1:1–17.

maze

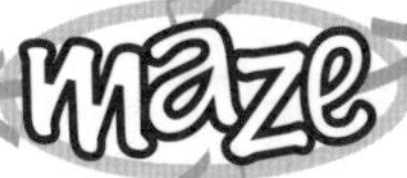

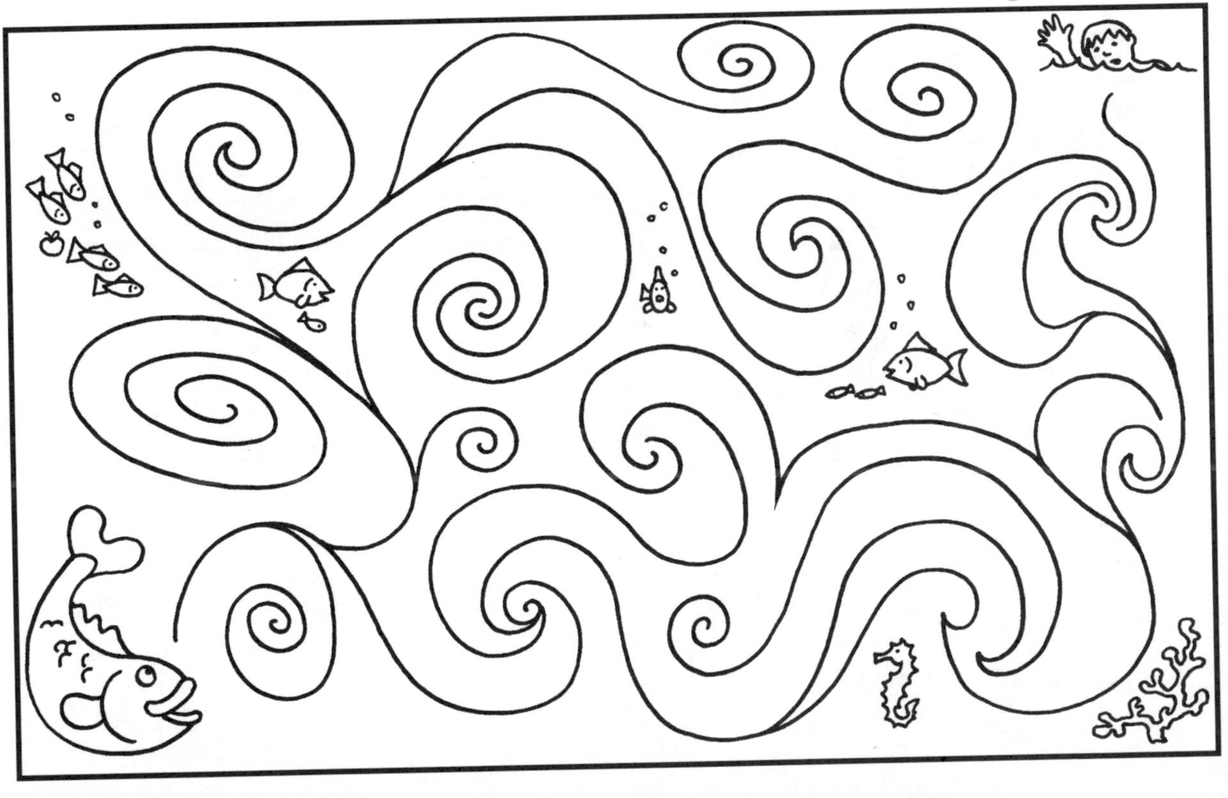

JULY

21

Here are 8 pictures of the wise men's gifts for Jesus. Which pictures are exactly the same?

Read this story in Matthew 2:1–12.
What were the wise men's gifts?

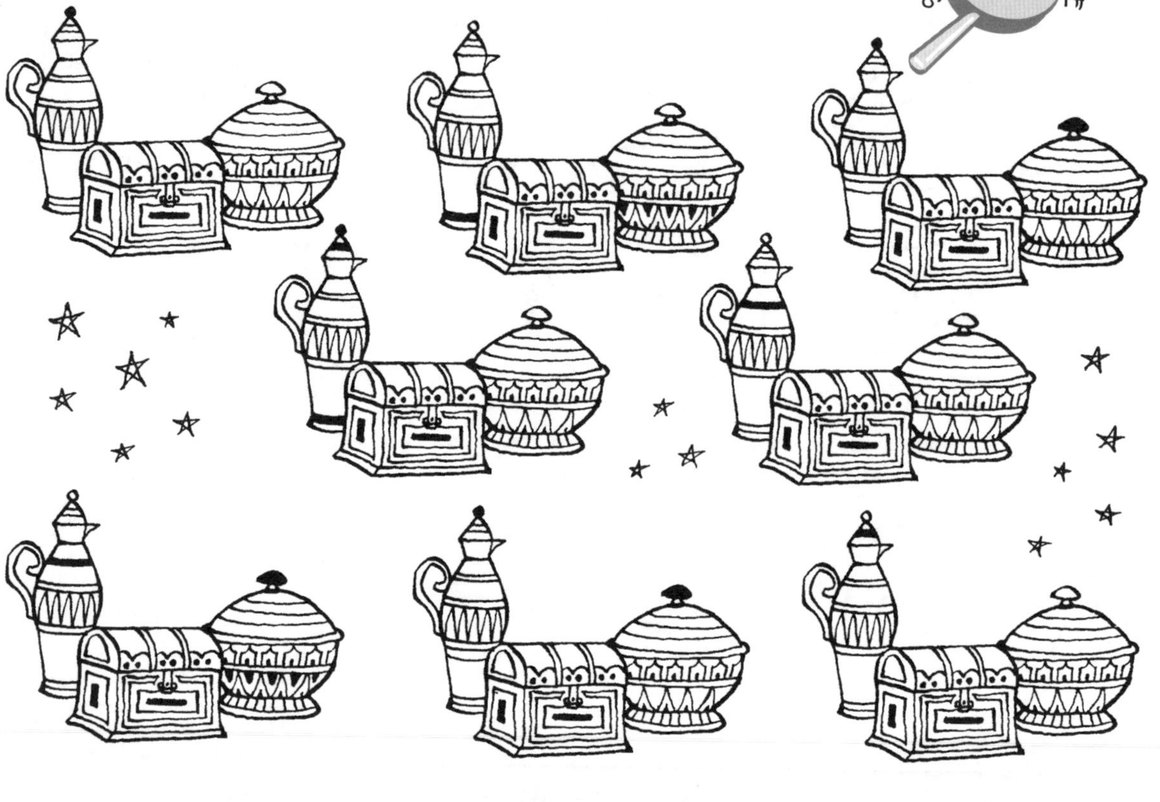

The great fish is about to swallow Jonah. Can you find 12 little fish hidden in this picture?

You can read this story in Jonah 1:1–17.

Color me!

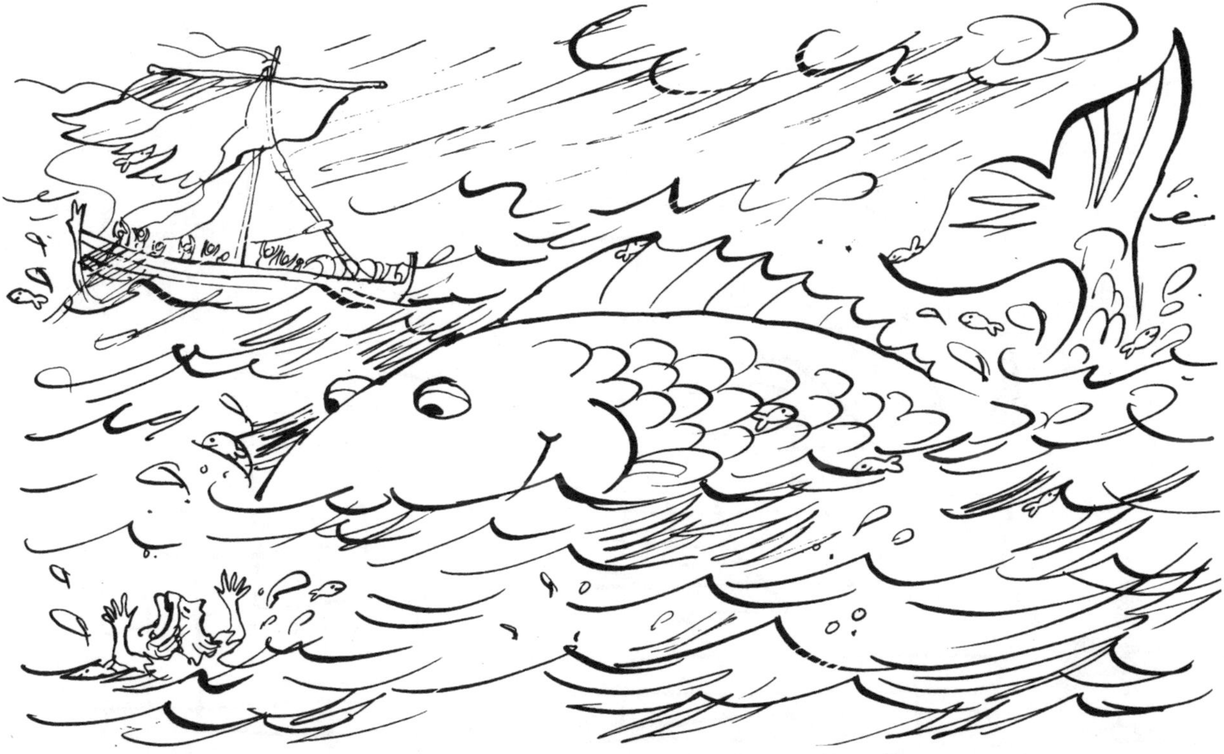

20

Which is the right route to Bethlehem? Show the wise men the best way to go. What can they see above the stable?

Read their story in Matthew 2:1–12.

puzzle

16
JUNE

Join up the dots to discover what is happening to Jonah here.

Is Jonah drowning?
Read the whole story in Jonah 1:1–17.

DOT-TO-DOT

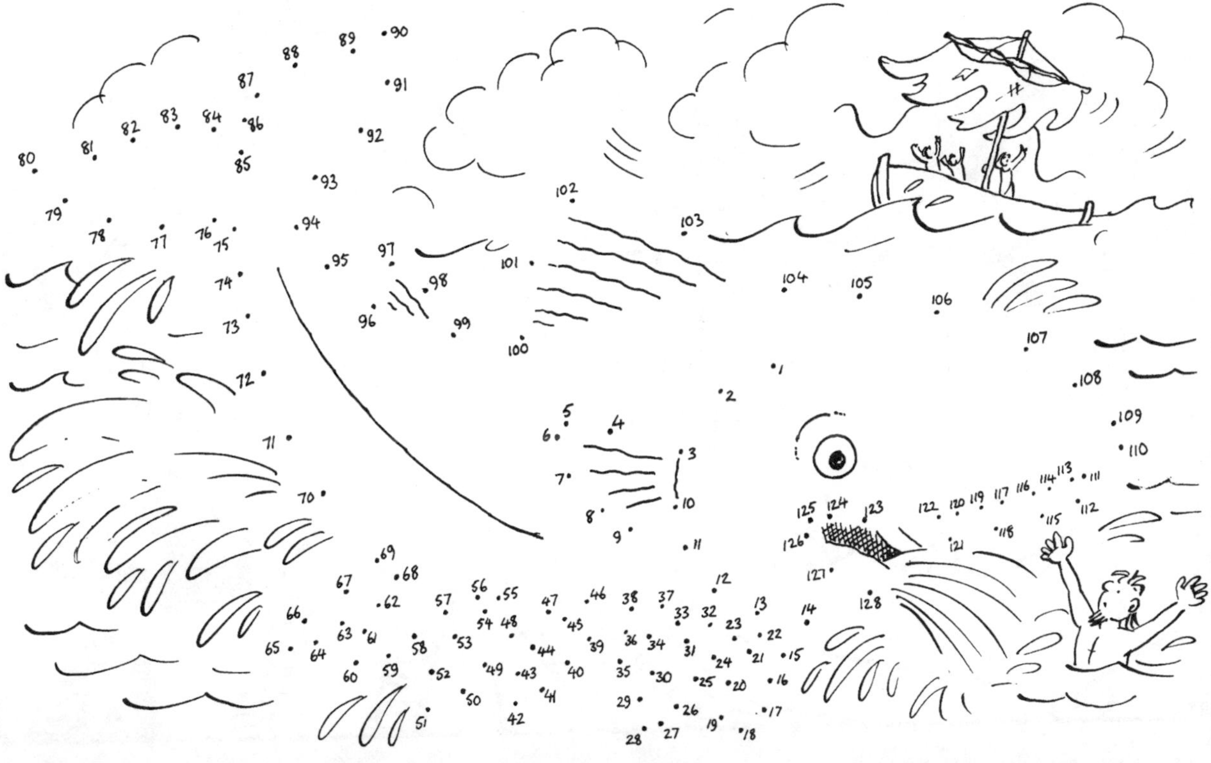

19
JULY

The wise men visited King Herod and asked him if he knew where they could find the newborn king.

Can you find 17 stars hidden in this picture? Was Herod a good king? Read this story in Matthew 2:1–12.

Puzzle

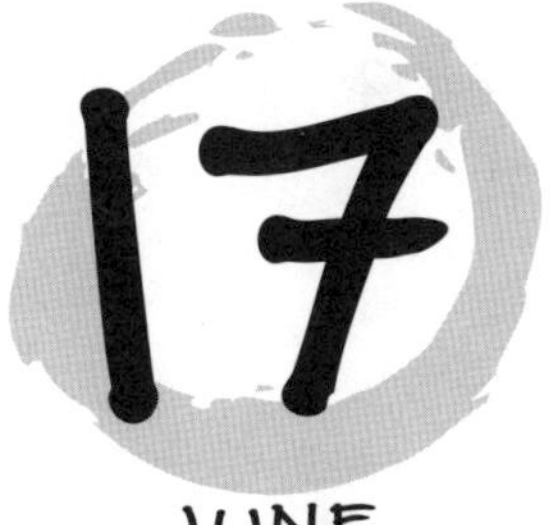

17 JUNE

At top left is a whole fish. Which of the other boxes has the right pieces to make the fish?

Read the story of the prophet and the great fish in Jonah 1:1–17.

Puzzle

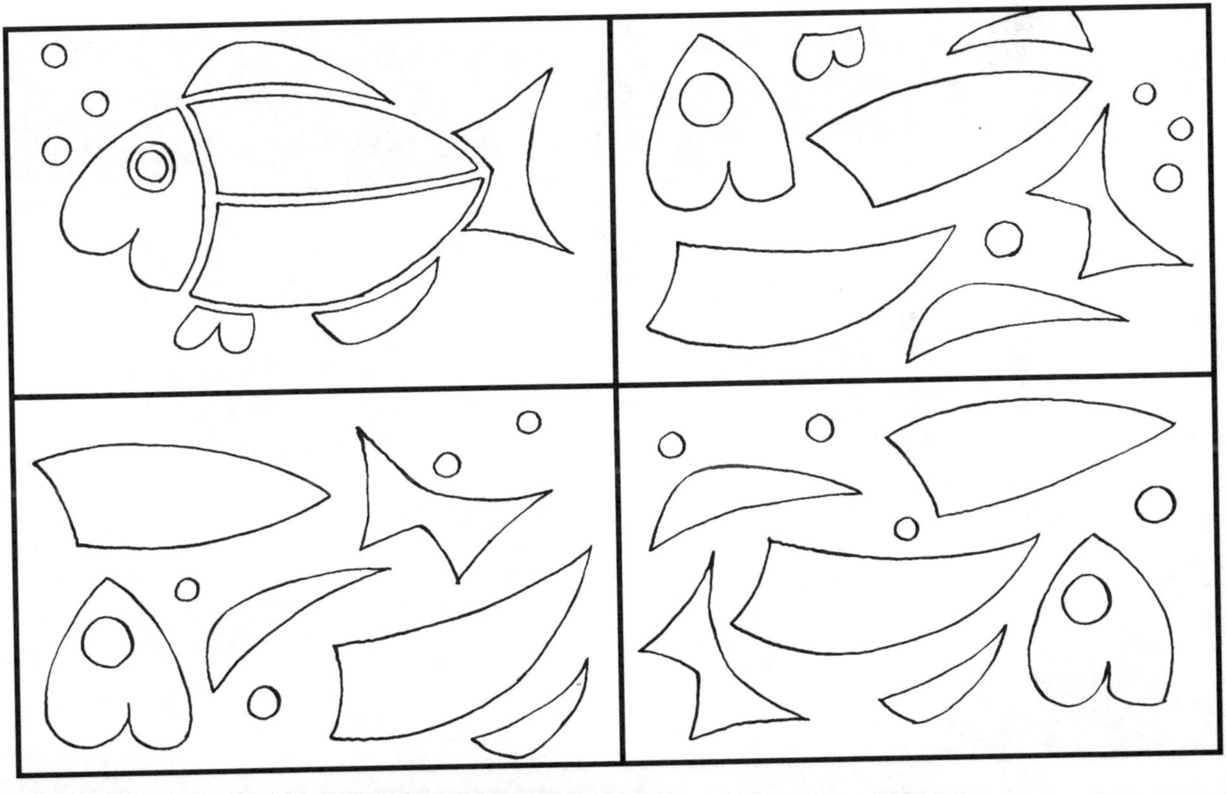

18

JULY

In this picture of the wise men seeking Jesus, the artist has made a lot of deliberate mistakes.

How many can you find? Should there be two special stars? Read their story in Matthew 2:1–12.

Puzzle

18
JUNE

The fish has swallowed Jonah. Help the fish reach land so he can throw him up again on the shore.

Read this story in Jonah 1:1–17, 2:10.

maze

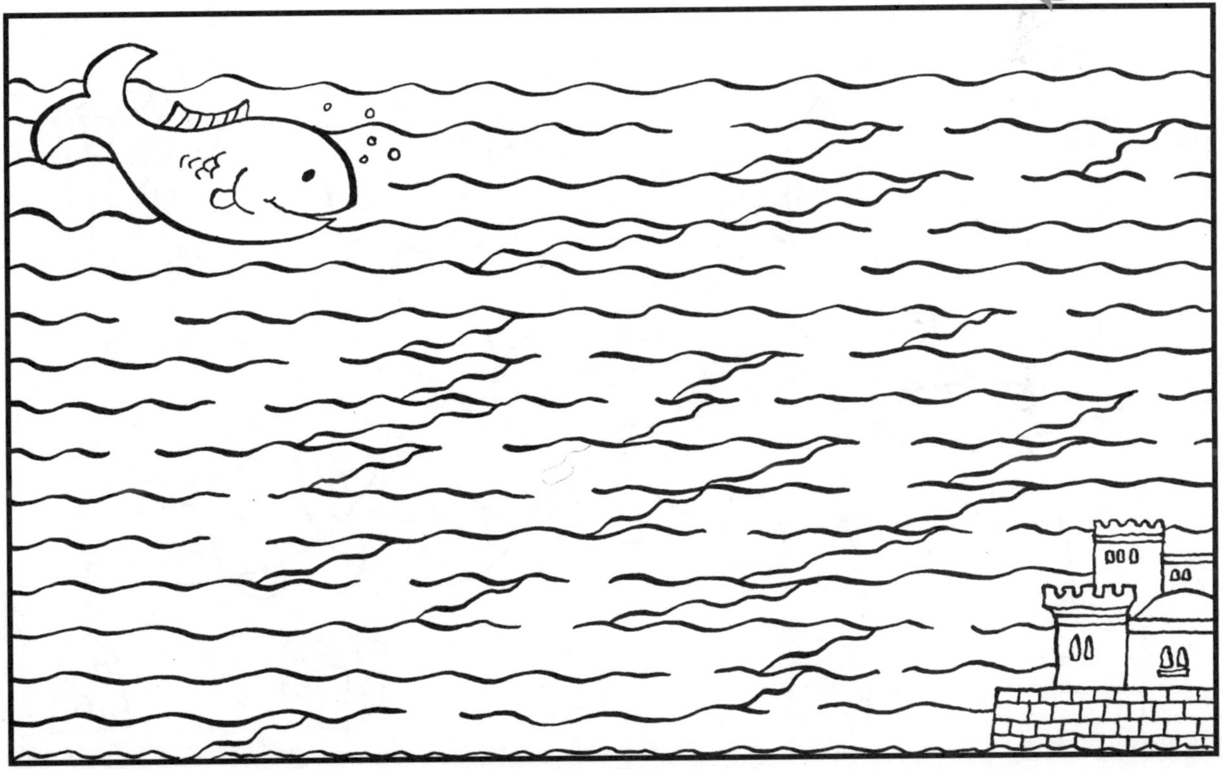

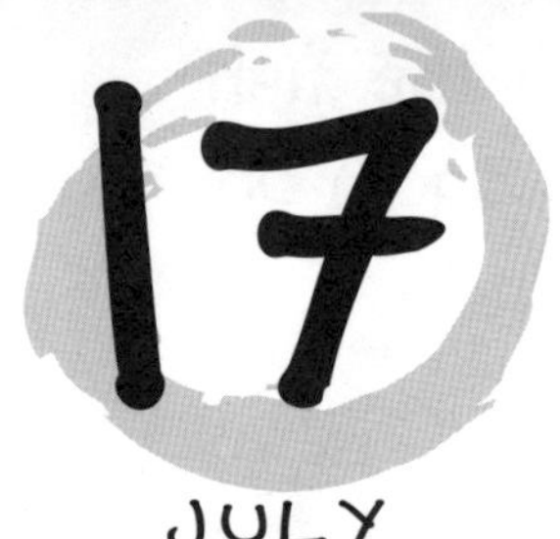

17

JULY

The wise men each brought a present for baby Jesus. Follow the lines to link each wise man with his present.

Read Matthew 2:11 to find out the gifts they brought.

Puzzle

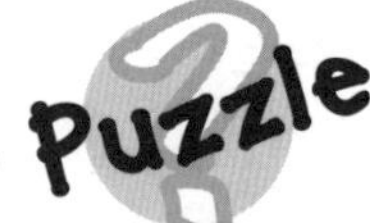

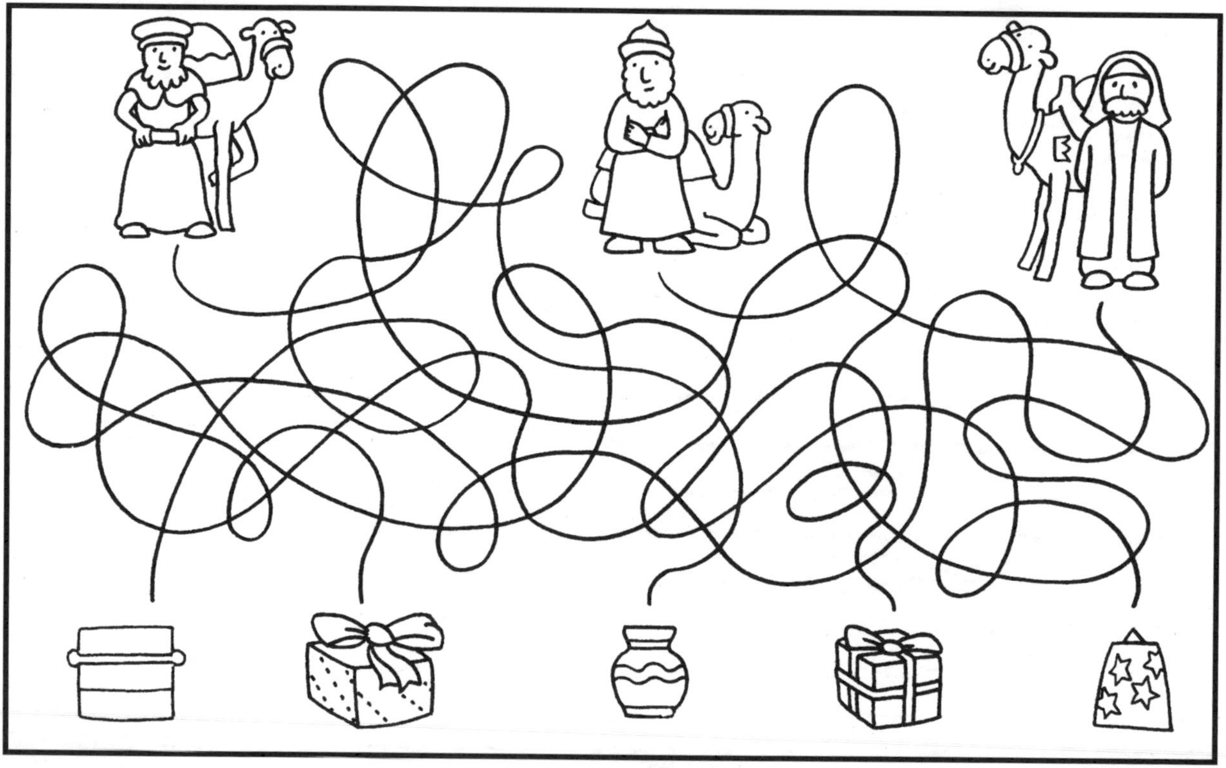

19 JUNE

The prophet Daniel looks a bit worried. Join up the dots to find out why.

Read this story in Daniel 6:6–23.
How long was Daniel in this pit?

DOT-TO-DOT

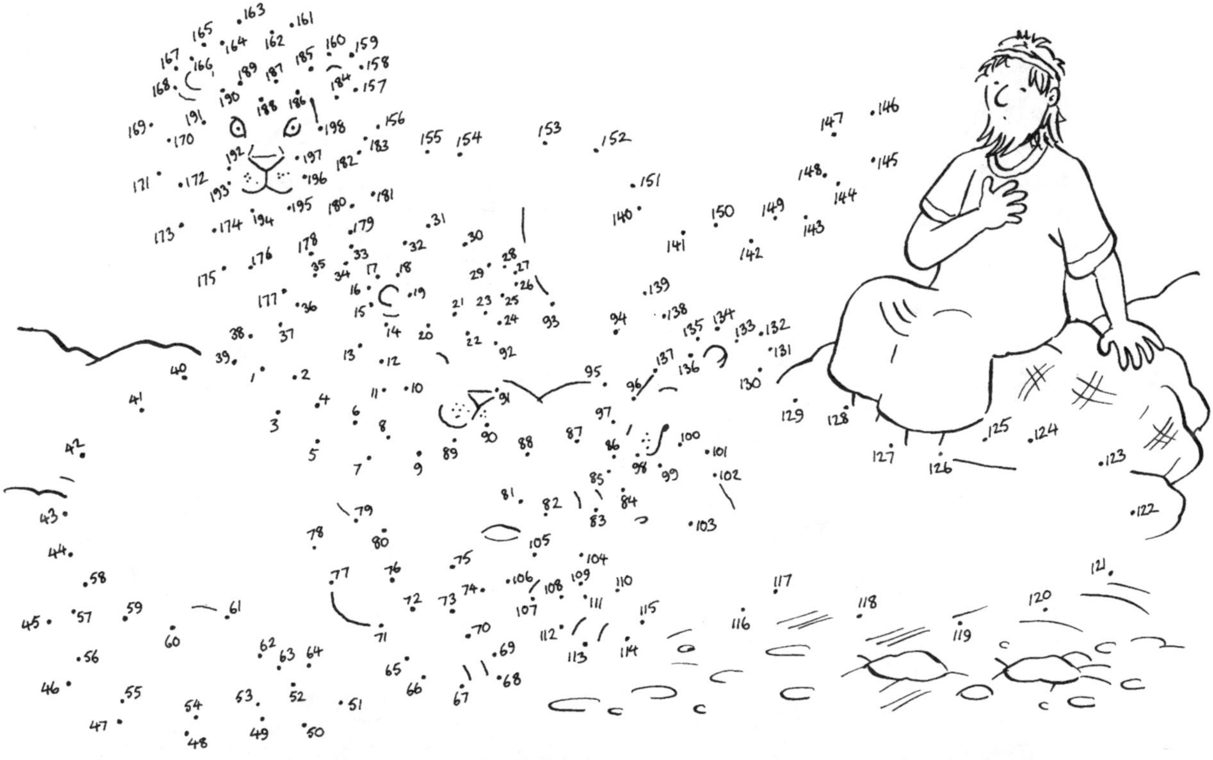

16
JULY

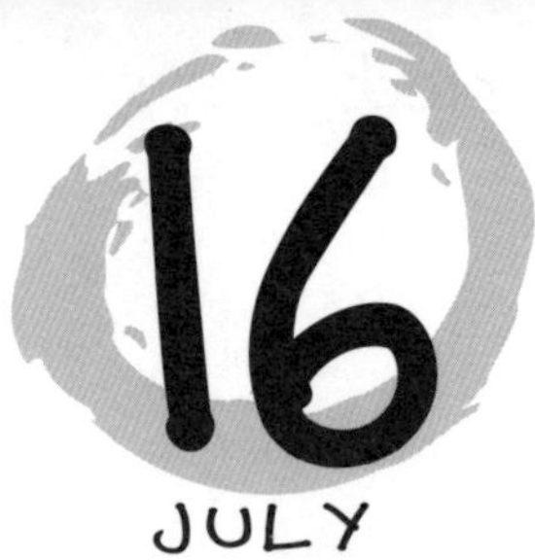

Here are 4 pictures of a wise man on his camel. Two are exactly the same. Which two?

Read this story in Matthew 2:1–12.

Puzzle

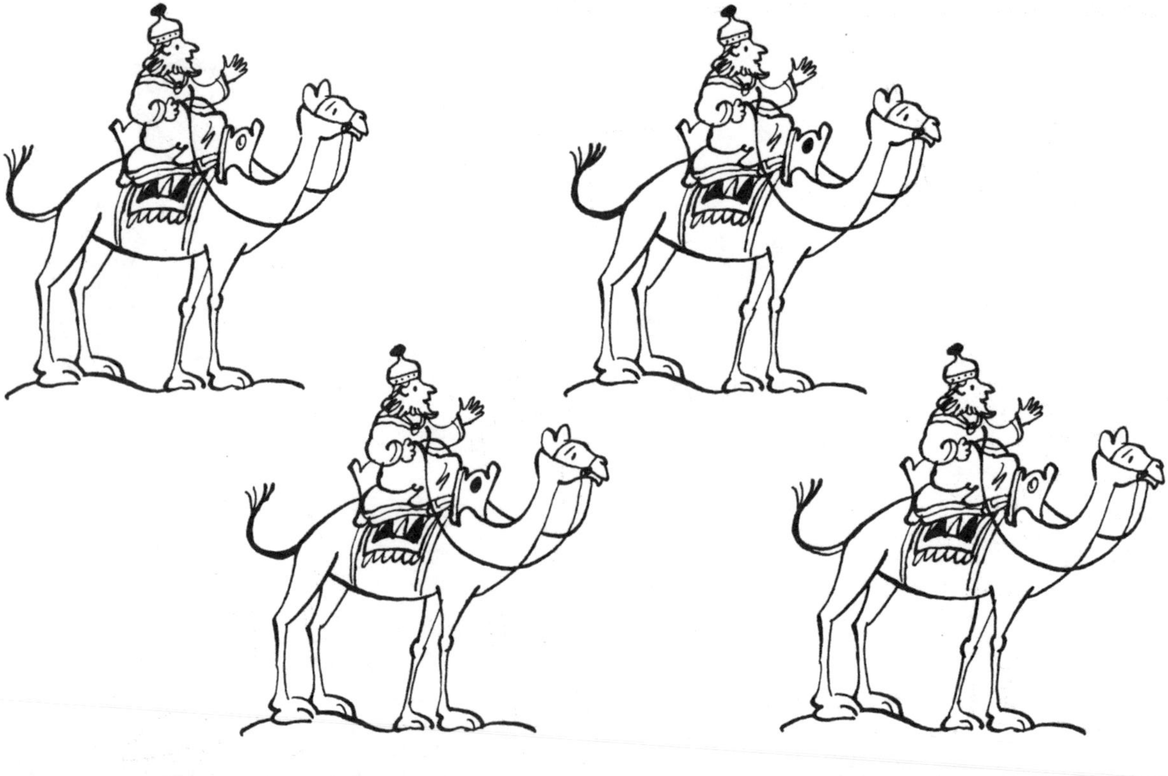

20

JUNE

King Darius was pleased that the lions' mouths were shut and that Daniel was kept safe in the pit of lions.

Can you find 10 bones hidden in this picture? Read this story in Daniel 6:6–23.

puzzle

15
JULY

The wise men saw a star and followed it to find the newborn baby. Join up the dots to see where they are going.

Read their story in Matthew 2:1–12.

DOT-TO-DOT

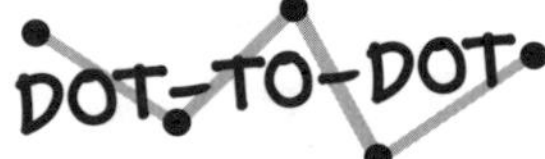

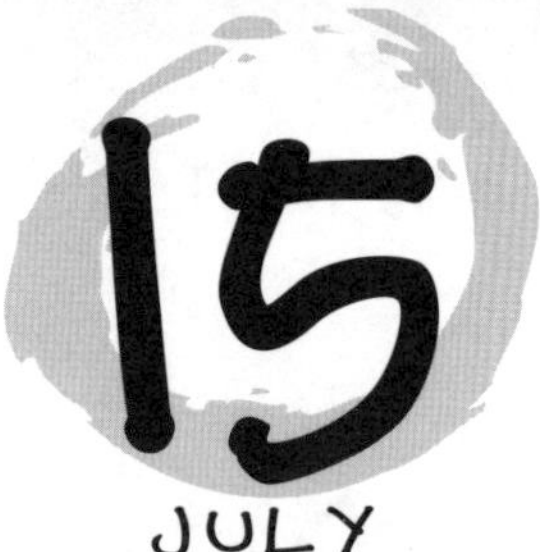

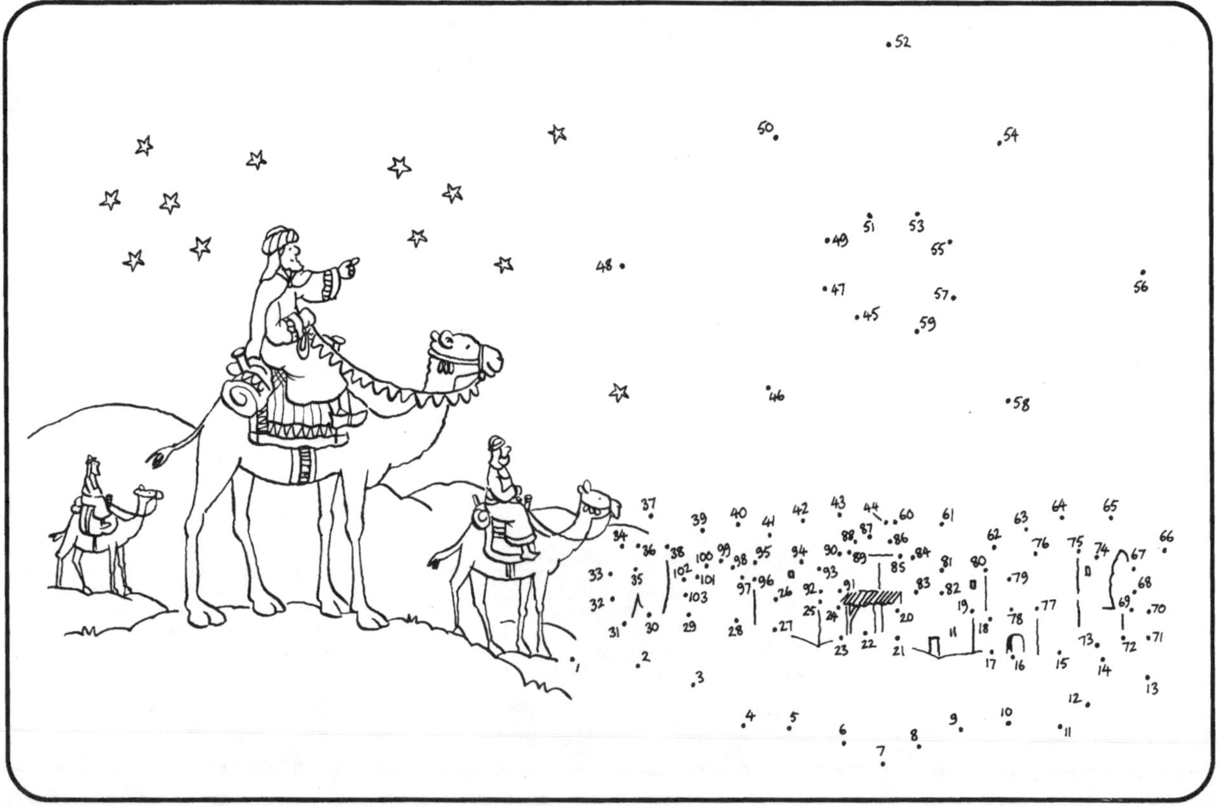

21

JUNE

Daniel was thrown into a den of lions. How many pairs of identical lions can you find here?

Read this story in Daniel 6:6–23.

Color me!

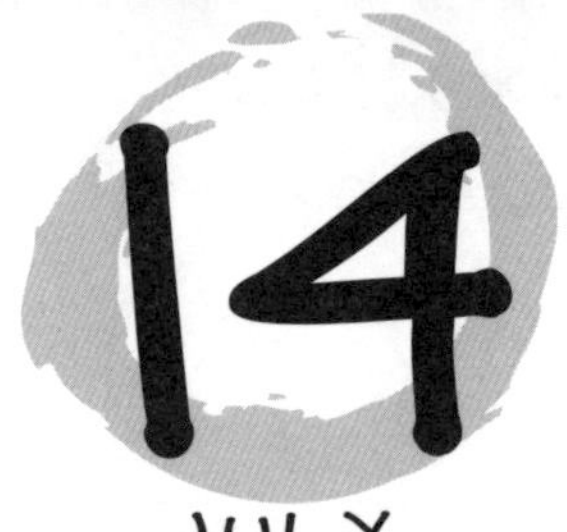

14 JULY

Wise men came to find baby Jesus. Join up the dots to discover how they traveled.

What is the man pointing at?
You can read this story in Matthew 2:1–12.

DOT-TO-DOT

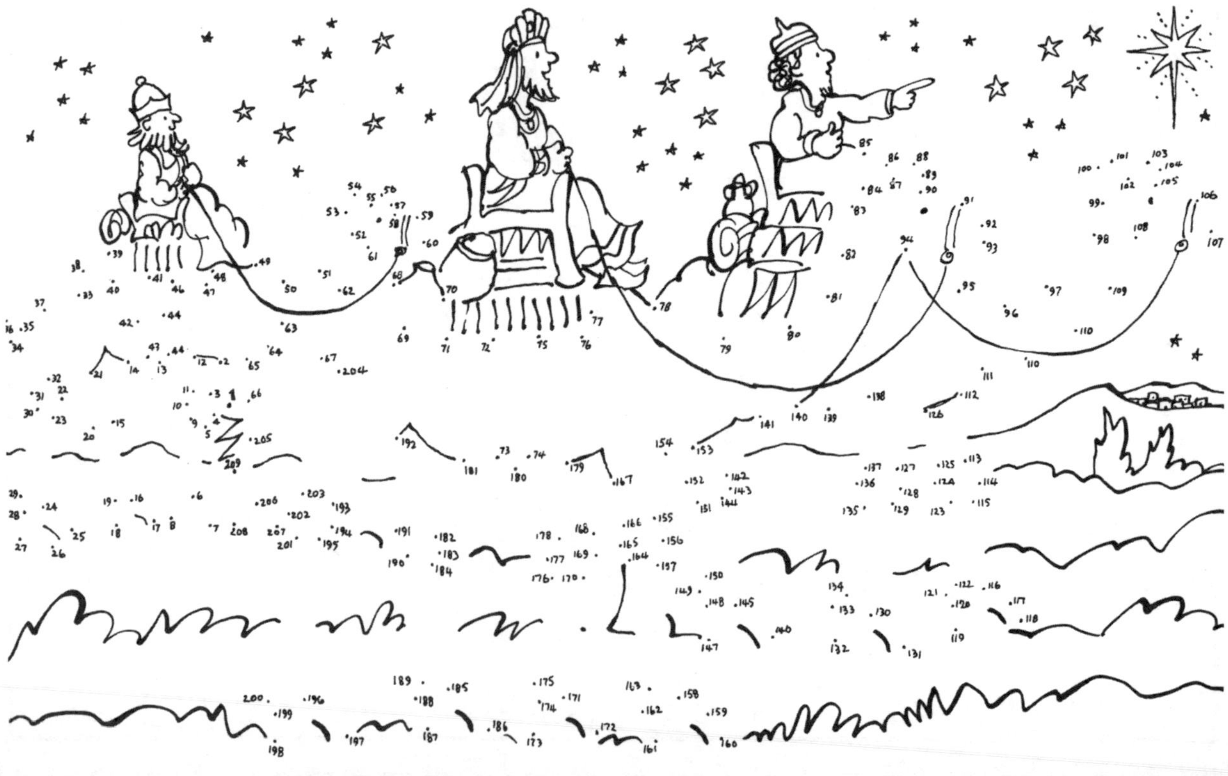

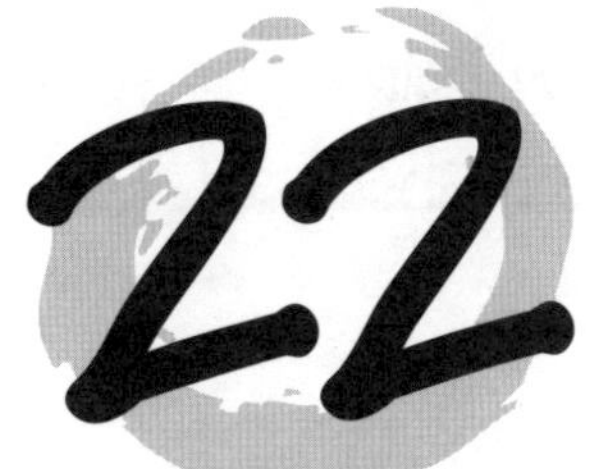

22

JUNE

Daniel, Jonah and Balaam are all linked with animals. Follow the paths to match the 3 men with the correct animals.

Read about Balaam in Numbers 22:21–35.

Puzzle

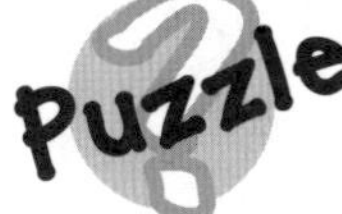

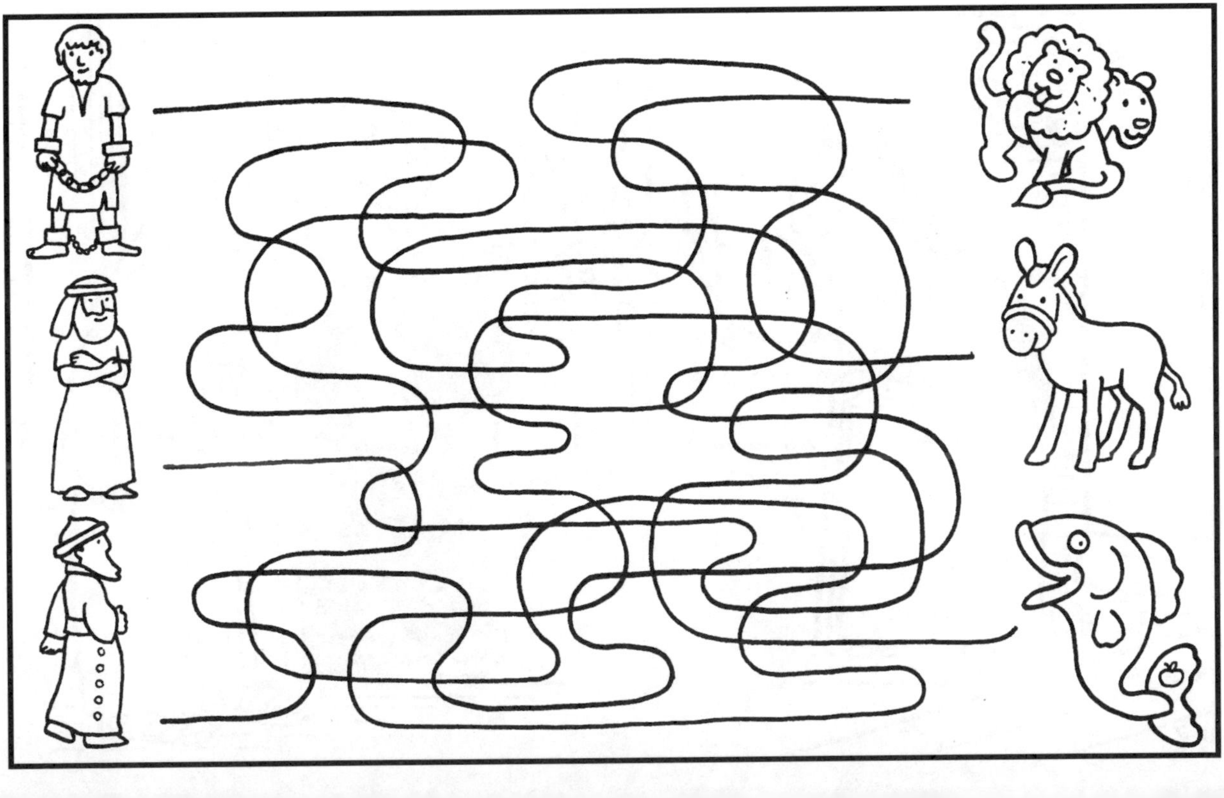

13

JULY

Anna was an old lady when she saw baby Jesus. She was very happy because she had been waiting for him to be born.

Can you find 11 doves in the picture?
Read about Anna in Luke 2:36–38.

Color me!

23 JUNE

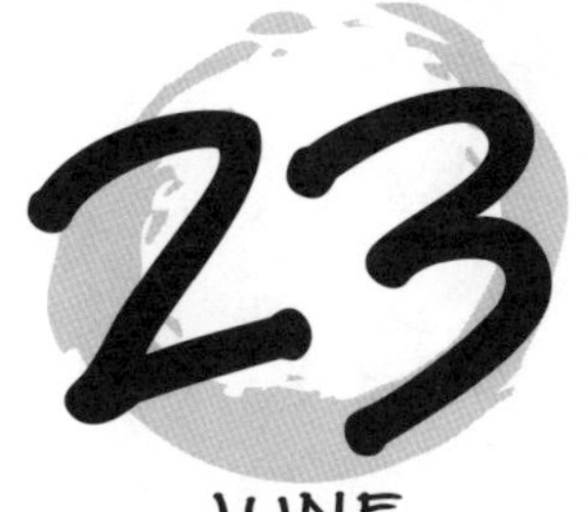

Mary lived in the little town of Nazareth. One day she had an unexpected visitor. Join up the dots to find out who her visitor was.

You can read this story in Luke 1:26–38.

DOT-TO-DOT

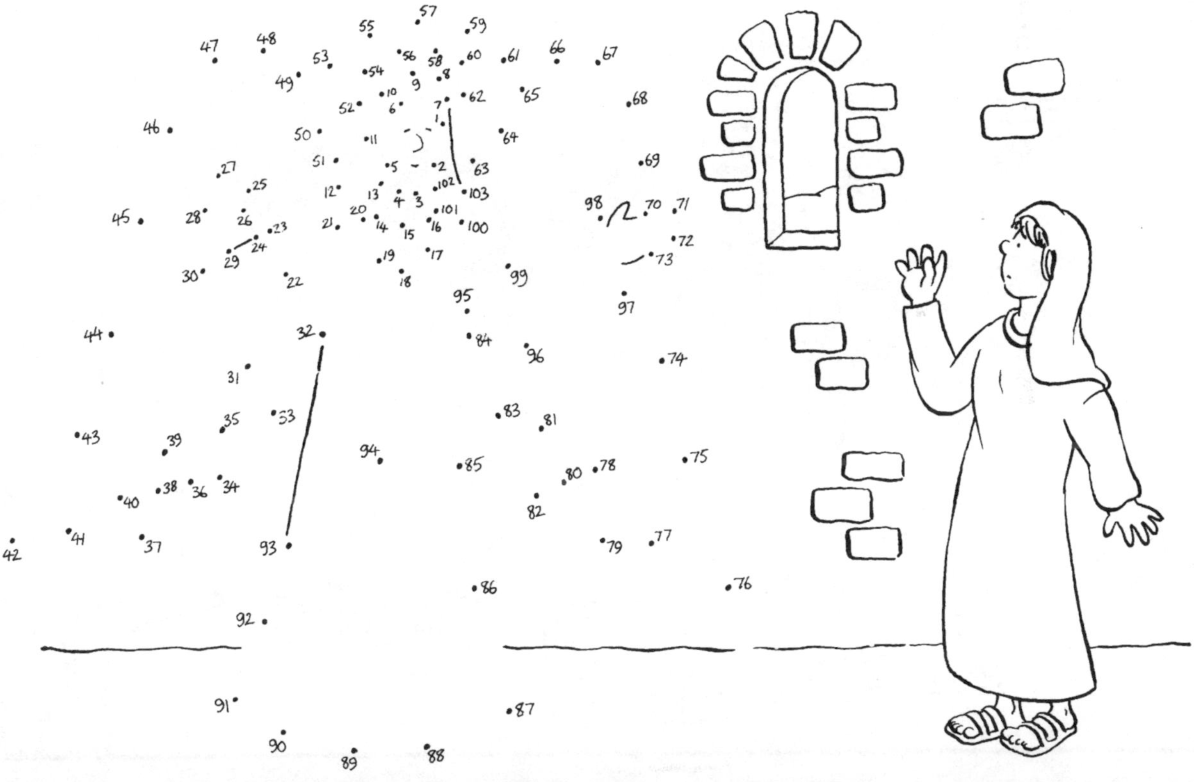

12 JULY

After the angels' visit, the shepherds rushed off into Bethlehem to find baby Jesus in the stable.

The artist has made lots of mistakes. How many have you found? You can read this story in Luke 2:8–20.

Puzzle

 **24**

Mary was astonished when the angel Gabriel told her that she would have a baby son, called Jesus.

Can you find 12 brooms hidden in this picture of Gabriel's visit? You can read this story in Luke 1:26–38.

Puzzle

11

JULY

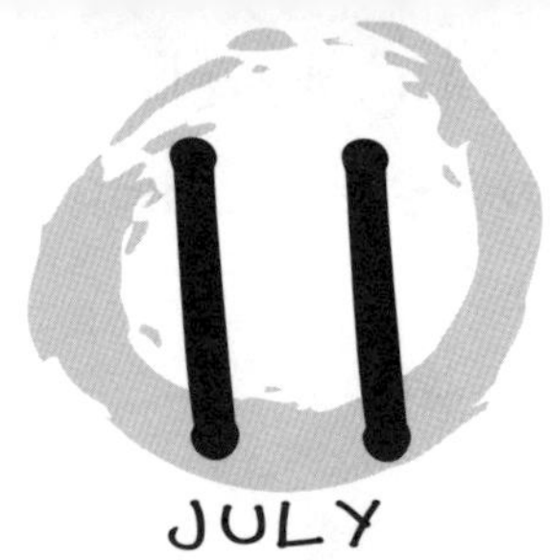

The shepherd at the top of the picture wants to visit baby Jesus in the stable. Which path will take him there without crossing any lines?

You can read this story in Luke 2:8–20.

maze

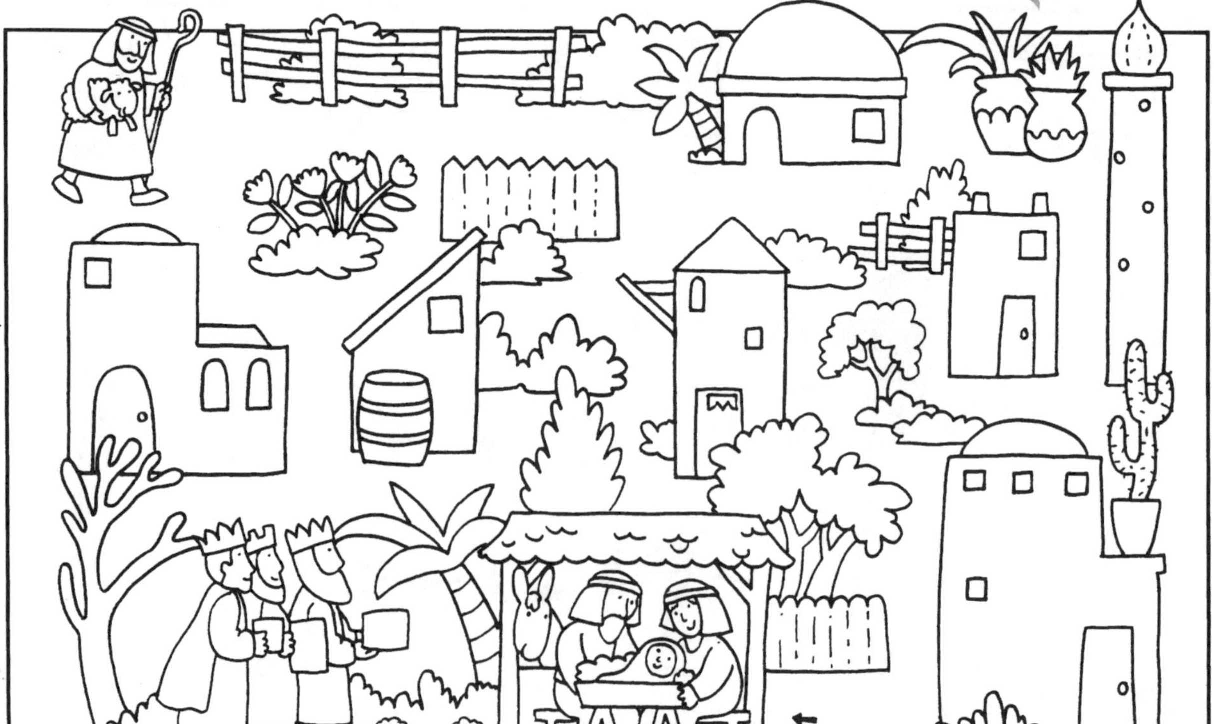

25
JUNE

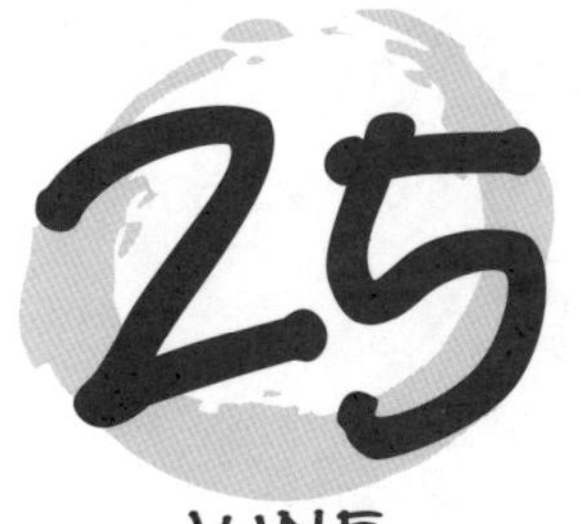

In this picture of Gabriel visiting Mary to tell her she is going to have a baby son, the artist has made lots of deliberate mistakes.

How many can you see? Which is the funniest?
You can read this story in Luke 1:26–38.

Puzzle

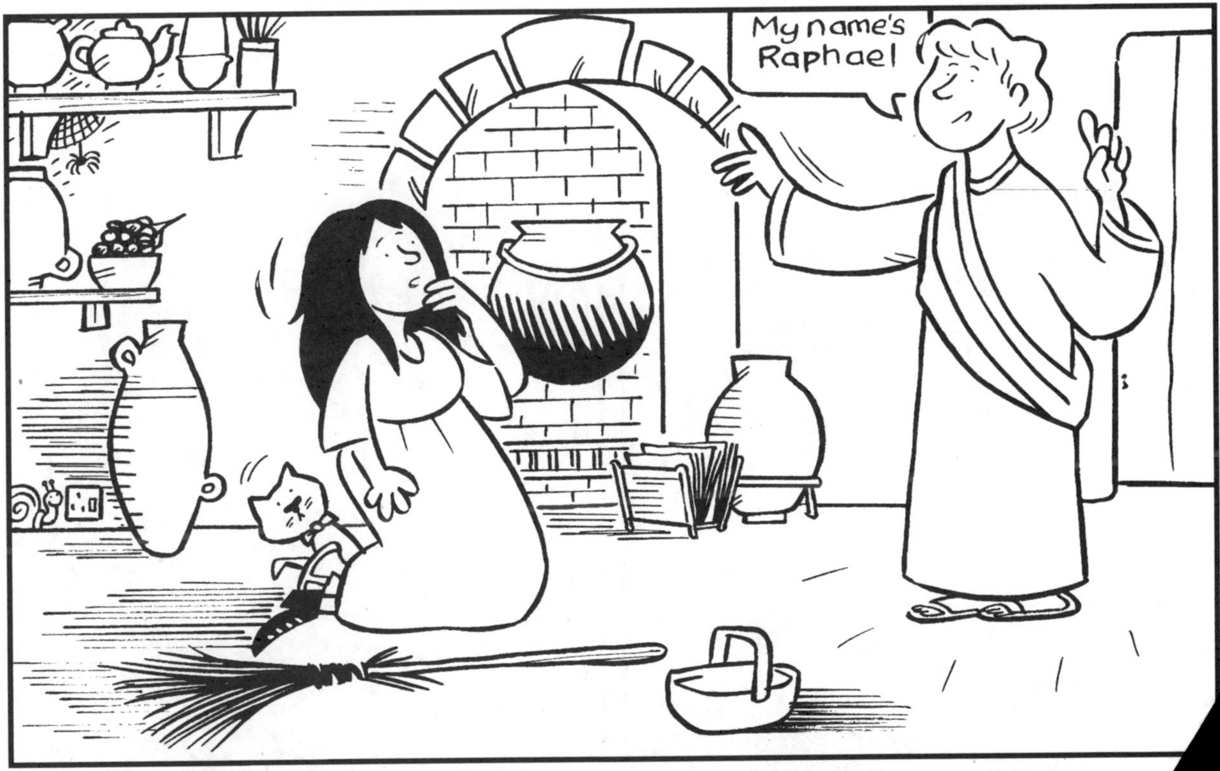

These two shepherds are rushing off to Bethlehem. There are 12 differences between the two pictures: can you find them?

You can read this story in Luke 2:8–20.

26

JUNE

Mary had a cousin named Elizabeth, who also had a baby boy. The boy's father couldn't speak, so he wrote the baby's name. It was 'John'.

Can you find 12 pencils in the picture?
See Luke 1:57–66.

Puzzle

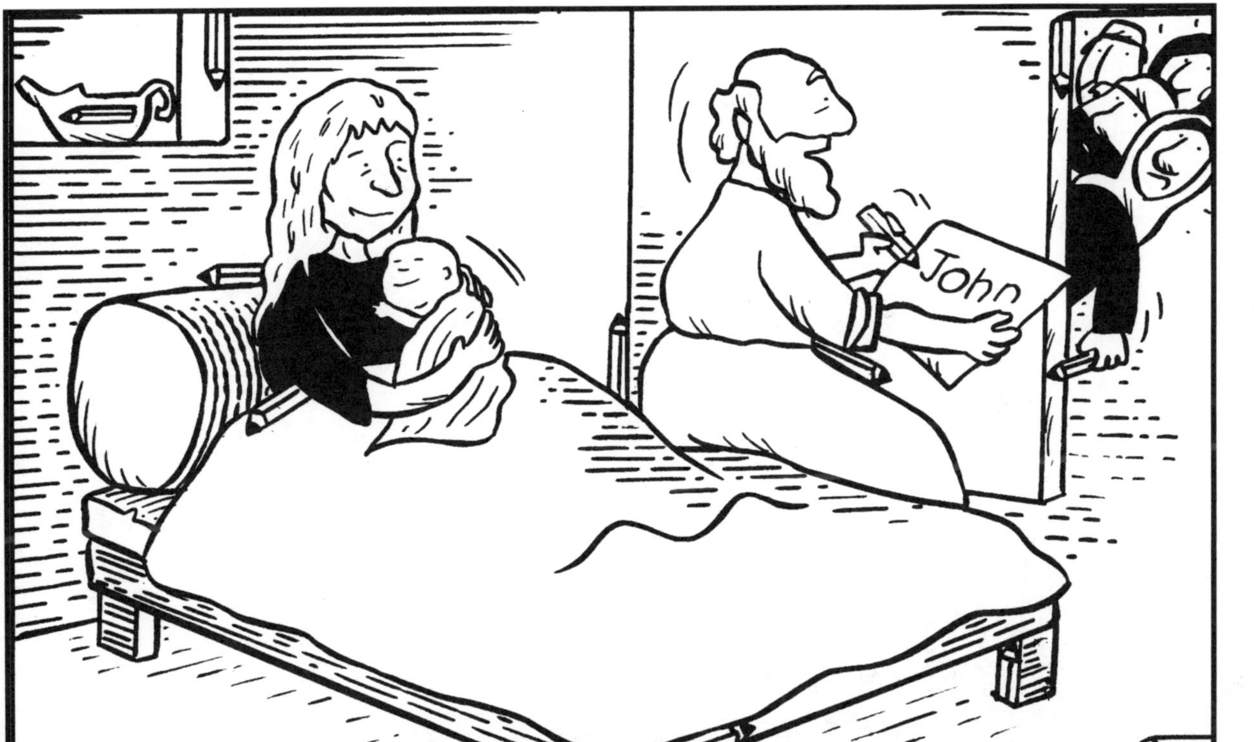

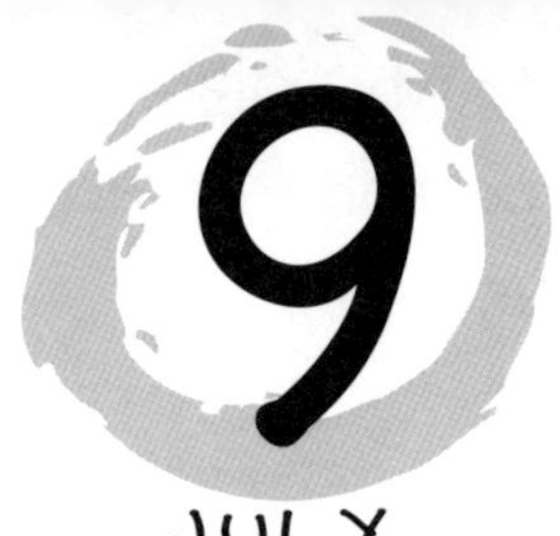

9

JULY

The shepherds look very surprised in this picture. Join up the dots to find out what they are looking at in the sky.

You can read this story in Luke 2:8–20.

DOT-TO-DOT

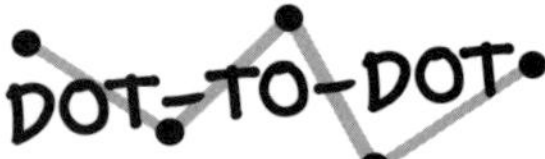

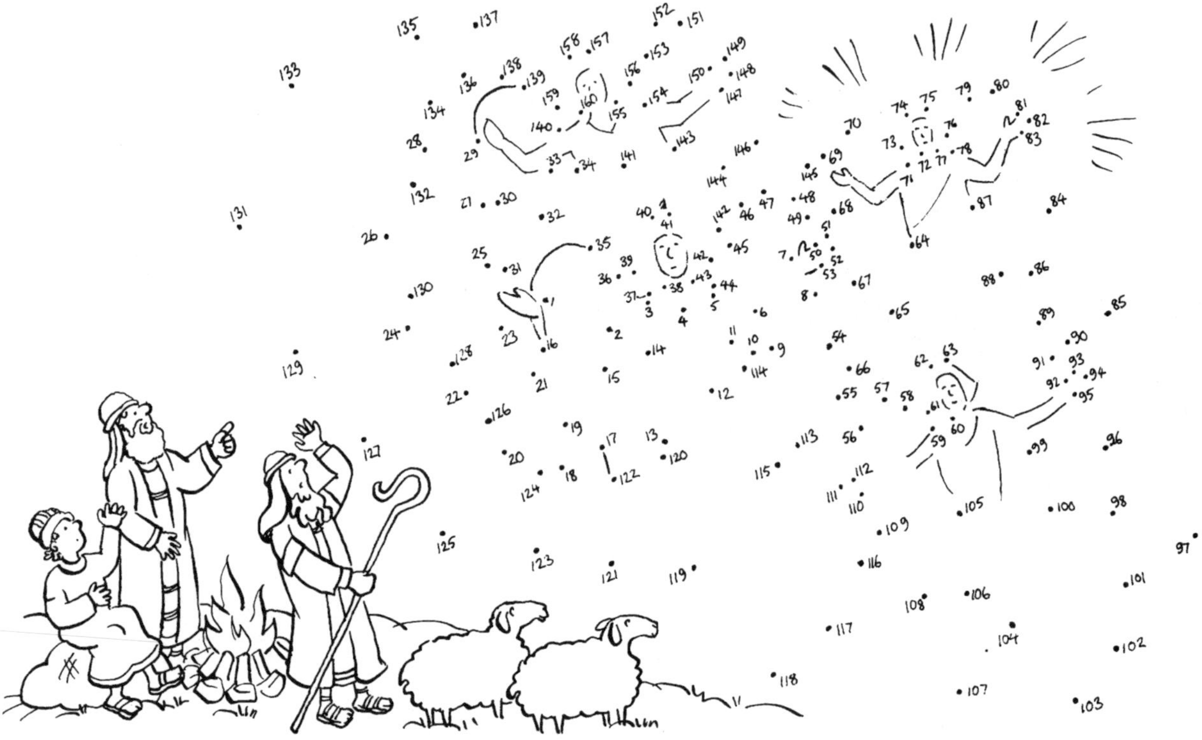

27

JUNE

In Jesus' time, people often wrote on scrolls that were wound around wooden handles.

Can you find 3 matching pairs of scrolls?

Puzzle

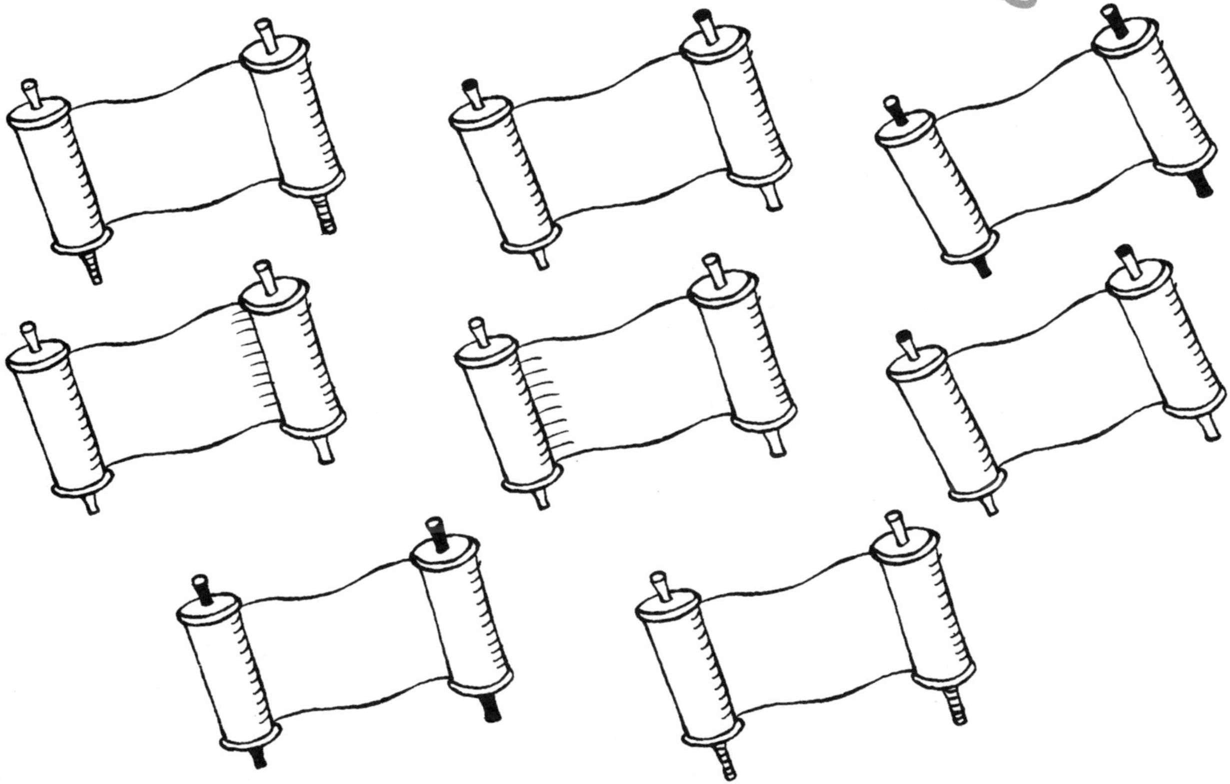

The donkey wants to visit baby Jesus in his Bethlehem manger (food box).

Which path must he take to reach the baby?
Read the story in Luke 2:1–7.

28

JUNE

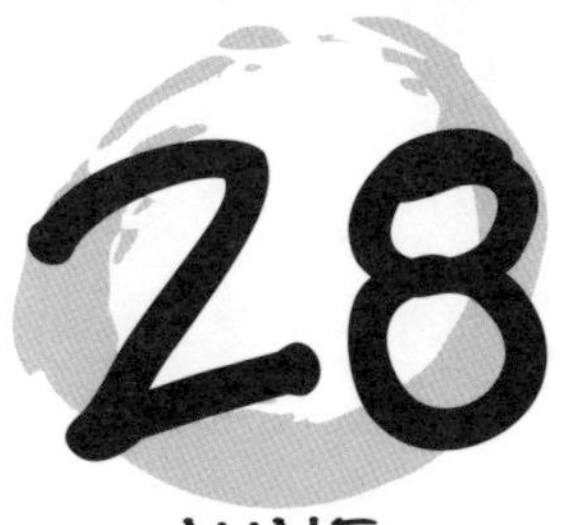

What is this man's job? Join up the dots to find out. Where does he live?

Find out his name and where he lived in Luke 1:26-27.

DOT-TO-DOT

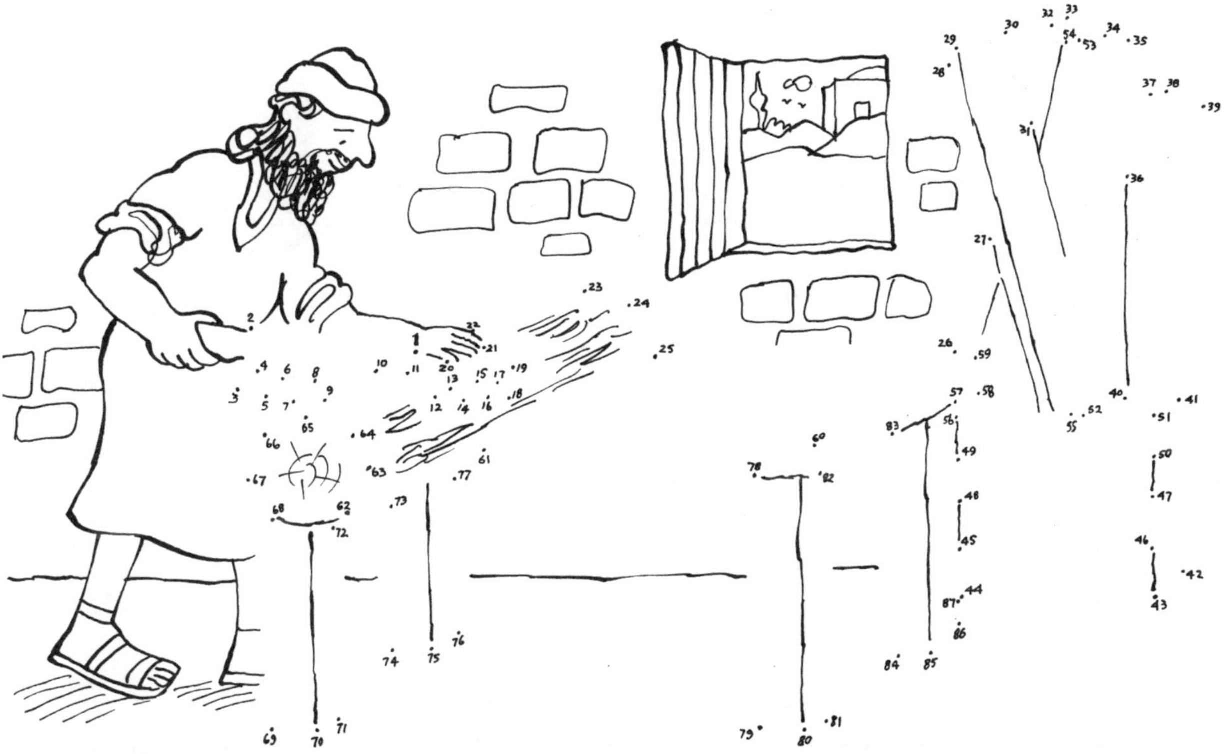

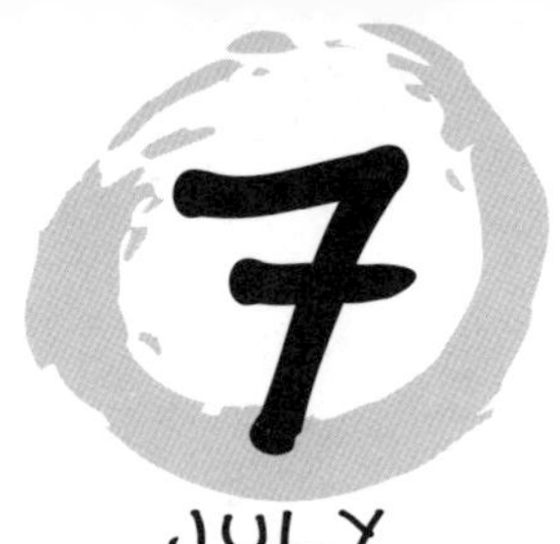

7

JULY

Here is another picture of the Bethlehem stable. The artist has hidden 10 lanterns. Can you find them all?

Read the story in Luke 2:1–7.

Puzzle

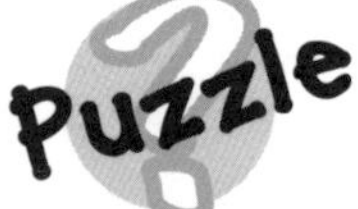

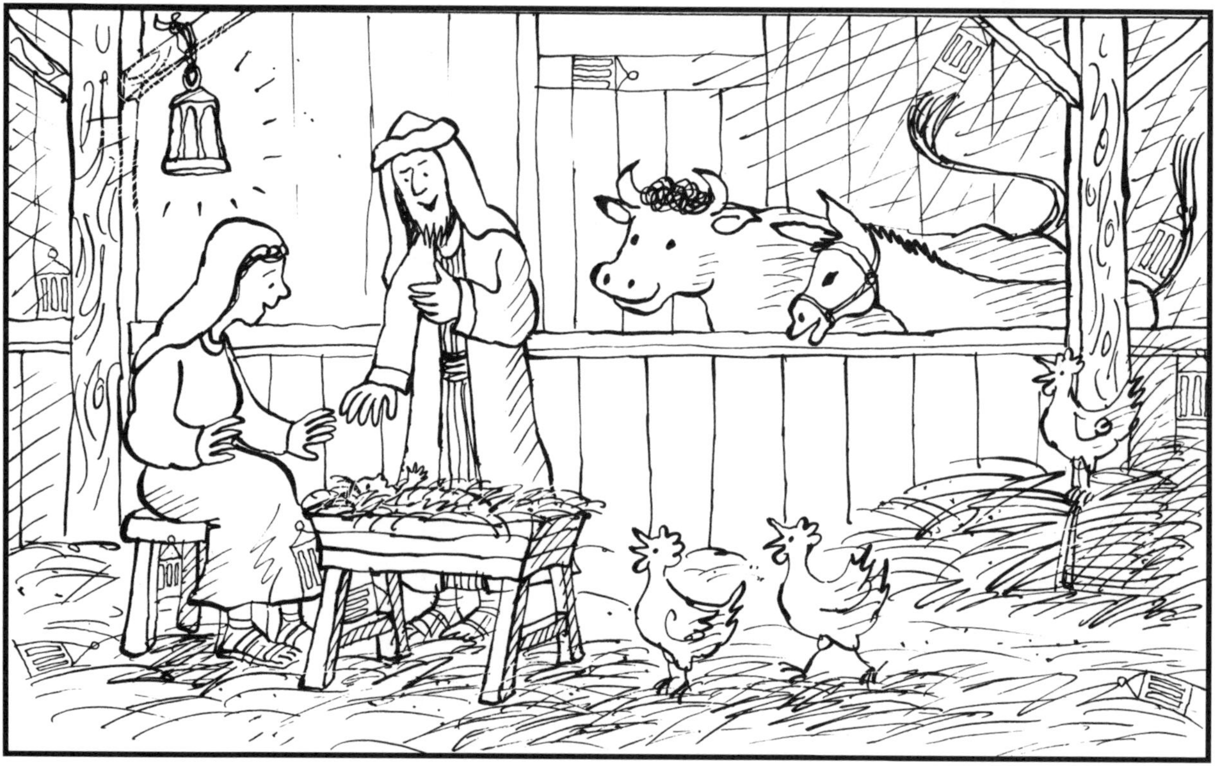

29

JUNE

Mary and Joseph had to go on a long journey just before Jesus was born. Join up the dots to see where they went.

You can read this story in Luke 2:1–5.
What is the name of this place?

DOT-TO-DOT

6

JULY

The innkeeper allowed Mary and Joseph to stay in his stable. Join up the dots to complete this picture.

What did Mary use as a crib for baby Jesus?
Read Luke 2:7.

DOT-TO-DOT

30
JUNE

The first box has a complete picture of Bethlehem. Which other box has all the bits to make the same picture of Bethlehem.

Read about Bethlehem in Matthew 2:1–6.

Puzzle

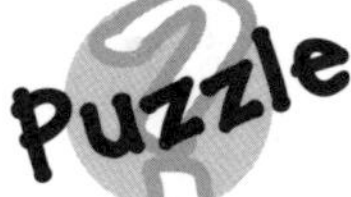

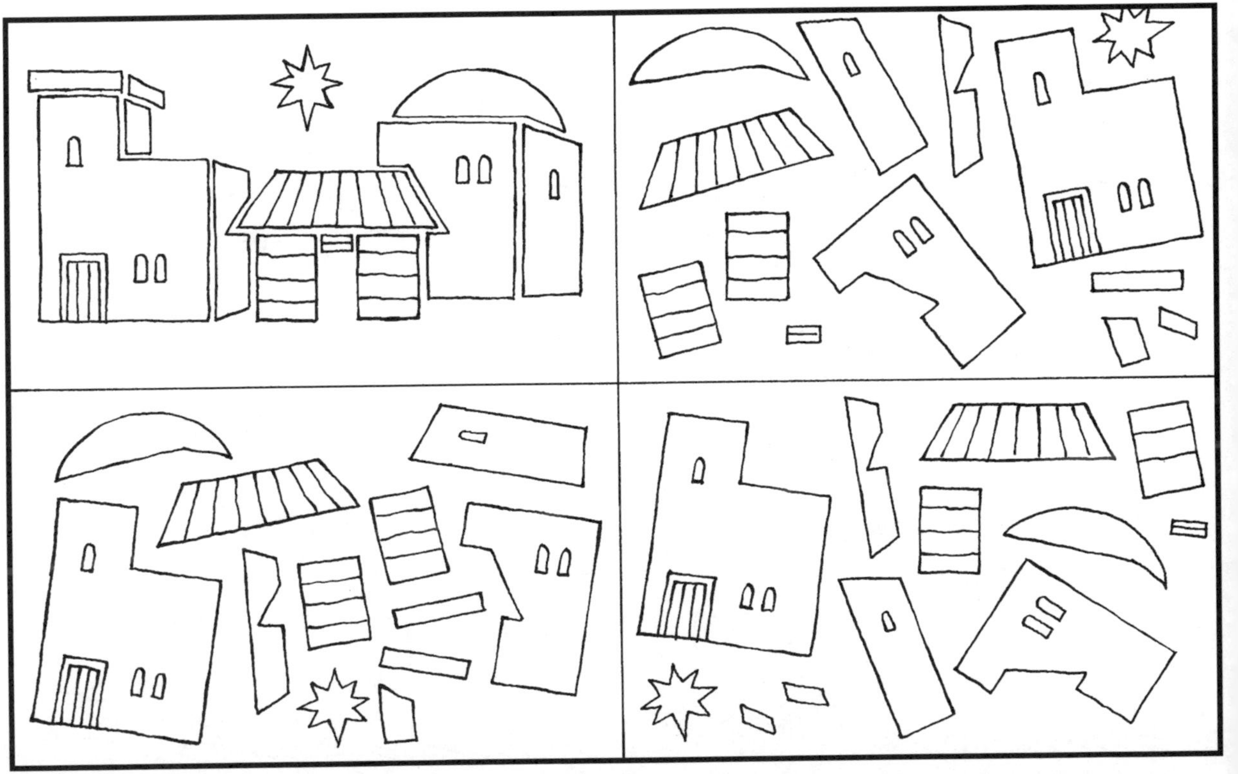

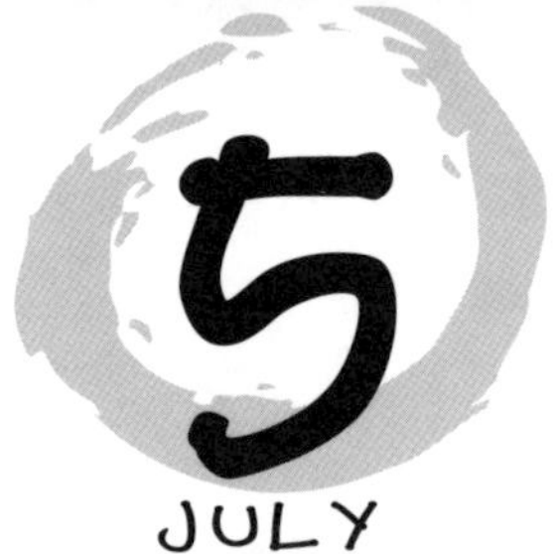

5

JULY

Here are 4 pictures of the animals in the Bethlehem stable where baby Jesus was born. Which is the odd one out?

See Luke 2:7.

SPOT THE DIFFERENCE

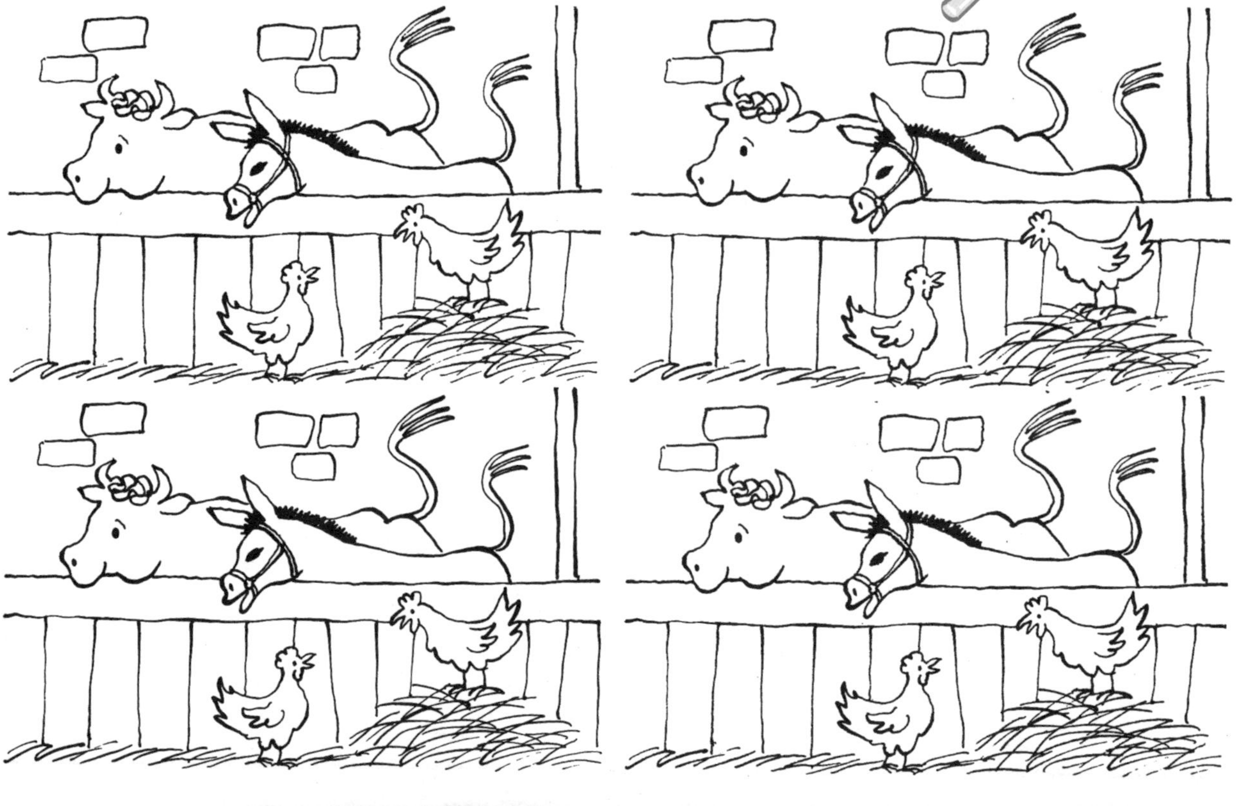

1

JULY

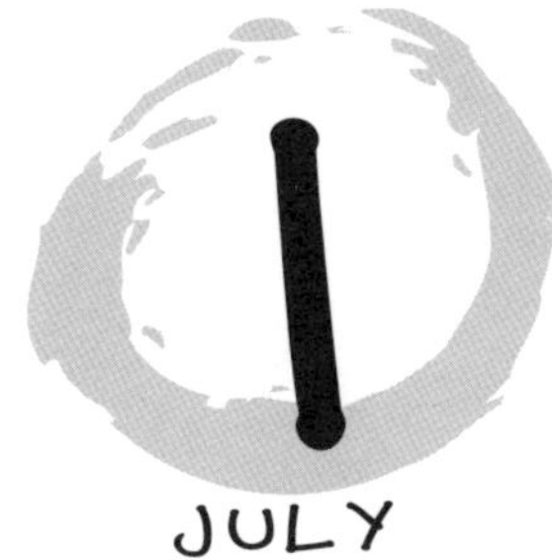

Why did Mary and Joseph visit Bethlehem? In this picture, the artist has deliberately made lots of mistakes. Circle all the ones you can find.

Luke 2:1–7 says why they went to Bethlehem.

Puzzle

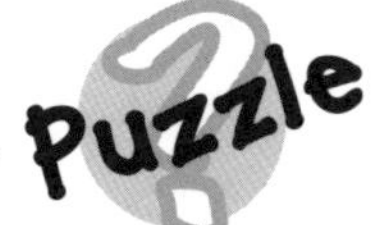

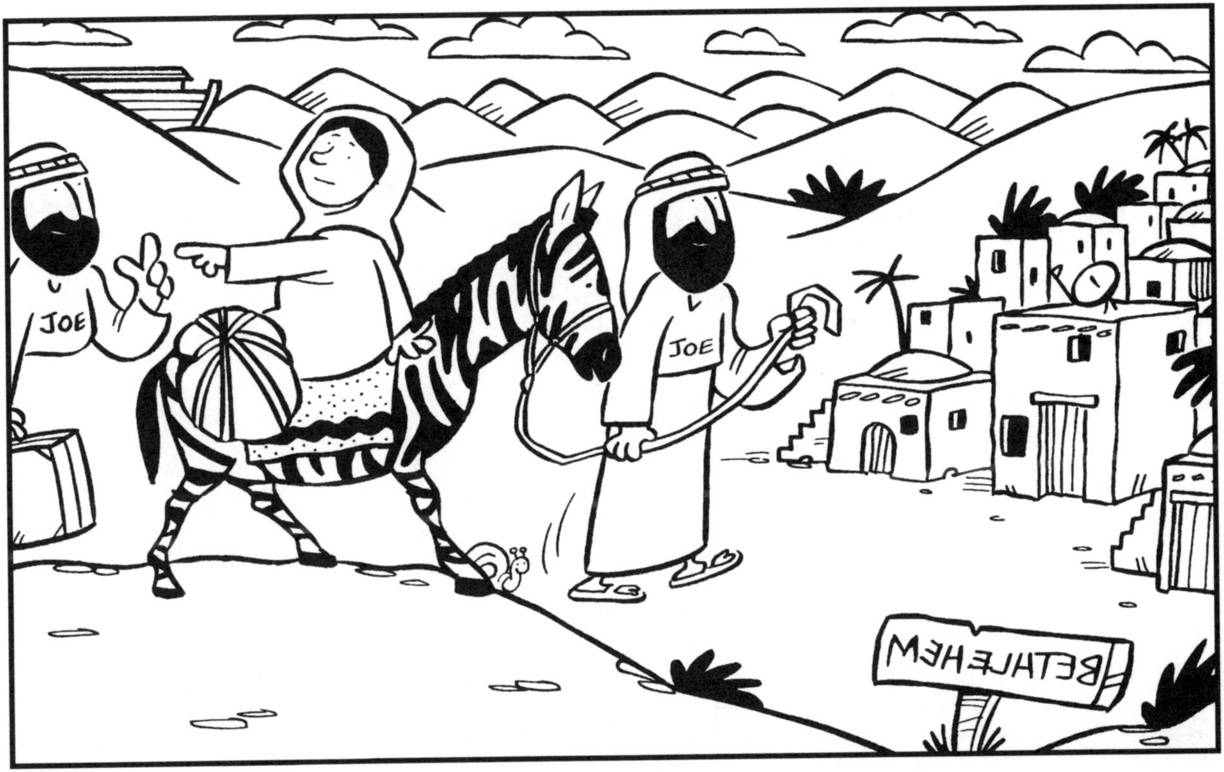

4

JULY

Mary and Joseph can see 3 inns at Bethlehem. Follow the paths to find out which inn they went to, to see if there was any room.

Read the story in Luke 2:1–7.

Puzzle

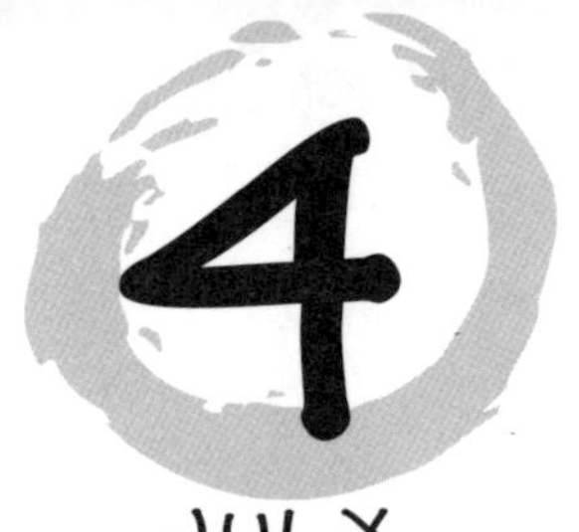

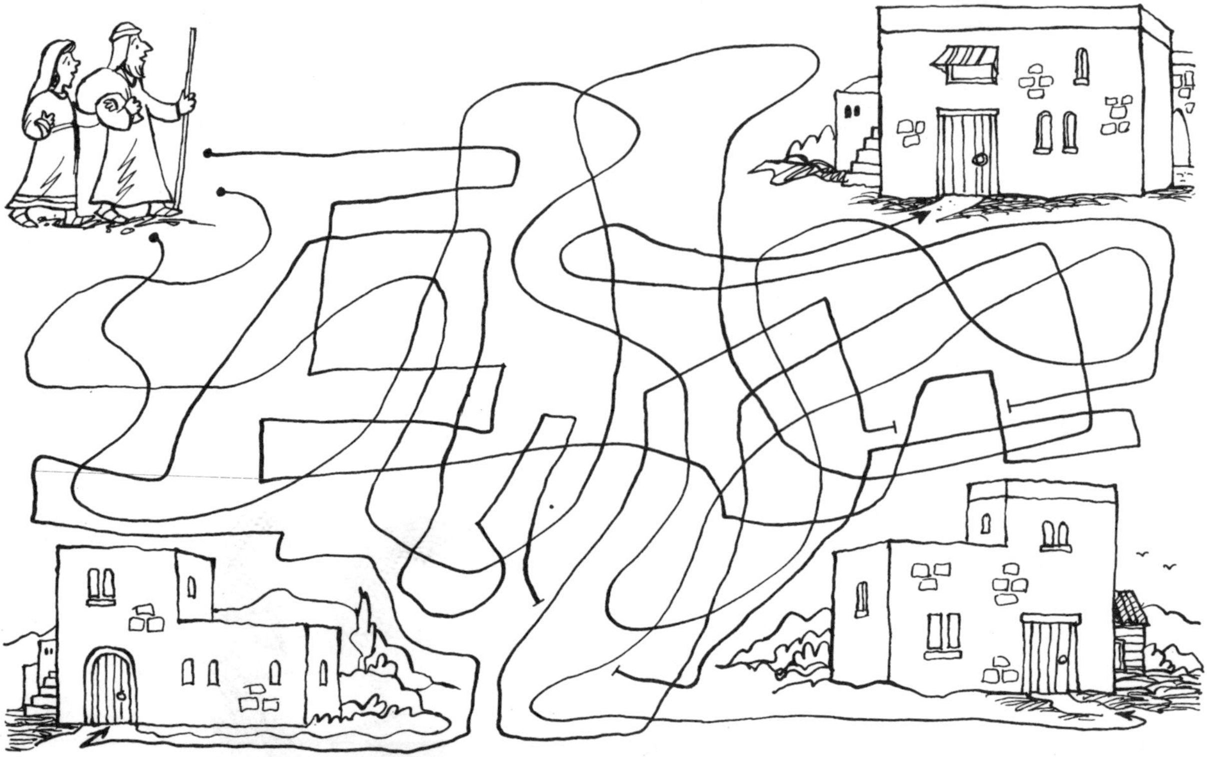

2 JULY

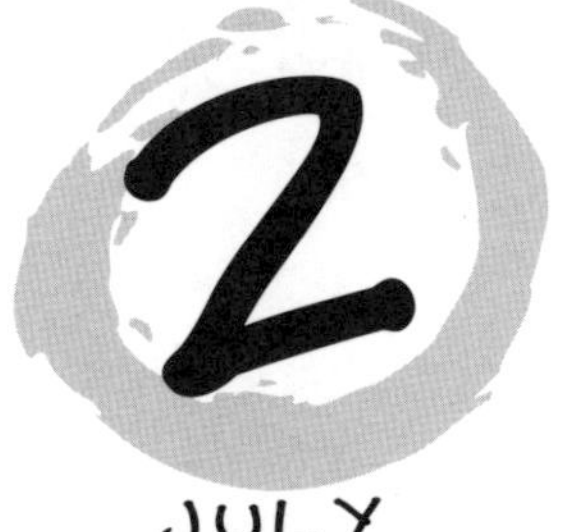

Joseph and Mary have just arrived at the inn at Bethlehem. The artist hasn't finished drawing the other houses.

Complete them—then color the picture with felt-tips.
Read the story in Luke 2:1–7.

Color me!

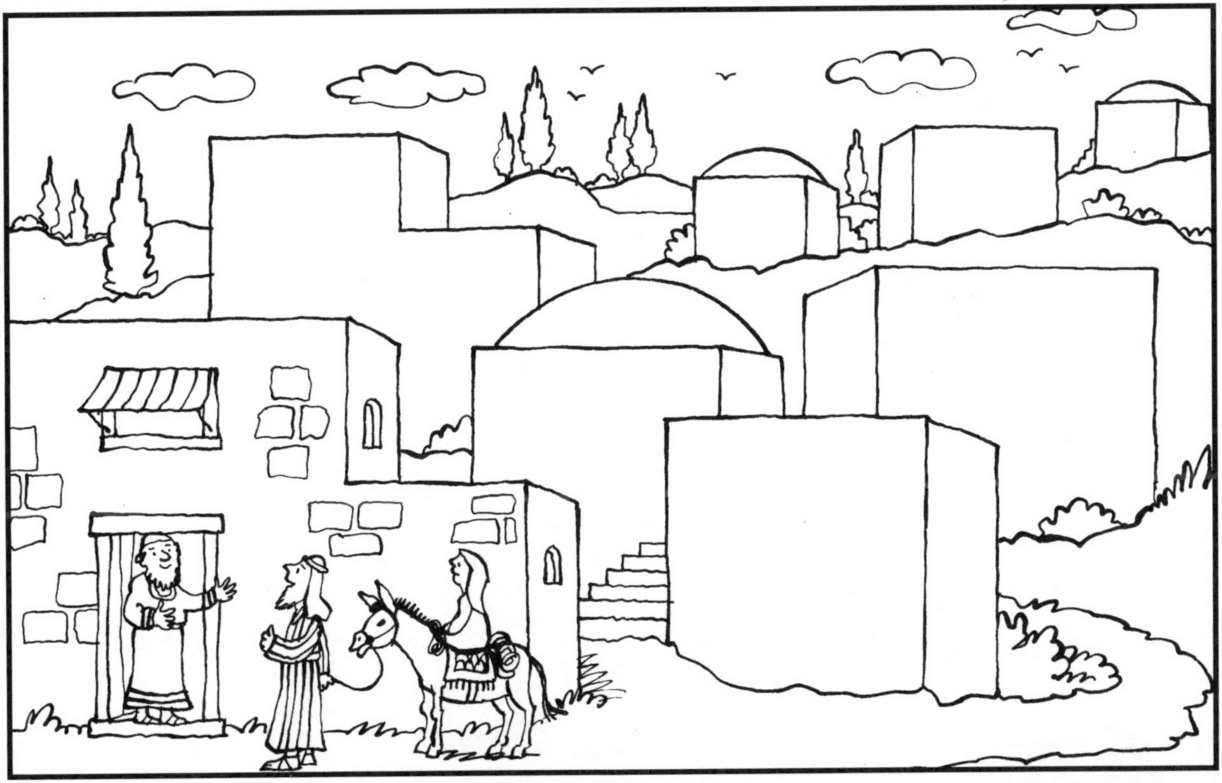

3 JULY

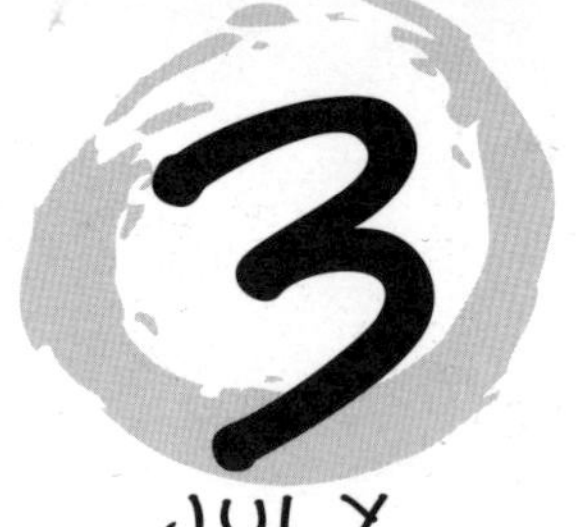

Join up the dots to complete this picture of Joseph and Mary at the door of the inn.

What is the innkeeper saying?
Read Luke 2:6–7 to find out.

DOT-TO-DOT

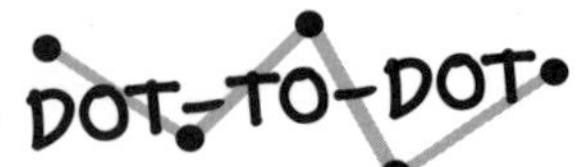

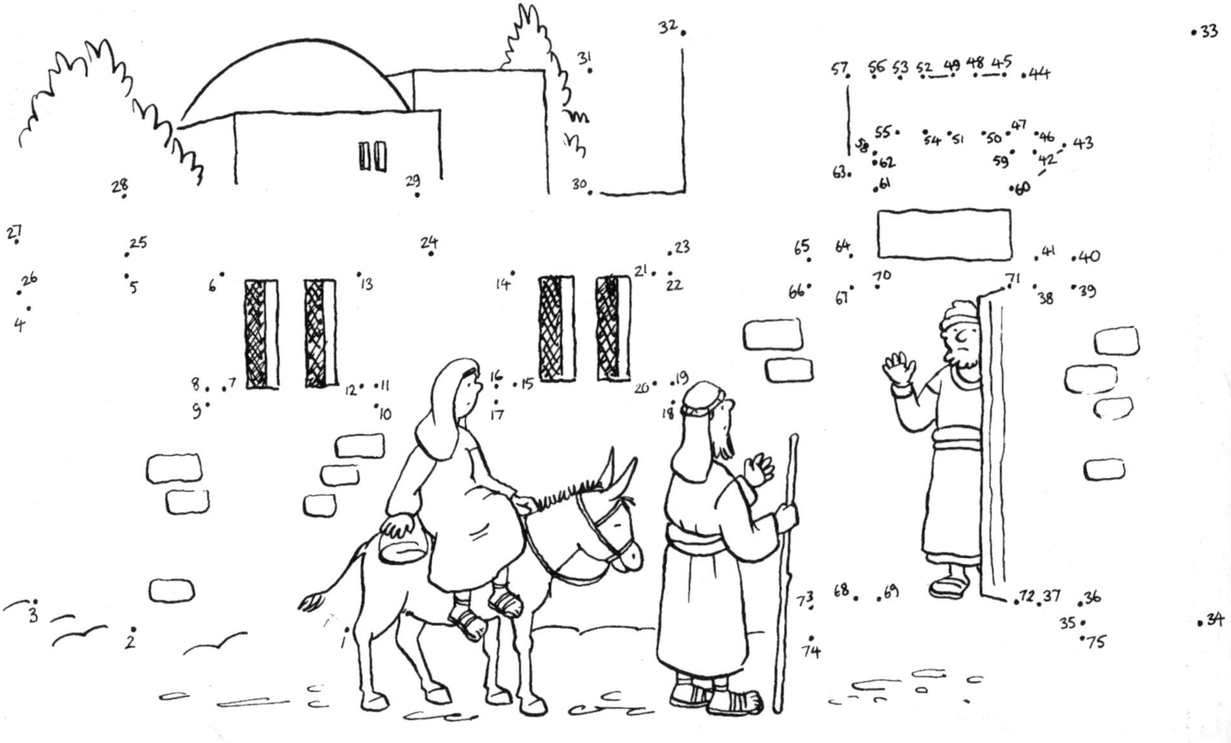